WESTMAR COLLEGE

Financing
the 1968
Election

Financing the 1968 Election

Herbert E. Alexander
Citizens' Research Foundation
Princeton, N.J.

Lexington Books
D.C. Heath and Company
Lexington, Massachusetts
Toronto   London

**To the memory of
my father**

Table of Contents

Appendixes

List of Tables

Acknowledgments

This is my third study of the financing of Presidential election campaigning. The earlier studies, *Financing the 1960 Election* and *Financing the 1964 Election,* were briefer and less comprehensive than the present one. Vast amounts of data regarding campaign costs and expenditures in 1968 were sought out and analyzed. Each successive study is an educational experience for the author and 1968 was notable in the diversity of ways and means found to raise, handle, and spend the large amounts of money used. This study updates and keeps active analyses and categories of data developed over the years by Professors James Pollock, Louise Overacker, and Alexander Heard, and by the Senate Subcommittee on Privileges and Elections (under the chairmanship of Senator Albert Gore) in 1956.

The data in this study were collected by the Citizens' Research Foundation. Special appreciation is due to many individuals for providing information in personal interviews, through correspondence, and by telephone. Many finance managers and others preferred to remain anonymous. It would be unfair to name some and not others, so I regretfully cannot name the many persons who graciously cooperated.

I am happy to acknowledge by name, and with many thanks, the assistance provided by members of the staff of the Citizens' Research Foundation. First and foremost, I appreciate the help of Genie Grohman Gans, who helped organize, draft, analyze, and edit the entire book. Others who contributed importantly to the final product were Caroline D. Jones, Barbara Sigmund, Mary Schoonmaker, Robert Durkee, Deborah Freedman, Frances Strayer, Dennis Durkin, Jean Soete, Theodora Radcliffe, Elizabeth Burns, Katharine Fischer, and Linda Sheldon.

None of those who were so helpful is responsible for errors of omission or commission; for those, as for interpretations, the author bears sole responsibility.

I am happy to acknowledge also the encouragement and forebearance of my wife, Nancy, and the good cheers of my children, Michael, Andrew, and Kenneth.

I always appreciate the cooperation and encouragement received from officers and members of the Board of Trustees of the Citizens' Research Foundation, but the presentation is mine and does not reflect their views.

This study was made possible by a grant from the Ford Foundation to the Citizens' Research Foundation.

Herbert E. Alexander

**Financing
the 1968
Election**

1 Introduction

The voting and financing patterns of the 1968 Presidential election were in sharp contrast: in voting it was one of the closest elections in history; in financing the Republicans outspent the Democrats by more than two to one. Unlike 1964, when a Republican financial advantage clearly did not affect President Johnson's reelection campaign, the Democrats in 1968 were seriously handicapped by their relative lack of funds. Overall, politics in 1968 set new records for expenditures, with the Presidential contests leading the increases.

Rising costs have been a feature of the American political system, especially since the mid-1950s, and the rate of increase has been accelerating. In 1952, the first Presidential election year for which total political costs were calculated, it was estimated that $140 million was spent on elective and party politics at all levels of government.[1] Total political costs rose to $155 million in 1956, $175 million in 1960, and $200 million in 1964.[2] This represents a 43 percent increase in 12 years. For 1968, the total estimated political costs were $300 million—an extraordinary 50 percent increase in four years.

Only a portion of all political expenditures are covered by federal and state reporting laws, and politicians are usually reluctant about divulging campaign fund information, so that precise data on all spending cannot be ascertained. However, the data which are available and the political conditions in 1968 support the estimate of a very significant increase in costs since 1964. Some of these data and conditions were:

the expenditures (total costs) of national level political committees (detailed in Table 1-1) increased 71 percent;
political broadcasting costs reported by the Federal Communications Commission increased 70 percent;
there were costly Presidential prenomination contests in both parties, unlike 1960 or 1964 when the competition for nomination was mainly in one party;
the ante was raised in both parties by the candidacies of Robert F. Kennedy and Nelson A. Rockefeller, both millionaires, for Presidential nomination;
there was protest activity both within and outside the two major parties—in the McCarthy campaign, the Wallace campaign, the New Party efforts, as well as the Black Panthers, Yippies, and others;
there were special efforts to gain control of state legislatures in order to control reapportionment after the 1970 census;
there was a general price rise of about 12 percent since 1964.

There were no known reductions in political expenditures that would offset the increases.

The national-level committees which are covered under Federal reporting laws include the major party national committees as well as labor and some Congressional and other committees which operate in more than one state on behalf of one or more Federal candidates in the general election. The number of such committees has been rising along with expenditures; there were 70 in 1960, 107 in 1964, and 222 in 1968. Table 1-1 details the expenditures of these committees.

Table 1-1

Summary of Political Spending at the National Level, 1968 General Election (in millions)

Committees	Gross Disbursements [a]	Lateral Transfers [b]	Total Campaign Costs	Transfers Out [c]	Direct Expenditures [d]
37 Republican [e]	$28.9	$ .1	$28.8	$3.4	$25.4
93 Democratic [f]	19.2 [g]	6.0	13.2	1.6	11.6
37 Labor [h]	7.1	1.0	6.1	4.2	1.9
3 Wallace [i]	7.2	— [j]	7.2	0	7.2
52 Miscellaneous [k]	4.3	.2	4.1	2.1	2.0
222 Total	$66.7	$7.3	$59.4	$11.3	$48.1

[a] Data derived from reports filed with the Clerk of the U.S. House of Representatives.

[b] Transfers between the Committees included in the table.

[c] Transfers to Senatorial, Congressional and other candidates, and to state and local committees.

[d] Including debts, if any.

[e] For further information, see Table 4-13.

[f] For further information see Table 4-14.

[g] Includes $2.8 million (received from contributions and loans) spent by state and local nonreporting committees for obligations incurred by the DNC; called constructive disbursements in financial report of DNC treasurer Robert Short.

[h] For further information, see Table 4-16.

[i] For further information, see Table 4-15.

[j] Less than $25,000.

[k] For further information, see Table 4-17.

The $59.4 million in total campaign costs of these committees compares with $34.8 million spent in 1964. Republican committee expenditures increased 68 percent from 1964, while combined Democratic and labor spending[a] increased 23 percent. Table 1-2 shows the relation of Republican and Democratic (and Wallace) committee spending for the last four Presidential election years. (The percentages are based on direct expenditures, as in the last column in Table 1-1, excluding miscellaneous committee spending.)

[a] Labor is combined with Democratic spending on the assumption that most labor money goes to support Democrats.

Table 1-2

Ratios of National-Level Direct Spending, 1956, 1960, 1964, 1968 (in percentages)

	1956 [a]	1960	1964	1968
Republican Committees	59	49	63	55
Total on behalf of Democrats	41	51	37	29
Democratic Committees:	37	47	34	25
Labor Committees:	4	4	3	4
Wallace Committees	—	—	—	16
Total	100	100	100	100

[a] Derived from Heard, *Costs*, p. 20, and *1956 General Election Campaigns*, Report to the Senate Committee on Rules and Administration, Subcommittee on Privileges and Elections, 85th Congress, 1 Session (1957), Exhibit 4, p. 41. 1956 deficits are listed by this Report as bills unpaid as of Nov. 30, 1956. Heard's figures for Republican and Democrats are for full calendar year 1956, but labor figures are for Jan. 1– Nov. 30, 1956. Heard's ratio for 1956 has been revised to include deficits.

Excluding spending by Wallace committees, the ratio of major party spending in 1968 was 65 percent for the Republicans and 35 percent on behalf of the Democrats (30 percent by Democratic committees and 5 percent by labor committees). Thus, the Republican financial dominance, customary in recent years, continued.

The costs of campaigning for the Presidency in 1968 were the largest component of the year's political bill, and the 1968 Presidential selection process was the most expensive in American history. The Presidential bill of $100 million (of which more than 90 percent can be accounted for fairly accurately) was an increase of 67 percent over the 1964 costs of $60 million, a significantly larger increase than even the 50 percent estimated increase for total political costs.

The Presidential bill for $100 million, which is one-third of the total political expenditures in 1968, included:

$37 million for national-level costs for Democrats and Republicans in the general election;
$25 million in the Democratic prenomination period;
more than $20 million in the Republican prenomination period;
$9 million for George Wallace's American Independent Party, beginning in 1967.

These known costs total $91 million. State and local spending on behalf of Presidential candidates in both the pre- and postnomination periods would make up a large part of the difference. In addition, one must count in party and delegate expenses related to the national nominating conventions, and spending by activists giving parties, travelling, and telephoning paid out-of-pocket directly by the individuals concerned.

Data on the expenditures of national-level committees primarily concerned with the Presidential general election are available from 1912. The figures in Table 1-3 exclude spending by labor and miscellaneous committees, which generally do not benefit the Presidential candidates. Although there were some unusual years, the rise in expenditures was gradual from 1912 to 1952. Since 1956, the rise has been even more rapid than the big increases in overall political costs, with 1968 again occupying a unique position.

Table 1-3

Direct Campaign Expenditures by National-Level Presidential and Party Committees, General Elections 1912–1968[a] (in millions)

1912	$2.9 [b]	1932	$5.1	1952	$11.6
1916	4.7	1936	14.1	1956	12.9
1920	6.9	1940	6.2	1960	19.9
1924	5.4 [b]	1944	5.0	1964	24.8
1928	11.6	1948	6.2 [b]	1968	44.2 [b]

Source: Citizens' Research Foundation.

[a] Data for 1912–1944 include transfers to states. Total for 1948 includes only the expenditures of the national party committees. For 1952–1968, data do not include transfers to states, but do include all national-level committees.

[b] Totals include significant minor party spending.

Calculations of the cost-per-vote for the Presidency since 1912 show a variable pattern for more than 40 years, and then a steady rise since the mid-1950s, culminating in an enormous leap for 1968.[3] From 1912 to 1956, the cost-per-vote ranged from a little more than 10 cents (in the wartime election of 1944) to around 31 cents (in the intense 1928 and 1936 elections); but after each rise, there was an almost comparable drop so that in 1912 the cost-per-vote was just over 19 cents and in 1956 it was just under 21 cents. By 1960, the cost-per-vote had risen to almost 29 cents and in 1964 it set a record at more than 35 cents. But for 1968, the record was shattered as the cost-per-vote jumped to 60 cents.

The 60-cent figure for 1968 includes Wallace spending beginning in February—which would normally be the prenomination period. But the American Independent Party had no convention, so no distinction can be made between primary and general election costs. If the Wallace votes and national-level expenditures are excluded from the calculation, the 1968 cost-per-vote was still a record high of close to 51 cents.

There are two sets of reasons for the extraordinary cost of the 1968 Presidential campaigns: one set is unique to the year; the other includes factors which must be considered continuing components of Presidential campaigns, likely to contribute to high costs in future years.

In the second category are the scientific and technological advances which have contributed to increased campaign costs in the 1960's, particularly in the areas of travel, polling, computers, and broadcasting. The ability to have more and wider contact with the electorate via jet plane first entranced Richard Nixon in his 1960 compaign, and has since become a standard and major expense in Presidential campaigns. Extensive private polling was first used by John F. Kennedy in that same year, and its use, importance, and cost are increasing as the candidates, the poll-takers, and the techniques have become more sophisticated. The use of computers in planning campaigns and simulating elections is at an early stage, but can be expected to grow.

The cost of political broadcasting is the most measurable of these technological factors. Television is much more expensive than radio, and its use and cost are continually increasing. Charges for political broadcasts in the general election for network television, which covers almost exclusively the Presidential contest, were $2.9 million in both 1956 and 1960, rose to $3.8 million in 1964, and then jumped to $7.4 million in 1968.[4] The total broadcast expenditures (radio and television, network and station) for the 1968 Presidential and Vice-Presidential prenomination and general election contests were $28.5 million, 2.2 times greater than the comparable 1964 expenditures.[5]

The one intangible component of the rising costs is the role of the President. For many reasons—including the increased role of the United States in the world during the last decades, the power potential which the President holds, a growing view of the President as the initiator as well as executor of the nation's policies, and the direct impact of federal policy on more people—the Presidency is more important today than previously, and therefore the stakes for achieving it are greater.

The major unique causes of the high Presidential costs in 1968 were the prenomination contests in both parties; the candidacy of a millionaire in each major party; protest activity both within and outside the major parties; and the Nixon-Humphrey contest, in which neither was an incumbent, and both were challenged by the Wallace candidacy.

In most Presidential years, the candidate of one party is fairly certain of winning nomination and there is little major opposition. In 1964, this was true for the Democrats, who had an incumbent President; in 1960, the Republicans had the Vice-President, who was heir apparent; and in 1956, the Republicans had an enormously popular President. Not since 1952 had there been real uncertainty and major contests in both parties for the Presidential nomination as there were in 1968, and for more than 20 years before 1952, the Presidential nomination in one (or both) of the parties was not seriously contested. For all these reasons, the costs of the 1968 Presidential campaigns reached the record-breaking total of $100 million; and some of the stated reasons suggest that costs of future Presidential campaigns cannot be expected to return to their pre-1968 level.

2 The Prenomination Campaigns

Costs

The Presidential prenomination campaigns of 1968 bore little resemblance to time past. In the Democratic and Republican parties combined, about $45 million was spent before Richard Nixon and Hubert Humphrey won the nominations, with the Democrats spending $5 million more than the Republicans. By comparison, the much-publicized clash between Hubert Humphrey and John Kennedy in 1960 seems, in retrospect, as if it took place in another era: the two candidates combined were reported to have spent only a little more than $1 million.[1] Both Humphrey and Nixon were candidates in both 1960 and 1968: in 1960, about $500,000 was spent in Nixon's prenomination campaign and about $250,000 on Humphrey's shorter one; in 1968, more than $10 million was spent on Nixon's nomination campaign and $4 million for Humphrey's—increases of twenty times from eight years earlier. Even the famous Eisenhower-Taft contest of 1952, costing at least $5 million,[2] and the bitter Goldwater-Rockefeller confrontation in 1964, which cost an estimated $10 million,[3] can hardly be compared to the $20 and $25 million spent by prenomination candidates in the Republican and Democratic parties, respectively, in 1968.

In most Presidential campaign years, there is competition in only one party for the nomination: the "in" party will nominate either the incumbent or his accepted successor. But in 1968, there were intense struggles in both parties. In addition, there were more than two major candidates in each party; there was an intensely felt issue (Vietnam) which brought many new people and much new money into the political process; and there were unusually wealthy candidates in both parties. Each of these factors acted to spur higher campaign spending, and they combined to create the most expensive prenomination process in American politics. There was more Democratic than Republican competition in the period of the primaries, particularly when Robert Kennedy was one of the contestants. In the Republican primaries, Nixon was without serious opposition from before the New Hampshire primary, when Romney withdrew, until Oregon, where Reagan was entered although not an announced candidate; competition heightened when Rockefeller finally entered. In the interim period, of course, Nixon had to spend to make a good showing and prove he could be a winner—much as he did in 1960—but this time at much greater expense and with a greater accumulation of liabilities. Humphrey, in 1968, was in Nixon's 1960 spot, an incumbent Vice-President with whatever advantages or disadvantages that meant. Nixon's 1968 drive was a long one, whereas Humphrey was able to run only after President Johnson withdrew. Although neither contested primaries, Humphrey's costs were lower than Rockefeller's; Humphrey was an incumbent with strong factional party support, whereas Rockefeller was a challenger. On the Democratic side, both McCarthy and Kennedy were challengers. And challengers, especially wealthy ones, often spend more.

The involvement of both a Rockefeller and a Kennedy in a single year did much to raise the ante for all the other candidates.[4] It is not only the actual spending of wealthy candidates which spurs spending by others; the possibility or threat of their spending also acts as a spur to higher spending. One of the ironies of this situation is that when a Rockefeller or a Kennedy is running, his fund raising is often handicapped by the feeling of many that the candidate can afford to spend his own money; then if he does spend substantially from his own resources, he is criticized for it.

Since Federal disclosure laws do not cover prenomination campaigns, most information which is available has been provided voluntarily by candidates or contributors. As might be expected, campaigners are usually more willing to disclose expenditures—how much they spent and on what —than the sources of their funds, particularly from large contributors. However, even the admittedly incomplete information available reveals bigger contributors, on the record, then at any time since the 1920s.

Sources of Funds

The largest known contribution was from a Rockefeller family member who gave more than $1.5 million to one committee (and might have given more which was not recorded). There are believed to have been at least three $500,000 contributors in the prenomination period: one each to the Nixon, McCarthy, and Kennedy campaigns. One contributor gave and spent a total of $300,000 in 1968, divided between Rockefeller (before he became an announced candidate) and McCarthy. There were also two, possibly three, $200,000 contributors to Romney's campaign, while McCarthy is believed to have had one $300,000 contributor and at least three other contributors of $100,000 or more. The Kennedy and Rockefeller campaigns also had $100,000 contributors outside the immediate families, and several dozen persons are known to have given between $50,000 and $100,000 to these and other campaigns. These contributions were for the most part not publicly reported, although there was more openness about giving, and more publicity given to who gave how much, than at any other time. The press seemed more aware in 1968; there were several luncheons or dinners widely reported at which very large sums were pledged, and in the McCarthy campaign, there were open rallies at which large pledges were publicly announced. More will be noted about individual large contributors to individual candidates in the sections below.

The combination of Kennedy, McCarthy, Johnson, Humphrey, Romney, and Rockefeller brought more left-of-center or moderate money onto the political scene than at any time in American history. Conventional belief has it that, apart from candidate family money, the liberals in American politics are relatively financially starved. Generally, Republicans, conservatives, and centrists have found their funding came easier; this seemed natural if one followed the simplistic notions that political money came mainly in large sums, that only the well-healed could afford to give in large sums, and that the wealthier elements tended to be more conservative and tended to give liberally to conservative candidates.

Prior to 1968, the Goldwater campaign of 1964 was one of the two most expensive prenomination campaigns on record (the other was Rockefeller's 1964 campaign, mostly family-financed); Goldwater was unique, however, in having 300,000 contributors in the preconvention period. That unprecedented achievement in financial participation did attract some ultra-conservatives previously outside the two-party political process, but in general it proved that hundreds of thousands of nonwealthy Americans would contribute to a political candidate.

If 1964 demonstrated that a conservative candidate could attract very large sums of money from thousands of small givers, 1968 demonstrated that with the proper mix of issues, events, and men, liberal candidates could also raise large sums of money from many relatively small contributors. No liberal Democrat had ever raised so much from so many— not John F. Kennedy nor Adlai E. Stevenson nor Estes Kefauver. Although the Kennedy, McCarthy, and Humphrey prenomination campaigns in 1968 all left deficits, in terms of the money actually raised, it was clear that political affluence and financial involvement in America had reached the liberals. (The Rockefeller and Romney campaigns left no deficits because the debts were paid by family and friends.)

The McCarthy mix of a few very large contributors and many small contributors may have been unique, but if it did nothing else it dispelled the notion that only Republicans or conservatives could find major, non-family financing. And with several moderate and liberal candidates in the 1968 Presidential race, the combined fund-raising record of center and left-of-center candidates was indeed impressive and unprecedented.

On the other side, of course, the two conservative candidates in 1968 (Nixon and Reagan) did very well in their fund raising. And outside the nominal two-party system, George Wallace did extraordinarily well in fund raising throughout 1968; he attracted an estimated 750,000 contributors, many of whom gave one dollar in order to sign petitions to get Wallace's American Independent Party on the ballot.

Cost Overstatements

Descriptions of the financing of the 1968 prenomination campaigns require two explanations, one general and one relating to the Democrats.

When travel costs for a campaign are given, there may be a considerable inflation of the actual cost. When finance managers say, for example, that travel cost $1 million, the statement may be true but does not take into account the fact that perhaps as much as half of the total is reimbursed by media travellers—newspaper, magazine, radio, and television reporters —who are charged for transportation by the campaign. The bulk of this reimbursed transportation is for riding in the candidate's plane (or another plane provided by the campaign), but some ground transportation may also be charged, such as press buses. When the candidate and staff fly with enough reporters, substantial portions of cost can be recouped, as figures relating to Nixon's general election campaign will show.

For the Democrats, the final disposition of the deficits from the McCarthy, Kennedy, and Humphrey campaigns will affect the spending totals. When campaign totals are given they represent committed costs, not actual cash expenditures. If outstanding bills are settled for less than their full amount —as has been done with at least some of the debts from the Kennedy, McCarthy, and Humphrey campaigns—the total real cost of the campaign will obviously be less. For example, the Kennedy campaign left a debt of $3.5 million, but efforts were made to settle accounts at an average of about 33 cents on the dollar. If all outstanding Kennedy campaign debts were settled at that rate, the total real cost of the campaign would be about 25 percent less than the listed, committed cost. After the November general election, the Democratic National Committee (DNC) assumed $1 million in debts from each of the Humphrey and Kennedy prenomination campaigns, and a very small amount from the McGovern campaign. These debts will presumably eventually be handled in conjunction with the more than $6 million in other debts of the DNC, which is discussed in detail below.

The Republicans

The Republican contenders spent more than $20 million in the nomination competition, with Nixon's winning campaign accounting for more than half the total. Rockefeller, without entering any primaries, spent more than $8 million; Romney spent $1.5 million in his aborted campaign; about $750,000 was spent on Reagan's behalf; and Harold Stassen's campaign cost $90,000. While most of this money was spent in 1968, some expenditures and much of the planning dated back to 1966-1967.

In some cases, Presidential hopefuls may begin working toward their goal as early as the preceding convention or election, as John F. Kennedy did after 1956 and Barry Goldwater after 1960, and some may truly be last-minute candidates, as Adlai Stevenson was in 1952 or Robert Kennedy was in 1968, but the usual beginning of Presidential speculation and organization is after the midterm Congressional elections. After the

1966 elections, three prominent Republicans were the subjects of Presidential speculation, and, in fact, were then beginning their campaigns. Two of them, Governors Romney of Michigan and Reagan of California, had just won impressive electoral victories, and the third, Richard Nixon, had been a tireless and effective campaigner on behalf of many Republican candidates across the country. Each of these three Presidential candidates held his first strategy meeting soon after the November elections, and the shape of their campaigns began to form.[5]

Romney

Early in 1967, an organization called Romney Associates was formed. Ostensibly, its function was to provide research and advice on whether or not Romney should run; in fact, it was the central planning organization for the campaign. A document dated July 20, 1967 showed Romney Associates had monthly expenditures of close to $40,000 in fixed costs:

Salaries	$25,500
Overhead	3,200
Telephone	2,000
Travel & Entertainment	5,700
Miscellaneous	1,000

Plans for the remainder of 1967 included the following expenditures beyond the fixed costs: summer conference at Macinac Island, $4,500; consultant fees, $6,000; trip to Europe, $20,000; trip to Asia (Vietnam), $20,000; polling, $50,000; public relations, wire service, $2,500; teleprompter, $1,500; miscellaneous, $1,500. Some of these projects were cancelled or cut back, but they give some idea of the dimensions of early planning, and of the fact that the best made campaign plans can go awry.

Romney's campaign budget, covering the period from September 1, 1967 to July 31, 1968, originally totalled $4.2 million: Romney Associates, $1.5 million; Romney for President, the main operating committee, $1 million; four primaries (New Hampshire, Wisconsin, Nebraska, and Oregon), $1.2 million; and activity in nonprimary states, $500,000. In addition to these expenses, however, there were the expenditures prior to September 1, 1967; costs at the Republican National Convention would have added at least $500,000; and exigencies undoubtedly would have required increasing the budget during the campaign.

But it was not to be. As early as April 1967, Romney's standing in the polls was sagging,[6] and four months later a nationwide syndicated column claimed that Romney's campaign was suffering from major problems in fund raising as well as from political difficulties.[7] Many observers believe that Romney never recovered from his highly publicized statement in late

August that he was "brainwashed" by military and diplomatic personnel in Vietnam,[a] Theodore White reports that Romney himself knew his campaign was doomed and wanted to get out in the fall of 1967.[9] Pushed by his supporters, however, Romney formally announced his candidacy in late November, only to withdraw 101 days later, 13 days before the New Hampshire primary.

The actual cost of George Romney's campaign was $1.5 million. Of the total, approximately $280,000 had been spent for the New Hampshire primary, $100,000 for activity in Wisconsin, and about $30,000 in Oregon prior to Romney's withdrawal. There are no detailed breakdowns of the total spent by expenditure category, but various items and monthly budgets are available.

One interesting budget document shows line items month-by-month from December 1, 1967 to March 15, 1968. December totals were budgeted at $190,764, broken down into more than 20 functional categories. Another document compared actual expenses, which were also listed by function, and totaled $189,445. An amazing projection and compliance for a political campaign! January and February (1968) budget projections were at $239,000 and $217,000, respectively, but in the heat of the campaign no comparisons of the actual costs with the projected costs were computed and interest in such comparisons wanes once a campaign ends.

The original plan and actual expenses for public opinion polling are of special interest. Plans were made for national as well as state polling and a budget document projected $154,000 for the polling (cost estimates were to be considered plus or minus ten percent). The total covered national polls, $50,000; eight primary states, averaging $8,000 per study, $64,000; and special studies for delegate persuasion, $40,000. In actuality, less than $100,000 was spent for one national and five state surveys (four in New Hampshire and one in Wisconsin).

Several documents regarding the New Hampshire primary contest show the anatomy of a campaign. The following summary was a projection of total costs made in early February:

Paid to 2-4-68	$105,100
Incurred but unpaid	32,000
Projected fixed costs	62,000
Contingency	10,000
Media	158,000
Total	$367,100

---

[a] A Louis Harris Survey reported that as a consequence of the statement Romney dropped from first to fourth place among Republican contenders.[8]

There were back-up figures for each of the categories. For example, the $105,100 paid to date was detailed as follows:

Organizational	$31,000
Candidate support	4,300
Direct mail	22,000
Media	37,200
Concord headquarters	5,700
Hanover headquarters	4,900

The $62,000 in projected fixed costs included expenses for the travel party of Governor and Mrs. Romney in the state, $20,000; field and advance men and Romney girls, $15,000; five New Hampshire staff salaries, $8,500. It is even possible to present further breakdowns of these amounts, for example of the travel party costs:

Press bus	$3,000
Hotels	7,000
Food	3,000
Press food and rooms	2,000
Mrs. Romney's party	2,000
Miscellaneous and contingency	3,000

Another document, dated March 27 (four weeks after Romney's withdrawal), showed the actual media costs in New Hampshire, which amounted to roughly 25 percent of the total costs in the state.

Newspaper Advertising[b]	$33,729.85
Television	12,308.15
Billboards and Posters	17.758.22
Radio	6,922.50
Total	$70,718.72

---

[b] In 1968, a special analysis of newspaper advertising was done by Media Records, Inc., a firm that specializes in counting newspaper advertising lineage, and then, from rate charts, determines the cost of the advertising. Special analyses of advertising by candidates in the New Hampshire and Oregon presidential primaries included weekly as well as daily newspapers. For Romney's New Hampshire campaign, the Media Records compilation was only $10,158; the discrepancy between this figure and the total listed by the Romney campaign ($33,729.85) cannot be explained. A similar comparison for the McCarthy campaign showed a discrepancy of only $809 on a total of about $31,000; and that could be explained by the possible insertion of advertising by individuals not connected with the official campaign. In Romney's case, there is no reason to doubt the figures as documented above.

Very detailed back-up figures for these amounts were also available, of which some examples follow.

Newspaper —Week of 2/18–2/24

Romney Column ads, 2 in all dailies (Contact Show)	$3,072.13
Telethon Tune-Ins in all dailies	3,132.44
Washington Day Speech ads, *Concord Daily Monitor, Manchester Union Leader*	340.47
Come and Meet ad, *Peterborough Transcript*	70.59
Total	$6,615.63

Television

Vietnam Show

Air time, WMUR, WMTW	$ 780.00
Pike Productions, editing, recording, taping, announcer, mixing tapes	2,685.97
WMUR-TV: studio time, taping with 5 men and cost of two video prints and tapes	1,106.89
UPI film	2,000.00
Total	$6,572.86

Mark Evans Show

Air time, WMUR, WMTW	$ 720.00
Fannell Studios, making of TV slide for minute break	18.18
Total	$ 738.18

Telethon

Air time, WMUR	$ 830.00
Air time, WMTW	420.00
60 seconds, WMUR	116.18
60 seconds, WMTW	75.00
Studio time and production	2,140.73
Talent fee for announcers	117.65
Total	$3,699.56

Ten-Second Spots

WMTW	$ 23.00
WCSH	73.00
WMUR	180.00
WGAN	120.00
Production costs of spot	607.42
Total	$1,003.42

Billboards

Cost of showing for two months	$13,254.80
Printing and production of first posting, 24 sheets	2,253.64
Printing and production of second posting, 24 sheets	1,111.22
200 2-sheeters, first posting	$ 387.77
200 2-sheeters, second printing	314.76
Fannell Studios, mechanical for billboards, posters, bumper strips, and photos	436.03
Total	$17,758.22

The Romney campaign in New Hampshire received national attention in early 1968 because a special profile of New Hampshire voters was prepared in a computer headquarters in Hanover. Information was detailed about every Republican voter in the state, some 150,000 strong. This project lent itself to both strategic and operational needs. It permitted mailings to any or all elements of the list; individuals could be invited to Romney appearances in their areas, or to visit the "home headquarters" planned in every city and village in the state. Prepared by a campaign management firm, Campaign Consultants, Inc., the profile was documented in a 121-page report accompanied by another volume of statistical tables two inches thick. These cost about $50,000. The same firm used the profile to direct the Romney media campaign in the primary.

Official reports filed in Wisconsin showed $84,458 spent before Romney's withdrawal; other expenditures related to the primary would bring the total to close to $100,000. One interesting sidelight to the Wisconsin campaign was that Romney had trouble lining up a competent advertising agency within the state because Nixon had already tied up the two major Republican-oriented agencies.

The financing for Romney's campaign came mainly from a half-dozen sources. One insider estimated that 85 percent of the money came from several people, including at least $200,000 each from George Romney himself, Nelson Rockefeller, and J. Willard Marriott. At least two other individuals were probably within the $50–100,000 range—J. Clifford Folger and Harold McClure, Jr. However, in the cases of Folger and McClure, and Max Fisher, another large giver, it is not clear how much they themselves gave and how much they raised from others. It is known that Folger personally gave several weeks pay to some staffers who were fired as soon as Romney withdrew.

The fund-raising chores were apportioned in an interesting manner. Fisher was finance chairman, he is Jewish and ostensibly raised money among Jews and other contacts; Marriott is a Mormon (as is Romney) with access to other Mormons; and Folger is a WASP with much experience in Republican circles. There was a division of labor, though jurisdictions overlapped and Fisher was the key man. There was much criticism of the operation. In one case, a breakfast for 200 top corporation executives was planned but follow-through at the top was lacking and the event fell through. At times, telephone calls that should have been made were not made, and although personal thank-you notes from the candidate were promised for contributions of $5,000 or more, in some cases, thank-you notes were not sent.

Special efforts were made to reach two immensely wealthy persons for contributions, but these also fell through for lack of proper follow-through by the candidate or his finance chairman. It happened that several close associates of Howard Hughes were Mormons, and ground work in that direction was laid. (McCarthy fund raisers also tried to get to the elusive Hughes, in the belief that his views on Vietnam were congenial, but this approach apparently was never consummated either.) Another Romney campaign operative regularly performed professional services for J. Paul Getty; groundwork was again laid, but apparently the effort was never clinched. These examples illustrate the gambits sometimes conceived to try to reach wealthy potential contributors.

A separate fund-raising operation and a bank account were set up in Phoenix, Arizona, independent of the Fisher operation. This effort raised about $70,000, which was to be used in the Oregon primary, but about $30,000 of the total was returned to donors when Romney withdrew. A separate Utah group had raised about $12,000 for Oregon before the withdrawal and then returned $3.80 to each contributor. The only major fund-raising event about which information is available is a breakfast which was held in Salt Lake City, at which about 50 people contributed a total of $26,000.

For the New Hampshire primary, virtually all the money came from the national campaign; there was neither the time nor resources to try to raise any money in the state, and only about $200 in unsolicited local contributions were received. Of the $83,100 reported in receipts in Wisconsin, only one $500 contributor from within the state was listed, and the remainder came from campaign operatives or as transfers from eleven committees located in Detroit.

The personal finances of Presidential candidates (indeed, of all political candidates) are the subject of much speculation, which often runs wild because of candidates' reticence to reveal more than very general information. In 1968, however, George Romney took the unprecedented step of making public his income tax returns for the previous twelve years, beginning in 1955.[10] No other candidates followed Romney's example of personal financial candor in such a comprehensive way, although Eugene McCarthy revealed some information on his income and net worth.

Nixon

At the outset, Richard M. Nixon had disabilities as a Presidential candidate resulting from his previous defeats. He had to build both confidence and a new image as a vote-getter in order to become a repeat-after-defeat standard bearer. His prenomination campaign included a judicious mix of selected primaries, avoiding expensive head-on clashes in a state like California, and careful cultivation of party regulars, particularly in the non-primary states. After the Republican disaster of 1964 and amid the tumult in the Democratic Party, Nixon knew his party wanted a pragmatist who would not alienate too much the Republican right or left.

In the circumstances, the prenomination financial campaign was notable: it was among the most expensive campaigns in history (in the same range as the McCarthy campaign costs), yet it was not the campaign of a candidate spending his own money and money was raised from a relatively broad base. While there were periods of difficulty in raising money, the campaign was financed without deficits and not a single fund-raising dinner was held throughout.

Early in 1966 an organization (Congress '66) was formed to support Richard Nixon's activities on behalf of Republican candidates in that year's Congressional elections. Nixon travelled 30,000 miles, campaigning in 86 Congressional Districts in 35 states. A total of $90,000 to cover the cost of this travel and one assistant was raised independently, as the Republican Party maintained strict neutrality by not aiding Nixon.[e] In November, the Republicans scored an impressive election result, which Nixon had not only worked for but also predicted, and Nixon thereafter became a major Presidential contender. The first planning session for the Nixon campaign was held in early January 1967. The basic strategy to win the Republican nomination was developed, and this included low visibility for the candidate during 1967.[12]

Nineteen months and more than $10 million later, Richard Nixon was the Republican nominee for President. Nixon's central national organization spent more than $8.5 million, mostly in 1968. Only broad categories of expenditure are available, as follows:

Advertising (some in primaries, some nationally) $2,500,000
Direct national organizational support of primaries 1,500,000
Convention 500,000
Organizing and funding citizens' organizations 400,000
Financial operation (not counting mailing costs) 150,000
Campaign management, including candidate travel,
   staff, regional organizational network,
   research, advance, women's activities,
   New York and Washington operations 3,500,000

---

[e] Witcover notes that Nixon claimed he was responsible for raising between $4 and $5 million, for the midterm elections, between 1964 and 1966.[11]

But substantial additional amounts were raised and spent independently in three of the major primary states—Wisconsin, Nebraska, and Oregon; by numerous state and local organizations in both primary and nonprimary states; by committees not controlled by the national headquarters; and by individuals. The total surely exceeds $10 million and may approach $12 million, if one includes the noncentrally supplied funds and all 1967 costs as well. To illustrate: a major three-floor headquarters, renting for $1,200 per month, was opened in Washington (one block from the White House) in April 1967; an office was opened in New Hampshire a full six months before the primary date; a locally supported write-in campaign in the New Jersey primary cost $80,000.

The estimated costs of the Nixon campaign in the major primary states are:

New Hampshire	$500,000
Wisconsin	500,000
Indiana	200,000
Nebraska	100,000
Oregon	500,000

These figures include direct payments for advertising from the national budget, mainly in New Hampshire and Oregon, but other advertising expenditures in those states not attributable to the national advertising budget were also made. The advertising expenditures in Wisconsin, Indiana, and Nebraska were part of the state budgets, but important parts of those funds came from national support of the primary efforts in those states. From late February, when Romney withdrew, until April 30, when Rockefeller entered, much of the pressure was off the Nixon campaign, and some national expenditures were cut back: for example, at least $50,000 worth of polling was cancelled.

Official Wisconsin reports show one interesting set of figures for the central Nixon primary campaign there. Payments to a public relations firm handling the Nixon account were broken down by time, space, and productions costs, as follows:

Production and advertising materials	$70,045
Newspaper advertising and radio	92,641
TV production	28,714
TV time	96,154
Outdoor advertising	32,657

This totals $320,211, bringing media costs to almost two-thirds of the total spent in the state. Another item put staff costs at $28,168.

In Oregon, one Nixon committee reported $173,000 in expenditures,[13] roughly categorized as follows: $50,000 for salaries and staff expenses,

$50,000 for mailing and postage, $30,000 in advertising, $20,000 for headquarters costs, and the rest in miscellaneous expenses. On the eve of the Oregon primary, "Nixon Now," a 30-minute documentary which had cost $100,000 to make,[14] was shown on nationwide television. In Oregon, it was followed by a 90-minute telethon to cap Nixon's primary contests.

The Nixon base of contributors for the national campaign was half the number of the Goldwater campaign in 1964, but the campaign raised and spent almost twice as much: about $2.2 million was raised from more than 150,000 contributors, with an average $14 contribution from a direct-mail drive numbering 5,000,000 pieces. The larger and main source of funds, however, came from contributors of $1,000 or more, who for at least that amount became members of Richard Nixon Associates (RNA). RNA had 1,200 contributors and provided more than one-half of the $8.5 million in nationally raised funds. It was a vehicle for recognizing large contributors at receptions, through special privileges at the convention, with gold lapel pins and a promised postelection advisory role. But it was not as widely publicized or criticized as the Democrats' President's Club, on whose operation it seemed modelled.[15]

Little is known about the membership of RNA in the prenomination period. One cannot assume that many of the largest contributors in the general election campaign were also big contributors in the prenomination period. There are four notable examples of major postconvention financial supporters who were in other camps earlier: Max Fisher was a big contributor as well as fund-raising chairman for Romney; Henry Salvatori gave to the Reagan campaign; Jack Dreyfus, Jr., was a major contributor to the McCarthy campaign; and John Hay Whitney gave to the Rockefeller campaign.

However, the largest known contributor to the Nixon banner in 1968 stayed throughout: he was W. Clement Stone of Chicago, President of Combined American Insurance Co., and counted by *Fortune* as a centimillionaire. In mid-1968, press reports indicated that Stone had contributed $500,000 to Nixon's prenomination campaign, and this figure was confirmed by an associate of Stone's and by Nixon aides. According to these sources, Mr. and Mrs. Stone gave $250,000 in $6,000 portions to numerous Nixon committees while the primaries were in progress. Another $250,000 was loaned in a single amount after the primaries but before the Convention; this loan was later forgiven and the money was dispersed as contributions to various Nixon committees. Early on, the Stone people admitted and publicized the $500,000 contribution figure, but because such a large amount from one source could be embarrassing to the Nixon campaign, the admissions were rescinded. Mr. Stone later acknowledged giving $200,000 during 1968, although the record shows that Mr. and Mrs. Stone gave at least $153,916 during the general election period alone. It seems most likely that the Stones' contributions to Nixon and other Republican candidates in 1968 were in the neighborhood of $700,000. The

$500,000 amount to a single candidate is the largest nonfamily contribution reported since the 1920s, although not the only one believed to have been made in 1968, and the $700,000 total is many times larger than any set of contributions from any individual or husband-wife team learned of in the Heard, Gore Committee, or Citizens' Research Foundation (CRF) studies over the last two decades.

There were unverifiable reports of other very large contributions to the Nixon prenomination campaign, and several people undoubtedly did give in the hundreds of thousands of dollars. One millionaire later appointed to the President's Cabinet was said by some to have given very large amounts, and there were similar reports about large gifts from a textile manufacturer.

Little notable data on sources of funds are available for the five major primaries which Nixon contested, although some comparable information was obtained for Wisconsin, Nebraska, and Oregon. Of the $460,000 officially reported to have been spent in Wisconsin, about $347,000 was transferred in from national committees, and this amount is included in the $8.6 million spent by the central organization. In Oregon, however, transfers of funds from these national committees accounted for only $65,500 of the $171,00 reported by one Nixon committee. For the Wisconsin primary, the bulk of large individual contributions came from people located out-of-state—only one contribution as high as $1,000 came from a person within the state. In Oregon, addresses of contributors are not given, but patterns of out-of-state large contributors for the three states are comparable.

The following individuals are known to have contributed the listed amounts to the Nixon primary campaigns in Wisconsin, Oregon, and Nebraska:

	Wisconsin	Oregon	Nebraska
Abplanalp, Robert H. Bronxville, New York	$3,000	$3,000	$1,000
Bobst, Elmer H. Morris Plains, New Jersey	3,000	3,000	1,000
Frick, Miss Helen Clay Pittsburgh, Pennsylvania	6,000	3,000	—
Garland, John J. Los Angeles, California San Marino, California	2,500	2,500	—
King, John M. Denver, Colorado	5,000	6,000	—
McGovern, Mr. and Mrs. Eugene Long Island, New York	6,000	3,000	1,000

	Wisconsin	Oregon	Nebraska
Olin, John M. St. Louis, Missouri East Alton, Illinois	3,000	3,000	1,000
Payson, Mrs. Charles New York, New York	3,000	—	1,000
Phipps, Mr. and Mrs. Ogden Palm Beach, Florida New York, New York	3,000	3,000	—
Russell, Fred J. Los Angeles, California South Gate, California	3,000	3,000	—
Stone, Mr. and Mrs. W. Clement Chicago, Illinois	9,000	9,000	1,000

The above amounts represent only those contributions on the record, and contributions by these persons, and others, to the national committees in the campaign, and to other primary states where information is not so readily available, may well be much larger. It is likely that any contributor to two or more primary state campaigns also gave to the national campaign, and the above contributors were probably among the largest to the Nixon prenomination campaign.

The money contributed by these and other individuals in Wisconsin, Nebraska and Oregon is in addition to the $8,500,000 raised and spent by the central campaign organization. This, plus more local spending not reported in these states, plus other state and local spending noted earlier, brings the Nixon expenditures total well within the $10-12 million range estimated.

There was one rather unusual appeal for help during the Nixon campaign. In June, 1968, when Rockefeller's massive and expensive media campaign was reaching its peak, the United Citizens for Nixon spent $500 on a classified advertisement in 17 newspapers around the country, asking for:

Volunteers to nominate and elect Richard Nixon; no pay, long hours; hard work; satisfaction of helping best-qualified American become President of the United States.[16]

Rockefeller

During most of the 1960s, Nelson Rockefeller was an acknowledged leader of the moderate wing of the Republican Party. However, because of his two unsuccessful Presidential bids and his refusal to support Goldwater after the 1964 convention, Rockefeller and his advisors believed that his candidacy in 1968 could not succeed and would only reopen bitter wounds in the party. Therefore, Rockefeller became one of the key political and financial backers of George Romney. As Romney's campaign floundered and finally collapsed, the pressure steadily increased on Rockefeller to run. On March 21, almost two months after Romney's withdrawal, Rockefeller announced he would not run, but the pressure only increased, and on April 30 he finally yielded and became a Presidential candidate.[17]

Throughout the winter of 1967–8 there had been many efforts to try to get Rockefeller to run—some at considerable expense—which generated considerable spontaneous support at the local level. In New Hampshire, at least $15,000 was spent on a write-in campaign for Rockefeller, including about $10,000 to mail sample ballots, $2,000 on radio ads, and $1,500 on newspaper ads. The Massachusetts primary was held on the day Rockefeller finally announced his decision to run, and he won in a write-in campaign which supporters claimed cost only $1,500. There were other primary states where spending occurred, almost all of it preceding and separate from the national campaign; at least $3,000 was spent in Nebraska and at least $8,000 in the District of Columbia. In Pennsylvania, Rockefeller had strong support in a write-in effort (and later at the Republican convention from that state's delegation). At least three major committees operated, raising more than $100,000, mainly from Pennsylvania sources. In Oregon, official reports show $124,770 spent for the primary there; $114,547 of that amount came in transfers from a committee named Northwest Republicans for Rockefeller, which undoubtedly received Rockefeller money from the East.

There were other local efforts which worked to get Rockefeller to run, or supported him after he did. One, a New York Draft Rockefeller Committee, spent about $15,000 in all, including one full-page newspaper ad. Another, the National Bipartisan Committee, spent at least the cost of its full-page ad which appeared in *The New York Times*. Additionally, four scattered New York committees filed reports in Albany, with combined spending of $36,000. Larger and more expensive efforts got under way after Romney's withdrawal left the moderate field open. Governor Spiro T. Agnew of Maryland went to some expense to open a National Draft Rockefeller '68 headquarters in Baltimore before Rockefeller pulled the rug out from under the effort by not announcing his candidacy as early as expected. On separate occasions, a group of Oregon supporters and a group of Republican leaders and public officials flew to New York to visit with Rockefeller to urge him to run.

Perhaps the most unusual, and certainly the most expensive, effort to draft Rockefeller cost one supporter $100,000. Stewart R. Mott, who was later to become one of Senator McCarthy's largest contributors, undertook his own campaign on Rockefeller's behalf in March. He bought newspaper ads, mainly in *The New York Times* and in eight Michigan (Mott's home state) papers, urging Rockefeller to run. In series, the ads totalled 21 full pages; they solicited contributions, and brought in about 7,000 replies, including $40,000 in cash and pledges for more. This led Mott to set up a Coalition for a Republican Alternative,[d] which, with the earlier ads and other expenses, spent a total of $140,000. Applying the $40,000 receipts to the total, the rest was paid for by Mott personally. This effort was largely ignored by the Rockefeller intimates. In the newspaper ads, Mott had offered to contribute $50,000 if Rockefeller announced by March 15, if he adopted an acceptable policy for withdrawal from Vietnam, and if readers pledged $100,000. But Rockefeller was not ready to announce then, and when he did, there was no effort to embrace Mott's operation. Mott persisted through the Coalition committee until June 1, but by then he was involved in the McCarthy campaign and did not contribute to the national Rockefeller campaign.

Once Rockefeller finally announced, no efforts were spared for want of money. He did not enter any primaries. The campaign was mainly a national media effort directed at influencing public opinion, to show through opinion polls that Rockefeller could win against potential Democratic nominees.[18] At the same time, major efforts were made to win delegates; the campaign tried to persuade prospects to hang loose and not be committed to Nixon or Reagan, even if they could not be committed to Rockefeller.

In 1968, the Rockefeller financial disclosure record was worse than it had been in 1964.[e] Rockefeller operatives consistently refused to give any information, even though all the other 1968 contenders had disclosed significant aspects of their finances. The only reason given for refusing to cooperate was that whatever figures were given would not be believed, and that members of the Rockefeller family were sensitive about divulging their share of the campaign. But it is curious that a major public figure for more than a decade, an enlightened man with a progressive record, a man criticized because of his wealth, fails to care about frank disclosure, or to see that it could be a most disarming tactic. Rockefeller and other wealthy candidates have been and probably will continue to be charged with attempting to buy nominations or elections, yet by refusing to divulge the facts, they are victimized by irresponsible charges as to how much they are actually spending. Endless speculation could be stilled if the truth were told. While there may well be strategic reasons during a campaign to divulge as little as possible, no purpose could possibly be served by secrecy after it is over, and especially in Nelson Rockefeller's case, when 1968 was undoubtedly his Presidential swan song.

By piecing together bits of information, it can be fairly estimated that

---

[d] Named after the Coalition for a Democratic Alternative, the New York dump-Johnson and, later, McCarthy organization.

[e] Of all the Republican and Democratic prenomination campaigns, the Rockefeller campaign was the least cooperative in providing information for this study.

about $8 million was spent by Rockefeller's central campaign. (One can imagine the cost had any primaries been contested!) The money was spent roughly as follows:

Advertising[19]		$4,500,000
Network TV	$1,000,000	
Spot TV	2,000,000	
Newspapers	1,500,000	
Organization		1,500,000
Travel (65,000 miles in 45 states)		1,000,000
Polls and Surveys		250,000
Convention		750,000

One of the few hard figures available seems to corroborate the advertising figures above. The Leading National Advertisers/Television Bureau of Advertising, an organization which monitors television advertising, listed Rockefeller television network spending of $906,000: the $100,000 difference between this figure and the one above would probably be due to production costs. Network advertising consisted of two half-hour programs and a series of one-minute participations and five-minute programs telecast from June 11 until August 2. The following excerpt from the network schedule gives some of the flavor of the Rockefeller media campaign.

Network Television

Date	Network	Program	Advertisement/Time
June 11	CBS	—	"The Presidential Man"/30 min.
June 13	ABC	"That Girl"	"Why I Run"
June 16	ABC	Sunday Movie	"Why I Run"
June 18	NBC	Tuesday Movie	"Johnny"
June 18	ABC	"N.Y.P.D."	"Why I Run"
June 20	ABC	"The Flying Nun"	"Johnny"
June 23	ABC	Sunday Movie	"River"/"Why I Run"
July 1	NBC/New Haven	"Today"	"Rocky"/5 min.
July 3	NBC/Nebraska	"Today"	"Rocky"/5 min.

In addition to the network television, there were one-minute spot announcements and five-minute programs on local television stations; some radio was also used. One source estimated that there were a total of 462 television spots a week on 100 stations in 30 cities. The newspaper advertising campaign included a series of seven full-page ads in 41 dailies in 33 cities, and totalled an estimated 377 pages in 54 newspaper in 40 cities.[20] The media plan was directed at a northern tier of 13 states, the District of Columbia, and Texas—reaching 60 percent of the nation's population. A special effort was made to persuade Governor Rhodes and the Ohio delegation. In that state, direct mail was used intensively, and a media campaign costing about $100,000 was mounted for a week prior to one of Rockefeller's trips to the state.

Polls and surveys were used, but not as extensively as one might have thought. One set of polls in eleven states was commissioned after Romney withdrew, and cost about $50,000. (As noted above, when Romney withdrew Nixon cancelled a series of state polls he had contracted for.) Rockefeller's decision on whether or not to announce his candidacy relied on the public national polls that Gallup and Harris were conducting, as well as on private polls. In addition, Rockefeller had to decide whether to run in the Oregon and Nebraska primaries; polls were done in Oregon but not in Nebraska to help make the decision.

The Oregon survey was part of a series of eleven polls that Rockefeller commissioned once he announced. Rockefeller strategy considered favorable poll results as crucial to demonstrate voter support among independents and Democrats, and the ability to beat Democratic candidates more handily than Nixon. Accordingly, Rockefeller challenged Nixon to a state-by-state comparison, in which Rockefeller expected the larger states with sufficient electoral votes would show him to be a winner. Nixon and the Republican Party refused to share the costs of polling in all 50 states, estimated at $500,000; this would have been technically difficult to carry out and would have put a strain on the major polling organizations. Rockefeller never did more than the eleven originally chosen, and these were in nine states. All were single polls, not waves, though some were split, half before a trip to the state, half afterward, to help measure impact. There were also two nationwide polls, one augmented in the South, and several riders on regularly scheduled polls. This set cost less than $200,000, which combined with the earlier polling, brought the total to about $250,000.

It is even more difficult to get information on the sources of Rockefeller's funds than on the expenditures, but one bit of hard data was obtained from an official filing in Albany which was as unusual as it was revealing. The document was unusual because in most Presidential prenomination campaigns, central headquarters committees handling large amounts of money are organized in states without laws requiring filing. As noted, there is no Federal law which requires filing in such campaigns, and committees are usually established in Delaware or Illinois or the District of Columbia where there are no state filing laws. For example, it was rumored that there were 34 Rockefeller committees established in Delaware to conceal finances. Committees such as these can be paper organizations existing only in the office of a local attorney, with actual headquarters elsewhere. As will be noted, only a few major McCarthy committees reported in New York and Massachusetts, and no central

Nixon or Romney or Humphrey or Kennedy committees are known to have reported under state laws.[f] But somehow one major Rockefeller committee reported in Albany.

The organization was called Rockefeller for President (New York), and its report covered a period from June 6 until September 18. Receipts totalled $1,840,627.25 and expenditures were in an identical amount. Mrs. Martha Baird Rockefeller, Nelson's stepmother, contributed a total of $1,482,625 in eight separate amounts, ranging from $425,000 on June 6 to $10,000 on September 18. Nelson gave $350,000 on August 15, and Laurence S. Rockefeller gave a total of $2,000 in two contributions. The remaining $6,000 was made up in contributions from outsiders (ranging from 25 cents to $5,000). It is worth stressing the financial implications of these Rockefeller contributions because they reveal the true costs of politics to wealthy individuals. A federal gift tax law applies to political contributions of more than $3,000 to a single candidate or committee. The rates are progressive and the counting of gifts is cumulative, whether made to others within a family or to an outsider or nontax-exempt organization. Presumably after many years of such giving, Mrs. Rockefeller would pay at the maximum rate of about 57 percent, which probably would make the total cost to her of helping Nelson's campaign through this committee about $2,323,000. And she may well have given to other committees as well in excess of $3,000.

On the other hand, tax lawyers claim that the $350,000 listed from Nelson himself probably does not fall under the gift tax, because it would be considered as merely an out-of-pocket expenditure by the candidate for his own campaign, and not constitute a gift. However, it would be considered a gift if Nelson's wife gave money. The conclusion is that it costs less if the candidate himself foots the bill than if other members of the family do so, but presumably families like to spread the burden.

The Albany filing revealed a series of expenditures but only to three recipients: $10.67 to the treasurer of the committee for an unspecified purpose; four items totalling $380,118.29 sent to another Rockefeller committee; and 21 payments totalling $1,460,498.29 to Jack Tinker & Partners, Inc., an advertising agency that did the campaign advertising.

The central Rockefeller campaign raised about $1.5 million outside the Rockefeller family. Of that amount, approximately one-half was given by perhaps a dozen persons, and another dozen gave about $500,000. Not more than $10,000 was raised from newspaper ads or was unsolicited. The remaining $6.5 million spent by the central campaign was apparently put up by the Rockefeller family (including the $1.8 million already noted). One published report states that each of the Rockefeller brothers agreed to limit his contribution to $750,000.[21]

---

[f] In some of the primary states, the candidates and their committees filed reports as required by state law, but here I refer to major national-level central committees, of which only a few McCarthy and one Rockefeller committee were found.

For a complete picture of the political finances of the Rockefeller family, one must add the contributions made by Nelson and perhaps other family members to Romney's campaign. Nelson Rockefeller alone is reported to have contributed about $300,000 to the Romney campaign. Combining his own Presidential expenses to his Romney contributions would surely put Nelson Rockefeller in the ranks of the largest financiers of politics in 1968.

Reagan

Although Ronald Reagan did not formally announce his candidacy for the Presidency until the first day of the Republican National Convention, planning for the campaign began immediately after his overwhelming victory in the 1966 California gubernatorial election. Theodore White claims that the original campaign plan drawn up by F. Clifton White (formerly Goldwater's key strategist) was never implemented,[22] but there is little doubt that a very deliberate noncandidate strategy was agreed upon and carried out throughout 1967 and 1968.[23]

About $750,000 was spent in the various authorized and unauthorized noncampaign efforts on behalf of the noncandidate. Some of the expenditures were not exclusively for Reagan, but were costs of the large California delegation (which was pledged to the governor as a favorite son), and some of the bills were picked up by wealthy delegates. There is no way of separating the purely Reagan expenses from those of his home delegation dedicated to furthering his cause.[g]

A major part of Reagan's strategy included his much-publicized travelling as a noncandidate to speak at various Republican functions across the country. One associate claimed a total of $3.8 million was raised for the party at these affairs between September 1967 and May 1968.[h] This activity was a means of gaining national attention, meeting potential supporters throughout the country, and exhibiting loyalty to the party at the same time. These travels on behalf of the party were the kind that paid off in the nomination of Barry Goldwater in 1964 and were similarly to pay off for Richard Nixon in 1968. Reagan's travels were financed through a trust fund set up under the direction of the Republican State Central Committee of California: money was raised by charging the sponsors of the dinners (or other affairs at which Reagan was to appear) either a portion of the gross receipts or a fixed fee arrived at by negotiation. In all, about $100,000 was raised and spent through the trust fund, but this amount is not included in the $750,000 actual campaign costs. The money was used to cover the travel costs of the governor and his entourage, as

---

[g] Much the same comment can be made about the New York delegation and Rockefeller expenses.

[h] Chester, Hodgson, and Page say that $1.5 million had been raised by January 1968.[24]

well as per diem expenses for political employees who helped with advance work, research, and other tasks.

A separate but similar fund of $250,000 was maintained for the costs of Reagan's appearances at Republican functions within California and for his activities as the state party leader. Money for the instate fund came from an assessment of 22½ percent of the gross income at the fund-raising events Reagan attended.[4] While these activities no doubt enhanced Reagan's standing as a potential candidate, they are not properly considered campaign expenses.

In the New Hampshire primary, Reagan disclaimed candidacy, but several thousand dollars were spent by self-starting supporters, of which $1,350 went into newspaper advertising. In Wisconsin, official reports of supporters show $6,540 was spent, but the total figure was probably closer to $10,000. In Nebraska, perhaps $25,000 was spent, mostly on television and mailings. In Oregon, a major effort, indirectly supported by Reagan's most intimate advisors, was undertaken. Official filings show $122,376 spent in that state, and it is probable that another $25,000 was spent independently and not included in the reported total. In the California primary, Nixon had agreed not to challenge Reagan, yet $100,000 was spent on a campaign to make a good showing for the governor, and to counter the recall effort in California which was embarrassing Reagan.

Beyond the travel and primary expenses, Reagan supporters hired F. Clifton White from February 1968 until the convention to advise the California delegation on national strategy and prospects for furthering their candidate. White's fee and expenses totalled more than $110,000, including $20,400 for travel, $12,800 for telephone, $10,900 for meetings, $60,000 for a portion of the field expenses, and $6,000 for some convention expenses. In addition to White's expenses, the Reagan campaign spent at least $150,000 at Miami Beach for a communications setup, a headquarters which was set up several months prior to the convention, a hospitality center, and receptions for delegates.

A national Reagan Information Center was located in Topeka, Kansas, because a key operative lived there and it served Reagan's purposes not to have headquarters in Washington or California. Much of the money for the Oregon primary came from the Topeka headquarters, which also probably sent money to Wisconsin and Nebraska. In addition to supplying funds for some of the primaries, the Topeka center spent more than $50,000 in campaign materials, and also spent about $90,000 for production and air time for a network television program, plus some local spots. The network production costs were minimal because the program consisted of a taped speech with only introduction and epilogue spliced in. A fund appeal on the broadcast brought in $50,000. Operatives claim the Topeka

[4] A separate third fund was maintained for the political travels of Lt. Governor Robert Finch.

funds came mostly from non-California sources, while the California and convention costs were covered mainly from California sources. It is probable that a small inner circle of Reagan friends put up most of the California funds.

There are several other Reagan supporters who were disclaimed by the Reagan organization, but who spent considerable additional funds. One, Walter J. Dilbeck, an Indiana millionaire, claimed to have spent $140,000 of his own money, starting in October 1967, to work up grass-roots support for Reagan; but only $57,000 was reported in official filings to have been spent in this effort,[j] which included opening a Washington office that was repudiated by Reagan.

Another supporter was a San Diego entrepreneur who published a book entitled *Reagan: A Political Biography*.[25] Some 200,000 copies were published as a commercial venture, and about one-third were sold to political committees or individuals who took it upon themselves to distribute the book as a campaign document. More than 40,000 copies were distributed in Oregon, and these costs are not included in the Oregon figures given. About 10,000 copies each were sent to Nebraska and Wisconsin. One of the committees that distributed the books was organized by the publisher, who then sold the books to the committee for distribution (and profit). Fund raising for the committee was carried on by mail, and claims were made that several thousand contributors helped out.

Stassen

In 1968, Harold Stassen waged a long campaign for the Presidency which is estimated to have cost $90,000. Most of the money was spent in travel and in the primary contests; in New Hampshire, about $10,000 was spent, including at least $5,520 for newspaper advertising, and in Wisconsin, official reports list expenditures of $43,417. In addition to these expenditures, there was the cost of a Washington office, only briefly open, and $7,000 was spent for a center at the convention.

Stassen himself contributed about $40,000 to his campaign, and the remaining $50,000 was raised from others, mostly in small contributions. In Wisconsin, the largest local contributor gave $1,200, while a supporter from Michigan was listed as a $3,000 contributor.

Vice-Presidential Campaign

The only campaign for the Vice-Presidency which is known to have involved significant amounts of money was that of Massachusetts Governor

---

[j] Filed with the Clerk of the House of Representatives. The report showed receipts of only $2,300; the rest was presumably made up by Dilbeck.

John Volpe.[k] An organization called "Friends of John A. Volpe" was set up in his homestate, to "further advance and promote the cause of efficient public service and responsive government." The organization admittedly had $263,000 in 1968, but it is not clear whether this was the total received and spent, or whether or not all the money was spent. Early in 1969, the officers of the organization refused to reveal the sources of the money, as requested by Massachusetts state officials, on the grounds that it was not a political committee because Volpe was not running for office.[20] Yet several weeks earlier, during the Senate confirmation hearings on his appointment to be Secretary of Transportation, Volpe had stated that the purpose of the fund was to promote him for the Vice-Presidency. At that time, Volpe said that $60,000 was spent on his gaining exposure outside the state, presumably through travel, and $70,000 was spent on his 1966 campaign debt and for contributions to Republican candidates in 1968. This rough accounting covers only about one-half of the known amount of the fund, and there is no information on if or how the rest of the money was spent.

The Democrats

The six Democratic contenders incurred costs of $25 million in their quests for the Presidential nomination, but the deficits and debt settlements noted above probably make the total actually spent about $21 million. McCarthy's effort was the longest and the most expensive, lasting nine months and costing about $11 million. Kennedy's 11-week whirlwind campaign, which included seven primary contests, cost $9 million. The combined campaigns of Johnson, Humphrey, and their Indiana and California stand-ins (Branigan and Lynch) cost close to $5 million, with Humphrey's effort accounting for more than 80 percent of that total. McGovern's brief campaign and Maddox's even briefer one cost, respectively, $74,000 and $50,000. Unlike the Republican campaigns, virtually all the Democratic spending occurred in 1968.

After the 1966 Congressional elections—the starting point for speculation about Republican hopefuls in the Presidential sweepstakes—the speculation about the Democrats was not about whom, but only about how Johnson would run his reelection campaign. Unlike the Republicans, there was no campaign planning at that time on the part of the President or any other Democrat. The main action in response to the 1966 Democratic election losses had been the hiring of two respected young political professionals at the Democratic National Committee, and they both left within six months.

---

[k] Volpe was one of Nixon's two or three final contenders for the job. Whether Volpe's campaign in any way influenced Nixon is not known.

Johnson

The campaign for the reelection of President Lyndon B. Johnson barely got up much steam before it was terminated. Because Johnson never formally declared his candidacy, there was little official or announced campaign activity.

The earliest reported activity was in mid-September 1967, when planning for the New Hampshire primary began;[27] six weeks later the State's Democratic Governor and Senator announced they would head a slate of delegates favorable to the President.[28] In mid-December, the overall strategy for the President's reelection campaign and counter offensive to McCarthy was described: Johnson would enter only those primaries where a state's law gave him no choice (Wisconsin, Nebraska, and Oregon); he would do little or no campaigning himself, maintaining an image of being above partisan politics; there would be campaigning by Vice-President Humphrey and other officials in the Administration; and there would be organizational effort by state Democratic officials where possible. In January 1968, some friends opened an office in Washington and began a program to encourage loyalty among influential party leaders and give assistance to favorable delegate slates or stand-in candidates. Not until February 21 did Johnson's unannounced campaign have an unannounced campaign manager (James H. Rowe), and only after McCarthy's remarkable showing in New Hampshire and Kennedy's entrance into the race did Johnson mobilize seriously for his campaign. Less than three weeks later, two days before the Wisconsin primary, it was all over. By then, March 31, 1968, major primary campaigns had been waged in New Hampshire and Wisconsin, significant activity had occurred in Indiana, and some preparatory work had been done in Nebraska, Oregon, and California.

The total cost of the Johnson effort was about $450,000 (treating the Branigan campaign in Indiana and the California campaign for the Lynch slate as separate operations, discussed under the Humphrey campaign). Apart from the primaries, the Washington organization probably spent $100,000; almost all the remainder was spent in the New Hampshire and Wisconsin campaigns.

In New Hampshire, Democrats loyal to the President ran an intensive write-in campaign on behalf of Johnson. Although a regular party organization is normally neutral in primary contests, this was certainly not true in New Hampshire (as it was also not true of the national party organization when it assumed the incumbent President would run again). Although officially the New Hampshire state party organization and the campaign organization were separate, most of the key people involved were the same, and the facilities and staff (but not the funds) of the party were used for the Johnson campaign. According to operatives in the state, about $64,000 was spent in New Hampshire, as follows:

Radio	$20,000
Newspapers	18,000
Brochures	10,000
Newsletters	2,600
Bumper stickers, etc.	2,500
Staff	2,500
Telephone	4,000
Miscellaneous	4,500

However, probably as much as $100,000 was actually spent (not including services provided by the state committee), and polls and other services supplies by the Washington committee added value to the campaign.

Wisconsin reports showed only $75,000 spent, of which $56,000 was paid to a public relations firm. However, Johnson supporters admit to spending close to $200,000 in the state, of which $125,000 was for media, and there were other expenditures from outside Wisconsin directed at the campaign. For example, a report of a national Citizens for Johnson-Humphrey Committee, a holdover from the 1964 campaign, showed direct expenditures of $54,500 in early 1968, of which many items were clearly for campaign expenses in Wisconsin. Milwaukee hotel bills, printing, and television costs were paid through a public relations firm, and there were travel costs charged by a Wisconsin airline. (Another official report, that of the 1964-holdover President's Club for Johnson Committee, showed $750 in research expenses for the Wisconsin primary.) Theodore White reports that the Democratic National Committee appropriated $200,000 of its funds for a final weekend media effort in Wisconsin,[29] although filed reports of the Democratic National Committee do not show recognizable payments that might account for this.

In Indiana, Governor Branigan had been persuaded to run as a stand-in for the President,[1] and some money had been spent by the Johnson organization before the President withdrew. Branigan—who had been talked into running only 15 days previously and had been informed of the withdrawal only a few minutes before the famous telecast—rejected Senator Edward Kennedy's suggestion that he withdraw from the race and ran, in effect, as a stand-in for Vice-President Humphrey.[31] In addition to the $150,000 spent directly in this effort, Branigan also had significant indirect state party organizational assistance, as had occurred in New Hampshire.

Another primary campaign with origins in the period before Johnson's withdrawal was the delegate slate in California headed by Attorney Gen-

---

[1] He had been reluctant to do so for many reasons, and in spite of a promise of $130,000 from the DNC to the state party.[30]

eral Thomas Lynch, the highest elected Democrat in the state. Some be-
ginnings were made: staff were assembled, headquarters opened, and
signatures gathered for the needed ballot petitions. Approximately $40,
000 was spent prior to Johnson's withdrawal. All the rest of the activity
and expenditures of the Lynch delegation will be noted in the discussion
of Humphrey's campaign.

Johnson's campaign supporters claimed that all of the money for the
New Hampshire campaign was raised in the state, but available evidence
seems to refute this claim. First, New Hampshire is not a wealthy state
and no other Presidential candidate has ever raised significant amounts
of money there. Second, one informant states that 25–35 people from
inside and out of the state donated at least $500 and constituted the finan-
cial base of the campaign. Third, there was a "District of Columbia
Committee for New Hampshire Democrats" to raise money for the campaign.[32] Finally, information from Wisconsin, where more data are available, raises questions about the extent of indigenous contributions to the
New Hampshire effort; the Wisconsin official reports show that much of
the money came from out of state. These reports also reveal much about
the personalization of fund raising for the President.

Of $139,000 received in Wisconsin in amounts of $500 or more, $105,
000 was transferred from the national Citizens for Johnson-Humphrey,[m]
various state affiliated Johnson-Humphrey Committees, and the Texas,
Illinois, New York, and California President's Clubs ($5,000 each). Fur-
ther, a parallel series of contributions were made to the national Citizens
from the various state Citizens affiliates and state President's clubs; in
spring 1968, of $84,300 contributed to the national Citizens, $80,800
came from these state groups. It seemed as if a Presidential word caused
the joint contributions of the state groups to the Wisconsin and national
Citizens organizations, and then of the national Citizens' contributions to
Wisconsin. The ability to command this kind of money, roughly $160,000
(adjusting for an intercommittee transfer of $25,000), is an illustration
of the leverage a President has in political-financial matters. The national
and state Citizens groups were holdover organizations from the 1964 campaign, and their funds had occasionally been used for Johnson or Humphrey political purposes. The involvement of the state President's clubs
reveals their development. Though they were established as Presidential
arms, they came to be recognized as national party fund-raising vehicles,
but in 1968 they reverted to their role as a personal Presidential finance
instrument.

Here the plot thickens, because $50,000 in special contributions are
known to have been made to the same state Citizens' and state President's
clubs before these organizations passed the monies on to the national Citizens and the Wisconsin Johnson committees. These special contributions

---

[m] $25,000 of which was not, incidentally, similarly recorded as an expenditure in the
official filing of the Citizens organization in Washington.

were made by the Seafarers International Union (SIU) in early April 1968, and were subsequently reported in official filings of the Union made with the Clerk of the House of Representatives; the SIU contributions were in the amount of $5,000 each and were sent to ten of the committees, which then passed the monies on as noted. (In addition to the $50,000 contributed to the Johnson committees, the Seafarers at a little later date also sent a series of ten $5,000 checks to as many committees supporting Vice-President Humphrey's Presidential aspirations. These $100,000 in Seafarers contributions were said to be linked to a favorable Johnson Administration ruling on an extradition case in which the union was interested.)[33]

While the Seafarers Union contributions accounted for $50,000 of the money used for Johnson's renomination campaign, at least $110,000 more came from the state Citizens' and President's clubs. Whether the rest was fresh money collected for the purpose, or was money previously collected by these state groups, the utilization of these channels illustrates ways contributions can be camouflaged through rerouting, and the ability of a President to manipulate funds through a network that could extend to many more states if necessary.

Once Johnson withdrew, a few contributors asked for the return of their President's Club gifts so as to redirect the money, presumably into Humphrey's prenomination campaign. Official fund raising by the Democratic National Committee (DNC) and the President's Club ceased, and national Club monies were mostly turned over to the DNC. Disposition of certain other state President's Club funds is unknown, and some may have found their way to help Humphrey.

The Dump-Johnson Movement

The roots of the McCarthy and Kennedy candidacies go back at least to the 1966 elections, when various antiwar groups supported nonincumbent peace candidates, all of whom lost, in either the primary or general election. Many political commentators and antiwar activists viewed these losses as an indication of the weakness of the antiwar movement. For example, the National Conference for New Politics (NCNP), one of the more radical antiwar organizations, believed the results proved that changes in the political leadership or the country's Vietnam policy were not possible within the dominant two-party system; they turned to strategies outside the electoral system, or at least outside the Democratic and Republican parties. The NCNP filed reports with the Clerk of the House, showing $106,840 spent in 1966.[n]

---

[n] The NCNP lated died a rather loud and publicized death at a September 1967 conference which was disrupted by its more radical elements. A few of its supporters ended up in the McCarthy campaign; most did not participate in the two major parties' activities in 1968, but became active in the fourth party effort. For 1967, the NCNP reported expenditures of $80,440.

But a few observers and antiwar activists believed that the large Democratic Congressional losses reflected growing anti-Johnson feeling, and began to see the possibility of an electoral strategy that would link the anti-Vietnam movement with the broader anti-Johnson sentiment in the country. In the spring of 1967, Allard Lowenstein (who was elected to Congress in 1968) and Curtis Gans of Americans for Democratic Action (ADA) were talking and meeting with various individuals and groups around the country, probing the depth of the anti-Johnson sentiment and advocating a political challenge to Johnson within the Democratic Party. During the late spring and summer, several state and local groups were formed, whose names illustrated their goals—Dissenting Democrats (California), Concerned Democrats (Michigan), Democrats for an Alternate Candidate (Colorado).

Meanwhile, in March, some people connected with the National Committee for an Effective Congress had arranged for Senator McCarthy to meet with a group of former Stevenson supporters, and the idea of a Presidential candidacy in opposition to Johnson was discussed. Other possible candidates were also discussed, while for the next six months, some of those people urged McCarthy to become the anti-Johnson candidate.

In August, California and New York sources contacted by Lowenstein pledged $3,000 to create a national dump-Johnson organization with a Washington office and hire Gans as a full-time organizer. The national Conference of Concerned Democrats was born on September 1, although it was not until six weeks later that $3,000 had been received, and only one-third of that came from the original pledges.

The Conference of Concerned Democrats (CCD) helped organize and coordinate groups in one-third of the states (most of which later became McCarthy campaign organizations), of which the largest and most famous was New York's Coalition for a Democratic Alternative (CDA). (The CDA raised considerable sums of money for the national McCarthy campaign in addition to supporting its own major campaigns for Democratic Convention delegates and for an insurgent Senatorial candidate.) In a little more than four months of active existence, the CCD and the state and local groups it spawned demonstrated the existence of a broad, committed base of support for an alternative Democratic candidate; a national conference staged by the CCD in Chicago in early December was a kind of miniconvention for the anti-Johnson crusade. McCarthy, who had announced his candidacy two days earlier, was the keynote speaker at the convention, and was endorsed by it.

The total expenditures and income of the CCD were $47,555.06. A few debts, some unreimbursed out-of-pocket expenses, and a donated ad would bring the total cost of this operation to about $53,000. Of the $47,555 in actual expenditures, about $26,000 was spent in staging the December convention (of which more than one-third was received in room and registration fees). The other $21,500 in organizing costs included $8,000 for travel, $4,500 for telephone, $3,000 for salaries, $4,000 for a press clipping service, and $2,000 in miscellaneous costs.

The CCD had one very large contributor, an example of the kind of previously nonpolitical individual whose antiwar beliefs led him to political involvement in 1967–68. Harry Roth, a clothing manufacturer, took out a full-page ad in *The New York Times* of September 26, 1967 (costing $7,800) in which he pledged $100,000 to any antiwar candidate who ran with Johnson's approval. When first approached by CCD organizers, Roth would not support an anti-Johnson movement, but he was later convinced and then gave $17,500 toward financing the December convention.

The other large contributions were relatively small by conventional political standards: they included one contribution of $1,475, one of $1,200, and eight at $500. There were also 12 contributions between $100 and $300. Small contributions, including responses to an ad in *The New Republic* and an ad in the Chicago *Sun-Times* in connection with the convention, and conference income accounted for about $12,000. A joint CCD-McCarthy fund-raising effort yielded another $2,000, and the McCarthy campaign later gave $8,000 to the CCD so that its staff would be able to stop separate fund raising to pay off existing debts and work instead for the McCarthy campaign.

McCarthy

When the Conference of Concerned Democrats was searching for an anti-Johnson candidate in the late summer and early fall of 1967, the obvious choice was Robert Kennedy because of his national prominence. His definitive (at the time) refusal led the antiwar leaders to other leading dove Senators, Frank Church, George McGovern, and Eugene McCarthy. Both Church and McGovern were willing to run if no one else did, but both were up for reelection in 1968 and were not eager to endanger their Senate seats in making the Presidential race. When the CCD leaders approached McCarthy, they found that he had independently come to believe that a political challenge to President Johnson had to be made, and was seriously considering making the move himself.[34]

McCarthy's formal declaration came on November 30, 1967. It was generally greeted with questions as to what he really expected to do, for few took his Presidential bid seriously. As late as February, the predominant tone in news articles about McCarthy was still one of questioning whether his candidacy was serious or whether he was a stalking horse for Kennedy. But when Romney withdrew, the lack of primary competition in the Republican Party resulted in more media attention to McCarthy's primary campaigns.

Although the McCarthy effort may at first have seemed to be only a policy campaign—an attempt to influence America's Vietnam policy—

many McCarthy staffers believed from the beginning that the nomination was a real goal, and certainly after the New Hampshire showing, the President's withdrawal, and the Wisconsin victory, the McCarthy "magical mystery tour" (a favorite staff epithet) was a serious campaign for the nomination. The Kennedy challenge helped escalate the campaign into a major financial effort.

The McCarthy campaign was unusual in several respects. Because it was based on efforts to change American policy in Vietnam and to find an alternative candidate to President Johnson, many of the antiwar groups, such as various Dissenting Democrats and Concerned Democrats, became McCarthy committees, and the early campaign benefited from their prior existence as operating committees ready to move quickly behind Mc-Carthy. In addition, the campaign was characterized by the greatest de-centralization of any modern campaign. In the financial operations, there were intrigues, espionage, and sabotage. Door locks were changed to pre-vent access by deposed managers; scores of different bank accounts were set up by different persons to further their favored projects; bootleg bank accounts were used to fund activities discontinued or no longer in favor; mailbags were captured to divert contributions to favored accounts; pro-grams were discontinued by authorizing payments in order to drain ac-counts and then not replenishing funds; certain large contributors were persuaded to support only favored activities.

In spite of the chaotic nature of the effort, or perhaps because of it, the McCarthy campaign was the most cooperative of any (except the aborted Romney one) in providing information for this study. Also like Romney, McCarthy early in the campaign made public some information about his personal finances. Unlike Romney, however—and unlike every other ma-jor Presidential candidate in 1968 except Humphrey—McCarthy is not a wealthy man: in addition to his Senator's salary of $30,000 (since raised to $42,500), he had other income of about $20,000 per year and his net worth was listed at only $30,000.

Before McCarthy announced his candidacy, elements of the antiwar movement had said up to $1 million was available for a peace candidate, and then this same amount was said to be available for McCarthy. Mc-Carthy himself said he thought that that amount would be enough, as John F. Kennedy had spent $1 million in 1960 and he (McCarthy) ex-pected to spend less than the 1960 total.[35] McCarthy soon found that the promised amounts were not negotiable dollars, and that the sum required for the campaign was going to be far in excess of any previous nomination effort.

McCarthy's central campaign included eight primaries (all except South Dakota were major efforts), lasted nine months, and spent about $8.6 million. In addition, locally financed primary campaigns in several other states and other local campaign activity in almost every state brought the total spent on behalf of McCarthy's candidacy to close to $11 million—in the same range as Nixon's costs.

Close to one-half of the total amount spent by the central campaign was spent in the primaries, including some New York and Massachusetts spending for New Hampshire. Virtually all money transferred from national headquarters was to the primary states; very little was transferred for delegate efforts in the nonprimary states.

New Hampshire	$280,000
Wisconsin	500,000
Indiana	700,000
Nebraska	160,000
South Dakota	30,000
Oregon	336,000
California	1,000,000
New York	700,000
Subtotal	$3,706,000

In addition, amounts for headquarters and supplemental accounts in New York and Washington, adjusted for transfers of funds, were as follows:

Washington:	
Headquarters	$1,600,000
Supplemental Accts.	400,000
New York:	
Headquarters	950,000
Supplemental Accts.	200,000
Television—network	250,000
M-Day	300,000
Convention	190,000
Debts°	1,000,000
Subtotal	$4,890,000
Total	$8,596,000

When McCarthy was still considering whether or not to enter the New Hampshire primary, his supporters there estimated a campaign would cost $55,000.[36] Five times that estimate was eventually spent in and for the New Hampshire primary, and more than one-half of that ($164,000) was spent by the central campaign, accounted for as follows:

° The listed debt at the end of the campaign was $1.3 million, but it included some bills from primary states which are already included in the primary state totals above.

Expenditures

Rent	$ 2,115
Headquarters expenses	8,847
Telephone	3,656
Personal expenses	3,647
Babysitters	880
Radio	35,856
Newspaper	30,929
Billboard	4,980
Production and Printing	36,812
Motels	8,847
Bus and Auto Rental	4,202
Mail	11,246
Miscellaneous	11,812
Total	$163,831

It proved impossible to determine the exact television expenses for New Hampshire, which were paid out of New York accounts, but they were probably close to $75,000. Moreover, at least $40,477 in expenses were incurred in Massachusetts by McCarthy accounts there, for television advertising directed at New Hampshire. So the total New Hampshire costs are listed at $280,000. The importance of trying to make McCarthy known can be gauged by the media effort: for the last three days of the campaign there were McCarthy spots every 30 minutes on every radio station in the state, and the television effort was comparable.[37]

In Wisconsin, very little is known of expenditures, excepting that at least $153,500 can be identified as media expenses for the major statewide and Milwaukee committees. But enough money is unaccounted for to make that figure a low one, and knowledgeable sources place the total at about $500,000.

In Indiana, less than one-half of the estimated $700,000 total cost can be accounted for. This includes $83,000 for operating expenses, $20,000 for staff salaries, $31,000 for newspaper advertising, $171,000 for television and other advertising, $3,700 for hotel and travel, $5,184 in miscellaneous costs, and $5,000 for "Oregon Primary Election Campaign Expense." It is probable that most of the remaining expenses in Indiana were for media.

For Nebraska, all but $12,000 of the $160,000 spent has been accounted for in detailed lists of funds disbursed by the Nebraska campaign committee and by the national committee for Nebraska. The following categorical summary of expenses shows a much heavier media emphasis, in contrast to local organization, than most of McCarthy's other primary campaigns.

Headquarters	$ 1,575
Telephone	17,406
Postage and Telegram	6,133
Travel (incl. hotels, airlines, cars)	13,951
Advertising (incl. radio, TV, printing, news service)	107,371
Miscellaneous	1,978
Total	$148,414

In Oregon, approximately two-thirds of the total expenditures are available in itemized form, and several items are of interest: about $135,000 went to the advertising agency working with the state campaign; $9,174 went for expenses for the advance staff, but some of these costs were actually publicity expenses incurred in advertising for meetings or rallies to be held; $395 were listed in expenses for election night; per diems for students were $14,719 while staff housing was listed at $3,465; statewide storefronts were listed at $3,138 total, and tricounty storefronts at $4,521.

Arrangements for financing the California primary were exceedingly complex. There was one major national bank account set up in San Francisco, through which $833,000 ran, but this partly paid for some media expenses in Oregon, and transfers of funds were made to other California accounts. The account was started with about $150,000 sent in from New York and Washington, but after the primary, about $135,000 was transferred back East.

In addition, there were three subsidiary national accounts, one in San Francisco and two in Los Angeles, which handled another $300,000 or so and was spent mostly on staff salaries and per diems; some of this money was transferred from the major account, but some, particularly in Los Angeles, constituted fresh money raised there. To complicate the financial picture, there were major accounts run by Californians in both the North and South, with transfers of funds back and forth. Combining the national and statewide accounts, and adjusting for transfers, about $1 million was spent in the California primary. But this does not include amounts raised and spent locally, as in Santa Ana and Santa Clara; in a state the size of California, this can mount up.

Details of the California media costs, which accounted for slightly more than one-half of the total, are available:

Newspaper advertising	$288,510
Television	116,562
Radio	93,145
Agency and production direct expenses	10,941
Total	$509,158

An additional $25,000 is known to have been spent on media by others. The heavy newspaper advertising came about for two reasons: a hard buying situation in radio and television created by earlier purchases of good time by the Kennedy and Lynch campaigns; and a late flow of funds, with money pouring in after McCarthy's Oregon victory a week earlier. McCarthy newspaper ads practically matched those bought for Kennedy ($290,000), though Kennedy outspent McCarthy on radio and on television in the California primary.

Over the summer, a unique approach to political advertising was developed by the Southern California McCarthy committee. Individuals could buy 30 seconds of radio time to state their own reasons for supporting McCarthy. The campaign committee first purchased 36 spots during one week on one radio station, and then expanded the program to other stations. The cost to the individual wishing to make his statement was $35, and all of the spots ended with the line, "Won't you speak out, too?"[38]

In its primary-to-primary orientation, the McCarthy campaign was hardly thinking about the Convention in late spring, when a young staff member proposed that he begin researching previous convention operations in order to develop a tentative budget. Since no one objected, he proceeded to do so, and after many weeks of careful research concluded that about $1 million was needed for an efficient and complete convention operation.[p] A proposed budget, dated June 14, totalled $946,303, including more than $300,000 for hospitality and almost $200,000 for communications. The McCarthy campaign, however, had neither the money, staff, nor desire for that kind of an operation, and a revised proposed budget, dated July 7, came to $582,498; two weeks later and a little more than one month before the Convention began, an operating budget of $250,000 was approved.

The actual expenditures of the McCarthy campaign at Chicago were less than the budget, totalling about $190,000. Because of the telephone strike,[q] it was impossible to install a communication system, and only about $42,000 of the budgeted $75,000 was spent for telephones, teletype machines, walkie-talkies, and communications consultants. The other big item was hotel rooms, which cost $70,000; only about $10,000 was spent on hospitality, although there was also at least that much spent on an airport rally for McCarthy's arrival. Staff and office costs in Chicago came to $22,000; the press and public relations effort, including a daily edition of *The McCarthy Advance,* cost about $13,000; and local transportation

[p] While totally out of line with what the McCarthy campaign could afford, this figure is not very unreasonable for an all-out convention operation. In 1968, Rockefeller spent $750,000 and did not have an elaborate communications system; Nixon spent $500,000 while being confident of having the nomination sewed up. A figure of $500,000 is probably a minimum for a comprehensive convention operation.

[q] The striking workers agreed to break their strike to install phones at the Amphitheatre itself, but nowhere else.

costs were about $10,000 (with costs of transporting staff to Chicago being paid for out of the Washington rather than the Chicago budget). By most standards, the McCarthy convention operation was indeed a frugal one.

There were locally financed primaries and delegate battles in several states; the information available from these states ranges from estimates to detailed data. In Pennsylvania, McCarthy supporters at the state and local level spent about $430,000 for the nonbinding Presidential primary there. In New Jersey, $112,000 was spent in supporting delegate primaries throughout the state. Of the total, $18,000 was spent on a fund-raising dinner, rally, and mailing (which returned $76,000); $48,000 for advertising; $9,400 for literature, buttons, stickers, and so on; $7,300 on salaries; and $29,000 on all other operating and campaign expenses. In Connecticut, a complicated challenge system of delegate selection was used for the first time in a Presidential contest; at least $120,000 was spent in this effort.

In Massachusetts, President Johnson chose to let McCarthy have the state's 72 votes on the first ballot rather than run or have a stand-in candidate run in the state's primary. Although no clear reasons for the decision were ever given, it was speculated that Johnson and his advisors "feared it might cost them $500,000 to wage a campaign to crush McCarthy."[39] The Massachusetts McCarthy committees spent $269,980 in the primary campaign. This, however, was only a part of the total amount Massachusetts McCarthy supporters raised and spent on behalf of their candidate. Excluding $91,350 transferred into the state, $652,529 was counted as income in Massachusetts by three major statewide committees. One of these, the Volunteers for McCarthy, was a Massachusetts account for the national campaign, and it received contributions from in and out of state. It transferred $123,520 mostly to Washington, New York, New Hampshire, and convention committees, and additionally, made substantial advances ($78,000), loans ($10,000), and contributions ($28,000) to McCarthy-allied candidates for the United States Senate or House. The other major Massachusetts committee, besides spending for the primary there, transferred $163,413, mostly to the New York headquarters. So Massachusetts was a major source of financing for its own primary as well as sending almost $300,000 to the national McCarthy campaign. After the campaign, a dedicated worker was able to reconstruct the complete financial picture of the Massachusetts effort from the myriad records of various amateur bookkeepers. This is included as Appendix A as an example both of an extraordinary state effort and of unusually precise campaign financial records.

In Illinois, a little more than $200,000 was spent within the state (excluding all convention expenses), mainly in support of several delegate primary contests. The $160,000 spent by the statewide McCarthy organization (the remainder was spent by local organizations) in the effort included $83,634 on advertising, $16,640 on salaries, $15,997 on postage, $9,803 on telephones, $8,464 on printing, and about $25,000 on office and other expenses. In addition, Illinois sent $77,000 to the national headquarters and primary states.

In Florida, $60,000 was spent in the statewide primary campaign there; the state also sent $20,000 to the national or other primary campaigns. In Ohio, probably close to $100,000 was spent in five Congressional District delegate contests. In Minnesota, about $60,000 was raised and spent in a campaign to win delegates through local caucuses. A similar effort in Iowa cost about $32,000. In Kentucky and New Mexico, it is estimated that $75,000 and $50,000, respectively, were spent in caucus battles, but in each of these cases all but about $10,000 was transferred in from other states. In Michigan, almost $150,00 was raised and spent on campaign activity within the state, including $50,000 for the massive rally at Tiger Stadium. Michigan also sent $26,000 to Wisconsin and a small amount to the national headquarters.

After the campaign was over, one of the McCarthy finance managers sent a questionnaire to finance operatives in every state to try to find out what had happened, and further inquiries were made in connection with this study. In addition to the individual state figures above, information was received from 18 other states and the District of Columbia. These 19 raised and spent a total of $275,000, ranging from $125 in Arkansas to about $50,000 each in Washington and Missouri. (Washington also sent about $20,000 to help the Oregon primary and Missouri also sent $50,000 to the national campaign.)

Adding this to the individual state figures, the total spent in all the locally supported campaigns was close to $1,825,000. And adding this to the costs of the national headquarters and the eight major primary campaigns, a total of more than $10.8 million was spent by McCarthy efforts in 38 states and the District of Columbia. Considering the remaining gaps in information—for twelve states (none of which had significant campaigns or expenditures) and for most activity at the local level (less than statewide)—the total spent on behalf of McCarthy was probably about $11 million.

Except in a Rockefeller or Kennedy campaign, where the money is centrally controlled, most campaigns are relatively decentralized in their fund raising, as they are in other activities. The Humphrey campaign, for instance, had major operatives working out of Washington, New York, and Minnesota; but some coordination was accomplished and two or three people in central command knew what was happening financially.

Not so in the campaign of Senator McCarthy, in which the decentralization reflected the composition of the campaign, with groups and individuals operating independently, with petty jealousies between various finance or campaign managers growing out of policy or strategy differences, with major personality conflicts, with frustrating competition for the Senator's favor.

In spite of the incredible decentralization and internal conflict, the McCarthy campaign managed to raise notable sums of money from a small number of very large contributors (very few of whom had given in such large amounts before), and a large number of very small contributors (perhaps as many as 150,000), but without many in between, in the $100 to $1,000 category. The lack of middle-range contributors gave the campaign a top-heavy and bottom-heavy structure, reflecting its inner tensions: between some of the biggest contributors who wanted a modern, television-oriented campaign, and others who saw McCarthy's greatest strength in the grass roots and wanted to nourish that remarkable phenomenon—preserving or stimulating the mood of youthful enthusiasm—by assisting student activities, putting or keeping young people on the payroll, or encouraging volunteer proselytizing across the land.

For the national campaign, as best as can be pieced together, about $2.5 million was raised from about 50 large contributors. But key finance operators still do not know in some cases the actual sources of funds in some accounts, that is, whether they came from personal contributions of fund raisers or from funds collected by them from others. There were numerous loans, some of which were repaid and some forgiven, and this complicates knowing who gave how much in certain cases; some large contributors and lenders received repayments from cash balances in early 1969.

The contributors were no doubt mainly attracted by McCarthy's stand on the Vietnam issue, and his courage in taking on first an incumbent President, then a wealthy Senator whose family name and record are legendary in American politics, then an incumbent Vice-President who was a political mentor coming from the same state. Of course, McCarthy also attracted money that was anti-Johnson or anti-Kennedy, for whatever reasons. Both Humphrey and McCarthy supporters admit that some Humphrey supporters channeled money to help McCarthy in order to hurt the greater threat, Kennedy, particularly in the Oregon and California primaries, but McCarthy insiders claim to know of only small amounts thus received. Some say more was arranged for but not forthcoming when McCarthy won in Oregon and the donors reneged, thinking enough damage had been done to Kennedy's prospects. Among the anti-Kennedy money, there was speculation about Teamster money pouring in to hurt Kennedy (Kennedy forces were bitter about both Teamster and other labor money that was intended to damage Kennedy) but McCarthy operatives minimize the extent of labor help, and are themselves bitter that more of labor did not join in the movement.

McCarthy also was reported to have attracted funds from special interests concerned about legislation before the Senate Finance Committee, of which he was a member, especially oil, drug, and mutual fund money. From the point of view of the industries, certainly there was a point to assisting McCarthy on the supposition that it would not hurt when he returned to Senate duties. Finance managers admit very little oil money was raised; though one fund-raising party at the Petroleum Club in Houston brought in about $40,000, it did not all come from oil sources. Many Wall Street people were involved as fund raisers and as large givers. This may have reflected some sentiment among elements of Wall Street that the American economy would be better off without the dollar and manpower drain into Vietnam. This, however, seemed more an individual motivation than an organized movement.

Throughout 1968, speculation persisted that some fund raisers from Wall Street in the McCarthy and other campaigns solicited other brokers with whom they did business. This took on potential significance in the case of mutual fund managers, who could give business to many other brokerage houses; moreover, complex deals known as "give-ups" permitted mutual fund managers to divert portions of commissions to houses that provided research services. The notion was that millions of dollars of "give-ups" were involved before being prohibited late in 1968, and that for such favors sizeable political contributions might have been asked.

It is probably fair to say that because most McCarthy money was contributed for ideological or Vietnam-policy-related reasons, it represented probably more money less touched with vested interest than in most other campaigns. Another element that pointed up the character of the McCarthy money was that many contributors (and other Americans) probably did not believe that McCarthy could get nominated, yet the money continued to flow in even at the Democratic Convention.

But the flow of money into the campaign was uneven, and was particularly influenced by events—by the New Hampshire showing, by occasional polls, by the Tet offensive, by LBJ's withdrawal, by Kennedy's entry, by the Oregon victory, by the last stand in California, and then by the surprising New York primary result. For example, in the first mail received after Kennedy's announcement, the New York McCarthy campaign received $19,343 from 917 contributors; 10,000 10-cent buttons and 35-cent posters were sold between Sunday afternoon and Monday morning.[40] On Wednesday, May 29, the day after McCarthy's upset victory in the Oregon primary, the campaign reportedly received $250,000; the desperately needed money was used for last-minute radio and newspaper advertising in the California campaign.[41]

For the New Hampshire primary, the sources of at least $95,000 of the $164,000 spent centrally can be accounted for. Of that, about $44,000 was transferred in from the Washington office, $38,215 from the New York Coalition for a Democratic Alternative, $2,000 from Vermont, $700 from North Carolina, and $400 from Rhode Island McCarthy groups. In addition, a New Jersey committee sent $15,720 to a special account (tallied above as part of the Washington supplemental accounts), but the money was actually spent in New Hampshire. The substantial monies spent from New York and Massachusetts accounts were raised in those states as part of the national effort. There were twelve individual donations of $500 or more, and money collected in New Hampshire for the central account amounted to about $4,000.

Wisconsin was perhaps the one state where the McCarthy campaign was not seriously short of money. Robert Kennedy's entry into the Presidential contests had a lot to do with that, bringing immediate funds from both McCarthy supporters and anti-Kennedy forces. In Wisconsin, where $322,488 can be accounted for in contributions and transfers of funds in sums of $500 or more to statewide and Milwaukee committees, the transfers from out of state account for $257,386, while the in-state transfers total only $10,313. Out-of-state contributions from individuals totalled $35,750 in sums of $500 or more, while those from in-state contributors totalled $14,740.

In Indiana, one committee accounted for the source of close to one-half the total expenditures. The Indiana Citizens for McCarthy committee listed less than $25,000 received in contributions from within the state, and more than $300,000 received from the national headquarters. Other committees estimated contributions of $100,000 from within the state.

For the Nebraska campaign, a detailed list of contributions received (to May 13, 1968 the day before the primary) covers virtually all the money spent by the Nebraska committee, which was about one-third of the total $160,000 spent for the primary. The remaining $100,000 was billed directly to the Washington headquarters. The Nebraska committee received $56,000 in amounts of $25 or more, of which $47,000 came from the national headquarters. The source of the remaining $8,800 gives a good flavor of the McCarthy campaign. About $4,200 was raised within the state; there were 40 contributions of more than $25, the largest was $530; more than one-half of the contributions (24) were for $50. The $4,600 which was received from out of state came from local McCarthy committees in five states (Arizona, Colorado, New Mexico, Washington, and Wisconsin) and from individuals in seven states (Colorado, Illinois, Michigan, New Jersey, New York, and Wisconsin). The largest local committee contribution was for $500, and the largest individual contribution was for $1,000.

In Oregon, various national committees in Washington sent at least $185,000 for the primary. Another $36,000 came from state or local committees in New York, Colorado, Wisconsin, California, Indiana, Massachusetts, and Washington (Seattle). Most of the remaining money—more than $100,000—was raised within the state, although there probably were a few contributors among them from out of state. Information is not available on the sources of funds for the California primary, although substantial amounts were raised within the state.

The period between the last primary in New York and the convention in Chicago was difficult for McCarthy to sustain politically, yet substantial sums of money were raised. There were staff controversies over the kind of campaign to run during the summer, and whether to keep on many of the students. Decisions were made and reversed, but finally financial problems dictated that many be dismissed. In mid-July, the campaign was reportedly facing a deficit of more than $1 million, and personnel and program budgets were to be cut by one-third.[42] The Senator toyed with the idea of travelling to Paris to learn first hand about the peace talks, but then dismissed that. Apart from some travelling, the main activities centered on two half-hour network television programs[r] and McCarthy-Day (M-Day) rallies, the latter being interconnected by closed-circuit TV in the 22 cities in which they were held on August 15.

In fund raising the usual means were employed and amenities followed. For large contributors, special gatherings were held before rallies or dinners, usually with the Senator present. Cocktail parties were held in luxurious apartments and homes; one such event in New York City was held in River House because people would go just to see the place. Early in the campaign, one contributor got a five-minute audience with Senator McCarthy for $1,000, over the protests of some schedulers. But there was near-consensus that McCarthy could have displayed more warmth toward large contributors and spent more time courting them than he did. One potentially very large contributor, a centimillionaire, was temporarily turned off because McCarthy failed to ask for money after prompting beforehand to make the pitch that the contributor anticipated; solicitation by others later did not produce as much as was hoped for.

There were the usual dinners, luncheons, and parties. One dinner in February, held in a New York hotel during the New Hampshire campaign, raised $45,000 from 97 persons present; this was clear profit because the bills were paid by the host. A businessmen's luncheon was held prior to the Wisconsin primary, also at a New York hotel, which was attended by 800 or more people and brought $75,000 or more to the campaign.

The distribution of sources of money raised by a large dinner held at the Waldorf-Astoria in late June is interesting. Roughly $500,000 was raised: one predinner party at an individual's apartment collected and pledged $85,000, another predinner party at the Waldorf hosted by Stewart Mott raised another $80,000, ticket sales accounted for $120,000, while pledges from the floor brought a spontaneous outpouring of $220,000 more in cash and pledges. Not all the pledges were fully redeemed—rarely are all redeemed—and some of the pledges may have been exaggerated to include money the person already gave, in order to inflate the total and urge on the uncommitted.

---

[r] There was an additional earlier network program before the Wisconsin primary, and a 5-minute network show featuring Paul Newman, the actor. Some of the television payments came from a Washington supplemental account.

But this dinner, plus the McCarthy-Day (M-Day) rallies, plus returns from broadcast and mail solicitations, and special preconvention fund raising, raised more than $1 million after the last, the New York, primary. The two broadcasts, one at the end of July and one about two weeks later, each brought in more than $90,000, enough to pay for the air time. One late mailing of 250,000 pieces brought in $85,000, and a special mailing to bank executives produced $30,000.

Mailings had been productive throughout. Some unusual direct-mail and telegram appeals were used quite successfully. The subscription lists of *Avant-Garde, FACT,* and *Ramparts* magazines were used, as well as the lists of somewhat more staid publications such as *Atlas, Commonwealth,* and *The New York Review of Books.* One series of direct-mail appeals—which included 250,000 letters from "Faculty for McCarthy" to colleges and universities around the country, the magazine lists, and the lists of several political organizations—cost $62,942 and the return was $198,483. A series of more than 1,400 telegrams to those who had already contributed $100 or more to McCarthy did even better: the costs were about $3,500 and more than $70,000 was received. As of July 12, the chief direct-mail and telegram effort had yielded an impressive return of better than four to one: $388,200 in income for $85,400 in costs.

Another means of fund raising consisted of literally thousands of local cocktail parties, coffees, and such, where $5 or $10 was expected of those attending. These were the main means of financing the primary campaign in Northern California, but they were widely used across the country.

The McCarthy campaign was able to do what few other campaigns can do successfully. There were several discotheques around the country raising money for the campaign. The first and most successful was "Eugene's" in New York, which at times netted as much as $11,500 per week; a "Eugene's" in Chicago, before and during the Convention, made a profit of about $3,500 per week for several weeks. It is unusual for campaigns to be able to sustain such operations over time.

The campaign also was successful in holding indoor and outdoor rallies productive both in ticket sales and collections.[s] These were held in Madison Square Garden,[t] in Fenway Park (Boston),[u] in Boston Garden,[v] in

[s] Ticket sales illustrate a major problem in estimating numbers of contributors to a campaign. At each of the Madison Square Garden rallies, for example, there were 18–20,000 persons attending. Tickets were sold for admittance, so 35–40,000 contributors could be counted at these events alone. (Additionally, collections were made inside and most probably gave again.) If these rallies are included, the number of McCarthy contributors would total more than 200,000 individuals.

[t] Receipts from 20,000 admission tickets totalled $100,000 and there were pledges, cash, and checks totalling $300,000. Expenses for the rally are not known.

[u] Where total receipts from ticket sales, contributions, and concessions, and a prerally cocktail party were $153,790; there were expenses of $55,984 for a net profit of $97,806.

[v] Where ticket sales and contributions totaled $61,411, expenses were $26,823, and net profit was $34,588.

Cobo Hall (Detroit),[w] and culminated in the M-Day rallies; these produced net profits totalling hundreds of thousands of dollars. A zeal and contagion were evident at several of the rallies, where barkers read off pledges and whipped up enthusiasm for giving.

There were some very large givers: at one of two Madison Square Garden Rallies, one $50,000 gift was reported by several knowledgeable people present to have been completely unpremeditated and spontaneous. This was typical of the spirit which existed among many active in the campaign. Many gave numerous times and a few gave very large amounts. In one case, an out-of-state contributor sent $500 in response to a newspaper ad. When a New York fund raiser happened to be visiting in the contributor's state, he called to thank the man personally. This conversation interested the contributor further and in a few days he sent in another check, this one for $50,000, but with conditions for its use. Two or three days later the same contributor sent in still another $50,000 and agreed to remove the restrictions on the use of the money. This contributor, who had once been a Republican, had never given so heavily, but he was motivated in 1968 to give as never before.

More information on more large contributors was provided more systematically by operatives of the McCarthy campaign than for any other Presidential prenomination campaign in 1968, and in fact, more than for any other such campaign in modern history. Some of the information was provided in lists that were made available and some in interviews, but interview data have been used only when verified by two or more reliable interview sources or by available contributor lists.[x] In all cases, the lowest verifiable amount has been used, and any doubts were resolved on the side of caution. In the cases of the very largest contributors—those of $100,000 or more—where specific amounts could not be determined, the notation "$100,000-plus" has been used.[y] In several cases, some informants stated a given person was a very large contributor, but other informants doubted that the person gave very much personally, believing that some of the money may have been raised from others and submitted in the fund raiser's name. In these cases, the amount is listed as "$10,000-plus" beause that is the minimal figure that all could agree on; the actual amount could

---

[w] Where William Clay Ford paid all the bills, so that the gate receipts and collections were pure profit.

[x] Some of the information from the interviews and on the lists overlapped, and special care was taken to reconcile the data so as to avoid duplications that would add amounts erroneously. The same care was taken with respect to the committee lists of contributors, for again there was overlap.

[y] For example, stories were plentiful and confirmed by several of the campaign's financial managers that at least three contributors gave several hundred thousand dollars each; but only Stewart Mott could be verified as one, and his contributions are noted. The other two are listed as contributors of $100,000 plus—to ensure accuracy, avoid exaggeration, and avoid unfairness—even though there are grounds for believing each gave considerably more.

have been anything between that figure and ten times more. Given the handling of the bank accounts, only one or two persons might know exactly who gave exactly how much, and they are unwilling to reveal that information.

The McCarthy campaign had at least five contributors who gave $100,000 or more. On the record, the largest contributor was Stewart R. Mott, philanthropist and son of a pioneer in the automobile industry, one of the founders of General Motors. After spending $100,000 trying to persuade Rockefeller to run, as noted earlier, Mott turned to McCarthy and contributed and spent, by his own calculations, approximately $210,000 on McCarthy's campaign. One gift of $100,000 was publicly and dramatically announced at the August 15 M-Day rally at Madison Square Garden. Mott also became coordinator for special gifts and helped to raise substantial amounts in addition to his own contributions. Mott also gave $43,700 to other Democrats and $11,000 to various miscellaneous committees, for a total of $364,700 in political contributions in 1968.[43]

Mr. and Mrs. Jack J. Dreyfus, Jr., are listed as $100,000-plus contributors, although some accounts say they gave as much as $500,000 and are considered by some to be the single largest contributors to the McCarthy campaign. Dreyfus was a senior partner of the Wall Street firm of Dreyfus and Co., and a business associate of Howard Stein, McCarthy's finance chairman. It is known that some of his money was given outright, some was given as loans but forgiven, and some loans are known to have been repaid. In addition to his McCarthy campaign contributions, Dreyfus gave $69,000 to Humphrey and other Democrats and $76,000 to Nixon and other Republicans in the general election period. These known contributions total $245,000, making him one of the largest political givers in 1968.

Another of the $100,000 plus contributors was connected with Wall Street (as were other large contributors): Ellsworth Carrington, a registered representative with Legg and Co., who also gave $5,000 to Paul O'Dwyer's campaign for the Senate in New York, and $1,000 to the New York Coalition for a Democratic Alternative. The other $100,000 plus contributors were Mr. and Mrs. Martin Peretz of Cambridge, Massachusetts (he is a Harvard professor), who also gave at least $10,000 to Paul O'Dwyer and $4,400 to other Democrats; and Allan Miller, a philanthropist in Boca Raton, Florida, who gave at least $108,000 to the McCarthy campaign.

There were at least six contributors in the $50,000 to $99,999 category, of whom one was connected with Wall Street: Mr. and Mrs. Daniel J. Bernstein—he is president of D.J. Bernstein & Co.—gave at least $75,100 to McCarthy, as well as $35,136 to Paul O'Dwyer's Senate campaign, $6,826 to the National Committee for an Effective Congress, $500 to the pre-McCarthy national Conference of Concerned Democrats, and an unknown amount to the New (Fourth) Party. Others in this category were

Blair Clark, journalist and McCarthy's campaign manager, New York, who gave at least $75,000; Martin Fife, president of Fife Industries in New York, gave $72,000; Mr. and Mrs. Samuel Rubin of New York, he is a retired executive of Faberge, gave $75,000; Mrs. June Degnan, a California philanthropist who had earlier given $500 to the Conference of Concerned Democrats, gave $60,000; and Robert Gimbel, of Saks Fifth Avenue in New York, gave at least $50,250.

Of the 183 Democrats in the $10,000 or more category of contributors, 25 were McCarthy givers. But this count, of course, distorts the national Democratic picture because similar information was not available for the Humphrey or Kennedy prenomination campaigns. In addition, for the Republican prenomination candidates, only the largest givers in the Romney, Nixon, and Rockefeller campaigns are known.

Of the 25 $10,000 and over McCarthy contributors, there were six others (in addition to Dreyfus, Carrington, and Bernstein) connected with Wall Street: Howard Stein, manager of the Dreyfus Fund; Yura Arkus-Duntov, president of the Equity Growth Fund, who gave at least $20,000 to McCarthy (and $500 to Senator Morse of Oregon); Richard T. Shields, an independent investment broker, who gave $18,000 to McCarthy and $1,000 to Senator Javits (Republican) of New York and $1,000 to Governor's Club of New York; F. Palmer Weber, president of F. Palmer Weber & Associates, who gave at least $10,000 to McCarthy; William L. Bernhard, who gave $16,500 to McCarthy and $2,500 to Humphrey-Muskie; and Randolph Compton, who gave $10,000 to the McCarthy campaign.

Much of the fund raising was pointed toward a specific primary, first New Hampshire, then Wisconsin, and so on. Local fund raising in some states made possible large transfers of funds to the primary state. For example, the New York Coalition for a Democratic Alternative was notably successful in raising money. Official filings in Albany showed $677,000 spent through June 1968, of which substantial amounts of money were sent to the various primary states:

January–April	New Hampshire	$ 38,215.00
March–May	Wisconsin	103,572.95
April–June	Pennsylvania	989.64
April–May	Indiana	19,313.00
May	California	102,000.00 (approx.)
	Oregon	21,685.00
		$285,775.59

Here again, everyone was his own strategist, and the New York group had to decide where money could be used most effectively. This was a determination not only as to what state to send money to, but what committee or what operative would use it most effectively for goals congenial to the sending group.

The remainder, plus other Albany filings for New York committees, account for the $600,000 spent by McCarthy forces substantially for the New York primary. The word substantially is used advisedly because certain CDA costs throughout the year could properly be allocated as national costs since the CDA operation was closely tied to the national McCarthy operation. Actual CDA expenditures in May and June relating to the June 18 primary were about $250,000.

The N.Y. CDA money was raised through parties—one attended mainly by Columbia University professors brought in about $10,000—but most successfully through a series of newspaper ads mainly in *The New York Times* and *The New York Post*. The ads were prepared by a volunteer professional advertising man, and some brought as much as eight or ten times their cost. The ads were run often, at key periods two or three times a week. This series was no doubt the most successful series in political history. In a six-month period, from March to August, 1968, fourteen ads grossed $174,877, from almost 8,000 contributors. (Earlier ads had also done well but accounts were not available.) Similar ads run in *The Los Angeles Times* were not as productive, and there is no explanation of why they were so successful in one place but not in the other.

An unusual example of McCarthy's kind of financial drawing power was demonstrated after he lost the nomination. A McCarthy Donors Fund raised $55,000, of which $37,200 came in amounts of under $100. The Fund used $15,000 toward the campaign deficit, and the remaining $40,000 was donated to eleven McCarthy-endorsed Congressional candidates.

McCarthy's limited and sporadic financial resources forced concentration on one state at a time, without much margin for early buildups in subsequent primaries. The McCarthy campaign demonstrated one of the virtues of the long string of state primaries spaced over a period of several months: one could build success upon good showings, each of which could be mounted with minimal staff moving from one state to another, whereas a national primary with focus on a single election would have required a national-size as compared with a state-size staff, and would not permit the slow buildup McCarthy was able to achieve, both financially and at the polls. As Chester, Hodgson, and Page noted: "The present primary system, for all its absurdities, does offer an opportunity for an insurgent candidate, with comparatively little money, to get into contention. The primary route is not cheap in the long run, but it starts comparatively inexpensively. A candidate who starts well can, with luck, pick up backers before he moves on to the next campaign. Such was the nature of Senator McCarthy's campaign."[44]

In September 1968, the McCarthy campaign owed to creditors as much as $1.3 million. Most of these debts were for the national campaign, but state committees, local treasurers left with bills and no way to pay them off, creditors late in sending bills who lost track of disbanded committees or could not collect from campaign staffers, all sent bills to Washington, where a central office was established to handle these matters, and stayed in operation into early 1969. One document made available showed $391,000 in income from September 1 until November 8, as follows:

Citizens for McCarthy—New York	$240,000.00
Miscellaneous and State Organizations	106,253.14
Press (for travel with the Senator)	36,341.75
Refunds	2,697.32
Literature and Button Sales	431.60
Miscellaneous—Sale of equipment	780.00
Contributions	4,381.91
	$390,885.72

Later about $75,000 was turned over from various Washington accounts. All bills for $400 or less were paid 100 cents on the dollar; the rest were negotiated. Hotel-chain bills were aggregated, as were auto rentals, telephone, and other such bills from around the country, and negotiations took place with the national parent corporation. There were some single companies that were owed in the hundreds of thousands of dollars. In some cases, partial payments were made with the understanding that further payments were not expected; in other cases, settlements were negotiated, and they averaged about 36 cents on the dollar.

There has been a saying that the winners pay their bills, the losers negotiate. Debt settlement in the Humphrey, McCarthy, and Kennedy campaigns, along with others at lower levels, no doubt will lead many creditors to reexamine their policies regarding extension of credit to political campaigns. Public utilities must provide services, but only broadcasters traditionally insist upon payment before service is rendered. Because of risks involved, political bills may tend to be toted as high as the toll will bear, but the experience in 1968 may lead to more demand for prepayments, or for large deposits (as utilities sometimes now require), or at the least to excessive charges on the reasoning that settlement for a fraction on the dollar may be necessary later. When bills are settled, the corporation is in effect making a form of indirect contribution to the campaign, which some companies may willingly do for good-will purposes. But when regulated industries, such as telephones or airlines, do so, they are opening themselves to federal tightening of the laws, or to litigation brought by stockholders or even customers who must pay full rates.

Kennedy

Throughout 1967, Robert Kennedy was torn between his growing opposition to the President's policy in Vietnam and his belief that a political challenge to Johnson would almost surely fail, and that even if it did succeed, it might destroy the Democratic Party and ultimately hurt the cause of peace. In late summer, Kennedy flatly said no to becoming the candidate of the dump-Johnson movement. However, in late October and again in early December 1967, he met with a group of political friends to discuss becoming a candidate; his entrance was probably inevitable after the Tet offensive and its political repercussions in early February 1968. Kennedy's announcement on March 16, four days after McCarthy's dramatic showing in New Hampshire, was geared in part to the legalities of getting on the ballot in California, but it drove the McCarthy New Hampshire story off the front pages of magazines and newspapers and contributed to unending bitterness from McCarthy supporters.[45] As one commentator noted later in reviewing two books about Kennedy: "Events caught Kennedy, too, unprepared, forcing him to make his move too soon by the conventional wisdom of the old politics and too late for the moral passions of the new."[46]

When Kennedy announced his candidacy, there was no formal campaign or campaign organization ready or even planned. The candidate took off on a whirlwind tour around the country, speaking mostly before universities, while his brother and brother-in-law (Senator Edward Kennedy and Stephen Smith) got the campaign organized.[47] The campaign was to last only 80 days, a little more than 11 weeks. In that time, almost $9 million in costs were committed, close to $1 million per week. However, counting the known settlements on bills owed to creditors and depending upon eventual action by the Democratic National Committee on the $1 million Kennedy debt which was assumed, the real costs were less than $7 million.

Some people claim that Kennedy campaigning never really ceases, and would include in Robert Kennedy's total campaign bill the cost of his activities and buildup prior to 1968. To some extent, however, this is true of all major political figures. For example, Reagan's 1967–68 speaking trips around the country certainly contributed to his later candidacy, and yet at the time they were perfectly legitimate activities of the incumbent governor of one of the country's major states. It is virtually impossible to separate any politician's activities into those which are part of his present position from those which may be pointed toward a future position or campaign. Although the Kennedys have undertaken more politically-related activities than many other public figures, they are probably more noticed not only because of their financial resources but because the press and public find them more interesting or newsworthy, and choose to follow their activities closely. One cannot document the financial or other advantages of this kind of continuous attention from the media, some perhaps encouraged by Kennedy forces, yet without cost to the beneficiary. Kennedy's 1968 campaign also benefited from the help of volunteering political professionals, who were able not only to donate their services but also to pay their own expenses.

The Kennedy style of campaigning was evident in 1968: many of the workers had their training in John Kennedy's earlier campaigns, some in Robert Kennedy's 1964 Senate race, and some in the preannouncement maneuvering in late 1967 and early 1968 to get Kennedy to challenge Johnson. The old hands were supplemented, and to some degree challenged, by the younger staff from the Senator's office, many of whom had views on how the campaign should be run which clashed with the more experienced elders. But overall, this campaign, like all Kennedy campaigns, was a combination of organization and media: there was strong emphasis on the nuts and bolts of politics—registration and get-out-the-vote drives conducted by telephone and by foot, and direct mailings to registered voters—as well as heavy media usage.

Just over one-half of the total committed costs—almost $4.6 million— was for the seven primaries in which Kennedy was entered (including New York, where $100,000 was spent before Kennedy's death). It has been possible to ascertain in a form rarely available, the media and production costs for those states, as well as the approximate total costs for the primary campaigns. The Kennedy campaign did not have any network broadcasts, as did the McCarthy and Humphrey campaigns, so these media figures are relatively comprehensive. The production costs were a national expenditure independent from, and in addition to, the media and primary state totals. Oregon was an exception: political circumstances there dictated that a local advertising agency be used. The production costs of $5,300 (for modifications of nationally supplied materials) in Oregon have been added to the national production figure in Table 2-1. The amounts in this table are fully verifiable; they show that the media and total costs were, in some cases, not nearly as high as many press stories alleged during the campaign.

The Kennedy media campaign production costs were exceptionally high —47 percent of the time and space costs. As will be seen in the general election section, this compares with production costs of about 25 percent for the Humphrey and Nixon postnomination campaigns. (The average production costs for commercial advertising are about 7 percent.) The big difference in the percentage probably reflects the larger volume of spending in the two general election campaigns, which averages down the production costs, rather than any major differences in style or method. (Although the instantaneous nature of Kennedy's campaign might seem

---

" For example, a *Washington Star* article on May 2, 1968 (five days before the Indiana primary) estimated Kennedy's total costs in Indiana at $1 million, of which media expenses were estimated at $500,000–$750,000. However, this was conservative in comparison to a $2 million estimated total which was used by many hostile newspapers, and a $3 million figure even surfaced in at least one story.[48]

Table 2-1

Kennedy Primary Campaign Costs: Totals with Media Breakdown

State	Total Primary (Approximate)	Media (Time and Space)
Indiana	$ 750,000	$ 288,000
		185,000—TV
		75,000—Radio
		28,000—Newspapers
Nebraska	$ 150,000	$ 68,000
		40,000—TV
		15,000—Radio
		13,000—Newspapers
D.C.	$ 40,000	$ 20,000
		10,000—TV
		10,000—Radio
South Dakota	$ 100,000	$ 35,000
		20,000—TV
		10,000—Radio
		5,000—Newspapers
Oregon	$ 277,000	$ 103,000
		51,000—TV
		23,000—Radio
		29,000—Newspapers
California	$2,400,000	$1,100,000 [a]
		450,000—TV
		230,000—Radio
		290,000—Newspapers
New York	$ 100,000	—
		$1,614,000
Media Production [b]		759,185
Total Primaries	$3,817,000	Total Media $2,373,185

[a] $130,000 discrepancy between the total and the TV, radio, and newspaper figures is unexplained.

[b] Production of film biographies cost $300,000; the rest of the costs were for preparation of radio and television spot announcements and newspaper materials.

to be a contributing factor to the high production costs, Humphrey's campaign was also a last-minute effort and yet those production costs were only slightly higher than Nixon's, whose campaign was one of the most planned in history.)

The media campaign was handled centrally (except for Oregon) by the advertising agency of Papert Koenig Lois (PKL). The campaign was a crash job, with the first spots on the air in Indiana on April 17, just a month and a day after Kennedy declared his candidacy. As many as 51 PKL employees were working on the campaign at one time, and during the California primary effort, there was a sizeable agency-in-exile working away from the New York office.

The Kennedy media campaign was notable in monitoring the television expenditures of the opposition. Documents were prepared summarizing and weighting the spot television of all the candidates, as shown in the following example:

Market: Rapid City, S.D. Time Zone: CTZ Dates: 5/31–6/3

	Kennedy	Humphrey	McCarthy
# of Spots	37	24	20
Daytime	5	8	4
Early and Late Fringe	11	8	6
Prime Evening	21	8	10
Weighted Total	90	48	46

Spot Weighting Values, Central Time Zone
Daytime (prior to 5:30 PM) = 1
Fringe (5:30–6:30 PM; after 10 PM) = 2
Prime Evening (6:30–10 PM) = 3

These were prepared market by market in Indiana, South Dakota, Nebraska, and California; several girls were assigned to compile this data day by day. This kind of market research is unusual in politics, but is probably the prototype of future campaigns. Most campaigns would not have the resources for this, but the assistance it offers in terms of tactical decisions regarding response and counteraction can be invaluable.

The Kennedy campaign also conducted two other kinds of surveys unusual in politics. One, in Nebraska, was a public opinion poll questioning respondents about whether and where they saw or heard advertising for Senator Kennedy, and what their reactions were as to topicality and credibility. Another compared reactions to Kennedy and McCarthy, in much the same terms.

Another survey in California explored voter responsiveness to a range of Kennedy television communications. Eight focussed group sessions of nine or ten people each were conducted, four in the Los Angeles and four in the San Francisco areas. The subjects were undecided Democrats in a range of income, occupational, and age groups. Each session took two hours and was guided by moderators skilled in group dynamics. An opening general discussion was followed by exposure to one-minute spots and five-minute programs used in previous primaries. Further discussion was developed to provide insight into both rational and emotional reactions. In some sessions, a 30-minute film reviewing the Nebraska campaign was shown, and again responses were sought out. This information was used to change or modify future advertising, and to stress items or issues favorably received.

It can be anticipated that techniques such as these will be refined and more commonly used in future campaigns. Several related questions result: will these techniques lead to more efficient as well as more effective campaigns, and if so, will this lead to reduced rather than increased campaign costs; if not, where will the money come from for these often expensive techniques?

Apart from the detailed financial (and substantial) information on Kennedy's media campaign, there are only limited data available about other costs in the primary states, and no specific information on the money spent outside the seven primaries, in Washington headquarters or elsewhere. Money never seemed an obstacle in planning or implementing the campaign strategy. One revealing example comes from Kennedy's first campaign trip to California on March 23: "An extra Boeing 727, complete with stewardesses, Bloody Marys, and sandwiches was prepared at a few minutes' notice to take an overflow of half a dozen reporters for a ten-minute flight [from San Francisco] to Sacramento."[49]

However, one account of the 1968 campaigns says that the California Kennedy campaign began "in a state of near-pauperism," lacking money even for buttons. There were two reasons for this situation, which are revealing of the Kennedy campaign style and some of its difficulties. According to this account, the national campaign was unwilling to give the California campaign manager, Jesse Unruh, sufficient money at the beginning. This was because Kennedy money was always "strictly under the control of the family," and not until Stephen Smith went to California did the money flow. Secondly, the party regulars had been solicited to support Johnson's campaign, and then Humphrey's campaign, as well as the Lynch slate; meanwhile, the ideological money had been tapped by McCarthy for close to two months before Kennedy declared his candidacy. "It was a vicious circle: because of the late start, it was hard to raise cash, and because there was a shortage of cash, it was hard to make up for the late start."[50] In view of the $2.4 million final cost of Kennedy's California campaign, however, one can assume the national campaign made up for any difficulties in fund raising within the state.

In Oregon, slightly more than one-half of the $174,000 nonmedia expenses can be ascertained. The expenditures included at least $64,000 to a firm that conducted the direct-mail drive (some of the payments were for printing), at least $5,500 for public opinion polling, and almost $21,000 in disbursements to county and city headquarters for local operations. One interesting series of payments listed on official reports was to state and county election officials for purchase of voter lists or named mailing tabs, a rarity which exists because Oregon is one of only two states that mail candidate information pamphlets to all registered voters. This state action, by the way, is intended to reduce campaign costs, but candidates generally continue to mail their own literature to voters anyway.

In the Oregon and California primaries, there was a mass migration of campaign staff and volunteers from the East, so much so that the Washington headquarters was practically stripped of personnel. The costs involved in transportation and lodging for these staffers were high, though exact amounts are not known. However, some of the California primary costs have been learned from several different sources and the total costs can be patched together quite accurately.

In addition to the media expenses of $1.1 million, a Kennedy-for-President Committee in California had spent, as of June 15 (11 days after the primary), a total of $684,238. This total is derived from a computer printout which is a researcher's dream of how political books should be kept. The entire June 15 statement is reproduced in Appendix C. Some of the expense categories included operations, $221,192; special groups, $95,893; registration drive, $27,698; candidate travel, $34,772; get out the vote drive, $175,822; polls and surveys, $10,289; subcategory items included bumper strips, $12,209; buttons, $10,307; brochures, $35,325. Four days later, on June 19, total expenditures were listed in a similar statement at $776,633, mainly as a result of additional payments in the operations category. Adding to this actual expenditure figure a deficit of $650,000 and the $1.1 million in media expenses gives a total cost of about $2.5 million, but even this figure does not necessarily include all the costs of the Washington headquarters relating to California, or Washington staffers, particularly their salaries, while in California.

Of the $650,000 debt in California, a telephone bill amounting to $100,000 was combined with national telephone bills remaining from the campaign for a reported total of more than $500,000 in all for this one category of expenditure. That left $550,000 in debts to be settled in California, which was not completed until June 11, 1969. All bills for less than $100 were paid full value. Most others were settled on the average at about one-third on the dollar. Thus, deficits of $550,000 were settled for about $180,000. One bill gained national attention: for $85,000 owed to the Ambassador Hotel, where Robert Kennedy was shot. Settlement was negotiated and thought accepted at $28,000, but somehow the Ambassador refused to go along and instead obtained a writ to attach the Kennedy bank account, then holding only $395. Finally, the Ambassador agreed to settle for $33,500, which wiped out all Kennedy debts in California.

The deficit of the Kennedy campaign, including that in California, amounted to $3.5 million, of which the Democratic National Committee assumed $1 million. Some creditors were friends of the Kennedy family or sympathetic in the circumstances and voluntarily pared their bills down. In other cases, negotiations took place. Among the deficits were $100,000 from the Indiana campaign, $400,000 owed to the advertising agency, and $200,000 to one of the television production firms. To the extent these bills may have been reduced, the real media costs were reduced, though the committed costs represent evidence of what it can cost to run a crash, national campaign for Presidential nomination.

While Kennedy aides were relatively cooperative in providing information on campaign expenditures, they were as silent as Rockefeller in revealing sources of funds. In addition to one rumored $500,000 contributor and another at $100,000, for which verification could not be obtained, the only other bit of information comes from the official report published by the State of Oregon.[51] Of the total of $310,620 listed in contributions to the Oregon-for-Kennedy Committee, there was one individual $500 contributor, $309,842 came from the national campaign, and the remaining less than $300 came in small contributions.

A fund-raising campaign was begun soon after the November elections to help pay off the deficit, and five dinners were held which grossed between $1.4 and $1.5 million. The approximate proceeds were: New York, Washington, and Boston, $375,000 each; Los Angeles, $225,000; and San Francisco, $115,000. Proceeds for the California dinners were disappointing; one reason was that the Los Angeles chairman became ill. Whether this money plus other postcampaign contributions and/or family resources totally retired Kennedy debt is not known.

Humphrey

In the support it gathered, the prenomination campaign of Hubert H. Humphrey was basically a continuation of the Johnson campaign, comprising the party loyalists, much of the labor leadership, and some traditional minority and liberal leadership and membership. Between the time of the President's withdrawal and Humphrey's formal announcement almost a month later (on April 27), the Vice-President and his political organization succeeded in preventing any bandwagon to Robert Kennedy and in fact started one of their own.

The campaign strategy included avoiding the primaries in the belief that "the risks of running and losing far outweigh the possible benefits of running and winning."[52] It counted on collecting political debts piled up in party fund-raising activities (as Nixon had done on the Republican side), as well as exploiting all of the anti-Kennedy (and to a lesser degree anti-McCarthy) opinions and fears among many party politicians and financial backers. Although Humphrey received no direct or indirect assistance from the President, personnel at the Democratic National Committee (DNC) were hardly neutral: Chairman John Bailey was reported having difficulty keeping Humphrey buttons off some DNC staffers, and others left the DNC to join the official Humphrey campaign.[53]

One of the major differences between Humphrey's 1960 and 1968 Presidential bids was financial: in 1960, Humphrey was overwhelmed by

Kennedy money; in 1968, he attracted substantial money because he was running against a Kennedy. Before he announced his candidacy, Humphrey was urged to run by a group of wealthy New York businessmen, some of whom were at the same time urging Rockefeller to run; their motivation appeared to have been primarily anti-Kennedy.[54] Throughout his campaign, Humphrey was plagued by conflicts on his staff between Johnson loyalists and others who urged him to disassociate himself as much as possible from the Administration. He was even urged by more than one friend to resign as Vice-President. In spite of all the inner tensions, however, the Humphrey campaign was able to carry on the concentrated delegate-wooing operation which resulted in the first-ballot convention victory for the Vice-President.

In the prenomination period, Humphrey inherited some funds existing in Johnson-oriented committees, such as in certain of the President's Clubs already referred to, and the state Citizens for Johnson-Humphrey. (Certain others, however, helped the DNC pay off bills.) One operative in California said that significant amounts—scores of thousands of dollars in that state—were transferred to be used by Humphrey once Johnson withdrew. Certain Johnson-oriented funds had gone into the Lynch delegation, and Humphrey was the beneficiary. Separability is impossible, but in combined Johnson, Humphrey, Branigan, and Lynch funds, close to $5 million was spent. Of this, the Humphrey campaign alone spent about $4 million, without entering any primaries. In addition to actual expenditures, labor assistance first to Johnson and then to Humphrey added incalculable amounts.

Humphrey's two major operating organizations, the United Democrats for Humphrey and the Citizens for Humphrey, committed expenditures of $3.2 million. A separate New York operation raised and spent $549,000. Additional committees in California and other states probably brings the direct Humphrey total to at least $4 million. There were large salary, per diem, and travel expenses because the campaign was designed to seek delegate strength, particularly in large blocs in states controlled by the party organizations, often in states in which no primary had been held to select the delegation membership.

Only a few details of the $4 million Humphrey total are available. Without primary campaigning and despite announced cutbacks in advertising, the central national campaign spent $881,000 for this purpose from July 24 until August 25. Television (no radio) and newspaper advertising expenses broke down as follows:

Local spots	$387,000	43.9%
Network programs	174,000	19.8
Network participations	171,000	19.4
Specials	8,000	.9
Newspapers	11,000	1.2
Production	130,000	14.8

Campaign materials were scarce throughout, and one source estimated that only $50,000 was spent (centrally) on buttons and bumper strips. At the height of the campaign operation, the payroll ran $40,000 per week. (After Kennedy's death, there were major cutbacks in staff.)

In Indiana, Governor Branigan's campaign as a favorite son cost $150,000 (not included in the $4 million total), but there are no details available on the expenditures. In Oregon, where Humphrey could not avoid being on the ballot but did no campaigning, the United Democrats-for-Humphrey in Washington transferred $22,301 for local use. In South Dakota, a total of about $50,000 was spent, including some for television. Before Kennedy's assassination, Humphrey's supporters in New York had spent several hundred thousand dollars in both state and national activities; national Humphrey committees transferred $111,125 to New York Humphrey committees between April 23 (four days before Humphrey's declaration) and June 3. The national campaign spent money on wining and dining delegates, who were flown to Washington in chartered planes; the only hard figure known, however, is $5,000 which was spent to entertain the Delaware delegation.

The story of the Lynch delegation in California is pertinent because it involved both the Johnson and Humphrey campaigns, and illustrates the politics of indirection. Although there were reports that as much as $500,000 was spent, the actual figure is probably about $275,000 (most of which is not included in the Humphrey total). The delegation was pulled together, and a staff assembled, before President Johnson withdrew; as noted earlier, about $40,000 was spent on staff and signature collection to qualify for the ballot. The staff was reduced after Johnson withdrew and most of the remaining expenses, about $200,000 went for media advertising the week before the primary.

Television ads cost at least $75,000—some were paid for directly by interested individuals and some by the national Humphrey campaign—and radio spots cost $40,000. There were also newspaper ads in at least ten papers covering most of the state for three days at a cost of $20,000 per day for a total of $60,000. About $40,000 was spent in holding a big gala in Oakland. (Another $100,000 was spent on registration activities in the April-to-September period by individuals associated with the Lynch delegation, but this money was not considered by them as direct campaign spending.)

The Humphrey campaign convention expenses in Chicago were estimated by one informant at about $275,000, partially as follows:

Hotels	$100,000
Communications (Walkie-Talkies)	25,000
Ushers	20,000
Convention Hall Operations	25,000
Newspapers—Newsletters	25,000
Hospitality Suite	25,000
Per diems	12,000

This amount is no doubt low and it is likely that additional amounts were spent at the convention and are included in the Humphrey deficit.

Almost all of Humphrey's campaign funds came from large contributors. Probably much of the membership of the various President's Clubs supported Humphrey (if not before the nomination, then afterwards). More will be said about the President's Clubs later, but here it bears stating that in the previous year or two, President Johnson had not devoted much time to the Club, but Humphrey had, so he inherited a good deal of good will from its membership. With only a few exceptions, the leadership and former staff of the President's Club was involved in raising funds for Humphrey, and this included Richard Maguire, former treasurer of the DNC, under whose guidance the financial policies of the Democratic Party underwent profound change in favor of large contributors, corporate contributions through program advertising books, and a policy of financial secrecy hardly worthy of a major national party. Maguire resigned as DNC treasurer, in no small part because of criticism of these policies, so it was surprising that he resurfaced so visibly on the Humphrey team. Yet it was symptomatic of the schizophrenia of the Humphrey campaign. Perhaps old treasurers don't fade away because they know where the skeletons are buried. (After Humphrey's nomination, John Criswell, one of Maguire's successors at the DNC, also helped raise funds for Humphrey.)

The Lynch delegation funds for northern California were raised for the most part from a gala at which Frank Sinatra entertained. This affair was held at the Oakland Auditorium and grossed $128,000, with the public sale of tickets bringing in more than $40,000. This included 400 who attended at $100 each and 1,000 at $25 each. The public sale of tickets was expensive, however, and the net cleared was only $80,000. The rest of the Lynch delegation funds was made up in individual contributions apart from the gala.

At the same time that fund raising for the Lynch slate was occurring, money was being raised in California for Humphrey's national campaign. One dinner at the Century Plaza Hotel in Los Angeles was attended by 30 people at $5,000 each. In southern California, there were probably six contributors of at least $25,000 each. In all, at least $500,000 was produced by the dinner and one other event. Several informants, some friendly and some antagonistic, agree that one fund raiser in southern California probably was responsible for raising $1 million for Humphrey in the pre-and postnomination periods combined.

The Humphrey money drive attracted segments of the business community that were not for Republican candidates, or were strongly anti-Kennedy. For example, Sidney J. Weinberg, the late Wall Street financier, conducted a one-man drive to raise funds for Humphrey by a personal letter-writing campaign; returns were less than expected. In addition, several lunches were held in New York City attended by major leaders of the financial and corporate communities. One luncheon, at Le Pavillon, was widely reported in the media as having raised $1 million in collections and pledges, but this was disputed by more than one who attended. Several informants gave accounts indicating how such reports can get inflated and yet be true. Pledges were called for and two persons promised $250,000 each. Then another promised $100,000, and so on. Each one is thinking of giving some money himself, but raising the rest from among friends and associates. The problem is that several pledgers are thinking of asking the same circle of friends. All cannot raise as much as they hope, and few give personally as much as the difference between what they pledge and what they collect. For example, one pledge for $50,000 was 80 percent fulfilled by the individual raising $35,000 and giving $5,000 himself; the remaining $10,000 was forgotten by all concerned. In the case of one $50,000 pledge, the person gave nothing and collected nothing, then complained when he was not sent tickets to a later fund-raising dinner. He was refused until he gave something, which was $5,000. At least three pledges were for 40 percent before nomination, 60 percent after. The Le Pavillon lunch eventually did produce about $1 million, but not all was collected as contributions; some loans and some direct payments for newspaper ads were generated as well. Another lunch was held at the 21 Club in New York, and the Humphrey campaign ran some unpublicized gatherings.

The campaign also held a series of fund-raising dinners and galas around the country, mostly in the summer. One dinner in Washington drew 2,500 people at $500 per plate, grossing $1 million; another dinner in New York grossed about $500,000. Five galas were headlined by Frank Sinatra and netted perhaps as much as $500,000. Although Sinatra's services were volunteered, fees for agents and accompanists and promotion costs made the galas rather expensive to run: they cost $40–50,000 each.

Income to the Humphrey campaign flowed unevenly, particularly after the death of Robert Kennedy. *The New York Times* reported in late June that 50 campaign aids (25 percent of the staff) had been laid off in one five-day period; the reasons for reduced contributions were said to be a belief that Humphrey had the nomination sewed up, and the fact that some of the contributors were primarily anti-Kennedy and would now support Nixon.[55] In late July, lack of funds put the advertising campaign at least weeks behind schedule when the campaign had been unable to make a down payment to Doyle Dane Bernbach, the campaign's advertising agency.

Throughout the prenomination period, there were strong intimations of some Democratic money going to Nixon—gifts made by persons who thought Nixon would be easier for Humphrey to beat. There were also rumors of tie-ins with Colorado supporters of Nixon who provided a plane and other assistance to Humphrey in return.

Labor's role was probably greater than ever before in an open Presidential nomination contest within the Democratic Party. Even before Humphrey announced his candidacy, there was one report that a high AFL-CIO official at a secret meeting "made it clear that labor is ready and willing to provide men and money for a drive to stop Sen. Robert F. Kennedy" and "talked of a $5 million national labor fund for the Vice-President."[56] Leadership elements worked openly to support President Johnson, Governor Branigan in Indiana, and Humphrey—and to oppose Senator Kennedy—although there was considerable rank-and-file support for Kennedy, as there was for Wallace. The national COPE (Committee on Political Education, of the AFL-CIO) leadership travelled extensively, including in the major primary states, to activate the grass roots and to organize manpower and assistance. Some of this is known to have occurred across state borders—in Illinois and directed at Indiana and in Washington and directed at Oregon. Where possible, party leaders were importuned to support Humphrey or at least not to support Kennedy, and labor was involved in influencing the choice of Democratic delegates in some states.

There should have been an embarrassment of riches for labor in 1968; in terms of domestic positions, Kennedy or McCarthy should have been as acceptable as Humphrey. But the labor leadership position on Vietnam, labor's long relationship with Humphrey, and rising antipathy to Kennedy, resulted in labor's making a huge effort on behalf of Humphrey. There were ironies, like the support of nonliberals such as Branigan as a way of advancing Humphrey's cause. A few voices questioned the legitimacy of investing funds to defeat prolabor candidates while the rank-and-file was widely split. Only a few labor leaders openly supported Senator Kennedy, and these were mostly dissidents within labor's ranks, mainly in the United Automobile Workers. Even fewer supported McCarthy although an anti-Vietnam policy labor committee endorsed him.

Labor in 1968 took the unprecedented action of contributing money directly to Presidential nomination candidates within the Democratic Party. Official reports filed in Washington show that 22 union committees contributed a total of more than $167,000.[57] The largest contributor was the Seafarers International Union, which gave $65,500 to Humphrey in addition to the $50,000 to Johnson already noted. The Seafarers are under indictment for having made some of these contributions directly from the union treasury, rather than from voluntarily contributed funds.

In addition, two industry-related committees contributed to Humphrey committees in the prenomination period: the Savings Association Political Education Committee gave $1,000, and the Committee on American Leadership (COAL, acronym for a coal industry group) gave $1,000 to Humphrey but also gave $1,000 to Nixon before his nomination.

More than $1 million in costs for Humphrey's prenomination campaign remained as a debt at the time of the Convention, and it was set aside so that the campaign could concentrate on fund raising for the general election campaign. In an unusual move, particularly in a losing campaign, Robert Short, the treasurer of the DNC but a Humphrey operative before the Convention, proposed in January 1969, that the DNC assume responsibility for one million dollars in deficit each for the Humphrey and Kennedy campaigns. His reasoning was that given the DNC deficit of $6 million from the general election campaign, there was need for united action to pay off that much. That entailed getting star speakers at fund-raising events, and minimizing competitive fund drives. Since Hubert Humphrey and Senator Edward Kennedy, two stellar attractions at dinners, each would be expected to assume responsibility for his own or his brother's debts, they could not devote their talents to helping the party. Accordingly, the DNC took over the additional two millions in Humphrey and Kennedy debts to make one enormous debt and, hopefully, to spur a unified effort to get back into the black. By the time Short's proposal was made, most of the McCarthy debts had been settled, and his workers were concerned that creditors might want to reopen negotiations on the chance they might get larger payments if his debts were also pooled. However, creditors generally remained satisfied, and McCarthy people were not anxious to hand over their problems to the party establishment. The DNC also took over the small McGovern deficit.

McGovern

The very brief campaigns of Senator George McGovern and Governor Lester Maddox illustrate how it is possible to spend $50,000 or $100,000 in only a few weeks. McGovern announced his candidacy just 16 days before the opening of the Convention; Maddox threw his hat in the ring one week later.

McGovern had been one of those approached by the dump-Johnson movement in the Fall of 1967 to be the movement's candidate. He had declined because he felt the challenge might seriously hurt his own Senatorial campaign and should be undertaken by a Senator not up for reelection, such as Lee Metcalf or Eugene McCarthy. Several months later, when Kennedy was reassessing his own decision during the week of the New Hampshire primary, McGovern reportedly was one of several Senators who urged him (Kennedy) not to enter the race, "not to split the peace wing of the Democratic Party."[58] In the period immediately following Kennedy's assassination, McGovern was urged by some former Kennedy supporters to take up the banner. McGovern first rejected the proposal but came under increasing pressure to act as a compromise candidate. McGovern was seemingly acceptable to the McCarthy forces because of his long-standing and outspoken opposition to Vietnam policy, to Kennedy forces who were still alienated by Senator McCarthy, and to the Humphrey forces because he retained his credentials as a regular Democrat who was committed to support the party's nominees. Yet, in fact, McGovern had no strong, organized support from any of these groups, and he surprised many observers when he announced his candidacy on August 10.

McGovern's 2½ week campaign cost more than $100,000, but reimbursed travel costs brought the net expenditures to $74,000. The following breakdown covers the actual McGovern campaign costs:

Travel (not reimbursed)	$12,000
Telephone and telegraph	8,000
Hotels (not convention)	8,000
Staff	6,000
Publications, buttons	5,000
Convention:	
Hotel and telephone	23,000
Ampitheatre	12,000

The Convention hotel costs included a bloc of 40 rooms, a hospitality suite for delegates and supporters, and a reception for Mrs. McGovern. At the Amphitheatre, the costs involved installation of a switchboard and partitioning rooms for a headquarters. In addition to the campaign costs, the effort benefited from considerable volunteer assistance.

(Although more than $100,000 in less than three weeks may seem high, the costs of the McGovern campaign were very small compared with the brief campaign of Governor William Scranton for the Republican nomination in 1964; that effort was about one-month long and cost more than $800,000. But whereas Scranton was the center of attention for moderates following Rockefeller's withdrawal, McGovern had somewhat less time and much less focus as a major factional candidate.[59])

Although the impetus for the McGovern campaign may have come in part from former Kennedy supporters, the rumors of Kennedy money backing McGovern seem unfounded. The campaign raised about $40,000: one New York contributor gave perhaps as much as $10,000, about $15,000 was raised at Chicago, and some money was raised in California (by Pierre Salinger) and in South Dakota. A fund-raising telegram sent to 4,000 persons, at a cost of $1.25 each, brought in only 25 or 30 responses.

The Democratic National Committee took over the $27,000 debt of the McGovern campaign when it assumed the Kennedy and Humphrey campaign debts.

Maddox

Governor Lester Maddox of Georgia announced his candidacy on August 17. What his purpose was in doing so is not known; its effect was to cause some slight embarrassment to Vice-President Humphrey (in light of the famous arm-in-arm photograph of the two in 1967) and bring even greater national attention to the personalities and conflicts in the Georgia delegation.[60]

Maddox's brief campaign spent about $50,000. Most of the costs were at the Convention, and some of them would have been incurred by elements of the Georgia delegation in any case. Other costs included travel to the Convention, and there were a few newspaper ads in Georgia for fund-raising purposes. The Maddox campaign had a few $1,000 contributors, more at about $100, and still more in the $10–$20 range. A few contributions were from out of state, but most of the money came from Georgia.

Financial Imperatives—The Primaries

One of the recurrent questions in politics, certainly a major one in 1968, is whether the amount of money spent affects the results of elections. If all other factors were equal, or nearly so, it might be possible simply to compare candidates' spending and the votes received and then answer the question. But it is rarely the case that two or more candidates have the same advantages or disadvantages except for money, and it certainly was not true in the 1968 Presidential primaries. Some of the nonmonetary factors which affect elections are: how prominent a candidate is, whether or not he has the support of the party machinery, and whether he is an incumbent and has the resulting advantage in free publicity. All comparisons must be considered in light of the nonmonetary advantages of each of the candidates as well as how much money each spent.

New Hampshire

In the first primary, the major attention was initially on the Nixon-Romney battle, billed as the first of several clashes which would eventually determine the Republican nominee. Before his withdrawal a week before the primary, Romney had spent $280,000, while Nixon spent $300,000 in New Hampshire. Nixon, on the ballot, received 80,667 votes, while Romney, a write-in candidate, received only 1,743 and Rockefeller, also a write-in, received 11,241 in a campaign which costs his supporters about $15,000. If any conclusions can be drawn from the New Hampshire events, it is probably that Romney's spending could not overcome his weakness as a candidate; he had sufficient financing to get an adequate test of his popularity. It might be noted that the Romney experience demonstrates another aspect of the value of a string of primaries: a candidate, even one with financial backing, can find he does not have the necessary drawing power in one or a few primaries. This is better than wasting the enormous sums it would cost to compete in a national primary to find out the same thing.

In New Hampshire, press attention turned to the Democratic contest when the Republican battle evaporated. The McCarthy campaign out-spent the Johnson write-in campaign by close to 3 to 1. In the voting, Johnson won by just under 4,000 on the Democratic side (7.2 percent); including Republican write-ins, Johnson beat McCarthy by only 230 votes. This is an example of a candidate's financial advantage being relatively unimportant in view of his opponent's other advantages: McCarthy was running against an incumbent President, he began the campaign virtually unknown in the state, and the state's Democratic elected and party leader-ship were strongly supporting his opponent. Another financial statistic is McCarthy's cost-per-vote in New Hampshire, which was an incredible $12. (It might be noted that there have been elections in this country when votes were bought outright for less than that!) There were only a few more than 100,000 registered Democrats in the state in 1968, and Mc-Carthy had all the disadvantages already noted, so that the resulting cost-per-vote was unusual. Disproportionate amounts of money are often spent in the New Hampshire primary because of the psychological lift it gives to the winner of the first one in the Presidential sweepstakes.

Wisconsin

In the nation's second primary, all attention was focused on the Mc-Carthy-Johnson battle, yet its outcome was somewhat distorted by the fact that the President withdrew two days before the voting. In the last days, the Johnson campaign still urged to vote for the President—there were even some special postwithdrawal ads—and most observers believe there was a significant pro-Johnson sympathy vote which affected the re-sult. McCarthy outspent Johnson by about 2½ to 1; in the voting, Mc-Carthy outpolled Johnson by more than 1½ to 1, winning by more than 20 percentage points. Johnson's nonmonetary advantages were considered to be much more significant than McCarthy's spending edge, and the re-sult was judged to be a smashing victory for McCarthy. On a cost-per-vote basis, the two contenders were not far apart: McCarthy spent about $1.20 and Johnson about 99 cents per vote received.

On the Republican side, the only major interest was how large a vote Nixon, who had no major opposition, would get. His goal was to demon-strate his drawing power, something believed to be crucial in convincing delegates that he should be the Republican nominee. The Nixon campaign aim was reportedly to get more votes than McCarthy. (Wisconsin has an open primary, and the McCarthy campaign had been urging Republican voters to demonstrate their opposition to the President's leadership and

Vietnam policy by voting for McCarthy.) Nixon spent as much as Mc-
Carthy, $500,000, and received about 20,000 fewer votes than McCarthy.
The only other point of interest in the Republican primary was Reagan.
He received 51,000 votes, 10 percent of the Republican ballots, after a
campaign estimated to have cost $10,000. While obviously not competing
with Nixon's campaign, the Reagan effort was part of a carefully designed
plan to show growing strength in successive primaries. (In New Hampshire, a few thousand dollars had been spent and Reagan had received
only 362 votes, .3 percent of the Republican vote.)

The McCarthy-Kennedy Competition

During the campaign, most of the estimates of very high Kennedy
spending, and of Kennedy outspending McCarthy, were exaggerated. In
the five primary states in which Kennedy and McCarthy met head-on in
direct battles, their total costs were very close in three of the states, and
significantly different only in California. (Actually, McCarthy hardly waged
a serious campaign in South Dakota, making only a one-day appearance
in the state.)

	Indiana	*Nebraska*	*Oregon*	*California*	*S.D.*
Kennedy	$750,000	$150,000	$277,000	$2,500,000	$100,000
McCarthy	$700,000	$160,000	$336,000	$1,000,000	$ 30,000

Indiana

The Indiana primary in 1968 was a good example of the fact that money
is only one factor in an election, and sometimes the least important factor.
Even if McCarthy, as the less well-known candidate, had spent significantly more, it is extremely doubtful whether he could have overcome
Kennedy's natural constituencies in the state. Kennedy beat McCarthy
by more than 100,000 votes, 15.3 percent of the Democratic total. However, it is Governor Branigan's campaign which really demonstrates the
value of nonmonetary factors, such as control of party machinery and local
patronage, as well as the unpaid publicity which an incumbent governor
receives from friendly newspapers. Branigan spent $150,000—between
one-fourth and one-fifth the amounts spent by Kennedy and McCarthy—
and came in second, with 31 percent of the Democratic vote.

On the Republican side, Nixon was officially unopposed, and with no
write-in voting allowed in the state, there was no unofficial competition
either.

Nebraska

McCarthy suffered his biggest defeat in Nebraska, while spending virtually the same amount as Kennedy. Here, too, money probably did not matter very much. Although Nebraska was not as natural a state for Kennedy as Indiana was, Kennedy had the advantage of a well-known name, and his campaign there was much better organized than McCarthy's. If McCarthy was to have done any better (he received 31 percent of the vote to Kennedy's 51.7 percent), the key was probably a longer, better campaign rather than significantly more money.

Since Nebraska is a state which puts the names of all generally recognized Presidential candidates on the ballot unless they formally decline (as Rockefeller had done before he changed his mind too late to get on the ballot), Reagan's name was on the ballot along with Nixon's. Here, in step three of Reagan's careful escalation plan, his unofficial campaign spent $25,000 in winning 21 percent of the vote. While this was a noticeable increase over Reagan's Wisconsin showing, it did little damage to Nixon, who won 70 percent of the vote after spending $100,000.

Oregon

Oregon, like Nebraska, automatically lists all generally recognized candidates on the ballot. However, neither Rockefeller nor Humphrey had announced or were recognized in time to get on the ballot, and there was not enough time to get Johnson's name off the ballot. The official expenditure figures show McCarthy outspending Kennedy, but it is likely that they both spent somewhat more, and that the difference between their expenditures was less than $50,000. McCarthy's victory by 22,000 votes (a six percent difference) was considered major in view of Kennedy's advantages in being better known and in having won his first two encounters with McCarthy.

On the Republican side, Nixon outspent Reagan's unofficial but organized campaign by more than 3 to 1 ($500,000 to $150,000) and also outpolled him by more than 3 to 1. This was clearly a setback for the Reagan effort, which spent six times more than in Nebraska, and received only 21,000 more votes, actually getting slightly less of the vote in Oregon (20.4 percent) than in Nebraska (21.3 percent).

California

California is the nation's most expensive primary, as it involves more voters and more delegates than any other binding preference primary. For the Democrats in 1968, California is the only primary for which one might question whether money had a decisive role. Kennedy outspent McCarthy by 2½ to 1 and he won by 4.5 percent—140,000 votes out of more than 3 million Democratic ballots. For the California primary, the comparable details of both the McCarthy and Kennedy media expenses are available; in both cases, the media accounted for about 50 percent of the total spent:

	McCarthy	Kennedy
Total California Expenses	$1,000,000	$2,500,000
Total Media Expenses	523,200	1,100,000
Television	116,600	450,000
Radio	93,100	230,000
Newspapers	288,500	290,000
Other, unspecified	25,000	130,000

After the campaign, some McCarthy aides said that if they had been able to run a media campaign for three weeks rather than one, the outcome might have been different. However, the positive effect of the McCarthy win in Oregon (one week before the California primary), and the negative effect of the McCarthy-Kennedy debate (although McCarthy may not have lost it as some claimed, it clearly did stop his momentum) may have had as much to do with the final outcome as the spending differences.

On the Republican side, Nixon had agreed not to challenge Reagan in his home state, and since there is no way to write in votes in California's Presidential primary, Reagan spent $100,000 and received all of the Republican votes cast.

3

Financing the Conventions

The Republican National Nominating Convention of 1968 cost $796,263, representing an increase of almost 20 percent from the $664,750 cost of the 1964 convention. The funds were provided as follows:[1]

City of Miami Beach	$235,000
Southern Florida Hotel & Motel Assoc.	65,000
Governor's Official Comm. of Fla.	350,000
1968 Convention Program Book	274,500
Total	$924,500

The balance of income over expenditures—$128,237—is being held for costs in connection with the 1972 Republican National Convention.

In comparison, the 1968 Democratic National Nominating Convention cost $1,746,301 in expenses paid or incurred. This amount is difficult to compare with 1964, because there remain doubts as to exactly how much the earlier convention did cost.[2] The funds for the 1968 Convention were provided as follows:

Chicago Host Committees	$750,000[a]
1968 Convention Program Book	274,500
Miscellaneous	14,667
Total	$1,039,167

Thus there was a deficit of $707,134, and this amount is included in the Democratic Party deficit of $8.6 million noted elsewhere.

The Republicans made available a full listing of Convention expenditures (Table 3-1), and the Democrats a partial listing (Table 3-2). Presumably, a large part of the remaining $811,839 in Democratic expenses was for salaries and travel.

No information is available on the costs of the safety and security measures taken for the Chicago convention, nor for the elaborate system of electronic surveillance of ingress and egress to and from the Arena, but these are known to have been very expensive.

Both Miami Beach and Chicago also provided fringe benefits not included in the above accountings. In addition to its $650,000 guarantee, Miami Beach agreed to provide facilities and services estimated to be

[a] About $350,000 of this came from the Chicago hotel tax fund, and about $400,000 was raised privately, largely at a single meeting held in the Mayor's Conference Room.

Table 3-1

Republican National Convention Expenditures, 1968

1. Salaries (for office personnel in Washington, D.C. office at Republican National Committee Office in Miami Beach and special professional and technical personnel required on part-time basis)	$ 58,787.59
2. Transportation (staff, Officers of Convention, superintendents of news media, arrangements for Committee Chairmen)	37,787.82
3. Subsistence (food, lodging & gratuities)	86,817.44
4. Office space	10,711.55
5. Office furniture, equipment rental & supplies	28,815.41
6. Telephone, telegraph, postage, & express charges	38,800.19
7. Printing (not including printing of tickets & Proceedings)	13,521.89
8. Manufacture of Convention badges	11,231.14
9. Printing of Convention tickets	14,701.22
10. Construction in Convention Hall	81,876.79
11. Special lighting	15,996.65
12. Ushering service	30,806.25
13. Custodial and protective services	25,589.71
14. Insurance	17,008.00
15. Technical services (prompting device and operation, make-up, platform design, placement of lights)	54,939.43
16. Signs	1,973.08
17. Music (orchestra, director, arrangements)	25,975.50
18. Convention Hall decorations	16,885.64
19. Reporting Services (including meetings of Committees)	14,712.25
20. Meetings on Convention planning	2,502.66
21. All expenses related to development of Platform (professional services, printing, travel, reporting, meetings, etc.)	32,254.79
22. Special events	14,583.08
23. Site Committee expenses	6,190.41
24. Miscellaneous	8,031.51
25. Expenditures connected with preparation of 1968 Official Convention Program	131,262.64
26. Anticipated cost of printing and distribution of Proceedings of 1968 Republican National Convention (work on this will not be completed until early 1970)	14,500.00
Total	$796,262.64

Table 3-2

Democratic National Convention Expenditures, 1968 (Partial)

Meetings and Conferences	$ 123,542
Construction of rostrum and interior work (not including television facilities)	214,108
Equipment rental	360,485
Printing	117,065
Hotel rental	119,260
	934,460
Uncategorized costs	811,841
Total	$1,746,301

worth more than $150,000, and hotels and motels agreed to provide certain office space and public room space, also without any additional charge. Chicago also provided $116,240 worth of fringe benefits, which covered air conditioning and seating at the Arena, various meeting rooms, and pre-Convention office space in hotels.

Program Books

The reader will note that the Republican and Democratic receipts from the 1968 Convention Program books were identical. This resulted from a special situation that led the two parties to establish a 1968 Convention Program Joint Committee, which solicited corporate advertising and, after costs, divided the proceeds equally to the respective Arrangements Committees for the Republican and Democratic Conventions. The background to this situation began in 1966, when the Congress enacted an amendment to a tax bill specifically forbidding corporations from claiming tax deductions for advertisements in political programs or publications.[3]

Traditionally, every four years, both major parties had sold space to corporations for advertising in Convention program books. In 1964, the Democrats charged $15,000 per page of advertising, three times higher than was charged in 1960. Many of the 1964 Democratic, as well as Republican, advertisers were corporations doing business with or regulated by the federal government. The success of the 1964 Democratic volume led the Republicans to publish a special program book, at $10,000 per page, in 1965. Then the Democrats published another, again at $15,000 per page, in late 1965. Press and Congressional criticism of these non-Convention journals led to the adoption of the amendment noted above, which was written and offered by Senator John J. Williams (and now known as the Williams Amendment). This choked off corporate advertising not only in program books and journals at the federal level, but also at the state and local levels, where there had been considerable dependence on revenue from such publications.

By 1968, it became apparent to the major national parties that revenue from program books would be a necessary addition to Convention funds provided by the host cities. Mutual agreement was reached by party leaders to seek bipartisan consent for a further amendment permitting advertising in program books in connection with conventions held to nominate candidates for President and Vice-President. Conditions were set that proceeds must be used solely to defray the costs of conducting such conventions, and that the amount paid for advertising be reasonable in light of the business the taxpayer may expect to receive directly from the advertising or as a result of the convention being held in the area in which the taxpayer has a principal place of business.

The amendment[4] was not enacted until June 1968, which left little more than a month to solicit advertising and give lead time for publication before the Republican Convention, which was held the first week in August. The parties set up a joint committee with offices in the Mayflower Hotel in Washington. Advertisers were sold space in both the Republican and Democratic books jointly, and the bipartisan aspect may have cut down sales. Only full pages were sold—at $10,000 per page black and white, $12,500 for four-color, $15,000 for inside front and back covers, and $25,000 for back cover. Total income from sales was $560,000, and after deducting administrative expenses of about $11,000, each Arrangements Committee got $274,500. Each program book, of course, contained editorial matter determined by each party independently. The production and distribution of the books were also the individual responsibility of each party, although there was prior agreement that each would produce 50,000 books and that the books would not be sold, as some had been in the past (sometimes to corporations). Because of the limited time available, space sales were lower and the actual production costs of the books were higher than otherwise might have been the case.

Indirect Costs

During 1968, particularly in Democratic politics, certain efforts were made to discredit the convention process and, indeed, the whole process of nomination. Criticism ranged from the manners of electing and selecting delegates at the state and local levels, where no doubt much hanky-panky has been perpetrated in the name of democratic selection, to the alleged rigging and managing of the national convention itself, where the elaborate security arrangements and the actions of the Chicago police lent themselves to the interpretation that national nominating conventions are not always fully open. The McCarthy forces were the source of much, though not all, of the criticism, which was pointed at both the Humphrey camp and at the supposed indirect control of the Convention by President Johnson. Much of the criticism became involved with candidate strategy, and even where voiced independently, was used for partisan purposes, and readily became an indirect campaign cost.

One example of this kind of cost was that of the Commission on the Democratic Selection of Presidential Nominees, headed by Iowa Governor Harold Hughes (now Senator). Generated by McCarthy supporters in late June, the concept of establishing an ad hoc commission consisting of Democrats representing various factions quickly gathered support. A McCarthy supporter put up $10,000 to finance the venture through his publishing brokerage house, in return for rights to develop the research product into a scholarly book which he would then publish. The *Report* of the Hughes Commission[5] served as a constructive force in the nomination process and laid the groundwork for the convention resolutions creating the postconvention McGovern and O'Hara commissions, to be discussed later.

Another example of an indirect cost at the Democratic Convention resulted from the clashes between police and demonstrators. Thousands of dollars were spent for bail and fines for people arrested during the disorders. Money was raised at meetings and by word of mouth during the Convention, and there were also some post-Convention appeals to cover the legal and court costs of cases still being litigated.

Candidates' Expenditures

In addition to the parties' expenses and the various indirect costs at the Conventions, there are, of course, the amounts spent by the candidates themselves to entertain and to try to win delegates to their side. During 1968, one frequent criticism of the Presidential nomination process was its high costs—even when primaries were not contested (as in the cases of Humphrey and Rockefeller)—and this was well illustrated by the expenses of the candidates in Miami and Chicago.

The Republican contenders spent $1.4 million, with Rockefeller's $750,000 leading the field. Governor and Mrs. Rockefeller held a reception for delegates that far surpassed in sumptuousness the one that Nixon held, and it cost about $80,000; friendly delegates were particularly well treated at Rockefeller expenses. Nixon's much more highly organized effort, including a delegate intelligence operation that was the envy of many, spent $500,000 at the Convention. Reagan (who had only announced his candidacy the day the Convention opened) spent $156,000 in Miami, while Stassen added $7,000 to the total.

In Chicago, the Democratic candidates spent much less than their Republican counterparts, a total of at least $550,000. There were only two major contenders in Chicago, and the campaigns of both were already deeply in debt. Humphrey forces admitted spending at least $275,000 at the Convention, and they probably spent a good deal more. The McCarthy campaign spent about $187,000. McCarthy's costs were held down somewhat by a unique approach to entertaining delegates: scores of Chicago area McCarthy supporters gave parties at their homes (some of them very elaborate) for delegates.[b] McGovern spent $35,000 at Chicago, and Maddox probably spent as much.

A national convention is a mass of paper. Press handouts, brochures, schedules, announcements by the various candidates and by the convention management, and other materials inundate the delegates. The McCarthy campaign published and distributed its newspaper, *The*

---

[b] The approach was not very successful; most delegates preferred the traditional hotel gatherings and going out on the town in Chicago to the McCarthy home parties.

McCarthy Advance, on a daily basis during the Democratic Convention. Rockefeller used newspaper (and television) advertising extensively in Miami, including a Sunday supplement in the Miami *Herald.* In addition to the flood of paper, all possible means of communication are used, particularly by candidates: local radio and television, closed-circuit television to hotel rooms, billboards, advertising on cars, trucks, buses, on any vehicle that moves, including airplanes trailing political tags or skywriting. In Miami Beach, even the plentiful waterways were used, with signs on boats of all descriptions. In Miami Beach, in fact, houseboats were used for lodging and entertainment. The Rockefeller riverboat, Biscayne Belle, took delegates for rides, but "Nixon's Navy" was more ubiquitous.

Big Contributors

National conventions are also the gathering place of large contributors. Many, of course, are delegates, but the convention attracts many others who are not, and VIP lounges are usually maintained by the national parties. Candidates for nomination also have special receptions or lounges for large contributors, and some candidates are still raising money at the conventions. The Democrats at Chicago had a special lounge and message center for major financial supporters, and members of the President's Club (and guests) were treated to free drinks and buffet dinners at the Stockyard Inn every evening the convention was in session.[e]

The Republicans took advantage of the Miami Beach setting for a $1,000 per ticket gala that grossed more than $1 million. Imitation orange tree decorations were provided free, and the gala expenses of about $150,000 left a nice profit to commence the Nixon campaign.

---

[e] But this could hardly compare with the lavish treatment big contributors received at the 1964 Democratic Convention.[6]

4 The General Election Campaigns

Political spending can be conceived as a function of availability of funds or willingness to go into debt, and the financial realities of 1968 illustrate the relationships between financing and campaigning. The Republican efficiency and availability of money led to greater campaign centralization than existed in the Democratic campaign, where funding was a serious problem throughout. In the Republican campaign, auxiliary committees at the national level were well integrated with the party committees; financial operations were moved to New York City where the prenomination Nixon campaign had been centered. In the Democratic campaign, the paucity of money led to considerable dispersal of function as some state groups were persuaded to cooperate in projects that the national campaign would have carried alone had money been available. Even so, the Democratic campaign was a professional one, whereas the Wallace campaign, despite its relative affluence, was not.

The sections immediately following outline the expenditures of the Nixon, Humphrey, and Wallace campaigns. The finances of the various national-level committees affiliated with these campaigns are shown in another context further on.[1]

Nixon

The most impressive part of recent Republican Presidential campaigns has been in their financing. It was the outstanding aspect of the Goldwater campaign, which raised and spent more money than any Presidential candidate of either party ever had, and still managed a modest surplus, while losing the election decisively. It was true of the Nixon campaign in 1968, which spent almost 60 percent more than on behalf of Goldwater, raising practically all that was needed.

Nixon's campaign was also one of the most carefully planned and efficiently run in history. Beginning in May, some Nixon staffers were put to work on planning for the general election campaign. The Nixon campaign efficiency was a favorite topic for political writers, both during and after the campaign, and often credited as the main reason for Nixon's victory. Yet with all the mechanical efficiency, opinion research, and computers, a basic strategy and tactics still depends on people, some of whom are good politicians and some of whom are not. Possibly because of the careful preplanning, the Nixon campaign suffered from a kind of rigidity which made it difficult to change strategy. For example, late in the race, in response to Humphrey's late surge, what was done was simply more of what had already been done. In the last week or so, the advertising budget was increased from $10 to $12 million, with $1.7 million going for additional 60-second television spots in 15 states, including the key states of California, Illinois, Michigan, New Jersey, New York, Ohio, Pennsylvania, and Texas.[2] (Nixon won four of these eight states.)

In spite of the most expensive campaign in history, the percentage of people who favored Nixon was almost exactly the same on voting day as it was revealed in public opinion surveys in May (43 percent). Theodore White calculated the composition of Nixon's support and concluded that during the entire campaign, Nixon did not or could not expand his base.[3] Another analysis suggests that the Nixon campaign was essentially a negative one, based on a "coalition of dissent" of the Johnson administration, and aimed at not saying much that would lose part of that coalition.[4] Whatever the explanation, the Nixon campaign was a very expensive effort which seems to have changed very few votes.

The Republican National Committee had entered 1968 in a strong financial position, with $695,000 in cash. By July 19, two weeks prior to the convention, $5,672,736 had been raised by national party committees (including the congressional campaign committees), of which $514,000 was clear and uncommitted for the postconvention effort. At the convention, a $500-per-plate gala raised more than $1 million, which with miscellaneous other receipts brought Republican income to a remarkable $7 million before mounting the general election campaign. According to a January, 1969 report to the Republican National Finance Committee, the Nixon-Agnew campaign raised more than $21 million;[a] adding this to other party receipts brought the Republican national-level income for the year to $29,653,931.[b] With adjustments for lateral transfers, Republican expenditures in 1968 were $28,851,000; Nixon's general election campaign accounted for 86 percent of the total, a record $24,870,000. Unfortunately, the breakdown in Table 4-1 is by operating division rather than function, so that it is difficult to compare certain categories of spending with the Humphrey campaign (or with the 1964 Republican general election campaign). Where comparisons are possible, the Nixon campaign spent at least 1½ times more, and the total cost was almost 2½ times the cost of Humphrey's campaign.

(Nixon had another advantage, even more lopsided than the financial one. He was endorsed by 483 daily newspapers which have a circulation of 20.7 million; Humphrey was endorsed by 93 daily newspapers which have a circulation of 3.9 million. However, the significance of such endorsements is not really known.)

The major thrust of Nixon's campaign was media, both in terms of

---

[a] Later reports raised this figure to $23 million.

[b] This figure varies only slightly with official filings made with the Clerk of the House.

Table 4-1

1968 Republican Presidential Expenditures

Division	Total Expenses
New York Office	$ 368,787
New York Mail Room	89,496
Washington Office	119,060
Staff—Nixon	128,003
Staff—Agnew	156,922
Scheduling	79,034
Tour	1,837,416(*)
Research	122,136
National Expense	119,746
Regional & Special	510,842
Key Issues Committee	37,247
Women	72,880
Polling	384,102
Neighbors for Nixon	1,156,283
Truth Squad	101,918
United Citizens	1,912,117
Surrogates	190,436
Victory '68	58,515
Minorities	371,177
Ethnic	83,861
Advertising	11,010,795
Campaign Materials	1,325,557
Finance	340,423
Payroll Taxes	60,397
Republican National Committee	1,362,885
Direct-Mail Fund Raising	1,566,117
$1000 Dinner Costs	216,705
Advances to State Committees	779,181
Payments for late (1969) bills, uncategorized	800,000
	$25,362,038
(*) Reimbursed from media travellers	—492,000
	$24,870,038

cost and strategy.[5] The charge given to the advertising agency executive who was to run the media campaign "was simply to work out a plan for reaching every voter in the United States who owned a television or radio set;" the cost did not matter.[6] In addition, Nixon's daily schedule was often geared to television schedules: the ideal day contained an event (almost any event) early enough to be reported on local or national evening news shows. While television was the main focus of the media effort, money was also no object for newspaper and magazine advertising. For example, about $130,000 was spent for one two-page ad in *Life* magazine on October 25, 1968.

In addition to all the media advertising, there was a unique special-projects operation for all the paraphernalia of the campaign. A centralized materials center designed, ordered, warehoused, supplied, billed, and controlled all the major items used. The operation was handled by Feeley and Wheeler, a New York advertising agency, at a cost of $1,124,626 (included in Table 4–1 under campaign materials). A catalogue was prepared for use throughout the country, and special kits were prepared for servicing 116 rallies with custom-packaged materials. The items and costs (to purchasers) give some illustration of a modern Presidential campaign.

20,500,000 buttons	$300,000
9,000,000 bumper strips	300,000
560,000 balloons	70,000
400,000 posters and placards	70,000
28,000 straw skimmers	30,000
30,000 brochures	
3,500,000 speeches & position papers	500,000
12,000 paper dresses	40,000
jewelry	50,000

The figures add up to more than the total cost given above because of markup and rounding; there was some income to the national campaign (through Feeley and Wheeler) from purchases of items by state and local campaign committees. Moreover, the figures above for speeches and position papers do not include many items handled by the office of the press secretary, Herbert Klein. Nor do they include the costs of two books of speeches and papers, *Nixon Speaks Out* and *Nixon on the Issues,* published by campaign committees.

Of the $364,000 spent for polling, $250,000 was used for the massive panel and telephone polling. The specifics of the Nixon polling, and other large political projects in 1968, are told elsewhere.[7] but there is a curious aspect to the heavy use of polling in Nixon's campaign. As eager as Nixon and his staff were to know what the polls revealed about what people thought, "everybody was anxious to make it clear that Nixon would not tailor his politics to fit what the research said people wanted—and, indeed, there is evidence that he did not do so."[8] Nixon—and many other politicians—pay out much money for polls, and then respond as much to unscientific and intuitive judgments as to the polls themselves.

A computer was used for an interesting and expensive individual communication project. Voters could ask Nixon questions, via tape records in local campaign offices, on any issue. The replies were "written" by a computer, whose memory bank held Nixon's position on 67 issues. The computer was programmed to give slightly different answers each time, in order to appear individual. This effort cost $250,000.

The net cost for the candidate's travel (subtracting the amount reimbursed by media travellers) was $1,345,416. The campaign plane was characterized by comfort and services, especially for reporters, and reflected the high degree of organization of the Nixon campaign tour.

Control radiated from the staff plane. Two open-circuit ground-to-air phones; seven internal phone circuits; six ground-to-ground press phones and four for staff, hooked up instantly where the plane alighted; a radio-receiving Xerox machine; an airborne teletype, receiving or sending at 100 words a minute; fifteen walkie-talkie machines with air-to-air or air-to-ground radii of five miles—all combined to create a web of invisible communication, about the plane, whether in flight or at rest, that made every input from New York headquarters or around the country instantly available, made questions and answers a matter of minutes.[9]

At every stop, there were at least two telexes in the hotel and an especially secure telephone for the staff. No other candidate had ever put together so much hardware.

One example of the efficiency of the preplanning of the campaign can be seen in comparing the projected budget with actual expenditures for one of the operating divisions. The United Citizens-for-Nixon, headquartered in two floors of the just-abandoned Willard Hotel in Washington, was the major nonparty campaign vehicle. There were 100 paid employees and about 400 volunteers directing citizen and volunteer activities around the country. The budget for this operation was $2 million; the actual expenses were $1,912,117—a small difference for a political campaign.

Humphrey

The financial campaign of Hubert Humphrey stood in stark contrast to that of Richard Nixon. While the Republican Convention had taken place in an atmosphere of relative calm and unity, the events in Chicago brought on further political and financial chaos to the already troubled Democrats. At the time of Convention planning, the Democrats were expecting to be renominating the President, and the Convention was scheduled for as late as possible. As a result, there was almost no time to heal wounds or adequately gear up to raise money between the Convention and the start of the general election campaign. Most important, there was no plan for raising the $10–$15 million which would be needed. Moreover, President Johnson did or was able to do less to help out financially than an incumbent President usually does. But from the polls which showed only about 30 percent of the voters favored Humphrey in September, there was, as the saying goes, nowhere to go but up.

The turning point on the issue of Vietnam, and consequently for the campaign, came on September 30. Campaign manager Larry O'Brien decided to spend $100,000—an enormous sum to the campaign at that time—for a half-hour national television broadcast; Humphrey would strike forward with a new position on Vietnam policy.[10] A plea for funds was tagged on at the end of the half-hour, with a card showing the number of a hastily arranged post-office box in Washington. The response was greater than anticipated: depending on which report one believes, that telecast brought in approximately $150,000 to $300,000.[e] In any case, the telecast not only paid for itself, but made a profit. It also marked the beginning of the upturn in Humphrey's campaign.

The contrast between the functioning and finances of the Democratic National Committee and the Republican National Committee were almost as marked as between the two campaigns. There is some dispute as to whether or not the Humphrey people inherited a debt when they took over the DNC. Johnson functionaries claim they had commitments of funds to pay off all bills, but apparently some of the money came in during the campaign and was hard to distinguish from campaign funds. There is no dispute that Humphrey inherited a moribund National Committee. The DNC had been widely criticized intermittently between 1965 and 1968 for sins of omission and commission, such as failing to seriously pursue small contributor programs, pursuing too vigorously and too secretively the President's Club, and publishing expensive program advertising books. After President Johnson withdrew, the DNC ceased almost all meaningful activity, including fund raising. The President's Club, the main source of money, was inactive after March 31, and the Sustaining Fund had not been pursued energetically enough to be productive.

The cash flow according to Humphrey operatives can be reconstructed about as follows:

September 1 inherited debt at DNC	$ 419,249[d]
Raised between 9/1–12/31	4,869,380
Reported borrowing as of 12/31	6,155,000
Deficit as of 1/17/69	6,166,218

The total national campaign cost, covering the DNC and 55 other committees, was $10,296,419. The breakdown is less detailed than that provided by the Republicans, but is by functional category, as follows:

Advertising	$6,304,030
Travel	875,600
Personnel	759,436
Communications	722,700

[e] According to Chester, Hodgson, and Page, and *Congressional Quarterly,* the telecast brought in $150,000; according to *Time* in one article, $200,000, and in a later article, $300,000; and according to White, $250,000.[11]

[d] Does *not* include $707,000 deficit resulting from the Chicago Convention.

Field expenses	578,656
Contributions to state and local committees	380,070
Polls and surveys	261,521
Office expenses	250,201
Miscellaneous	164,205

The most detailed disclosure of advertising expenses in a Presidential campaign was made for the Humphrey campaign, covering close to 90 percent of the $6.3 million spent.[12] The $762,000 discrepancy between the total advertising costs and the amount for which details were provided can be explained by the limitations of the DNC's advertising agency role. There were some newspaper ads, campaign materials, and other advertising which were not bought through the agency, and also some which were brought by campaign committees other than the DNC and the central headquarters committees.

The campaign switched advertising agencies shortly after the Convention, from Doyle Dane Bernbach (which Humphrey had been using since May) to a special unit spun off by Lennen and Newell, Inc. While there were many rumored and some plausible explanations for the unusual last-minute switch, one reason was clearly financial: DDB wanted the usual fifteen percent commission, while L & N were willing to do the work on a fee basis. (The agency fees eventually came to less than seven percent of the cost of the advertising handled by Lennen and Newell, Inc.)

Almost everything about Humphrey's campaign differed substantially from that of his Republican opponent. In connection with a Humphrey visit to Texas late in the campaign, Rep. Henry Gonzales noted, "We've had no radio, no television spots, and I dug into my own pocket to pay for 10,000 Arriba Humphrey buttons and 75,000 leaflets." The Nixon campaign not only had a substantial media campaign, but also had 12 full-time Mexican-American workers in the state for three months.[13]

Even such staples as buttons and bumper stickers were in chronically short supply. Partly because they were still owed for materials provided before the Convention, button-makers would not supply the goods on credit, and O'Brien could not scrape up $100,000 to buy the first order (of designs which had been ready for weeks) until September 23.[e]

An example of the relative inefficiency of the Humphrey campaign can be seen in comparing the travel statistics to those of the Nixon campaign. The two Presidential candidates visited almost exactly the same number of cities and states—Humphrey visited 36 states and 116 cities while Nixon visited 35 states and 118 cities—but Nixon outspent Humphrey by a ratio of more than three to two. The Humphrey style of travel was definitely

---

[e] The Indianapolis AFL-CIO produced and distributed 300,000 handbills in little more than a month, rather than wait for materials produced by national headquarters.[14]

tourist class compared to that of the luxurious and efficient Nixon entourage.

Without money, or any idea of how much or when it might be coming, a campaign cannot be planned. In particular, media time cannot be bought without cash in hand. And without media exposure and well-planned and well-coordinated candidate appearances (which also take money), a campaign may not catch on and will have even more trouble raising money. Theodore White calls this the "push-pull" or "resonant" effect in politics.[15] Humphrey himself, in retrospect, said: "It's not the amount of money you get, it's when you get it."[16]

Wallace

At the beginning, in late 1967 and early 1968, the Presidential campaign of George C. Wallace was considered by many electoral analysts to be an interesting political sideshow. From late Spring to early October of 1968, it was viewed as a very serious threat to the two-party system or to the Constitutional method for selecting a President. By election day, no one seemed sure of its significance for 1968 or the future.

After his surprising showing in three Democratic primaries in 1964, Wallace seemed destined to play some role in national politics in 1968. Like McCarthy, Wallace may have begun with an issue-oriented campaign, but his strategy was flexible and evolved with growing success. Clearly, this would be more than a Southern regional candidacy, and as developments unfolded, there was indeed a chance of disrupting the electoral college system. Whatever his strategy and intentions, however, Wallace's support seemed to increase whenever there was decreased confidence in the government and in traditional politics. Hence, Martin Luther King's assassination and the subsequent riots, Robert Kennedy's assassination, and the Chicago convention violence each resulted in increased support for George Wallace. On the other hand, President Johnson's withdrawal was seen as a blow to Wallace's campaign. Beginning in the fall of 1967, when Wallace's campaign seriously got under way, the Harris polls showed a steady rise for Wallace: 10 percent in October; 12 percent in December; in late March, 15 percent in a Johnson-Nixon race and 19 percent in a McCarthy-Rockefeller race; and in mid-July, 16 percent in a McCarthy-Nixon race and 17 percent in a Humphrey-Nixon race. Gallup's polls were similar: 11 percent in late February, 14 percent in early May, and 16 percent in mid-July. By late spring, these poll percentages, if translated into votes, might well have meant that neither of the two major-party candidates would get enough electoral college votes to win—and Wallace's peak had not been reached. In late September, Gallup's second post-Convention poll gave 43 percent to Nixon, 28 percent to Humphrey, and 21 percent to George Wallace. And then the bubble burst.

Wallace's standing in the polls dropped from 21 percent in mid-September to 13 percent in late October; his final percentage of the vote was 13.5 percent. The reasons for Wallace's October decline are varied, and the relative importance of each is unknown. Wallace's choice of General Curtis LeMay, named on October 3, clearly hurt the campaign.[f] Humphrey's October surge also hurt Wallace to the extent that the Democratic party and workers were mobilizing and working. Most important was probably the extraordinary labor union effort on behalf of Humphrey; it was not that union leaders said anything new about Wallace, but that they had credibility with blue-collar potential Wallace supporters who were traditionally Democrats.

Wallace's top campaign staff was exclusively Southern, and almost exclusively Alabamian. None had had any previous experience in national politics. Although *Time* magazine said the campaign was "perhaps the most amateurishly organized drive . . . in modern American history—by contrast, Eugene McCarthy's 'children's crusade' was a model of efficiency and professionalism,"[18] it is impossible to dismiss lightly the first minor-party effort which succeeded in getting on the ballot in all 50 states. The only failure was in the District of Columbia. Below the top staff level, members of various extremist groups, such as the John Birch Society, the Citizens Councils of America, Inc., and even the Ku Klux Klan, provided a significant amount of the local manpower and direction to the campaign.[19] In 1968, George Wallace received 13.5 percent of the popular vote and 45 electoral votes. On a popular vote basis, this can be considered a notable showing; on an electoral vote basis, it reveals the advantages of a regional candidacy where votes are concentrated in certain states.

Financially, the campaign of George Wallace was by far the costliest minor-party effort in American history. The available records of national committees show only $665,420 spent for the Roosevelt Progressive Party in 1912, and $236,963 for the La-Follette Progressive Party in 1924.[20] For 1948, records of receipts by national committees show $1.1 million for Henry Wallace's effort and a mere $163,000 for Thurmond's campaign.[21] While these were not the totals spent at all levels, they hardly compare with the almost $7 million reported by the national Wallace campaign, even considering price differentials. Nor is there much comparison with the percentages of funds coming in small sums. The financial success of the Wallace campaign is not in doubt, and there is no doubt that there were surpluses. There also were reports of intention to pay all bills in full, something few of the other campaigns ended up doing.

The Wallace campaign had no formal pre- or postnomination periods,

---

[f] While most observers have suggested that LeMay's big handicap was his outspoken views on the use of nuclear power, which the vast majority of Americans do not share, Theodore White offers another reason. LeMay, he suggests, represented the establishment, and offended many pro-Wallace people whose basic attraction was essentially anti-establishment.[17]

since the mid-September Dallas Convention of the American Independent Party (AIP) was a very informal two-hour gathering. Wallace's running mate was not even chosen until two weeks later, although the AIP did publish a formal party platform. The Wallace command had toyed with the idea of holding a major convention in order to obtain free television coverage. Consideration was also given to publishing a convention program book, because the corporations which advertised in the Republican and Democratic convention program books might feel bound to advertise in the Wallace one as well.[g] Comparable revenues to those received by the Democratic and Republican program books probably would have paid for a major convention had one been held.

Because there was no prenomination period, there was legal question as the campaign unfolded as to whether the Wallace campaign should be filing official fund reports under federal law. The assumption was that political activity in January or June was pointed toward the November election, not an August convention or any primary victory. In this view, the Wallace campaign would not be exempted from reporting, as candidates for nomination are exempted, and reports would be required because the Wallace campaign was working, as the law states, for the purpose of attempting to influence the election of presidential and vice-presidential electors in two or more states. This argument was used in some press stories, and when the preelection filing dates came around in October, the Wallace campaign did file a report (dated October 24) going back to February 7, the day before Wallace's formal announcement of candidacy, while protesting that they were filing voluntarily and had not violated the law earlier. The filing, covering a nine-month period, was voluminous, and was not made by several committees but solely by "The Wallace Campaign." The filing was accompanied by a letter, addressed to the Clerk of the House of Representatives, W. Pat Jennings, which answered the press allegations, and warrants full coverage here:

Dear Sir:

Enclosed please find a report of The Wallace Campaign disclosing receipts and disbursements from February 7, 1968, through October 21, 1968.

As you know, former Governor Wallace is a candidate for President of the United States seeking election in the November 5, 1968, General Election. Governor Wallace has no campaign committee or committee-like organization functioning on his behalf as do the Presidential candidates of the Republican and Democratic Parties. Campaign contributions have been received and disbursed in his behalf by duly authorized agents. Legal counsel advises that the Corrupt Practices Act of 1925, as amended, is not applicable to his candidacy for the Presidency of the United States. In other words, there is only a re-

---

[g] In the McCarthy campaign, serious consideration was also given to publishing their own convention program book with advertising, but the idea was dropped.

quirement under the law that any committee, association or organization which accepts contributions or makes expenditures for the purpose of influencing or attempting to influence the election of candidates for Presidential or Vice-Presidential electors in two or more states must make an accounting. Governor Wallace has no such committee and, of course, candidates are not required to file.

Governor Wallace, however, in the interest of full public disclosure and in the interest of being fully in good faith with the American public, is pleased to file the attached.

Very substantial portions of the listed expenditures were used in ballot position campaigns in the various states and would, therefore, not be attributable to the actual campaign for President of the United States.

We shall appreciate your acknowledging of the report.

With kind regards, we are

Sincerely yours,

_____

Seymore Trammell
National Campaign Director

_____

Cecil C. Jackson, Jr.
National Campaign Director

Enclosure

Federal law requires a political committee to have a chairman and a treasurer, but there was no admission that a political committee was filing. Federal law prohibits a political committee from receiving or disbursing more than $3 million, but the single Wallace filing reported more, and interpretation turns on whether or not what reported was a political committee. In any case, the press and scholars were pleased that the reports were filed as far back as February, which is more than was available for Nixon or Humphrey or other candidates in the prenomination months. And the October filing was followed up with a January 1969, cumulative report (but no further reports in 1969 to show disposition of bills and funds).

From February 1968, "The Wallace Campaign" reported expenditures of $6,985,455, but only about $5.4 million of the almost $7 million in expenditures was itemized and can be accounted for. As with the major-party campaigns, the largest expense was for advertising, although the percentage spent for this activity was slightly lower than for other Presidential campaigns. The national Wallace campaign reported spending $3,085,000 for advertising, about 44 percent of the total. Of this, a little more than $200,000 was for printing, $500,000 was for supplies and materials, and $2,378,000 was for advertising—presumably radio, television, and newspaper time and space, and production costs. All but $80,000 of the $2.4 million was paid to Luckie and Forney of Birmingham, the advertising agency used throughout the campaign. Data from the Federal Communications Commission show just under $2 million spent by "other" party Presidential candidates in 1968, all of which was spent by Wallace.[22] Extrapolating from this and the total advertising figure, it would seem that less than 19 percent of the expenses were for production costs and agency fees, which is a very low figure for political advertising.

The next major expense category was travel. While at least $1,235,000 (according to the filed report) was spent on airplanes, rental cars, hotels, and so on, less than one-half of the amount can be detailed.

United Air Lines	$149,375
American Flyers Airline	235,000
Aerodyne	98,000
Dallas Aero Service	17,885
New York Hertz	67,065
Miramar Hotel (California)	20,423

Wallace began his campaign with a DC-7, which was either loaned by or rented from Henry Seale, a Texas oil millionaire and owner of Dallas Aero Service. Later, a DC-3 was added to the campaign, and in early October, two Electra propjets were acquired. If Nixon's travel accomodations were luxury class and Humphrey's were tourist class, then Wallace's must certainly be economy class.

General LeMay, Wallace's running mate, received a salary of $12,000 during the campaign. Since he was only a candidate for one month and two days, the salary might seem a little high. However, LeMay had been fired from his job with an electronics firm in Southern California shortly after his Vice-Presidential candidacy was announced, so he had suffered financially because of his candidacy. Records of all other salaries come to only $266,000.

The Wallace campaign spent at least $192,000 for telephone and telegraph, $132,000 for postage, $66,000 for rentals (halls for rallies, and so on), and $100,000 for office expenses, supplies, insurance, and so on. Wallace's campaign headquarters in Montgomery, however, were donated rent free; the three-story block-sized building had 60,000 square feet of space. Unlike the other Presidential campaigns, polling was not a significant expense; only $37,000 for polls was shown in the report.

Expenses reported by the Wallace campaign in the categories "legal expenses" and "state qualification costs" give some indication of the costs of getting on the ballot in all 50 states. These figures are not complete, and only represent expenses specified by the Wallace campaign as having been incurred for these purposes. The legal costs, which presumably involved paying for legal counsel and/or assistance in various states, totalled $118,175. There were legal expenses in 26 states, but two states accounted for almost 60 percent of the total: $35,000 was reported as spent in Ohio, where Wallace's challenge went all the way to the U.S. Supreme Court which ordered his name on the ballot; and $33,054 in California, where more than 65,000 voters had to reregister as members of the American Independent Party in order to secure a ballot position for Wallace. Of the other 24 states in which there were legal expenses, the costs in 19 of them were under $2,000. The exact meaning of state qualification costs is not known, but the Wallace campaign spent a total of $169,180.25 in seven states. Costs in two states accounted for 97 percent of the total: $50,000 in New York and $115,000 in Massachusetts.

In addition to the report filed by the national Wallace campaign, two smaller Wallace committees also filed with the Clerk of the House. One was a California committee and the other the Western headquarters of Youth-for-Wallace. These two committees spent $258,000 and raised about the same. Their expenditures included about $42,000 for printing and mailing, $19,000 for radio and television, $10,000 for billboards and signs, and $4,000 for advertising in 44 newspapers. Most contributions to these two committees were in amounts of less than $100 and the only notable income was $48,000 in literature sales.

Miscellaneous reports were filed in Connecticut, showing expenditures there of Americans for Wallace, $2,519; George Wallace Party, $10; and the Norwalk George Wallace Campaign, $1,917. A Wisconsin filing showed $133 spent. Doubtless thousands of such committees raising and spending sums in these ranges existed throughout the country, and if they could be tallied, they would add hundreds of thousands if not millions of dollars to the Wallace totals.

Moreover, it is necessary to stress that the Wallace campaign commenced seriously in mid-1967, and considerable money must have been spent between then and February 1968, when the national reporting began. In California, for instance, the drive to get on the ballot took place in the Fall of 1967, and the campaign admitted it cost at least $500,000. Campaign officials estimated that during 1967–68, the organizational and legal efforts to get Wallace on the ballot in the 50 states cost $3 million, only part of which would be included in the February-November 1968 report. Costs were in preparing petitions, gathering signatures, legal fees, and campaigning. The campaigning was inseparable from the task of seeking ballot qualification because Wallace would spend time in the state—to attract attention, to whip up enthusiasm—in order to get enough signatures to qualify.

The campaigns for ballot qualifications ranged from the expensive months-long California operation, which climaxed in early January 1968, with 107,000 newly registered AIP members, to Nebraska, where it took "just seven and a half minutes to get on the ballot" in early March.[23] In Georgia, $20,000 was spent in organizing for 200,000 signatures.[24] Managing to attain ballot status in all 50 states was a prodigious legal precedent and perhaps the most lasting achievement of the Wallace campaign.

If one accepts the calculation of $7 million plus 1967 costs for ballot qualification, the Wallace campaign cost a total of at least $9 million. This figure would seem to be confirmed by a postelection campaign headquarters' estimate of $9 million and a campaign aide's estimate of $10 million spent.[25] All analysts are agreed that the campaign ended with a surplus.

Campaign urgencies bring political expenditures for a variety of purposes, and several outstanding categories of expenses in 1968 are highlighted in the pages that follow.

Campaign Publicity

The Humphrey and Nixon staffs made available breakdowns of advertising expenses for the national-level general election campaigns, which are

Table 4-2

National-Level Nixon and Humphrey Advertising Expenditures, General Election, 1968

	Humphrey	Nixon
Time and Space		
Television	$3,525,000	$ 6,270,000
Network	2,151,000 [a]	
Regional Spot	1,374,000	
Radio	425,000	1,870,000
Network	123,000	
Regional Spot	302,000	
Newspapers	429,000	880,000
Refund	−150,000 [b]	— [c]
Total Time and Space	4,229,000	9,020,000
Media Production		
Radio and Television	1,043,000 [d]	
Newspapers	62,000	
Refund	−45,000 [b]	— [c]
Total Production	1,060,000	1,980,000
Agency Fees	378,000	
Refund	−125,000 [b]	— [c]
Total	$5,542,000	$11,000,000

[a] Divided approximately $1 million for programs and $1.1 million for spot announcements.

[b] Details of the $320,000 in advertising agency refunds are: $45,000 for overestimated production costs; $150,000 in rebates for network time ordered and paid for but where local station clearances could not be obtained; the remaining $125,000 was from advances to the agency bank accounts and could not be categorized.

[c] The Nixon campaign had some refunds but details are not known.

[d] Including about $300,000 spent on preparation of film biographies.

generally comparable though more detailed in the Democratic case. These disclosures are particularly valuable because they relate time and space charges to production costs. These figures are lower than the FCC figures used in the discussion of political broadcasting that follows, because the latter reflect all network and station charges, including those for broadcasts placed by state and local Nixon or Humphrey committees not controlled by national-level headquarters.

The advertising agency the Democrats used, a special unit spun off by Lennen and Newell, Inc., worked on a fee basis, rather than charge commission fees, because they felt a seven-week campaign of such volume would mean an inordinate commission. The item listed as agency fee covered costs for about 68 workers in New York and six in Washington.

At least on the Democratic side, the advertising expenses appear to indicate that there is some levelling of political campaign costs on occasion. The production and time/space costs of the Humphrey campaign were very much in line with those reported for broadcast media by the Goldwater national-level campaign in 1964: $1,066,484 and $4,542,151, respectively.[26] Comparable figures were not available for the Johnson-Humphrey campaign of 1964, but reports at the time were in the same range, near $5 million. However, this apparent levelling in Democratic media spending in 1968 can be attributed to limited Democratic funding, and it is certain that the Democrats would have liked to have spent more, and would have if they had dared go deeper into debt or could have raised the money.

Political Broadcasting

Political broadcast expenditures continued their steep rise in 1968. The total of $58.9 million spent—representing all network and station charges for both television and radio usage by candidates and supporters at all levels for both primary and general election periods—was 70 percent higher than $34.6 million spent in 1964.[27] Unlike the period from 1960 to 1964, when both radio and television expenditures increased by 73 percent, from 1964 to 1968 radio showed a greater rise than television. Radio expenditures rose 93 percent (from $10.8 million in 1964 to $20.9 million in 1968) while television expenditures rose 60 percent (from 23.8 to $38.0 million). The larger rise in radio expenditures was particularly marked for the primary period, in which the 1964–68 increase was 105 percent compared to 73 percent for television.[28] Overall, political broadcasting increased from 17.3 percent of the estimated total of all political spending ($200 million) in 1964 to 19.6 percent (of $300 million) in 1968, ensuring its position as the largest single cost in political campaigns.

In addition, however, there are both production costs and promotion costs incurred in connection with broadcasting. Because of the hurried nature of most political advertising, production costs tend to be high.

Production costs in normal advertising agency commercial work run about seven percent of time and space charges, but 20 to 50 percent production charges are not unusual in politics, because of the crash nature of campaigns, overtime, new issues cropping up, and the scrapping of undesirable spot announcements.

In Richard Nixon's general election campaign, for example, production costs of almost $2 million (although including an unknown amount for print production) were listed on a little more than $8 million worth of media time purchased by the central national campaign; this amounted to 24 percent of media time. The unplanned nature of Hubert Humphrey's campaign[h] or its lower volume may account for slightly higher known production costs of 27 percent: almost $1 million costs for $3.7 million in media time. Data on the advertising expenses of Robert Kennedy's campaign reveal the very high production costs of a sudden campaign. In six primaries, Kennedy's television and radio time costs were $1.25 million (there were no network broadcasts). The listed production costs were $760,000, but that included costs for newspaper as well as for broadcast production. However, since print production is a small fraction of the total, the broadcast production costs were surely at least 50 percent of the broadcast time costs. Hubert Humphrey's prenomination campaign incurred costs of only 14.8 percent for production in relation to air time.

If average production costs and agency fees for only 20 percent are added to the total broadcast expenditures of $58.9 million for 1968 reported by the FCC, the cost of broadcast advertising to candidates was approximately $70 million. To this figure must be added the cost of "tune-in" ads in newspapers and other promotion expenses. Thus, at least $75 million, one-quarter of the estimated total of all political spending, is directly related to political broadcasting, making it by far the largest functional political expense. If one were to add other allied costs—travel to the broadcast city, speech-writing, and other such planning and preparation—then a total of 50 percent more than time costs would not be unreasonable, making broadcast-related expenses as much as $90 million.

Primary and General Election

The total spent by Republicans and Democrats at all levels for both television and radio for primary and general elections was the same, $27.9 million,[30] but this reflected the usual pattern of greater primary expenditures by Democrats and greater general election expenditures by Republicans. In the primaries, both parties almost doubled their expenses over 1964, so that the Democrats maintained their edge of close to 2.5 times the Republican expenditures. In the general election, however, Democratic spending

---

[h] Of $3.4 million spent by Humphrey's national campaign for television advertising, $2.75 million was spent in the last week.[29]

increased by only 41 percent over 1964, while Republican spending was up 73 percent. The great difference in spending patterns of the major parties is best revealed by the fact that while Republicans in the general elections spent more than 400 percent as much as they spent in the primaries, Democrats spent only 25 percent more in the general election than they did in the primary period. Total expenditures by party for 1964 and 1968 are shown in Table 4-3.

Table 4-3

Total Television and Radio Network and Station Charges for Political Broadcasting by Election and Party, 1964, 1968 (in millions)

| | 1964 | | 1968 | |
	Rep.	Dem.	Rep.	Dem.
Primary	$ 2.9	$ 6.8	$ 5.4	$12.4
General Election	13.0	11.0	22.5	15.5
Total	15.9	17.8	27.9	27.9

Sources: FCC, *Survey 1964,* Table 1; *Survey 1968,* Table 1.

In the general election, $40.4 million was spent by all candidates for broadcasting, a 64 percent increase over the amount spent in 1964 and almost three times the amount spent in 1960.[31] The 1968 total was nearly seven times the amount spent in 1952, the year broadcasting first became a major expense item in national campaigns: television expenditures in 1968 were nine times the 1952 level, while radio expenditures had more than quadrupled in the 16 years.

The disparity in general election expenditures between the major parties was much greater than ever before, and for the first time there were significant expenditures for political broadcasting by minor parties (mainly the Wallace campaign). Table 4-4 details the expenditures for broadcasting

Table 4-4

Distribution of General Election Costs for Broadcasts by Party and Facility, 1952, 1956, 1960, 1964, 1968 (in millions)

	1952	1956	1960	1964	1968
Republicans	$3.5	$5.4	$ 7.6	$13.0	$22.5
Democrats	2.6	4.1	6.2	11.0	15.4
Other	—	.3	.4	.6	2.5
Total	6.1	9.8	14.2	24.6	40.4
Television	3.0	6.6	10.1	17.5	27.1
Radio	3.1	3.2	4.1	7.1	13.3

Sources: 1952, Heard, *The Costs of Democracy,* p. 22. 1956–68, FCC, *Survey 1968,* Table 3.

in the last five Presidential-year general elections (equivalent figures for the primary periods are not available for 1960-56-52).

The Campaigns for President. The total spent on political broadcasting by all Presidential and Vice-Presidential candidates in both the primary and general elections was very high—$28.5 million—and it accounts for 48.3 percent of all political broadcasting costs.[32] The Republicans spent $15.6 million and the Democrats spent $10.9 million, with $2.0 million being spent by minor parties.[33]

The pattern of greater Democratic primary spending and greater Republican general-election spending was evidenced in the Presidential campaigns and the disparity was particularly marked in the general election. The Democrats outspent the Republicans $4.8 million to $3.0 million in the primaries (nonmajor party candidates spent $300,000), while the Republicans outspent the Democrats $12.6 million to $6.1 million in the general election (nonmajors, $1.6 million).[34] The pattern of spending by facility was nearly the same for both parties, with about 2.5 times as much being spent for television as for radio. Table 4-5 details the Presidential broadcast costs.

Table 4-5

Network and Station Charges for Presidential and Vice-Presidential Candidates by Party, Primary and General Elections, 1968 (in millions)

	Rep.	Dem.	Other
Primary			
Television	$ 2.5	$3.4	$ .3
Radio	.5	1.4	.1
Total	$ 3.0	$4.8	$ .4
General Election			
Television	9.0	4.5	1.1
Radio	3.6	1.6	.5
Total	$12.6	$6.1	$1.6

Source: FCC, *Survey 1968*, Tables 1, 9, 20.

The intense Presidential primary competition in both parties and the close general election in 1968 were reflected in the significantly higher political broadcasting expenditures compared to four years earlier. The $28.5 million total in 1968 was 123 percent higher than the $12.8 million spent in 1964. The percentage of total broadcast costs devoted to the Presidential contests increased from 37 percent in 1964 to 1968's 48.3 percent: television expenditures for the Presidential contests increased from 42 percent to 56 percent, and radio expenditures increased from 25 percent to 36 percent of the total political broadcasting costs.[35] The 1964 and 1968 costs by facility are compared in Table 4-6.

Table 4-6

Network and Station Charges for Presidential and Vice-Presidential Candidates by Facility, Primary and General Election, 1964 and 1968 (in millions)

	1964	1968
Primary Election		
Television	$ 1.2	$ 6.2
Radio	.6	2.0
Total	$ 1.8	$ 8.2
General Election		
Television	$ 8.9	$14.6
Radio	2.1	5.7
Total	$11.0	$20.3

Sources: FCC, *Survey 1964,* Tables 1, 9A, 22A; *Survey 1968,* Tables 1, 9, 20.

These figures reveal the extraordinary intensity of the 1968 Presidential primary campaigns. Broadcast expenditures for the primaries increased 356 percent over 1964, while the general election expenditures increased 85 percent. Broken down by party, the 1968 expenditures were startling in relation to 1964: with contests in both years, Republican primary spending increased 131 percent; with only minor contests in 1964 (between Governor Wallace and President Johnson's stand-ins in three states) Democratic primary spending increased 1100 percent.[36] The Democrats paid a high price for their bitter 1968 prenomination battles.

Richard Nixon's local panel shows were a new technique in Presidential campaigns.[37] The unrehearsed shows featured Nixon answering questions from a group of local citizens before an audience of dignitaries and supporters. In addition to the live television coverage in the local region, the shows were taped and turned into radio and television commercials, sometimes as soon as 72 hours after the original show.[38] There were ten live telecasts. Production costs for these varied from $11,000 to $27,000, and consisted mostly of costs to build the set (like theatres-in-the-round) and to interconnect the various stations. Time costs for these shows were relatively low because they were bought on a local basis.

Both parties scheduled two-hour election-eve telethons, another first in Presidential campaigning. The Democrats paid $284,000 for their time, and the Republicans paid $293,500.[39] The Republicans' total cost, including production, was $450,000. Nixon in fact did two two-hour shows, answering questions live for two hours while the telethon was being shown to the East and Midwest and then again for two more hours while the show was beamed to the West Coast, Alaska, and Hawaii. Hawaii was reached by communication satellite, the first time a paid political program had been sent by satellite.[40] Both telethons featured celebrities, and the candidates answered questions telephoned by viewers.[41]

The Republicans had a rating of 26, meaning that 26 percent of those households watching television were watching the Nixon telethon; the Democrats' rating was 22. The estimated total audience was 15 million for Nixon and 14 million for Humphrey. Almost 90 percent of each audience were of voting age.[42] A national interview study reported that 15.6 percent of those who watched the election-eve broadcasts said that they decided for whom to vote either that night or election day.[43]

In style, the Nixon and Humphrey television campaigns were noticeably different. The Republicans focused on the man. The Democrats tended to focus on an issue, and then identify Humphrey with that issue.

The Democrats and Republicans each had one commercial which was attacked by the other party, and both of them were extraordinarily well placed. Hubert Humphrey had a five-minute spot attacking Nixon's position on the nuclear nonproliferation treaty (which the Republicans later charged was misrepresented) following the network showing of the movie "Dr. Strangelove." The Republicans had a one-minute spot which mixed pictures of a smiling Humphrey with pictures of war, poverty, and riots; it was shown on Rowan and Martin's "Laugh-In," which was first in the Nielsen rating that week. The Democrats protested and the commercial was not shown again on network television.

Broadcasting Discounts

Broadcasters can affect a candidate's choice of time purchased by giving discounts on some kinds of time and not on others. In 1968, there were two interesting examples of how broadcasters shaped some of the political dialogue. The Columbia Broadcasting System network gave a discount for 5-minute trailers used at the end of 25-minute abbreviated half-hour programs, in effect charging about one-third as much as for a one-minute participation (spot announcement) in a regular prime-time network program. The National Broadcasting Corporation gave 50 percent discounts for one-minute participations; in some cases the minute was added to an already sold commercial schedule, thus adding profit to the network.

Candidates were of course grateful for any discounts, and were obviously likely to use more of the discounted time than of nondiscounted kinds of media time. One might well question whether public decisions as to political broadcasting should be made solely by the broadcasters. Consideration of the candidates' opinions of what kinds of media best suit their styles or needs get subordinated to the broadcasters' marketing or profit-making motives. Judgments as to what kinds of time best suit or best inform the public get subordinated to other considerations also.

There was no suspension of Section 315 of the Federal Communications Act—the so-called "equal time" provision—for the 1968 Presidential campaigns. Suspension of Section 315 would have been necessary if 1960-style debates between the major party candidates were to be held. It was even proposed that Section 315 be suspended prior to the nominating conventions because of the number of major candidates in both parties, and the fact that with some candidates competing in primaries (Nixon, Kennedy, and McCarthy) and some not (Humphrey, Rockefeller, and Reagan), there was no way for the electorate to make meaningful comparisons. However, as the Congressional maneuvering over various suspension bills dragged on into the late spring and early summer, various political and broadcasting commentators suggested other kinds of joint candidate appearances which would not be covered by the "equal time" restrictions.

The possibility and legality of this approach was demonstrated by the McCarthy-Kennedy debate three days before the California primary. The two candidates appeared on a special Saturday night version of ABC's "Issues and Answers." A regularly scheduled news show, such as "Issues and Answers," is specifically excluded from coverage under the "equal time" provision and, fortunately for ABC, no other candidates raised questions about the McCarthy-Kennedy national telecast. Although Jack Gould, *The New York Times'* television critic, called the debate an "electronic tennis game, in which Senators Robert F. Kennedy and Eugene J. McCarthy played on the same side of the net,"[44] and most observers did not think either candidate won, the debate clearly showed the possibility of some kinds of joint candidate appearances even if Section 315 were not suspended. However, the only other attempt to follow this approach was a planned one-hour special version of "Meet the Press" in late August, on which McCarthy and Humphrey would have each appeared separately in 30-minute segments; McCarthy cancelled his appearance partly because he felt the back-to-back format would give an illusion of a debate without the reality.[45]

A different approach was tried in late August (right before the Democratic National Convention), when plans were made for a one-hour McCarthy-Humphrey debate to be carried on all three television networks. Before the two candidates jointly agreed to cancel the debate (for a variety of reasons), Senator George McGovern and Governor Lester Maddox requested that they be included since they, too, were candidates for the Democratic nomination. The networks responded with an offer of 30 minutes each for McGovern and Maddox, to be used separately or in a joint hour appearance, which McGovern rejected. Whether or not the separate time would have fulfilled the "equal time" requirement of

Section 315 had not been decided by the FCC when the debate cancellation mooted the issue.

Ironically, there also was one three-way face-to-face meeting of Humphrey, McCarthy, and McGovern, which incidentally proved that "there is more than one way to stage a debate."[46] The event was a caucus of the California delegation at the Democratic National Convention to which the three candidates had been invited (Governor Maddox was not invited). All three television networks could and did choose to cover the caucus as a legitimate news event: the caucus was not arranged by the networks, and it was not subject to the "equal time" provision.

The possibilities of applying these experiences to the future can usefully be pursued. Aside from these several instances of new approaches to political appearances, all attention was focused on the question of suspension of Section 315. In 1968, it was the Republicans who made sure that the bill to suspend Section 315 was bottled up in Congress, as the Democrats had in 1964. By early fall, it was clear to the Republicans that their party and candidates would be in a relatively strong political and financial position, facing a badly divided and financially weak Democratic Party. Confident of sufficient funds for the media time they wanted to buy, the Republicans saw no reason to ensure availability of more free time which would help the Democrats, who were likely to have much less money available for their campaign.

In addition to financial considerations, Richard Nixon's personal view of debates was probably negative. Most observers believe he lost the 1960 debates with John Kennedy, which in turn may have cost him the election. The extraordinary exposure of debates is normally more valuable to the underdog or less well-known candidate. Nixon was clearly expected to be the front-runner (as he was at the beginning of the 1960 campaign), and saw no reason to jeopardize that position. Nixon no doubt preferred the planned regional telecasts he could control.

Nixon's aversion to appearances not controlled by him extended beyond debates. Unlike other candidates in recent years, he turned down all invitations for interview shows (for example, "Meet the Press") from early 1967 until late in October 1968. In contrast, Hubert Humphrey accepted as many invitations for local and regional (as well as national) interview and even talk and call-in shows as he could find. On such shows, Humphrey would say he was the first major candidate who had ever put himself in these totally open situations. Often the show's moderator would then note that Nixon had refused to participate on the program.[47]

The Democrats made Nixon's unwillingness to debate an issue in the campaign, although it was embarrassing since the Republicans had done the same thing when President Johnson responded negatively in 1964. Nixon was chided for his refusal to debate, and there were some unfavorable editorial comments on the subject. Humphrey tried to pressure Nixon with offers to debate with or without Wallace, on or off television, on paid or free television; he offered to pay for half, and then all, of an hour for a debate without Wallace on October 20.[48] Nixon's refusal to debate[‡] was difficult to defend because of a *Saturday Evening Post* article in 1964 in which he had said debates were to serve the public, not the candidates, and that they brought about a better campaign.[49] Nevertheless, he did not relent and Humphrey used the October 20 hour on his own, attracting one of the largest political audiences of the campaign.[50]

While there is no reason to believe that the election result in 1964 would have been different had there been debates and/or more free time, it is an open question with regard to the 1968 general election. The Republicans had an enormous advantage in media exposure. They outspent the Democrats 2 to 1 on both radio and television[51] and the Democrats had to cancel all local spots during the third and fourth weeks of the campaign (the end of September) and cut network television in half for the weeks of October 7 and 14 because of lack of funds.[52] Given the closeness of the vote, one can only speculate as to the outcome if the Democrats had had more media exposure.

What is clear from the events of 1964 and 1968 is that if the question of suspension of Section 315 is considered anew every four years, the decision will be based largely on the political situation and advantage of the moment, and on which party controls the Congress. The larger question of what may be in the public interest gets ignored.[53] If there is any hope of diminishing partisan and immediate-advantage considerations, the decision on Section 315 may have to be made for more than one election at a time, and probably at least a year prior to an affected election.

Sustaining Time

Certain network interview and documentary programs are exempt from the "equal time" provisions of Section 315, and in these categories, time can be provided to one candidate without obliging broadcasters to provide precisely equal time for other candidates. Some of these programs, such as "Meet the Press," are commercially sponsored and others are simply donated by the broadcasters. In the latter case, the time provided is called "sustaining time." In the sustaining category in 1968, the television networks offered only three hours and one minute of free time, down more than 25 percent from 1964 and less than 10 percent of the amount of time made available in 1960. Radio networks did a little better in 1968. Seven networks provided 24 hours and 17 minutes of sustaining time, which was a small increase over the time provided by four networks in

---

[‡] Nixon's public reason for refusing was that under the equal time provision Wallace would have to be offered the opportunity to buy matching time, and he (Nixon) did not want to do anything to weaken the two-party system by providing Wallace with the possibility of additional exposure.

1964.[54] A comparison of network sustaining time provided in the general elections for the last four Presidential election years is given in Table 4-7. (All of the time was for Presidential or Vice-Presidential candidates or supporters.)

Table 4-7

Network Sustaining Time Provided to Candidates and Their Supporters, General Election, 1956, 1960, 1964, 1968 (in hours and minutes)

| Year | Total Time, All Parties and Candidates | |
	Television [a]	Radio [b]
1968	3:01	24:17
1964	4:28	21:14
1960	39:22	43:14
1956	29:38	32:23

Source: FCC, *Survey 1968*, Table 4.
[a] Three networks.
[b] Seven networks in 1968; four networks in all other years.

The candidates themselves received relatively more of the sustaining time in 1968 than they had in 1964. Of the three hours and one minute of television network time in the general election, two hours and twenty-eight minutes were used for appearances of Presidential and Vice-Presidential candidates.[55] Four years earlier, less than one-third of the time had been for the candidates themselves. In the 1968 primaries, candidates themselves received 12 hours and 48 minutes of the total television network sustaining time of 13 hours and 16 minutes.[56] All of this sustaining time on television represented only 16 percent of Presidential and Vice-Presidential candidate appearances, as is shown in Table 4-8.

Table 4-8

Television Network Appearances of Candidates for President and Vice-President, 1968 (in hours and minutes)

	Primary	General Election	Total
Time paid for by Candidates or Supporters	7:32	24:29	32:01
Time on Commercially Sponsored Programs (e.g., "Meet the Press")	26:49	21:55	48:44
Sustaining Time	12:48	2:28	15:16

Source: FCC, *Survey 1968*, Table 6.

The major parties are normally the beneficiaries of the sustaining time which is exempt from "equal time" requirements. However, in 1968, of the sustaining television network time in the general election (3:01),

Republicans received 1 hour and 5 minutes, the Democrats received 39 minutes, and minor parties received 1 hour and 17 minutes. The radio networks provided 6 hours and 41 minutes to the Republicans, 10 hours and 56 minutes to the Democrats and 6 hours and 40 minutes to minor parties.[57] The minor party time reflects mostly time devoted to George Wallace's candidacy.

In the primaries, however, television networks provided 13¼ hours to Presidential candidates and their supporters: almost 4 hours to Republicans and just under 9½ hours to the Democrats. Radio networks provided 31½ hours: 10 hours to Republicans, 20½ hours to Democrats, and 1 hour to minor parties.[58]

One of the key arguments of those advocating repeal of Section 315 is that broadcasters would give more time to major party candidates if they did not have to give equal time to minor party candidates. The evidence from 1968 raises questions about this argument. An analysis of United States Senate races shows that in 25 states where there were only two candidates in the general election, 34 percent of the television stations in those states gave some free time; in 7 states where there were three or more candidates, however, 45 percent of the television stations gave some free time. Similarly, in 12 states which had only two candidates for Governor, 35 percent of the stations gave some free time, and in 9 states which had 3 or more candidates for Governor, 48 percent of the stations gave some free time.[59] While repeal of Section 315 may be desirable in Presidential campaigns when there will invariably be many candidates, at other levels it seems clear that the existence of minor–party candidates is not a significant deterrent to providing free time. The broadcaster's record, especially in two-candidate races, is not impressive.

Spots and Program Time

Presidential and Vice-Presidential candidates in the primary and general elections spent little more for program time than for announcement time on the television networks, $4.6 million to $4.2 million. On network radio, they spent $240,000 for program time and $452,000 for announcements.[60] However, this relative balance of program time and announcements was not duplicated at other levels of political broadcasting.

On television stations (nonnetwork programs), candidates at all levels spent $25.1 million for announcements and $4.0 million for program time, a ratio of more than six to one.[61] On radio stations, the ratio was 40 to 1, with $18.7 million being spent on announcements and $500,000 being spent on program time.[62] The relative spending on announcements has been steadily increasing; the overall ratio of 10 to 1 on radio and television stations in 1968 compares to 6 to 1 in 1966, 4 to 1 in 1964, and 3 to 1 in 1962.[63]

States. Radio and television station (nonnetwork) charges for political broadcasting totalled $49.3 million; they ranged from $63,000 in Mississippi to $5 million in California. More than $2 million was spent in each of nine states—California, Florida, Illinois, Missouri, New York, Ohio, Pennsylvania, Texas, and Wisconsin—and more than $1 million in each of five other states—Indiana, Michigan, North Carolina, Oregon, and Tennessee.[64]

Republicans and Democrats at the state level followed the overall pattern of primary and general election spending, as shown in Table 4-9.

Table 4-9

Radio and Television Station Charges (Nonnetwork), Primary and General Election, 1968 (in millions)

	Primary	General Election	Total
Republican	$ 4.3	$17.8	$22.1
Democrat	11.9	12.8	24.7
Other	.7	1.8	2.5
Total	$16.9	$32.4	$49.3

Source: FCC, *Survey 1968,* Tables 11, 12, 22, 23.

Democrats spent most in California ($2.7 million) and least in Wyoming ($19,000); and Republicans spent most in New York ($2.1 million) and least in Mississippi ($7,000).[65]

In the primaries, Democrats spent more than one-half million on radio in three states, California ($660,000), Texas ($638,000) and Wisconsin ($1,012,000), while the Republicans spent that sum only in Ohio ($515,000). For television, Republicans' largest expenditure was in California, where they spent $299,000; Democrats topped that amount in six states: California ($879,000), Florida ($407,000), Louisiana ($358,000), Missouri ($420,000), New York ($443,000), and Texas ($998,000).[66] It is interesting that of the states in which there were closely fought Democratic Presidential primaries, only California is one of the states of highest television spending. In some of the other states (such as Wisconsin and Indiana), the non-Presidential Democratic primary contests did not involve high broadcasts costs, so that the total primary expenditures were not as high as those states with very high non-Presidential, though no (or low) Presidential primary broadcast costs.

In the general election, comparison of television expenditures by party shows that the most spent by Democrats was $767,000 in California, while Republicans spent more in five states: California ($1.1 million), Indiana ($851,000), New York ($1.3 million), Ohio ($827,000), and Pennsylvania ($826,000). The disparities in radio expenditure were almost as great:

Democrats kept California in number one position, spending $432,000; Republicans topped that in four states: California ($548,000), New York ($510,000), Tennessee ($980,000) and Texas ($434,000).[67]

Conclusion

Viewed in terms of costs, political broadcasting is an ever-growing component of national campaigning. Viewed in terms of candidate selection, the impact of broadcasting on our political life, at least at the Presidential level, is probably less than some have warned. Many political commentators during the 1960s voiced the fear that candidates would be nominated on the basis of their television personality or image. Yet in 1968, when more money was spent on television and radio than ever before, neither major Presidential candidate was a television candidate. Both were party men, with few assets considered important for television campaining. Richard Nixon's television presence was an improvement over 1960, but he was hardly a TV idol, and his appearances were carefully controlled. Hubert Humphrey, who talked too much and in a gravelly voice, appeared at his best in filmed documentaries which were carefully photographed and edited; he did not appear in his spot announcements. The Vice-Presidential candidates of the major parties could not have been chosen on the basis of television appeal either, for younger, more physically appealing politicians were available.

If one tries to judge the impact of political broadcasting on the outcome of the Presidential election, contradictory conclusions can be drawn from the evidence of 1968. On one hand, some political experts believe that Humphrey would have won the election if he had had sufficient funds to properly plan and fully execute his television campaign. It is suggested by these observers that lack of adequate television exposure caused by lack of funds cost Humphrey the election.

On the other hand, it has been noted by some observers that in spite of the most massive television campaign in history, and the biggest television spending advantage over his opponent in history, Nixon's rating in the polls was virtually unchanged from May to November (ranging around 42 percent). This could mean that Nixon's nonsupporters or waiverers may have been largely unaffected by his expensive media campaign and that his media campaign served mainly to reinforce the favorable tendencies of his existing constituency.

It is impossible to resolve these two conflicting views on the importance of television on the basis of the 1968 Presidential election. One can conclude that other factors are probably at least as important, and that very little is really known about the way and the degree to which television influences voters.

Newspaper Advertising

In 1968, the Citizens' Research Foundation commissioned several analyses of political advertising in selected newspapers from Media Records, Inc., (MR), a firm that specializes in measuring advertising linage and expenditures. One survey included 361 daily and Sunday newspapers in 139 cities, covering 62 percent of total daily and 78 percent of total Sunday circulation in the United States. The survey did not constitute a scientific sample but rather a survey of the major newspapers in most of the major cities. Because most of the newspapers covered are large papers, their advertising rates are high, and therefore, the total monies the survey found to have been spent on political advertising are probably a larger percentage of total political advertising in newspapers than the 62 or 78 percent seemingly represented in the survey.

The period from July 1 through election day, November 5, was covered by the survey, because this time span is comparable to similar analyses done by MR in 1964 and 1956; unfortunately, no survey was conducted in 1960. For the July-November period in 1968, a total of $11.6 million worth of advertising was placed in the surveyed newspapers by candidates and committees at various levels. This was 50 percent more than the $7.7 million spent in 1964, and 170 percent more than the $4.3 million recorded in 1956.[68]

For 1968, in addition, the CRF commissioned two special analyses of newspaper advertising by candidates in the Presidential primaries in New Hampshire and Oregon, covering weeklies as well as dailies and Sunday newspapers. Newspaper advertising costs in New Hampshire totalled $103,998, whereas in Oregon they totalled $214,814. These two limited state studies, plus the national totals noted above, account for $11.9 million in newspaper advertising from MR sources. These data, however, can be combined with selected spending estimates obtained from individual candidates' campaigns, which will allow us to develop fuller estimates as we proceed.

Presidential Primaries

In addition to the data available from Media Records for the New Hampshire and Oregon primaries,[j] hard figures on newspaper advertising

---

[j] In New Hampshire, nine dailies and 28 weeklies, plus Boston Sunday newspapers were surveyed from January 1, 1968 through March 11, 1968. In Oregon, 21 dailies and 105 weeklies, including Sunday papers were surveyed from March 1 through May 27. Rates used for each daily newspaper are open line rates for General or National advertisers as shown in Standard Rate and Data Newspaper Rates and Data publication, January 1968. Rates used for each weekly newspaper are obtained from Editor and Publisher 1967 Year Book (published in April). Rates in the publication are quoted by inch. The rate per line is found by dividing by 14 lines (to the inch), which is a recognized formula.

Table 4-10

Expenditures for Newspaper Advertising New Hampshire, Oregon, and California Presidential Primaries, 1968[a]

	N.H.	Ore.	Calif. [b]
Democrats			
Johnson/Humphrey	$ 8,482	—	$ 60,000
McCarthy	31,738	65,222	288,510
Kennedy	—	29,274 [c]	290,000
Total	40,220	94,496	638,510
Republicans			
Romney	33,730 [d]	—	—
Nixon	41,403	84,550	—
Rockefeller	1,533	25,831	—
Reagan	1,530	14,083	— [e]
Total	78,196	124,464	—
TOTAL	$118,416	$218,960	$638,510

[a] Data from Media Records, Inc. unless otherwise indicated. Expenditures for minor candidates, not included in the table, totalled $9,334 in New Hampshire and $1,178 in Oregon.

[b] California data for Democrats from the candidates' campaigns; for Republicans, no data are available, but costs are assumed to be none for all candidates except Reagan since he was unchallenged in the primary.

[c] As reported by the Kennedy campaign.

[d] As reported by the Romney campaign.

[e] Not available.

were obtained for the three contending Democratic slates in the California primary. This information is presented in Table 4-10.

Including the $9,334 spent in New Hampshire by minor candidates, a total of $127,750 was spent for newspaper advertising in that state's Presidential primary, of which the Romney, Nixon, and McCarthy campaign together accounted for 85 percent of the total.[k] The total represented 80 cents for each vote cast, which is very high. As noted earlier, political costs in New Hampshire tend to be disproportionately high because of

[k] There are two corrections in the Media Records data, one each for New Hampshire and Oregon, which raise the possibility that there is a general underestimating of costs. In New Hampshire, MR showed $10,158 spent on newspaper advertising for Romney, whereas the campaign records showed $33,729. There is no reason to doubt the accuracy of the figure supplied by the Romney campaign, and it has been used instead of the MR figure. A similar comparison for the McCarthy campaign in New Hampshire showed a discrepancy of only $809 on a total of over $30,000, and this could be logically explained by the insertion of advertising by individuals not connected with the central campaign. In Romney's case, the difference is far too large to be explained this way. In Oregon, a similar discrepancy of about $7,000 was found in the figures on the Kennedy campaign (on a total of almost $30,000), and the campaign figure was used.

the psychological advantage to be gained by winning the first primary. In addition, both radio and newspapers tend to be used relatively more in New Hampshire because of the difficulties in reaching the population through television. The only television station in the state reaches a small percentage of the voters, and out-of-state stations either reach only a small portion of New Hampshire voters, as those in Maine and Vermont, or are expensive, as the Boston stations. (Boston Sunday newspapers have wide circulation in New England also.)

In Oregon, the cost-per-vote for newspaper advertising in the Presidential primary was 32 cents. The Republicans outspent the Democrats, as they had in New Hampshire, but with more voters on the Democratic side, the Republicans cost-per-vote was 40 cents compared with 25 cents for the Democrats. In California, where information is available only for the Democrats, the cost-per-vote of the newspaper advertising was 20½ cents in the Presidential primary.

For the other contested primaries—Wisconsin, Indiana, Nebraska, and South Dakota—and the rest of the prenomination period, only fragmentary information is available on expenditures for newspaper political advertising.

For the Nixon campaign, $93,000 was officially reported as an expense in the Wisconsin primary for "newspaper advertising and a little radio"; there is no other information on newspaper advertising for Nixon. For Rockefeller, the amounts in Table 4-10 for New Hampshire and Oregon newspaper advertising represent spending in primaries in which he was not an active candidate. But after he announced his candidacy, an estimated $1.5 million was spent nationally on newspaper advertising as part of Rockefeller's media effort. Part of this amount would be included in the total reported for all political advertising in July (see Table 4-12), but there is no way of calculating how much of the $1.5 million should be counted as pre-July spending. The costs of newspaper advertising for Reagan's campaigns elsewhere are not known, but one of his major costs in the Oregon total was for an eight-page color supplement in Sunday newspapers whose circulation exceeded 600,000.

For the Democrats, there is no information available other than that in Table 4-10 on newspaper advertising for the Johnson, Humphrey, or McCarthy campaigns. The Kennedy campaign, as noted earlier, made available details on all media spending in the primaries. In addition to the information in Table 4-10, Kennedy spent $28,000 in Indiana, $13,000 in Nebraska, and $5,000 in South Dakota on newspaper advertising.

Presidential General Election Campaign

Newspaper spending on behalf of Presidential and Vice-Presidential candidates in the general election period, from the August nominations until

Election Day, totaled $2.8 million in 1968, as shown in Table 4-11.[1] This was roughly one-eighth of the amount spent on the broadcasting media for a comparable period.

Table 4-11

Expenditures on Newspapers by Nixon, Humphrey, and Wallace, August–November, 1968

	August	September	October	November	Total
		(Thousands of Dollars)			
Nixon	$18.2	$347.2	$286.9	$581.2	$1,233.5
Humphrey	0.7	39.3	543.7	613.0	1,196.7
Wallace	34.0	97.9	154.7	91.9	378.5
Total	$52.9	$484.4	$985.3	$1,286.1	$2,808.7

The three Presidential candidates accounted for 24 percent of all political spending on newspaper advertising (in the newspapers covered in the MR survey) in the general election period, as shown in Table 4-12.

The Media Records study shows that the Humphrey campaign came relatively close to matching Nixon's newspaper advertising expenditures, in marked contrast to Nixon's two to one advantage in broadcast expenditures. One major difference in the Nixon and Humphrey newspaper strategies can be seen when the spending of the two campaigns is analyzed geographically. For Humphrey, 63 percent of his newspaper advertising was accounted for in the ten largest advertising markets, while only 43 percent of Nixon's spending was in the largest markets. George Wallace's share of total spending in these ten markets was an even smaller 35 percent of his total newspaper spending.

There were also marked differences in the Nixon and Humphrey patterns of spending over the course of the general election campaign. The effects of the Democrats' severe money crisis early in the campaign is reflected in the negligible amount spent on newspaper advertising in September; the Nixon campaign spent nine times as much for the month. However, while the Democratic broadcast expenditures did not catch up to the Republicans until the last week of the campaign, in newspaper advertising, the Democrats caught up to the Republicans in October. Although the Democrats outspent the Republicans almost two to one in October, the two candidates were more equally represented if measured in terms of linage. This was because the Democrats used wide tune-in advertising—shorter, more ex-

---

[1] Although the general election period is usually considered to be from September 1 to Election Day, most of the August spending for Nixon was in the postnomination spending period, and should properly be counted as general election costs. For Wallace, of course, since there was no formal nominating convention, any time designation for the general election is arbitrary.

pensive ads—to maximize the audience for Humphrey's fewer television appearances.

As has been the pattern for the last several Presidential campaigns, the bulk of the advertising spending by the national campaigns in 1968 was for broadcasting, with relatively less attention given to newspapers. (At the local level, the Presidential campaign committees are more likely to have money for newspaper advertising than for television.) A notable exception to this pattern was the formation by the Republican national campaign of the Field Advertising Service, whose primary responsibility was to coordinate the national committee's advertising campaign with the campaigns of Richard Nixon and Spiro Agnew. Approximately $1,000,000 was spent by FAS on preparation of newspaper mats, commercials, and posters for placement by local planners.

An unusual aspect of the 1968 campaign was the amount of precampaign selling which was done by the newspapers and the Bureau of Advertising of the ANPA as their national selling arm. Long before the national conventions, the Bureau made presentations to the chairmen of the Democratic and Republican parties. The Bureau also prepared a booklet describing effective ways to use newspaper advertising. Nearly 12,000 copies of the book were distributed to candidates by the Bureau and its member papers. During the national conventions, the Bureau presented each of the Presidential candidates with a newspaper-size brochure that made various sales points in favor of newspapers and contained suggested layouts that the candidates could use.

The national Nixon campaign purchased several full-page advertisements in 50 top markets. Reprints and mats of these ads were then furnished to the other 1,600 member newspapers of the ANPA which could in turn sell the ads to their local Republican or Nixon-Agnew committees. In the final days of the campaign, ads were placed in selected major cities.

The national Humphrey campaign reported expenditures of $429,000 on newspaper space placed by the national committee. Nearly all of this amount was used for tune-in ads in connection with network TV programs. Large-space ads (300–1,000 lines), appearing in 132 papers, were used to announce the Vice-President's paid appearances.

The Democrats paid out $50,000 to John L. Loeb, senior partner of Loeb, Rhodes, and Company, Wall Street investment bankers, for several newspaper advertisements. Loeb had made a $100,000 loan to the Humphrey campaign. In the last few days of the campaign, full-page ads signed by Loeb, seeking business support for Humphrey, were published in several leading newspapers, including *The New York Times, The Washington Post,* and *The Wall Street Journal.* Loeb paid for these with the returned $50,000.

The Humphrey campaign also listed a newspaper production figure of $62,000, which included the preparation of eight full-page ads which were distributed to local committees throughout the country to place in newspapers.

Total Newspaper Spending

For the July 1—Election Day period covered by the Media Records studies, the total expenditures figures were broken down into three categories: Republican, Democratic, and "Miscellaneous." These are shown in Table 4-12. These figures included any identifiable Republican or Democratic advertising for any candidate or ticket at any level, and they subsume the Nixon-Humphrey-Wallace figures noted above. The Miscellaneous category includes minor-party spending, but consists for the most part of political advertising for which a candidate but no party is mentioned. In

Table 4-12

Expenditures on Newspapers by Political Candidates at All Levels, 1956, 1964, 1968

	July	August	September	October	November	Total
		(Thousands of Dollars)				
1968						
Republican Party	$821.0	$148.9	$462.8	$ 884.8	$1,332.0	$3,649.5
Democratic Party	170.3	397.8	222.3	1,073.1	1,282.0	3,145.5
Miscellaneous ^a	247.8	220.6	498.6	1,592.8	2,260.9	4,820.7
						$11,615.7
1964						
Republican Party	$ 70.8	$ 50.8	$165.7	$ 837.6	$ 628.4	$1,753.3
Democratic Party	29.1	98.5	225.5	922.2	634.0	1,909.3
Miscellaneous ^a	134.9	174.1	265.8	2,107.6	1,398.0	4,080.4
						$ 7,743.0
1956						
Republican Party	$ 16.8	$ 27.2	$ 39.3	$ 348.5	$ 636.7	$1,068.5
Democratic Party	19.4	43.2	39.4	250.2	393.3	745.5
Miscellaneous ^a	276.9	197.7	283.4	693.6	1,017.5	2,469.1
						$ 4,283.1

^a Includes minor-party spending, but consists for the most part of advertising for candidates which was not allocable by party, that is, for which no party was mentioned.

the three years—1956, 1964, 1968—for which data are available, the Miscellaneous total has invariably been greater than that for either the Republican or Democratic parties, and in 1964 it was larger than both combined. Since the bulk of the Miscellaneous total must consist of unidentified Republican or Democratic expenditures, it is difficult to give much weight to trends in the relatively small allocated Republican and Democratic totals. But the fact that such a high proportion of political advertising in newspapers appears without a party label is in itself an interesting commentary on the extent of nonparty identification in the

United States. In 1964, for instance, there may well have been much Republican dissociation from Goldwater, leading many candidates to advertise without a party label at all; in 1968, this same phenomenon occurred to some extent in dissociation from Humphrey.

In 1968, MR shows Republican spending on newspapers of $3.6 million, twice the 1964 total of $1.8 million and more than three times the $1.1 spent in 1956 (Table 4-12). Reported Democratic spending rose by 65 percent, from $1.9 million in 1964 to $3.1 million in 1968, from a low level of $745,453 in 1956. The Miscellaneous category shows a much smaller increase, from $4.1 million in 1964 to $4.8 million in 1968, or 18 percent (corroborating the assumption that there was less party identification in 1964 than in 1968); the level in 1956 was $2.5 million. In 1968, the Republicans outspent the Democrats by 16 percent. (The Republican lead in linage was somewhat greater, seemingly a result of their greater use of less expensive, smaller-city newspapers.)

In order to calculate the total spent on political newspaper advertising for the entire year, by all candidates at all levels, it is necessary to estimate amounts spent in the prenomination period. To isolate general election spending, the total spent in July (Table 4-12) and the total spent by the Democrats in August before the Chicago convention would not apply and must be subtracted from the $11.6 million, which gives a total of $10 million. If one assumes that the relation of pre- to postnomination spending is the same for newspaper advertising as for broadcasting advertising, where primary spending accounted for one-third of all spending, then the total for newspaper advertising in the primary period would be $5 million. The known prenomination spending totals $2.5 million, covering the bulk of Presidential campaign advertising, but nothing for other campaigns at other levels. However, since spending by other than Presidential candidates in the general election period was three quarters of all spending, a figure of $5 million for the prenomination period would mean that non-Presidential contenders accounted for one-half of all newspaper advertising costs, which is certainly a conservative estimate. Therefore, the total spent for newspaper advertising by all candidates at all levels for 1968 would probably be at least $15 million for the newspapers in the MR survey. Because that covers only 62 percent daily and 78 percent Sunday circulation, we would need to add a minimum of another 25 percent, or $3.75 million, bringing the total to at least $18.75 million. To that total must be added political advertising in weeklies, which would bring the total conservatively to $20 million for all candidates and committees at all levels.

Newspaper Advertising Rates

Media Records reports that the average open line rate of the newspapers in its sample rose by 36 percent between 1956 and 1968, or about 3 percent per year. This compares with rate increases in the broadcasting industry over the same period of 5 percent per year for network television and 8–9 percent for spot television.

Newspapers frequently specify rates—usually higher—for political advertisers. For instance, the *New York Post*'s political rate, according to Standard Rate and Data, is 30¢ a line more than the open rate. The broadcasting media, in contrast, are prohibited by federal law from charging more to a political advertiser than they would to a commercial customer for equivalent use of their facilities, and a few states specifically prohibit newspapers from charging excessive rates for political advertising.

Private Public Opinion Polls

Because there are so many varieties of public opinion polls and surveys, and so many candidates, committees, and individuals purchasing them, it is very difficult to calculate the total spent for private political polling. What is spent for candidates should not be confused with the fewer but well-publicized national private polls—Gallup, Harris, and other newspaper polls—which are conducted for public consumption.

It seems likely that the total for all candidates at all levels came to about $6 million in 1968, which is $1 million more than was estimated for 1964. While there seemed to be more sophisticated and expensive polling services in 1968, there was also wider use of more inexpensive telephone polling. The estimate would break down to 1,200 polls at an average cost of $5,000, which does not seem excessive either as to the number of polls or the cost, which varies from a few thousand dollars up to as much as $10,000 for a comprehensive statewide poll.

Presidential General Election

The three Presidential contenders spent at least $683,000 on polling in their general election campaigns: Nixon spent $384,000; Humphrey, $262,000; and Wallace, only $37,000. Nixon had two major polling operations being conducted simultaneously: the first cost about $250,000 and was carried out by the Opinion Research Corp. (ORC) of Princeton; and the second was a counter-checking effort carried out separately under one consultant, Joseph Bachelder, also in Princeton.

The ORC operation was the longest, most costly, and most complex polling project in campaign history.[69] There were two parts to the operation, both conducted in what the campaign believed were the key states: New York, New Jersey, Pennsylvania, Ohio, Michigan, Missouri, Illinois, Wisconsin, California, Texas, and a southern unit which included a combined sample of voters in Virginia, North Carolina, South Carolina, and Florida. One part of the program ran from July to election eve, based on wave polling of a panel of about 500 persons in each state, selected after preliminary interviewing and screening of about 2,000 people in each state. The purpose of the wave technique (repeated interviews with the same respondents rather than new samples for each survey) is to measure changes in people's view over the course of the campaign.

The second part of the ORC operation consisted of virtually continuous telephone polling in those same states, from six special WATS-lines (Wide Area Telephone Service, bought on a monthly rather than a per-call basis) which were in use ten hours a day, seven days a week, from mid-September to election eve. A total of more than 12,000 people were interviewed at the rate of about 250 per day. This part of the operation was reportedly billed to the campaign at a rate of $10,000 per month. This operation provided the campaign with instant data. For example, within three hours of Humphrey's September 30 Salt Lake City speech on Vietnam, Nixon had a reaction from a sample of almost 1,500 people. Detailed analyses of the impact of the speech were available within 72 hours, record time for most polling operations, and when President Johnson announced the Vietnam bombing halt, Nixon had detailed polling data within 48 hours.

The importance of the polling data in devising campaign strategy is, of course, the key question, and the answers are, at best, sketchy. According to the most informed sources, Nixon's choice of a running mate was influenced by ORC's first polls, which showed Nixon running better alone than with any possible running mate; if no one could help the ticket, his choice need not consider that factor. In addition, Nixon's strategy on the Wallace campaign—raising questions on the impossibility of Wallace's winning rather than attacking the man or trying to co-opt his strongest issues—was said to be based at least partly on polling information, as was his skillful handling of the Vietnam issue. Nixon's polls also identified Humphrey's late surge, but whether they were able to help Nixon in countering it is not known.

According to *The Analyst,* the Humphrey campaign developed a polling plan much like that of the Republicans, but never completely carried it out. Humphrey's polling did not begin until well after the Democratic convention, and was abruptly stopped in mid-October due to lack of funds. A planned national telephone panel never was launched. Instead of mainly using one large commercial firm as the Republicans did, the Democrats contracted with six, smaller firms. Very little information about Democratic polling is available, so it is not known what the Humphrey campaign got for its $282,000 expenditure, or how much it influenced the campaign strategy.

In addition to the polling carried out by the major party Presidential campaigns, the local segments of those campaigns or even individuals may commission their own polls. Little of this is publicly reported, but there are two examples of these kinds of polls in 1968. Early in August, a group of ten New York Democrats, headed by R. Peter Straus, a friend of Humphrey, hired the John Kraft organization to do a state poll, comparing Humphrey and McCarthy as the candidates against Nixon and Wallace. The study cost $10,000.[70] In mid-June and mid-September, the Nassau County Republican Committee hired the Oliver Quayle Company for a poll which included questions on Presidential and Senatorial preference along with those for local offices. The cost of the first poll is not known, but the September one cost $2,500.[71] Undoubtedly, there were many such locally sponsored polls during 1968.

Presidential Preconvention

In the Presidential prenomination period, there is no information available on amounts spent for polling by any of the Democratic contenders. Humphrey and McCarthy are believed to have done relatively little polling, while Kennedy used polls more extensively. President Johnson's decision to retire is reported to have been influenced by a Gallup poll which said only 26 percent of the people approved his handling of the Vietnam war, and by a private Wisconsin poll. Kennedy's decision to become a candidate was reportedly cinched by a private California poll which said he would beat the President in that state.[72]

In the Republican prenomination campaigns, the biggest user of polls was Rockefeller, who is estimated to have spent $250,000 for polling. Rockefeller's initial decision not to run, when Romney withdrew, was based on three Oregon polls which showed his rating there decreasing. After he did enter the race, the major thrust of his effort was a heavy media campaign which, it was hoped, would influence the public and then be reflected in public opinion polls, which in turn would influence the delegates. There were two nationwide and nine state polls, in addition to riders commissioned onto regularly scheduled polls.[73]

While no detailed financial data are available for Nixon's prenomination campaign, it is known that ORC did a total of about $450,000 worth of polling for Nixon in 1968, of which $250,000 is known to have been spent in the general election; therefore, Nixon must have spent about $200,000 on polls before the Miami convention. The campaign had probably planned to spend more, since Nixon is known to have cancelled several polls, including some in Wisconsin and Oregon, when Romney withdrew.

During his brief campaign, Romney spent considerably less than $100,000 on polling. His decision to withdraw from the Presidential race was based almost solely on the polls in New Hampshire, both public and private, which showed him being overwhelmingly defeated by Nixon.

There is no information on polling done by Reagan's supporters, but it is unlikely that significant amounts of money were spent for polls.

In total, then, the Republican contenders for the Presidential nomination spent about $550,000, while their Democratic counterparts probably spent no more than $400,000. Therefore, the total spent on polls in the 1968 Presidential contests, pre- and postnomination, would be about $1.6 million, with almost 60 percent of the total being spent in the prenomination period.

Nonpresidential

On the Congressional level, the Republicans undertook a very large, coordinated polling effort for eight Senatorial and 50 key Congressional races, at the cost of about $400,000.[74] Early in 1968, the Republican Senatorial Campaign Committee and the Republican Congressional Campaign Committee hired an experienced electronic data processing firm, Datamatics, a subsidiary of the Spencer-Roberts campaign management firm in California. In turn, Datamatics developed very detailed specifications for the polls and invited bids from selected polling firms. The polls were to be in three waves, and there were also to be two in-depth interviews with at least 400 people in each state or Congressional District. The Market Opinion Research Company (MOR) of Detroit, a long-time polling organization which had done extensive work for Romney, received about one-half of the Datamatics-coordinated Republican project.

The Congressional Democrats did not have a coordinated polling program, and the amounts spent for polls by Democratic Senatorial and Congressional candidates in 1968 is not known. The Quayle organization said it did work for 75 contests in 30 states, while the Kraft organization reported working in at least 30 contests. The cost of this work could have cost close to $500,000, averaging perhaps $5,000 per race covered.

Only one other figure is known for polling in 1968. The cost of all of ORC's political work for the year was $600,000 (more than twice the amount of ORC's political billings in 1964), of which $450,000 was for Nixon and $50,000 was for Rockefeller. Therefore, there is an additional $100,000 not covered by the Presidential contests, and it is believed some of this work was done for the RNC during the year. As far as is known, the DNC did not undertake any polling projects apart from Humphrey's Presidential campaign.

There are few polling organizations with political billings strictly for polls larger than ORC's. Some polling is done by organizations which are not exclusively pollsters, so some billings include consulting and campaign services not properly counted as polling.

National-Level Committees

National-level committees are those which operate in two or more states to affect the outcome of any Federal election. In 1968, there were 222 such committees, which reported spending $59.4 million,[75] accounting for about one-fifth of the total estimated political expenditures of $300 million for the year. Some of these committees give funds to local or state committees or candidates and some spend all of their money themselves. There are no rules and few consistent patterns for the activities of these committees, except that they must file financial reports with the Clerk of the House of Representatives.

This section includes a brief description of the expenditures of the various categories of committees, tables listing them, and an analysis of their allocations to Presidential and Congressional candidates.

Party, Nonparty, and Wallace Committees

Tables 4-13 and 4-14 detail the receipts and expenditures of all national-level party and nonparty committees in 1968. The party committees are the Republican and Democratic National Committees, all the general elec-

Table 4-13

Receipts and Expenditures—Republican National Campaign Committees, January 1–December 31, 1968 (in thousands of dollars)

Committee	Gross Reported Receipts	Adjusted Receipts[a]	Gross Reported Disbursements	Total Transfers Out	Direct Expenditures[b]
National (RNC)	2,542	2,540	2,938	86	2,852
National Senatorial (NRSC)	833	799	860	460	400
National Congressional (NRCC)	2,879	2,828	2,905	736	2,169
Congressional Boosters (RCBC)	800	799	1,298	1,256	42
5 Miscellaneous National Committees[c]	4,588	4,550	4,624	110	4,514
Subtotal	$11,642	$11,515	$12,625	$2,648	$9,977
Nixon-Agnew Campaign Committee	2,401	2,401	2,385	50	2,335
Nixon-Agnew Finance Committee	2,983	2,980	2,979	142	2,837
Nixon-Agnew TV Committee	2,158	2,158	1,743	75	1,668
Victory '68	2,426	2,421	2,219	0	2,219
18 Miscellaneous Nixon-Agnew Committees[d]	7,356	7,344	6,930	555	6,375
Subtotal	$17,324	$17,304	$16,256	$ 822	$15,434
6 Miscellaneous Nonparty Committees[e]	$ 54	$ 48	$ 36	$ 25	$ 11
Total[f]	$29,020	$28,867	$28,917 [g]	$3,495	$25,422

ᵃ Adjusted for lateral transfers from national-level Republican, labor and miscellaneous committees included in this table and tables 4-16 and 4-17.

ᵇ Determined by subtracting Total Transfers Out from Gross Reported Disbursements.

ᶜ National Federation of Republican Women	$ 68,147
National Republican Finance Advisory Committee	375,219
National Republican Finance Committee	694,918
National Republican Finance Operations Committee	1,051,079
Republican Campaign Committee	2,434,762

All figures are gross reported disbursements.

ᵈ Agnew for Vice-President	$ 97,721
Americans for Good Government	163,934
D.C. Nixon-Agnew Dinner	93,463
Democrats for Nixon-Agnew	64,750
Grassroots for Nixon-Agnew	141,960
Independents for Nixon-Agnew	128,915
Nixon-Agnew Committee	1,298,071
Nixon-Agnew Communications	101,994
Nixon-Agnew Election	519,011
Nixon-Agnew Victory	1,587,612
Republican Victory	1,319,537
R.N. Associates	238,050
Thurmond Speaks	130,774
Thurmond Speaks for Nixon-Agnew	8,743
TV for Nixon-Agnew	362,327
United Citizens for Nixon-Agnew	625,574
Vote Getters for Nixon	13,070
Women's Finance Committee for Nixon-Agnew	34,422

All figures are gross reported disbursements.

ᵉ Committee of Nine	$18,969
Committee for a Republican Congress	–0–
Committee for Forward-Looking Republicans	73
Committee for Republican Research	7,656
Republican Candidates Committee	–0–
Republicans for Progress	8,847

All figures are gross reported disbursements.

ᶠ Minor discrepancies between totals and component items are due to rounding.

ᵍ To arrive at a meaningful net disbursement figure, $66,000 laterally transferred between Republican committees must be deducted, for a net of $28.851 million.

tion Presidential campaign groups (except those organized in only one state), and the House and Senate campaign committees of the major parties. "Nonparty" committees are those which are not officially connected with either major party, but which make contributions to candidates of only one of the two parties.

While both parties raised and spent more in 1968 than they had in 1964, the Republican gains were generally larger than the Democratic. In net receipts, Republican committees took in 61 percent more than they had in 1964, Democratic net receipts (including loans) were up 47 percent, and Democratic gross disbursements increased by 75 percent (compared to 68 percent for Republican committees), but these figures are misleading because the Democrats transferred so much money back and

Table 4-14

Receipts and Expenditures—Democratic National Campaign Committees, January 1–December 31, 1968 (in thousands of dollars)

Committee	Gross Reported Receipts	Adjusted Receipts[a]	Gross Reported Disbursements	Total Transfers Out	Direct Expenditures[b]
National (DNC)	2,040	1,219	2,613	394	2,219
Senatorial Campaign (DSCC)	430	382	596	500	96
Congressional Campaign (DCCC)	375	333	465	421	44
National Congressional (DNCC)	38	20	135	0	135
Democrats for Sound Government	199	155	170	119	51
Subtotal	$3,082	$2,109	$3,979	$1,434	$2,545
Humphrey for President Committee	1,620	1,217	1,574	515	1,059
Humphrey-Muskie Media Committee	2,204	37	2,204	272	1,932
Humphrey-Muskie National Finance Committee	671	409	212	93	119
Humphrey-Muskie Weekly TV Committee	3,125	1,345	1,446	267	1,179
76 Miscellaneous H-M Committees[c]	6,760	6,060	6,503	4,798	1,705
"Constructive Receipts/Expenditures"[d]	2,800	2,800	2,800	—	2,800
Subtotal	$17,180	$11,868	$14,739	$5,945	$ 8,794
3 Johnson-Humphrey Committees[e]	$ 129	$ 124	$ 140	$ 25	$ 115
5 Miscellaneous Nonparty Committees[f]	$ 332	$ 304	$ 325	$ 186	$ 139
Total[g]	$20,723	$14,406	$19,184[h]	$7,590	$11,593

[a] Adjusted for lateral transfers from national-level Democratic, labor and miscellaneous committees included in this table and tables 4-16 and 4-17.

[b] Determined by subcontracting Total Transfers Out from Gross Reported Disbursements.

[c] All of the following committees were adjuncts of the national organization unless otherwise indicated by asterisk (*). The dollar figures indicate gross reported disbursements.

Advertising Executives for Humphrey-Muskie	$ 15,070
Architects for Humphrey-Muskie	13,000
* Arts & Letters for Humphrey-Muskie	16,989
Builders for Humphrey-Muskie	189,616
Businessmen for Humphrey-Muskie	204,044
* Businessmen for Humphrey-Muskie	82,032
Businesswomen for Humphrey-Muskie	148,507
Chemists for Humphrey-Muskie	13,011
* Citizens for Humphrey	45,661
Citizens for Humphrey-Muskie	101,203

* Citizens for Humphrey-Muskie	289,208
* Citizens for Humphrey-Muskie	25,000
Conservationists for Humphrey-Muskie	15,012
Co-op Leaders for Humphrey-Muskie	10,032
County Officials for Humphrey-Muskie	157,573
D.C. Citizens for Humphrey-Muskie	12,415
D.C. Friends of Humphrey	17,415
D.C. Humphrey for President Club	30,415
* D.C. Salute to Humphrey	12,415
Dentists for Humphrey-Muskie	16,005
Doctors for Humphrey-Muskie	13,078
Economists for Humphrey-Muskie	18,042
Educators for Humphrey-Muskie	179,580
Entertainers for Humphrey-Muskie	179,614
Friends for Humphrey-Muskie	216,631
* Gala Committee for Humphrey	9,733
Get Out the Vote for Humphrey	137,000
Humphrey for President Club	401,000
Humphrey-Muskie Campaign Materials	89,683
* Humphrey-Muskie Victory	41,976
Independents for Humphrey-Muskie	218,161
Industrialists for Humphrey-Muskie	184,505
Insurance Executives for Humphrey-Muskie	15,137
Jewelers for Humphrey-Muskie	10,044
Lawyers for Humphrey-Muskie	179,628
Librarians for Humphrey-Muskie	15,026
* Maine Democrats for Muskie	6,211
Mayors for Humphrey-Muskie	142,550
* McCarthy Supporters for Humphrey Now	1,038
Minnesota Citizens for Humphrey-Muskie	64,926
Minnesota Friends for Humphrey-Muskie	62,704
Minnesota Humphrey for President Club	70,948
Minnesota Salute to Humphrey	51,426
Minorities for Humphrey-Muskie	42,354
Musicians for Humphrey-Muskie	13,100
* Muskie for Vice-President	34,195
National First Americans for Humphrey-Muskie	13,062
National Coordinating Committee for Humphrey	32,231
* National Coordinating Committee for Humphrey-Muskie	35,905
* National Coordinating Committee for Nomination of Hubert Humphrey	36,337
New Englanders for Humphrey-Muskie	10,433
* N.Y. Citizens for Humphrey-Muskie	476,226
* N.Y. Humphrey for President Club	295,769
Pharmacists for Humphrey-Muskie	174,081
Pilots for Humphrey-Muskie	13,035
Professional Men for Humphrey-Muskie	194,567
Public Administrators for Humphrey-Muskie	10,051
Real Estate Dealers for Humphrey-Muskie	19,160
Retailers for Humphrey-Muskie	165,832
Rural Electric Americans for Humphrey-Muskie	148,510
Rural Workers for Humphrey-Muskie	15,076
Scientists & Engineers for Humphrey-Muskie	179,500
Senior Citizens for Humphrey-Muskie	160,510
Small Businessmen for Humphrey-Muskie	174,539
Social Workers for Humphrey-Muskie	15,097

	10,038
Sport Stars for Humphrey-Muskie	10,038
* United Chiropractors for Humphrey-Muskie	2,753
Veterans for Humphrey-Muskie	174,517
* Veterans for Humphrey-Muskie	8,887
Victory Committee for Humphrey-Muskie	32,571
Volunteers for Humphrey-Muskie	52,670
Wholesalers for Humphrey-Muskie	15,050
Women for Humphrey-Muskie	170,543
* Women's Voice for Humphrey-Muskie	7,951
Young Americans for Humphrey-Muskie	23,060
Young Executives for Humphrey-Muskie	21,967

[d] See explanation, Chapter 5, The Democrats.

[e] Citizens for Johnson-Humphrey	$87,740
Independent Citizens for Johnson-Humphrey	–0–
Presidents Club for Johnson Committee	51,971

All figures are gross reported disbursements.

[f] Broadway for Peace, 1968	$70,693
Congressional Peace Campaign Committee	28,900
McCarthy Donors Fund	66,800
1968 Campaign Fund	97,884
Non-Partisan Committee to Elect the Best Men	60,463

All figures are gross reported disbursements.

[g] Minor discrepancies between totals and component items are due to rounding.

[h] To arrive at a meaningful net disbursement figure, $6.014 million laterally transferred between Democratic committees must be deducted, for a net of $13.170 million.

forth between committees. Comparing direct expenditures, which includes both lateral transfers of funds between committees and transfers out, the Democrats spent 49 percent more in 1968 than in 1964 while the Republicans' direct expenditures were up 59 percent.

As noted earlier, the Wallace campaign filed a financial report claiming it was not a political committee. In addition to the main campaign report, two other Wallace-related groups filed reports; although technically not national-level committees, they were regional committees directly connected to and part of the Wallace effort, and are therefore included in Table 4-15.

Table 4-15

Receipts and Expenditures—Wallace Campaign Committees, February 3–December 31, 1968 (in thousands of dollars)

Committee	Gross Reported Receipts	Adjusted Receipts[a]	Gross Reported Disbursements	Total Transfers Out	Direct Expenditures
National Campaign	$6,714[b]	$6,714	$6,985	$20	$6,965
California Campaign	214	194	215	—	215
Youth for Wallace	47	47	43	—	43
Total	$6,975[b]	$6,955	$7,243	$20	$7,223

[a] Adjusted for lateral transfers.

[b] Not a total, however, as the final report omitted data on contributions under $100.

Table 4-16

Receipts and Expenditures—Labor National Committees, January 1–December 31, 1968

Committee	Gross Receipts	Adjusted Receipts[a]	Gross Disbursements	Total Transfers Out	Direct Expenditures[b]
Active Ballot Club—Retail Clerks International Ass'n	$ 49,991	$ 49,991	$163,877	$ 80,044	$ 83,833
Amalgamated Meat Cutters and Butcher Workmen[c]	88,351	88,351	127,563	122,766	4,797
Amalgamated Political Education Committee	62,580	62,580	84,268	78,040	6,228
American Federation of Musicians Political Fund	24,876	24,876	38,348	30,434	7,914
Boilermakers—Blacksmiths' Legislative Education—Action Program	94,208	94,208	84,262	41,887	42,375
Brotherhood of Painters, Decorators & Paperhangers of America	66,221	56,221	63,321	55,187	8,134
Building & Construction Trades Department, AFL-CIO	47,999	27,999	63,970	63,570	400
Carpenters Legislative Improvement Committee	65,231	65,231	105,674	102,445	3,229
Committee for Good Government[d]	79,266	79,266	250,680	218,480	32,200
Committee on Political Education, AFL-CIO (COPE)	873,336	873,336	1,206,736	1,026,150	180,586
Communication Workers of America	145,933	145,933	194,792	194,792	0
Democratic, Republican, Independent Voter Education Committee, International Brotherhood of Teamsters (DRIVE)	138,383	138,383	210,565	174,437	36,128
International Brotherhood of Electrical Workers—Education Fund & Contribution Fund	93,353	8,250	116,158	106,123	10,035
International Ladies Garment Workers Union—1968 Committee & Wind-up 1966 Committee[e]	1,177,232	1,177,232	1,077,469	399,124	678,345
Laborers Political League	96,265	81,265	92,517	84,290	8,227
Machinists Non-Partisan Political League—Educational Fund & General Fund	479,235	464,235	572,360	340,035	232,325
Marine Engineers Beneficial Association—Combined Funds	264,568	222,237	261,786	238,227	23,559
National Maritime Union Fighting Fund	255,203	255,203	84,255[f]	84,255	0
Oil, Chemical & Atomic Workers International Union	43,538	43,538	50,933	50,933	0
Railway Clerks' Political League	133,053	133,053	128,327	125,050	3,277
Railway Labor's Political League—BLF & E Division	26,832	26,832	47,070	38,000	9,070

Table 4-16 *(Continued)*

Committee	Gross Receipts	Adjusted Receipts[a]	Gross Disbursements	Total Transfers Out	Direct Expenditures[b]
Seafarers International Union—COPE & SPAD	618,896	618,896	946,766	582,297	364,469
Sheet Metal Workers International Association	22,691	22,691	37,445	33,000	4,445
Textile Workers Union of America	23,292	20,292	34,911	34,275	636
Trainmen's Political Education League	140,440	140,440	214,669	214,669	0
United Auto Workers—COPE[d]	250,179	250,179	308,509	216,245	92,264
United Steel Workers of America	150,834	148,334	239,882	228,999	10,883
Subtotal	$5,423,635	$5,230,701	$6,679,550	$4,840,988	$1,838,562
10 Miscellaneous[g]	$ 110,200	$ 56,201	$ 245,210	$ 217,018	$ 28,192
Total[h]	$5,622,186	$5,375,253	$7,052,323	$5,180,772	$1,871,551

[a] Adjusted for lateral transfers from national-level committee groupings included in the tables (herein largely COPE).

[b] Determined by subtracting Transfers Out from Gross Disbursements.

[c] Late in the third quarter of 1969, the Amalgamated Meat Cutters and Butcher Workmen filed a single report for the six reporting periods of 1968.

[d] The Committee for Good Government and UAW-COPE are both political action committees affiliated with the UAW. The CGG receives its contributions from staff members and UAW-COPE from the union membership.

[e] 1967 receipts could not be broken out of the 1968 report. Expenditures are for 1968 only.

[f] Transfers only; this is not a total. No total available.

[g]

Brotherhood of Maintenance of Way Political League	$ 7,500	Rural Political Education Committee	$ 17,464
Engineers Political Education Committee	271	United Association Political Education Committee	12,849
International Brotherhood of Firemen and Oilers	8,787	United Auto Worker Districts	163,657
International Chemical Workers Union	10,699	United Plant Guard Workers	5,188
The International Typographical Union	6,745	United Rubber, Cork, Linoleum and Plastic Workers of America	12,050

All dollar figures indicated are gross disbursements.

[h] Minor discrepancies between totals and component items are due to rounding.

Table 4-17

Receipts and Expenditures—Miscellaneous National Committees, January 1–December 31, 1968

Committee	Gross Receipts	Adjusted Receipts[a]	Gross Disbursements	Total Transfers Out	Direct Expenditures[b]
Action Committee for Rural Electrification	$ 88,393	$ 88,393	$ 87,220	$ 73,295	$ 13,925
American Conservative Union	213,269	213,269	228,733	0	228,733
American Medical Political Action Committee (AMPAC)	450,969	450,969	681,965	620,742	61,223
American Nursing Home Education & Political Action Committee	58,801	58,801	89,717	32,600	57,117
Americans for Constitutional Action	200,364	200,364	239,061	1,000	238,061
Business—Industry Political Action Committee (BIPAC)	360,304	360,304	568,332	519,700	48,632
Christian Nationalist Crusade	343,170	343,170	298,568	0	298,568
Committee for Action	118,491	118,491	103,894	71,350	32,544
Committee for Economic Growth	41,160	41,160	49,650	41,200	8,450
Communist Party National Campaign Committee	16,484	16,484	16,227	0	16,227
Council for a Livable World	131,645	131,645	154,022	36,785	117,237
Effective Government Association	46,400	46,400	46,375	46,060	315
Exchange Firms Campaign Committee	186,753	181,753	146,888	146,300	588
Life Underwriters—Education Fund & Political Action Committee	75,739	75,739	70,431	35,500	34,931
National Committee for an Effective Congress	526,792	523,292	491,520	289,535	201,985
National States Rights Party	26,088	26,088	24,727	0	24,727
Savings Association Political Education Committee	41,793	40,293	39,394	36,200	3,194
Socialist Labor Party of America	99,347	99,347	80,130	0	80,130
Socialist Workers 1968 Campaign	38,117	38,117	40,418	0	40,418
Truck Operators Non-Partisan Committee	56,642	56,642	73,456	72,775	681
United Congressional Appeal	123,321	123,321	113,771	93,000	20,771
United Republicans of America[c]	475,453	475,453	496,361	47,103	449,258
Subtotal	$3,719,495	$3,709,495	$4,140,860	$2,163,145	$1,977,715
30 Miscellaneous[d]	$ 177,862	$ 177,862	$ 191,077	$ 159,482	$ 31,595
Total[e]	$3,897,357	$3,887,357	$4,331,937	$2,322,627	$2,009,310

Table 4-17 (Continued)

Committee	Amount	Committee	Amount
American Dental Political Action Committee	$ 760	Freezers Political Action Committee	$ 961
Bankers Congressional Committee	9,846	Fund for Good Government	9,250
Bus Industry Public Affairs Committee	3,621	Government Improvement Group	17,368
Canners Public Affairs Committee	5,400	Home Furnishings Political Committee	1,723
Citizens Committee for Improved Government	8,200	Linen Supply Political Action Committee	1,599
Committee for a Conservative Congress	1,893	Lone Star Executives Political Fund	10,909
Committee for American Principles	7,462	Motel Development Committee	2,528
Committee of Automotive Retailers	10,176	Nineteen Seventy-six Committee	310
Committee of the Hundred	0	North Street Good Government Group	8,750
Committee on American Leadership	20,944	Pro America	3,645
Communications Political Action Committee	4,834	Public Affairs Committee for Farmer Co-Operation	6,844
Construction Equipment Political Action Committee	3,913	Savings Bankers Non-Partisan Committee	1,074
Employment Education Committee	3,913	Scrap Political Action Committee	1,405
Food Processors Public Affairs Committee	4,468	Shoe Manufacturer's Good Government Committee	15,250
Forest Products Political Education Committee	24,035	Taxpayers Committee to End Foreign Aid	(No Info)

[a] Adjusted for lateral transfers from national-level committee groupings included in the tables. Transfers very limited in this category.

[b] Determined by subtracting Transfers Out from Gross Disbursements.

[c] Not a Republican committee, despite name.

[d] Largely committees identified with an industry, business, or profession. All dollar figures indicated are gross disbursements.

[e] Minor discrepancies between totals and component items are due to rounding.

Labor and Miscellaneous Committees

Tables 4-16 and 4-17 detail the receipts and expenditures of labor and all other national-level committees in 1968.

Labor.   The extent of labor's role in the 1968 elections was greater than ever before, and the nature of that role was different in several ways.[76] In gross disbursements, labor committees expended 92 percent more than they had in 1964, and they spent more of it themselves: direct expenditures increased 171 percent. In 1964, labor committees had directly spent only 19 percent of their total expenditures, while in 1968, their direct expenditures were 27 percent of the total. Another unusual aspect of labor's role in 1968 was the degree to which they allocated funds to the Presidential contest, which is detailed below.

Miscellaneous.   The expenditures of all the other national-level committees, which includes business and professional, minor party, and the others, increased 115 percent between 1964 and 1968, from $2 to $4.3 million. There was a doubling in the number of such committees—from 26 in 1964 to 52 in 1968—and an increase in the expenditures of virtually every committee which was active in both years. The miscellaneous category is broken down further into subgroups—business and professional, minor party, and others—in the following.

Business and Professional.[77]   Business and professional committees accounted for just under one-half of the total of the miscellaneous committees, a little more than $2 million. The allocations of these committees to Presidential and Congressional candidates is covered below.

Minor Party.   The five minor parties excluding the Wallace data—the Christian Nationalist Crusade, the National States Rights Party, the two Socialist parties, and the Communist Party—spent $460,000 in 1968, an increase of only 18 percent from 1964. The minor-party committees did not allocate funds to other committees or candidates; all of their disbursements were made directly.

Other.   This category includes all national-level committees which are not covered in any other category. Such committees range from the conservative United Republicans of America[78] to the liberal National Committee for an Effective Congress. The committees spent a total of $1.8 million in 1968, but the six largest—the American Conservative Union, Americans for Constitutional Action, the Council for a Livable World, the National Committee for an Effective Congress, the United Congressional Appeal, and the United Republicans of America—spent more than 90 percent of the total, $1.7 million.

Allocations to Presidential Candidates. Except for the party national committees and the various Presidential campaign committees, national-level committees usually allocate none or very little of their funds to Presidential candidates. This pattern can be seen in the allocations of all the miscellaneous committees in 1968: of their total disbursements to candidates or committees, $2.3 million, they gave about one percent, a mere $24,310, to Presidential candidates. But labor committees in 1968 broke with precedent and gave considerable sums to Humphrey committees, and broke other precedents by giving a substantial portion of those contributions in the prenomination period.

National-level labor committees contributed $540,900 to Humphrey committees,[m] or slightly more than 10 percent of their total disbursements to candidates or committees ($5.2 million). Almost one-third of the labor contributions were made during the prenomination period. While more than 80 percent of all labor committees contributed to Humphrey's campaign, there were a few union committees which accounted for most of the money.

The political action committees of three of the unions shown in Table 4-18 contributed more than $80,000 each to Humphrey, and accounted for 69 percent of the total he received from all such committees. These same union committees each contributed $49,000 or more in the postconvention period, accounting for 72 percent of the general election total of $373,369. In the prenomination period, there were three committees which gave Humphrey $20,000 or more each, accounting for 71 percent of the $167,531 total Humphrey received from all labor committees before the convention.

Table 4-18

Largest Labor Committee Contributions to Humphrey Committees, Pre- and Postconvention, 1968

Union Committee	Prenomination	Postconvention	Total
Seafarers (COPE & SPAD)	$65,000	$110,425	$175,925
Committee for Good Government [a] United Auto Workers—COPE	8,000	109,020	117,020
ILGWU	32,400	48,938	81,338
Railway Clerks	20,260	1,600	21,860

[a] Both UAW committees; see note d to Table 4-16.

The Seafarers' committees alone accounted for almost one-third of all the national-level labor money contributed to Humphrey, and those contributions also represented close to one-third of the Seafarers' total disbursements to candidate or campaign committees. The combined UAW

---

[m] There were also some early contributions to President Johnson's reelection campaign.

128

contributions to Humphrey were 27 percent of their total disbursements to candidates. The Humphrey contributions of the ILGWU and the Railway Clerks also represented a significant portion of their candidate allocations: 20 and 17 percent, respectively.

The degree of involvement of labor in the Presidential contest was one of the unusual features of the 1968 elections. It will be interesting to see whether labor continues to pay a prominent role in Democratic Presidential election campaigns, or whether 1968—because of labor's strong likes and dislikes (Humphrey, McCarthy, Kennedy)—will stand as a unique year.

Allocations to Senatorial and Congressional Candidates

The total amount received by identified Senatorial and Congressional candidates from national-level committees in 1968 was $6,603,376.[79] There were 362 Republican candidates who received $3,032,541; 417 Democratic candidates received $3,570,835; one Independent, three Conservative, and one Liberal Party candidates received $33,528; and there were $44,250 in labor committee contributions and $10,000 in miscellaneous committee contributions for which the recipients cannot be identified.

An additional amount of at least $1.3 million was allocated by national-level committees to state affiliates for them to allocate to candidates. This method of disbursing national funds makes it impossible to determine the actual recipients from the reports filed with the Clerk of the House of Representatives; in order to find out what candidate finally received the funds it would be necessary to examine reports (if they are required and are available) at the state level. The AFL-CIO Committee on Political Education (COPE), the largest labor committee (measured by gross disbursements), allocated $709,728 to state organizations in this manner. The American Medical Political Action Committee (AMPAC), the largest miscellaneous committee, allocated $583,540 to state affiliates. While it is likely that the majority of COPE money went to labor-oriented, liberal Democratic candidates, and that AMPAC money went mostly to conservative Republican candidates and some to conservative Democratic candidates, the actual recipients of these funds are not known.

For the $6,603,376 in direct allocations to identified Republican and Democratic candidates, Table 4-19 shows the source, by kind of committee, and the recipients, by party and office.[] It should be noted that contributions made to candidate committees with generalized names, such

[] In addition to the direct allocations to identified candidates, labor committees gave $45,500 to Republican Party campaign committees and $51,900 to Democratic Party campaign committees which were presumably given in turn to candidates, and thus would be included in the amounts in Column 1. Miscellaneous committees did the same, giving $59,100 to Republican committees and $79,500 to Democratic committees.[80]

as the Committee for Improved Registration, for which the recipient candidate cannot be determined are not included. The fund totals used here comprise only a small portion of the contributions from all sources, estimated to have been at least $50 million for all Senatorial and Congressional campaigns in 1968.[81] The direct allocations reflect the financial resources and priorities of the national committees, not the amounts spent by any one or all of the candidates.

Table 4-19

Patterns of Allocations to Senatorial and Congressional Candidates from National-Level Committees, Primary and General Elections, 1968[a]

	Party Committees	R & D "Nonparty" Committees[b]	Labor Committees	Misc. Committees	Total
Republican Candidates					
Senatorial	$ 622,229	$ 12,850	$ 65,479	$190,194	$ 890,752
Congressional	1,695,431	—	78,618	367,740	2,141,789
Total	2,317,660	12,850	144,097	557,934	3,032,541
Democratic Candidates					
Senatorial	492,523	103,700	922,778	117,935	1,636,936
Congressional	519,119	22,700	1,251,205	140,875	1,933,899
Total	1,011,642	126,400	2,173,983	258,810	3,570,835
Combined Total	$3,329,302	$139,250	$2,318,080	$816,744	$6,603,376

[a] Does not include $33,528 to Liberal, Conservative, and Independent Party candidates, and $54,350 to unidentified candidates.

[b] Defined and listed in note e, Table 4-13 and note f, Table 4-14.

Republican candidates received 46 percent of the funds contributed by national-level committees, while Democratic candidates received 54 percent. However, if the totals are broken down by office, very different patterns of party support are evident, reflecting an unusual political situation in 1968: Republican Congressional candidates received proportionally more than Democratic Congressional candidates, while Democratic Senatorial candidates received proportionally more than Republican Senatorial candidates.

Of the $4,075,688 received by Congressional candidates, 328 Republicans received 53 percent ($2,141,789) and 372 Democrats received 47 percent ($1,933,899). Senatorial candidates received $2,527,688 from national-level committees: 34 Republicans received 35 percent of the total ($890,752) and 45 Democrats received 65 percent ($1,636,936).

The pattern of more funds going to more Democratic Senatorial candidates reflected the high proportion of Democratic Senators whose terms were up in 1968, and the fact that incumbents usually receive more national-level support than nonincumbents. In 1968, there were 23 Democratic Senators and only 11 Republican Senators whose terms were expiring.

The emphasis on Senate Democrats is also apparent in the average amounts received by House and Senate candidates. The average amount received by Republican Senatorial candidates was $26,199, while their Democratic counterparts received an average of $36,376. The pattern was reversed on the House side: Republican candidates received an average of $6,530 while Democratic candidates received an average of $5,199 from national-level committees.

The financial attention of national-level committees, however, was not enough to prevent greater losses for Senate Democrats than for Senate Republicans. There were 20 incumbent Democrats who ran for reelection (three retired); 13 won and two other seats remained Democratic when challengers beat the incumbents in primaries and then also won the general election. Of the eight Republican incumbents who ran for reelection (three retired), only one was defeated, so the net change in the Senate was a gain of five seats for the Republicans. On the House side, there was a net gain of only four seats for the Republicans.

Comparative Sources of Candidates' Support

Of the $6.6 million allocated to Republican and Democratic candidates, as shown in Table 4-19, party and nonparty committees contributed 53 percent, labor committees contributed 35 percent, and miscellaneous committees contributed 12 percent. However, the pattern of sources for Republican candidates and for Democratic candidates was strikingly different, as shown in Table 4-20.

Party and nonparty committees accounted for 77 percent of Republican funds, and only 32 percent of Democratic funds. The Republicans also received relatively more from miscellaneous committees. These Republican advantages were offset by the contributions of labor committees, which accounted for 61 percent of Democratic candidates' funds and only 5 percent of Republican candidates' funds.

In 1960, a similar analysis of national committee allocations was done,[82] and a comparison of the sources of funds reveals a pattern of decreasing relative importance of the party committees, although in terms of aggregate dollars, the party committee amounts have increased. The total amount allocated by national-level committees increased from $1.9 million in 1960 to $6.6 million in 1968; the proportion contributed by party committees decreased from 70 percent to 53 percent. In 1960, Democrats received two percent more from labor committees than from party committees; in 1968, labor committees contributed almost twice as much to Democratic candidates as did party committees. For Republicans, a decrease in the proportion of party funds was balanced by a significant increase in funds from miscellaneous sources, and a slight increase in labor committees support.

Table 4-20

Comparison of National-Level Sources of Funds, 1960 and 1968 (in percentages)

	1960	1968
All Candidates		
Party Committees[a]	70%	53%
Labor Committees	24	35
Miscellaneous Committees	6	12
Republican Candidates		
Party Committees[a]	94	77
Labor Committees	1	5
Miscellaneous Committees	5	18
Democratic Candidates		
Party Committees[a]	45	32
Labor Committees	47	61
Miscellaneous Committees	8	7

[a] Includes nonparty committees for 1968.

In 1968, labor committees were somewhat more important for Democratic Congressional candidates than for Senatorial candidates. Democratic Congressional candidates received 65 percent of their total national committee funds from labor committees, while Senatorial candidates received 56 percent from that source. For Republican candidates, there were no significant differences in sources of national committee funds between Congressional and Senatorial candidates.

Largest Senatorial Contributions

There were not only more incumbent Senate Democrats than Republicans up for reelection in 1968, but many more Democratic incumbents did not have safe seats. The resulting emphasis on incumbent Democratic Senators can be seen in a comparison of the top Democratic and Republican recipients of national committee funds. The top six Democratic recipients all received more than the top six Republican recipients. Of the top six Democratic recipients, five were incumbents; of the top six Republican recipients, only one was an incumbent (see Table 4-21).

The six largest party committee contributions to Senatorial candidates were not significantly different for Democrats and Republicans. For Democratic candidates, the top contributions ranged from $24,000 to $51,500; for Republican candidates, the top contributions ranged from $30,385

Table 4-21

Largest Total Contributions to Senatorial Candidates, 1968

Democrats	
* Wayne Morse (Ore.)	$206,469[a]
John Gilligan (Ohio)	204,594[b]
* Birch Bayh (Ind.)	108,045
* Gaylord Nelson (Wisc.)	105,439
* Joseph Clark (Pa.)	74,899
* Daniel Brewster (Md.)	66,420
Republicans	
Robert Packwood (Ore.)	$60,010
* Everett Dirksen (Ill.)	53,300
Richard Schweiker (Pa.)	52,452
William Saxbe (Ohio)	51,675
Thomas Curtis (Mo.)	51,389
Charles Mathias (Md.)	46,965

* Denotes incumbent.
[a] Includes primary, general election, and recount contributions.
[b] Includes primary and general election contributions.

to $40,110. But the six top Democratic recipients of party committee funds were all incumbents (Frank Church, George McGovern, Morse, Nelson, Abraham Ribicoff, J. William Fulbright), and none of the six top Republican recipients of party committee funds was an incumbent (Packwood, Schweiker, Saxbe, Max Rafferty, David Stanley, and George Hansen).

There were some notable differences in the six largest contributions to Democratic and Republican Senatorial candidates from miscellaneous committees. The amounts received by the Democratic candidates (of whom five were incumbents) ranged from $5,050 to $25,600. The amounts received by the Republican candidates (of whom only one was an incumbent) ranged from $11,050 to $20,519.

It was the labor committee contributions that created the major difference in the amounts received by Democratic and Republican Senatorial candidates. Only one Republican candidate received more than $10,000 from labor committees, while seven Democratic candidates received more than $45,000 from that source (see Table 4-22).

The top five Democratic recipients in total national committee contributions (Morse, Gilligan, Bayh, Nelson, and Clark) were also the top five recipients of labor committee funds, and the labor money accounted for more than one-half of the total amounts they received. There were also three Republicans who were on the list of top recipients of labor funds (Dirksen, Saxbe, and Mathias) who were also among the top recipients in all national committee funds, but their labor money accounted for only about one-eighth of the total each received.

There was also significant duplication among the top recipients on the

Table 4-22

Largest Labor Contributions to Senatorial Candidates, 1968

Democrats	
John Gilligan (Ohio)	$180,344
* Wayne Morse (Ore.)	137,496
* Birch Bayh (Ind.)	79,645
* Gaylord Nelson (Wisc.)	61,250
* Joseph Clark (Pa.)	47,299
Alan Cranston (Calif.)	45,750
* Daniel Brewster (Md.)	45,570
Republicans	
* Thomas Kuchel (Calif.)	$31,279
* Jacob Javits (N.Y.)	7,000
* Everett Dirksen (Ill.)	6,700
William Saxbe (Ohio)	6,500
Charles Mathias (Md.)	5,500

* Denotes incumbent.

other lists of committee contributions. Two Democrats (Morse and Nelson) and three Republicans (Packwood, Schweiker, and Saxbe) were among the top six recipients of both party and overall committee contributions. All six Republicans (Packwood, Dirksen, Schweiker, Saxbe, Mathias, and Curtis) and three Democrats (Morse, Nelson, and Clark) were top recipients of both miscellaneous committee funds and overall committee funds. The same three Democrats and three of the Republicans (Dirksen, Saxbe, and Mathias) were on the lists of largest contributions from both labor and miscellaneous committees.

Largest Congressional Contributions

The top Congressional Democratic recipients also received more than their Republican counterparts, but the difference was not as pronounced as for Senatorial candidates (see Table 4-23).

In party committee contributions, the top Republican Congressional recipients were significantly ahead of their Democratic counterparts. The six Republicans received between $13,800 and $18,500; the six Democrats received between $6,500 and $7,200. This Republican advantage was more than balanced by the top labor committee contributions. The top six labor contributions to Democratic candidates ranged from $17,000 to $28,927; the range of the top six contributions to Republican candidates was from $3,250 to $6,275. The top contributions from miscellaneous committees slightly favored the Republicans: six Republicans received between $5,600 and $7,400; six Democrats received between $3,100 and $7,100.

Table 4-23

Largest Total Contributions to House Candidates, 1968

Democrats	
Charles Vanik (Ohio)	$36,527
Frederick Stant, Jr. (Va.)	24,500
Joseph Karth (Minn.)	22,634
Jacob Gilbert (N.Y.)	22,156
Bertram Podell (N.Y.)	21,019
Arnold Olsen (Mont.)	20,450
Republicans	
E. Ross Adair (Ind.)	$18,550
Robert Rust (Fla.)	18,500
Jim Collins (Tex.)	18,250
James Smith (Okla.)	18,250
Robert Podesta (Ill.)	17,900
Bill Teague (Cal.)	17,700

An analysis of the top Democratic and Republican Congressional recipients on each of the committee lists reveals far less duplication than among Senatorial candidates. Of the six Republicans who received most in total contributions from all national committees, four (Rust, Collins, Smith, and Teague) were also among the top recipients of party committee contributions: Smith and Teague received more than half and Rust and Collins received all of their totals from party sources. The Democrats had only two candidates (Vanik and Karth) on the list of the top party committee recipients who were also on the list of the top Democratic recipients from all sources. For these two Democrats, however, the party committee funds accounted for, respectively, only about one-sixth and one-third of their total funds.

Four of the top six Democratic recipients of labor committee funds (Vanik, Stant, Gilbert and Podell) were also among the top six recipients in overall contributions. None of the top six Republican recipients of labor funds was also among the top six in all committee funds. Only one Republican (Podesta) and no Democrats were on both the list of top recipients of miscellaneous committee funds and the list of top overall recipients.

For the Democratic Congressional candidates, only Vanik, a top overall recipient, was one of the top six on both the party and the labor recipient lists. There was no duplication of top labor committee recipients and top miscellaneous committee recipients in either party.

Conclusion

The reason for the greater diversity of national-level committee funds among Congressional candidates, as compared to Senatorial candidates, may simply be the fact that there are many more Congressional candidates.

It is also possible that the patterns of contributions for Senatorial candidates reflect the unusual nature of the 1968 elections: the Democrats were concentrating on those incumbents whose seats were doubtful, and the Republicans were concentrating on those challengers who were considered to have a good chance to win the doubtful seats. The latter would seem to be true from the pattern of top Senatorial recipients on all lists.

Of the 13 Democrats and 11 Republicans in the Senate group who were the top recipients on one or more of the committee lists (party, labor, miscellaneous, and total), seven Democrats and eight Republicans were in direct competition. (There was one "extra" Republican because Kuchel and Rafferty were both competing for the same seat; Kuchel received top labor funds in his losing primary campaign, and Rafferty was then among the top recipients of party committee funds in the general election.) Four of the seven Democrats in direct competition were incumbents, and only one of the eight Republicans was an incumbent. The election results revealed no obvious pattern: three Democrats, one incumbent and two nonincumbents, won; and four Republicans, all nonincumbents, won.

Democratic Senatorial and Congressional candidates receive more money from national-level sources than do their Republican counterparts, but this tends to balance out because in the overall patterns of financing, Democrats have less dependable sources of funds at the local level. In most areas of the country, Republicans have more systematic and productive local sources of funds. Liberal Democrats, in particular, are substantially dependent upon national-level labor funds. Some Democrats also receive local money not counted in this analysis. As shown in Table 4-19, labor committees gave Democrats almost as much money as party committees gave to Republicans. Of course, the impact was significantly different because almost all of the Republican party money was given in the general election period, whereas the labor money to Democratic candidates was disbursed in both primary and general election periods. Particularly in the cases of Morse and Gilligan, labor contributed very large amounts in their primary races, in which they faced very strong opponents.[83] Clearly, labor fills a void that Democratic party committees cannot seem to fill.

Presidential Campaigns in Selected States and Localities

Presidential campaigns are vastly decentralized, and are carried on simultaneously by party and ad hoc committees in 50 states. With the growth of organized groups and the multiplication of political interests, nonparty committees undertake significant campaign activity. Many such committees make no accounting of their funds to a high body.

To survey each of the 50 states would be an immense undertaking, but some indication of the amounts spent in some states and localities can be given. Information is taken from official documents, as in Oregon and Kentucky, press clippings usually based on official filings, research papers, and other sources. Only committees specifying Nixon-Agnew, Humphrey-Muskie, or Wallace-LeMay are included. Excluded are state or local party committees, committees which include the names of Senatorial candidates, and all prenomination information. There may be some duplication if state or local groups transferred funds to each other or to national-level committees whose totals have been noted in the main body of this study. The data are incomplete and unrepresentative, but are selected examples of the range of Presidential campaign financial activity that occurs in addition to the national-level data which this study mainly contains:

Republican

	Receipts	Expenditures
Connecticut		
United Citizens for Nixon-Agnew	$ 43,847.00	$ 43,417.00
Nixon for President Committee	15,198.00	16,524.00
Norwich United Citizens for Nixon-Agnew	748.00	996.00
Stanford Citizens for Nixon-Agnew	2,341.00	2,307.00
Florida		
Nixon-Agnew Committee	354,729.05	352,646.78
Nixon for President Campaign	27,007.94	35,822.62
Michigan		
Genesee County Nixon Rally	5,463.00	4,875.94
New Mexico		
Citizens for Nixon-Agnew	2,285.00	2,163.50
Oregon		
Oregon United Citizens for Nixon-Agnew	115,901.60	128,575.69

	Receipts	*Expenditures*
Baker County Citizens for Nixon	260.00	260.00
United Citizens for Nixon-Agnew Douglas County	701.37	701.37
Nixon Committee Gilliam County	184.25	184.25
Lane County Nixon-Agnew Committee	2,806.85	2,806.85

Pennsylvania

	Receipts	*Expenditures*
United Citizens for Nixon-Agnew	$ 56,827.00	$ 63,359.00
Citizens for Nixon-Agnew	21,069.00	22,047.00
Citizens for Nixon-Agnew Bucks County	6,810.00	6,019.00
Citizens for Nixon-Agnew Columbia County	9,494.00	9,494.00
Nixon-Agnew Victory Team Dauphin County	81,960.00	86,645.00
Citizens for Nixon York County	7,160.00	7,160.00
Nixon Welcome Committee Allegheny County	7,371.00	7,371.00

Democratic

	Receipts	*Expenditures*

California

	Receipts	*Expenditures*
Californians for Humphrey	$154,674.60	$142,580.40
Humphrey-Muskie Public Relations Fund	42,385.00	31,738.00
Humphrey-Muskie California Campaign	21,639.00	17,943.00

Massachusetts

Humphrey-Muskie Ad Committee	3,199.00	3,199.00

	Receipts	*Expenditures*
Michigan		
Citizens for Humphrey	36,762.04	109,710.02
New Mexico		
Albuquerque Lawyers for Humphrey-Muskie	312.50	312.50
New York		
Greater N. Y. Liberal Republicans, Democrats & Independents for Humphrey	16,825.00	18,792.00
N. Y. Volunteers for Humphrey-Muskie	38,584.00	38,584.00
N. Y. State Humphrey-Muskie Campaign	11,144.00	11,093.00
HHH T V & Film Committee	47,430.00	47,430.00
Oregon		
United Citizens for Humphrey Committee	22,368.31	22,361.78
Citizens for Humphrey	4,727.50	4,472.15
Citizens for Humphrey Clackamas County	514.60	514.60
Pennsylvania		
Citizens for Humphrey of Philadelphia	5,449.00	3,172.00
Humphrey-Muskie Citizens Telephone Campaign (Philadelphia County)	22,549.00	30,165.00
Citizens for Humphrey Philadelphia County	5,449.00	7,823.00
Citizens for Humphrey-Muskie Allegheny County	6,696.00	6,461.00
Texas		
Texas Citizens for Humphrey-Muskie	59,060.00	42,426.00

Wallace

	Receipts	Expenditures
Oregon		
Citizens for Wallace	$ 1,238.33	$ 1,238.33
Oregon Campaign, Wallace for President	2,885.88	2,885.88
Oregon Wallace Campaign American Party, Inc.	2,184.12	2,005.41
Wallace for President Committee	2,193.60	2,193.60
Wallace Campaign	155.09	155.09

Following the election, there were several state and local committees reporting debts derived from the Presidential campaigns, and there were reports of state party committees complaining about debts incurred in supporting the Presidential candidates at the top of the ticket. Some committees sent bills to Washington headquarters. Given the Democratic debts, of course, the national party would not assume further obligations. The Republicans, however, did accept some obligations owed by state and local affiliates. Also, some state and local party committees in 1969 indicated difficulty in raising funds and attributed the cause to the draining of contributors for the Presidential campaigns.

New Movements in 1968

The McCarthy and Kennedy campaigns were germinal in that they produced the basis for several political movements, offshoots as it were, that resulted in additional political spending. Several of these, such as the New Democratic Coalition and the groups related to the Peace Moratorium were essentially issue organizations, but several others undertook direct political activity, raising and spending reportable money. One of the latter was called the McCarthy Donors Fund, and another was the so-called New Party.

The McCarthy Donors Fund was an effort to channel post-Chicago energies and monies to support a limited number of peace candidates for Congress in the fall of 1968. A solicitation letter was sent to still-warm lists of McCarthy donors asking for funds. The mailings were paid for by the National Committee for an Effective Congress. The appeal, which at first was promising, soon tapered off, bringing in a total of $67,600, of which $66,800 was disbursed. There was a $15,000 contribution to the

McCarthy Finance Committee for debt reduction, and the rest of the funds were given to about 15 peace candidates.

During the summer of 1968, when it seemed certain that the Chicago convention would nominate Hubert Humphrey, some of the more radical antiwar groups and a few McCarthy supporters undertook to start a new party variously called the Fourth Party and then the New Party. (After the Convention, however, the greater part of the McCarthy movement leadership moved into local campaigns and issue-oriented or Democratic factional groups, such as the New Democratic Coalition, rather than into the abortive fourth party effort.) Partly organized as a potential vehicle for an independent candidacy for Senator McCarthy if he desired one, but in no way encouraged or aided by him or his staff, the party also cast about for other alternative candidates, including Benjamin Spock and Dick Gregory.

Representatives were active at both Miami Beach and Chicago, holding meetings and plotting strategy, but another important activity consisted of attempts to get the party on the ballot in various states. Following the precedent set by George Wallace in getting on the ballot in all the states, the New Party succeeded in qualifying in at least 10 states. Court suits were brought in six states to achieve ballot status. Unable to fund or agree upon a national candidate and finding it too expensive to build up a little-known candidate, the New Party ended up working mainly through some local groups where candidates were on the ballot, or through write-in campaigns already organized. For example, a McCarthy-Lindsay slate of electors in Arizona received 2,013 votes.

Almost $50,000 was raised and almost $53,000 was spent in the New party effort. There were perhaps a half-dozen major contributors, of whom one gave at least $20,000 to the effort. Significant spending went for travel and legal fees.°

The emphasis in this study upon the reporting minor parties should not cause the reader to overlook the other minor party efforts not reporting with the Clerk of the House.ᵖ Spending little money, many of these efforts were able to receive significant media exposure as legitimate news events. While these groups and individuals certainly posed no voting threat to the dominance of the two-party system—those that were on the ballot in 1968 together received only one-third of one percent of all the votes cast

° The New Party did not file a report with the Clerk of the House of Representatives, but did provide an accountant's audit.

ᵖ These included the Peace and Freedom Party on the ballot in six states, with Eldridge Cleaver its candidate in four states, the Universal Party, the Theocratic Party—and however identified, the so-called candidacies, serious and spurious, sober and humorous, of Pigasus (the black pig standard bearer of the Youth International Party), Louis Abolafia (the naked love candidate), and Pat Paulsen (the comic whose antics caused CBS some anxious moments about equal time resulting from his appearance on the Smothers Brothers Show).

—their existence certainly indicated at least some dissatisfaction with the two major parties, as did the Wallace movement. Another such indication was the fact that only 61 percent of the estimated voting-age population voted in 1968, which was not only low but also a decrease from both 1964 and 1960.

Sources of Funds

Two of the country's major public opinion research organizations have regularly asked questions about political contributions. According to both the Gallup Poll and the Survey Research Center (SRC), a large increase in the number of contributors occurred during the 1950s and then the number remained steady during the 1960s: from four percent of the population in 1952 to between nine and twelve percent from 1956 to 1964. For 1968, however, SRC data show a decline in contributors to less than eight percent (7.6), and, unfortunately, the Gallup organization inadvertently did not include questions on political contributions in any of its 1968 surveys. Table 5-1 shows solicitation and contribution data for each of the Presidential years since 1952.

Table 5-1

Percentage of National Adult Population Solicited and Making Contributions

Year	Organization	Solicited by:			Contributed to:		
		Rep.	Dem.	Total^a	Rep.	Dem.	Total^a
1952	SRC				3	1	4
1956	Gallup	8	11	19	3	6	9
1956	SRC				5	5	10
1960	Gallup	9	8	15	4	4	9
1960	Gallup						12
1960	SRC				7	4	11
1964	Gallup				6	4	12
1964	SRC	8	4	15	6	4	11
1968	SRC	8	6	20^b	3	3	8^c

Sources: Survey Research Center, University of Michigan, data direct from Center or from Angus Campbell, Philip E. Converse, Warren E. Miller, Donald E. Stokes, *The American Voter* (New York: John Wiley and Sons, 1960), p. 91; Gallup data direct or from Roper Opinion Research Center, Williams College.

^a The total percentage may add to a different total than the total of Democrats and Republicans because of individuals solicited by or contributing to both major parties, other parties, nonparty groups, or combinations of these.

^b Includes 3.5 percent who were solicited by both major parties and 1 percent who were solicited by Wallace's American Independent Party.

^c Includes .6 percent who contributed to Wallace's AIP.

Applying these percentages to the adult, noninstitutionalized population gives an indication of the numbers of individuals who said they made a contribution at some level to some campaign. According to the data, there were approximately:

3 million individual givers in 1952
8 million individual givers in 1956
10 million individual givers in 1960
12 million individual givers in 1964
8.7 million individual givers in 1968

There is no explanation for the decline in 1968. It is particularly puzzling in view of the facts that one of the Presidential candidates, George Wallace, is believed to have had more contributors than any other campaign in history, and that the intense Democratic prenomination contest drew large numbers of contributors, particularly to Eugene McCarthy's campaign. There may have been a decline in contributions at the state or local level, but there are no political or financial data which would indicate this happened.

According to SRC, a sampling variability in the 1968 survey could mean that anywhere between 7 million and 10.4 million persons contributed in 1968; the same margin of error or variability factor applied in earlier years. The lower range in the earlier years could be considered to match the upper range in 1968—say in the area of nine to ten million persons—but this would require previous estimates to have been consistently high. In any case, the 1968 finding occurred in the face of an apparent increase in the number of people who were asked to give, from 15 percent in 1964 to 20 percent in 1968.[a]

When contribution rates were analyzed by party identification of the contributors, Republicans showed a sharper decline than Democrats. Among Republican-identifiers, 13.6 percent made a political contribution in 1968, compared with 19 percent in both 1964 and 1960. Among Democratic-identifiers, 6 percent gave in 1968 compared with 7 percent in both 1964 and 1960. One interesting statistic for 1968 is that 6.3 percent of those who consider themselves independents made political contributions. This seems consistent with recent polls showing more individuals considering themselves as independents, and indicates that at least some of these independents are politically active.

Slightly more Republicans than Democrats gave to their own party in 1968; independents gave slightly more to Democrats than to Republicans. Some Republican-identifiers, but no Democratic-identifiers or independent-identifiers, gave to both major parties in 1968. Table 5-2 shows those who contributed and to whom they gave, by party identification.

In 1968, for the first time, SRC ran a supplementary survey of blacks only and then combined it with its full national sample for 1968. Table 5-3 campares the solicitation and contribution rates for blacks and for the

[a] The total number of people in the SRC sample survey was 1,557. Of these, 310 said they or a member of their household was asked "to give money or buy tickets to help pay the campaign expenses of a political party or candidate," and 119 said they did give money or buy tickets.

Table 5-2

Party Identification of Contributors, 1968

Contributors	Rep.	Dem.	Contributed to: Both	Wallace	Other[a]
Republican-identifiers	80%	10%	4%	2%	4%
Democratic-identifiers	5	76	—	12	7
Independent-identifiers	39	42	—	15	4

[a] Includes contributions to other parties, nonparty groups, unions, and undetermined.

entire survey group including blacks. While, proportionately, only one-half as many blacks were solicited and only one-half as many made contributions, the breakdown by party shows rather different patterns. The Democrats solicited a slightly higher proportion of blacks than of the population at large, and had a slightly higher percentage of contributors among blacks only. Republicans had a much lower rate of solicitation of blacks—one-eighth of the overall rate of solicitation—and received no contributions from the blacks in the sample survey.

Table 5-3

Solicitation and Contribution Rates: A Comparison of Blacks and the Total Population Surveyed, 1968 (in percentages)

	Blacks Only	Total Sample
Solicited by:		
Republicans	1	8
Democrats	7	6
Total [a]	10	20
Contributed to:		
Republicans	—	3
Democrats	4	3
Total[a]	4	8

[a] Total may be more than the sum of major-party rates because of solicitations by and/or contributions to other parties or combinations of parties.

One of the interesting statistics from these periodic surveys is the relatively high number of those who are solicited who give. In 1968, 38 percent of those who were asked to give did so. Perhaps most interesting is the fact that the rate of contributions among those who were solicited and gave was exactly the same for blacks as for the whole survey group: 38 percent of the blacks who were asked to contribute did so.

The high response rate among all individuals solicited would seem to mean that either campaign solicitations are somewhat limited to those who can be expected to give, because of past contributions or degree of involvement, or that an enormous reservoir of untapped potential exists for political contributions. In fact, other surveys indicate that the latter explanation may be true. From time to time, Gallup has asked people if they would contribute $5 to a campaign fund of the party of their choice if they were asked. Throughout the 1940s and 1950s, approximately one-third of people surveyed said that they would be willing to contribute. In both 1966 and 1968, more than 40 percent of the people Gallup surveyed said they would give $5 if asked.[1] If even a small portion of this potential could be realized, many of the financial problems of the parties would be eliminated.

The Republicans

In 1964, the Goldwater general election campaign had inherited a small deficit at the National Committee. In 1968, the Nixon campaign inherited a surplus resulting from the excellent preconvention Republican fund-raising record. Adding Convention gala funds (already referred to) to the cash balance, the Nixon campaign had close to $1.5 million to start with in August. This provided a nice cushion giving time to get the postnomination fund raising going. Unlike the Democrats, no borrowing was necessary throughout the campaign.

The fund-raising effort was as carefully planned and executed as the rest of the campaign. "[Finance manager Maurice] Stans knew exactly what had been spent, what was going to be spent, where the money had come from and where the rest of the money would be coming from . . . It was all programmed: there was the root-Republican money, the hate-Johnson money, the smart money, the little money; and then there was the big, big money from the large, classic contributors, nursed out of them personally by regional chiefs who spread over a geographical and ideological spectrum from arch-reactionary Henry Salvatori in California [who had been a major backer of Ronald Reagan] to liberal Max Fisher in Detroit [a major finance operative for George Romney]."[2]

The fund raising consisted of three main elements: a mail drive utilizing the large base provided by the RNC Sustaining Fund and supplemented with lists of the Nixon prenomination contributors; a large gifts drive that was incredibly successful; and a series of 22 simultaneous dinners held on September 19.

There were a total of 450,000 contributors to Republican mail drives during all of 1968 (and some individuals gave more than once). Of the $6.6 million raised from this source, $4.2 million came in the postconvention period.[b] As might be expected, the Nixon-Agnew mailings in the gen-

---

[b] Overall, the direct mail costs amounted to 38 percent of the total raised.

eral election period were somewhat more successful than the regular sustaining fund mailings in the preconvention period, as shown below:

	Number Mailed	Cost	Raised
Preconvention Sustaining Fund	9,000,000	$1,000,000	$2,400,000
Postconvention Nixon-Agnew	13,000,000	1,500,000	4,200,000

On the basis of net amount returned per letter sent, the preconvention mailings raised 16 cents per letter and the Presidential campaign mailings raised 21 cents per letter sent. Overall, about two percent of the letters mailed brought a response (which is very productive for direct-mail appeals). Returns from some mailings were better than others, and some ranged as high as $17 average contributions. The dollar returns were higher on computer letters which were personalized for each addressee. However, the costs of computer letters are about twice the costs of non-personalized letters, sometimes rising to more than $100 per thousand sent out.

The average dollar returns in 1968 were higher than in 1964, though from fewer contributors. There were also fewer new contributors in 1968, but these plus the old givers gave a very large base of potential contributors. Comparing 1964 and 1968 mail drives, it appears that the candidate was a greater draw in 1964 than in 1968 but that the Party was a greater draw in 1968 (when it returned to its centrist position) than in 1964:

	1964	1968
Preconvention Mail Income	$1,100,000	$2,400,000
Postconvention Mail Income	4,700,000	4,200,000
Total Raised	5,800,000	6,600,000
Total Contributors	651,000	450,000

Despite the continued success of Republican mail drives in 1968, the percentage of funds coming from this source was substantially less than it had been in 1964 because so much more money in big sums was raised. In 1964, only 28 percent of the dollar value of all individual contributions had come in sums of $500 or more; in 1968, the comparable figure was 47 percent. (The Democratic percentage for 1968 also rose, from the already-high 69 percent level of 1964, but 1968 Democratic figures are thrown off by the large borrowing program they pursued.)

The September 19 fund-raising dinners were held in 22 cities and linked by closed-circuit television. They were the only fund-raising dinners Nixon held during the entire campaign, pre- or postconvention. The dinners grossed almost $6 million, and netted $4.6 million to the campaign. Only

148

limited proceeds went to local committees, averaging not more than 10
percent, so the national campaign benefited by more than $4 million from
this source alone.

The costs of the fund-raising effort are a good example of the need to
spend large sums of money in order to raise even larger sums of money. The
total fund-raising costs for the Nixon campaign in the general election
period were $3.5 million. This included $340,423 for running the finance
office, direct-mail costs of $1,566,117 (which also included costs of ac-
knowledging contributions), national costs of $216,705 for the fund-raising
dinners (discussed below), and local costs of $1.4 million for those dinners.
For this substantial investment, however, the campaign raised $24 million
—a return of $6.66 for each dollar spent.

Theodore White alleges that the campaign was so sure of its income that
finance manager Stans did not have to promise any favors, appointments,
or even courtesies to the large contributors.[3] The Nixon campaign had a
blacklist of perhaps close to one hundred people from whom contributions
would not be accepted. While this was never officially admitted, most
observers believe that the major exclusions were John Birch and Klan
sources. Analyses of all available data on large contributors to the campaigns in 1968 will be found below.

The following table details the sources of Republican funds in 1968.

Table 5-4

Sources of Republican Funds, 1968

	Amount	Percent
Preconvention		
Sustaining	$ 2,414,545	42.57
Associates	745,838	13.15
State Payments	17,789	0.31
Speakers Commission	24,275	0.43
Committee Payments	2,084	0.04
Congressional	891,284	15.71
Boosters Club	724,052	12.76
Leadership Dinner	852,867	15.03
Total Preconvention	$ 5,672,734	100.00
Postconvention		
Nixon-Agnew Campaign	$21,250,000	88.61
Republican National Committee	601,566	2.50
Congressional Committee	1,527,260	6.36
Boosters Club	76,300	0.31
Senatorial Committee	526,071	2.19
Total Postconvention	$23,981,197	100.00
Total	$29,653,931	

This breakdown, which was distributed at the January 18, 1969, meeting of the Republican National Finance Committee, gives some slightly different figures than those already given in this study, or those reported with the Clerk of the House, but the variations result from slightly different definitions of what to include and exclude. Yet the table shows graphically the success of Republican fund raising during 1968, and puts to shame the Democratic effort.

Items of special interest are "Speakers Commission" and "Committee Payments." These show the lack of dependence which the national Republicans have on state payments within the quota system, or on fees charges for providing speakers to local fund-raising events. Practically all national Republican fund raising was direct in 1968, without reliance on state payments, and continues to be so. The Republicans maintain a quota system, as they have traditionally, but now it is more a credit system whereby contributions from whatever source—mail, tickets, direct contributions—are credited to the state quota of the donor's state. Results of this system for 1968 are shown in Table 5-5 with its illustration. Residents of 17 states or areas oversubscribed in response to various solicitation efforts. Among them were the major states of New York and California. One interesting aspect is the rankings of several Southern states: of the 17 states surpassing their quota, eight were Southern or Border states.

Many major committees of the Nixon campaign failed to file on time the official fund reports required by federal law just prior to the general election. These late October filings are supposed to give some preelection notion of who is giving and spending how much. The failure to file on time attracted considerable press attention, which was understandable in view of the great amounts of money obviously being spent in the Nixon campaign and the contrariness to usual Republican efficiency. The incident became embarrassing after Nixon won the election and only five of twenty reports were filed. Only one had been submitted on time. Some thought that the Republicans were reluctant to admit their high spending, but actually Republican officials had divulged publicly the aggregate amounts of money being spent. Some Democrats thought the Republicans purposely withheld reports so as not to divulge names of contributors, whom the Democrats could then have solicited on the grounds that Humphrey was coming up and was a possible winner. Some charged the Republicans with failing to live up to the principle that laws should be obeyed; it is ironic to get caught up in one's petard about "law and order."

The case became unique when for the first time the Clerk of the House of Representatives sent an official notification of the Republican violations (and one Democratic one as well) to the Attorney General. The Democratic-controlled Justice Department directed the FBI to investigate reports of 21 late-filing committees, ranging from 9 to 23 days late, but in other respects moved so slowly that the investigation was still going on when the Republicans took control on January 20, 1969. It is an interesting com-

Table 5-5. Status of Republican Fund Raising, December 1968

Rank	State	% of Quota	National Quota
1.	Virgin Islands	967.8	100%
2.	Mississippi	255.0	97%
3.	District of Columbia	181.3	
4.	Puerto Rico	176.7	
5.	New York	170.5	
6.	Texas	145.3	
7.	Tennessee	131.2	90%
8.	Virginia	128.1	
9.	Maryland	118.2	
10.	Alaska	116.8	
11.	California	113.3	
12.	Georgia	109.8	80%
13.	Hawaii	106.9	
14.	Oklahoma	106.5	
15.	South Carolina	105.7	
16.	Rhode Island	101.1	
17.	Kentucky	100.7	70%
18.	Delaware	96.0	
19.	Minnesota	92.5	
20.	Colorado	91.7	
21.	Illinois	91.6	
22.	New Mexico	91.6	60%
23.	Nebraska	90.9	
24.	Wyoming	88.5	
25.	Florida	84.0	
26.	Arkansas	82.2	
27.	Pennsylvania	81.2	50%
28.	Arizona	79.8	
29.	Nevada	79.4	
30.	Idaho	78.0	
31.	Massachusetts	77.8	
32.	Missouri	77.1	40%
33.	North Carolina	75.7	
34.	Louisiana	74.8	
35.	Ohio	74.6	
36.	Connecticut	74.2	
37.	Michigan	74.0	30%
38.	Montana	68.7	
39.	Kansas	67.4	
40.	Washington	65.1	
41.	New Jersey	64.3	
42.	Indiana	60.5	20%
43.	Alabama	58.7	
44.	Wisconsin	57.3	
45.	Utah	51.7	
46.	Vermont	49.1	
47.	Oregon	47.0	
48.	New Hampshire	46.0	10%
49.	South Dakota	44.9	
50.	Maine	43.6	
51.	North Dakota	42.9	
52.	Iowa	41.7	
53.	West Virginia	38.3	

Source: Republican National Finance Committee.

mentary that the matter was not raised at all at the hearings on the nomination of John Mitchell, Nixon's campaign manager, to be Attorney General, or of Maurice Stans, Nixon's finance manager, to be Secretary of Commerce. The Justice Department later closed the case without action.

Republican explanations of the late filings rationalized the infractions. Apparently, a computer made some mistakes by double-listing some contributions, and a decision was made to favor accuracy over timeliness; some reports were prepared on time but not filed until others could be filed simultaneously; some reports were notarized before the election but not filed until later; and some were held up in the mails. (There was some truth to the statement of one Republican official that he was too busy raising money to worry about meeting the deadline; Republican reports filed in January 1969, showed at least $6 million reported received between November 1 and December 31, much of it just before Election Day.) When finally filed, however, some of the reports were not up to the usual Republican standards of accuracy; the CRF accounting showed disparities of at least $500,000 between reported totals (which were higher) and schedules with back-up or detailed information (which were lower than reported totals).

In fairness, Democratic and Republican filings had often been late in the past. Whatever the reasons for the Republican incident in 1968, it appeared to be a conscious decision to delay. This incident served as a precedent for the Clerk to report violations, and in the future committees and candidates could be put on notice early that violations will be reported.

The Democrats

Although the Humphrey campaign received a respectable number of individual contributions (93,195), of which 95 percent (88,596) were for amounts of less than $100, the bulk of the money came from very large contributors and from loans. The Democratic campaign of 1964 had left a deficit not erased until 1967. By that time, President Johnson's low popularity began to cut into the party's appeal to both large and small contributors. During the 1960s, the Democrats came to rely upon large contributions and failed to pursue vigorously their small-gift campaigns, the Dollars for Democrats program and the DNC Sustaining Fund program. There was no successful small-gifts program comparable to the Republican mail drive to fall back on when in a desperate campaign or when out of power. Accordingly, the Humphrey campaign had to rely heavily on large contributions and loans.

During the Humphrey campaign, a formal organization for large contributors, called the Humphrey-for-President Club, rose "phoenix-like from the ashes of the defunct President's Club."[4] For a gift of $1,000 or more, contributors received a card which entitled them to membership in a new

President's Club if Humphrey were to be elected. (When he lost, the contributors got cuff links.) The members were solicited from among the thousands who had belonged to the President's Club at some time.

Started in 1961 by President Kennedy, the President's Club was originally an excuse to formalize and institutionalize the seeking of large contributions, and to give large donors status and contact with the President.[5] But it soon became in effect a finance arm of the Democratic Party and an operating committee for the President. Its peak membership was reached during 1964, when there were about 4,000 members, that is, individuals who contributed a minimum of $1,000 each. From 1965–1967, the President's Club became the mainstay of Democratic national fund raising. However, membership fell to about 2,000 persons in each of those years. In early 1968, President Johnson, as noted above, used President's Club funds in the New Hampshire and Wisconsin primaries. When Johnson bowed out from the 1968 fray in late March, most national party fund raising, including that of the President's Club, was suspended until the Presidential nominee was chosen.

But the Humphrey-for-President Club and other sources of large contributions proved woefully inadequate for the general election campaign. The total raised from all sources was less than $5 million, and the campaign had to be financed in large part by borrowing. The first $1 million in contributions had not been received until October 10, ten days after the Salt Lake City speech turnaround; by that time, the campaign was already into its second million dollars in borrowing.

At least one half, and perhaps more, of Humphrey's general election campaign expenses were paid for through contributions and loans from about 50 individuals. The exact amounts borrowed are in dispute, as will be shown, but reports filed with the Clerk of the House showed itemized loans totalling $3,125,000 from 43 persons. The itemizations were by name, address, amount, and date of the loans. Names of lenders, their identifications, and amounts of loans are listed in Appendix J. Discussion of lenders and identifications is combined with the section on Large Contributions.[6]

In no case was an individual loan of more than $5,000 made to a single committee. There were, for example, two lenders of $240,000 each on the record,[c] but these were itemized as 48 different loans of $5,000 each. Thus, 48 committees were used as receiving agents, and some of the receiving committees had no funds other than loans. Normally, loan funds were then transferred to operating committees which spent the money. In addition to the two lenders of $240,000 each, there were 19 lenders of $100,000; one of $95,000; four of $70,000; four of $50,000; two of $37,500; eight of

---

[c] News stories at the time of the loans stated the two largest lenders each loaned $250,000. However, careful checking of reports actually filed show only $240,000 each. Throughout this study, the amount $240,000 is used although there is no reason to doubt that the $250,000 figure is the more likely one and the correct one.

$10,000; and three of $5,000. Some of the lenders were also substantial contributors.

Some of the loans were distributed to the 48 or 20 or 2 receiving committees in a unique way. Rather than require the lender to make out and sign 48 or 20 or 2 checks, he could send the full amount, $240,000, or $100,000, or $10,000, to a lawyer who was not considered a political committee (and thereby was not subject to federal law applying to political committees) but who was in effect a Humphrey agent for lenders. He would deposit the loan and redistribute it in $5,000 lots to appropriate committees. Some lenders handled the loans in their own way, dividing up their own checks. Some borrowed the money themselves, individually, but some reportedly borrowed the money from a major bank which acted as grand lender (purportedly lending several million dollars). The DNC agreed to pay the interest. The text of the letter to potential lenders has been obtained, and in startling detail sets forth the conditions of the loans:

Dear _____:

I have been informed that you have expressed a willingness to lend funds to the attached list of independent committees for Humphrey and Muskie. It is further understood that this loan would continue until such time as the committees receive contributions sufficient to carry out their activities.

This is to inform you that in the event any of the committees listed on the attached list do not receive sufficient funds to meet their expenses and repay their loans and any interest thereon, the Democratic National Committee has pledged to these committees the anticipated receipts of its fund-raising program to assure payment of all loans to those committees. Anticipated receipts pledged by the Democratic National Committee to all such independent committees will not exceed five million dollars ($5,000,000).

All payment for reduction of these loans will be made PARI PASSU with similar loans that have been made and will be made to such independent committees during the course of this campaign.

Sincerely,

Robert E. Short
Treasurer

In addition to the unusual practice of reporting these loans in amounts no greater than $5,000 each, there were elements of ambiguity in the procedures followed which explain the discrepancy between the $6,155,000 in money owed and the $3,125,000 in loans actually itemized. This was partially accomplished in the official filings of one of the Citizens for Humphrey-Muskie committees, which carried two notations. One, a single item listing $2,800,000 in receipts, was explained as

Received constructively from various local, state and national committees
when obligations contracted for by this committee were liquidated in whole
or in part by direct payment of this committee's obligation in the above
amount.

The other, a listing of $2,800,000 in expenditures, was slated as

Disbursed constructively by this committee when various obligations contracted
for by this committee were paid in whole or in part by various local, state
and national committees in the above amount.

These notations mean that $2,800,000 was received in loans or contribu-
tions by state and local committees not reporting under federal (or, presumably, state) law, and that $2,800,000 was spent by these committees
on behalf of the national Humphrey campaign. Democratic officials admitted that some campaign bills were paid directly by individuals or non-
reporting committees because some people did not want to be known. Some
of them were the same ones openly disclosed as lenders or contributors,
but who did not want to be recorded as lending or giving as much as they
actually did to reporting committees.[7]

The practice of burying names of contributors is not unusual in Presidential campaigns, and can be accomplished readily by forming committees
in certain states without reporting laws.[a] These committees then receive
and disburse money in secrecy but at the command of the national campaign headquarters. Thus, the requirements of federal law that name, address, amount, and date of contributions or receipts of $100 or more be
itemized are evaded. Conceivably, some of the money was reported under
certain state laws, though it is difficult to trace. What was unusual about the
Democratic practices in 1968 was the admission that such activity occurred,
and that the total amounts involved were disclosed. The notations in the
financial report, moreover, were useful both in documenting the practice
and also in disclosing the total amounts of receipts and expenditures controlled by the national campaign.

Records of repayments reveal several interesting cases. John Loeb,
partner in Loeb, Rhodes and Co., investment bankers, lent $100,000 and
was repaid $50,000 for a specific purpose: to enable payment for full-page
newspaper ads seeking support for Humphrey, signed by Loeb, and placed
in several leading financial papers, including *The Wall Street Journal,* just
prior to the election.

---

[a] This practice was revealed in the March 1969, official filings of eleven Republican
committees, which showed six Illinois committees with similar names and contributing
patterns giving them a total of $268,610. None of the contributing committees had
been listed in any of the Republican financial reports in 1968, and there was no
information on who had contributed to the Illinois committees, or what if any function they had in the 1968 campaign. Illinois has no state reporting law, and press
inquiries failed to turn up information.

In another case, payment of $50,000 was made to Norman Cousins, editor of the *Saturday Review* magazine, and its purpose was given as repayment of loan, but the original loan was never listed. Cousins also was listed as a $50,000 contributor, but the timing suggests that the $50,000 originally lent was repaid and then contributed. If other 1968 loan repayments to individuals not originally listed as lenders are ever reported, as in this case, then eventually the secret lenders to the nonreporting committees could become known.

The January 1969, filing of the DNC reported $6,155,000 in contingent liabilities (covering borrowing to December 31, 1968) to various individuals. This amount included the $3,125,000 in itemized loans plus at least that portion of the $2.8 million in constructive receipts owed to lenders at state or local levels and not itemized in reports to the Clerk of the House. In any case, the DNC had assumed liability because most of the loans were made to ad hoc or bootleg committees which expired after the campaign. Certain repayments of loans were made in late 1968, and more repayments were made in early 1969—but none since.[8] The March 1969, filings showed DNC contingent liability down to $5,028,028.69. There was some discrepancy between this listed liability total and the total of itemized repayments, but there had been double borrowing, that is, further borrowing to repay earlier short-term loans, so the effective amount borrowed is not certain. However, from the March 1969, filing to this writing, no repayments of loans have been reported. Given the Democratic problems in raising funds since, undoubtedly some if not all loans will eventually be written off and considered as contributions.

To summarize from the figures given: $3,125,000 in loans were itemized by lender and $2,800,000 was reported in constructive receipts (some of which were hidden loans). This totals $5,925,000, while Democratic reports admit contingent liabilities to individuals totalling $6,155,000. Accordingly, $230,000 is unaccounted for, but this may be explained in part by simple inadvertence or by double borrowing.

The disbursing of the loans in $5,000 lots brought on an incredible amount of transferring of money from nonoperating committees receiving the loans, which often passed through several committees before reaching operating committees that spent the money. There was so much shuffling of money, in fact, that numerous adjustments had to be made to avoid duplication, which would have inflated total campaign receipt and expenditure tallies. The shuffling was so ingenious that it has been extremely difficult to reconstruct a meaningful description of what happened.

Robert Short's virtuosity in variations on the committee system has been noted by others.[9] Each of about 20 committees had similar lists of contributions, lenders (usually a variation on the basic group), and transfers out. Two committees, Entertainers-for-Humphrey and Lawyers-for-Humphrey, included exactly the same people and filed identical financial reports. There were three different Educators-for-Humphrey committees and numerous Citizens-for-Humphrey-Muskie groups.

Whatever comments one may make on the implications of borrowing so much money for a Presidential campaign, two points are clear. The borrowed money was in similar magnitude to the amounts spent for the Humphrey media campaign; without the borrowing, the campaign would not have been able to advertise as it did, for broadcasters demand payment in advance and do not give credit. The lending operation was reported, for the most part, to conform with the federal $5,000 limitation on individual giving (of anything of value, specifically including loans). In the past, lending had at times been reported in a less frank manner; for example, a single item might have specified a $1 million loan from a named bank.*
This procedure would not have disclosed the cosigners of the loan, nor revealed anything when repayments were made, for it would not have been possible to determine whose portion was being repaid.

In 1960, the Kennedy campaign incurred a deficit of $3.8 million, until then the largest campaign deficit in American history. In 1964, there were conflicting accounts of the size of the deficit from the Johnson campaign, but DNC debts were subsequently incurred in 1965 and 1966, and by 1967 there were claims that the Democrats owed as much as $4 million. But at least, the Democrats controlled the White House after 1960 and 1964. After 1968, including the assumed debts from the Humphrey and Kennedy prenomination campaigns, the DNC owed a total of $8 million—$9.3 million by 1970—and did not control the White House. (The Humphrey general election debt was owed not only to the remaining lenders, but also to some very large creditors, including telephone, hotel, and airline companies.) The Democrats strained financially to meet continuing obligations for staff and operations of the DNC, while also preparing for the 1970 and 1972 elections, and have not been able to pay off much of the debt owed to lenders or creditors.

In only one area did the Humphrey campaign have something that Nixon did not have, and that was the very substantial contribution by the labor movement. While the Democratic Presidential campaign undoubtedly benefited from some of the money spent by labor committees in the 1968 elections, or contributed directly, the more important benefit was the manpower provided. As Theodore White says, the strategy was simple and results unprecedented. The strategy was to register working people, reinforce their natural tendencies to vote Democratic, and then get out the vote on election day. The results included: 4.6 million voters registered by

---

* The United Citizens for Nixon-Agnew of Massachusetts was recorded on an official filing in Massachusetts as follows: "10/9/68 Proceeds of Loan First Nat. Bk. Secured by Signatures of Eugene Clapp, Richard R. Robie, John A. Volpe, Lloyd B. Waring $30,000." This loan from a national bank was illegal under federal law, but at least in this case the cosigners were listed. The cosigners later claimed they personally borrowed the money.

labor's efforts, 115 million pamphlets printed and distributed by national and local union organizations, more than 8,000 telephones in 638 localities manned by almost 25,000 union members and their families, and more than 72,000 house-to-house canvassers. Much of the pitch was anti-Wallace, using facts and figures to give lie to his appeal as a friend of the working man. And as Wallace faltered in October, Humphrey gained. Finally, on election day, the labor movement provided more than 94,000 volunteers— driving cars, distributing materials, baby-sitting, telephoning, and poll-watching.[10]

The financial support Humphrey did not get is as interesting as that he did get. Many of the wealthy liberals who usually contribute heavily to the Democrats had been thoroughly fished by the record-breaking costs of the McCarthy, Kennedy, and Rockefeller prenomination campaigns, and many who still had money to give were unresponsive because of Humphrey's Vietnam position, or perhaps his lack of a coherent position.

One of the antiwar liberals was Stewart Mott, an early backer of a draft-Rockefeller movement and later one of McCarthy's major financial supporters, who continued his record of unorthodox political activity with a rather unusual offer to Humphrey. On October 13, Mott wrote to Humphrey, on behalf of himself and ostensibly a group of McCarthy financial supporters, in anticipation of a meeting scheduled three days later between the group and Humphrey. In the letter,[11] Mott introduced himself and the others with a few biographical and personal financial details, and proceeded to tell Humphrey how much they could raise for the campaign if he (Humphrey) could convince them to support him. Hence, they had decided to give him "a personal private interview of one hour's length—in order to question you about our own view of the nation's future and what it ought to be." (The letter is reproduced in its entirety as Appendix D.) The scheduled meeting did not take place, and most of the other members of the group repudiated the letter and Mott's role in trying to arrange the meeting with Humphrey.

Theodore White summarized the story of the noncontributors rather succinctly:

But the hate-Kennedy money which had financed Humphrey until Kennedy's death had dried up; the hate-Johnson money which had financed Eugene McCarthy had also dried up; there was no Texas money, as there usually is in a Democratic campaign; there was no "smart" money from the great corporations and operators who usually bet on both sides, if both sides have a chance. There was only the old "love-Hubert" money, chiefly out of New York and Minnesota, and that had been used up or was not enough.[12]

Most of the "love-Hubert" money was contributed for reasons of personal attachment; many of the big givers were close friends of Humphrey or close friends of Johnson whom Humphrey had cultivated through President's Club and other appearances.

One promising source of the funds Humphrey needed turned out to be impossible to get. As a consequence of widespread criticism of a Democratic program advertising book in 1965, in which corporate advertising was placed at the rate of $15,000 per page, the Democrats decided to let the dust settle before spending the $600,000 or more profit from the book.[13] Accordingly, the money was put in a bank and there it stood throughout 1968. Since the money had originally been planned for use in registration and voter education, there was reason to spend the money early enough to assist registration drives. However, following President Johnson's withdrawal, there was some danger that funds would be spent in ways that could be interpreted as aiding one candidate over the others. After the convention, the Humphrey people tried to spring the money loose, but ran into problems. Since the money was hot in 1965, it had been put on ice under control of at least one trustee who was associated with a public relations firm doing work for the Democrats, and there may have been additional trustees. The attorneys for the same trustee raised substantial legal questions as to the conditions under which the money could be released, and how it could be spent.

By 1968, the accumulated interest added to make the total about $700,000. Humphrey operatives were willing to spend the money for registration and election-day expenses, but were unable to get the money released. Late in September, a magazine item headed "LBJ-HHH: $700,000 Misunderstanding" alleged that Johnson was withholding the money in order to keep Humphrey in line,[14] and the charge was repeated in a syndicated column by Evans and Novak a few days later.[15] Both the DNC and the White House denied the charge, stating that there were still substantial legal questions about the conditions under which the money could be released. Despite continuing and protracted negotiations, the money was not freed during the campaign. Indeed, efforts had been made to free the money as early as 1967, and often since then, and the money has still not been freed at this writing.

The Wallace Campaign

The financing of George Wallace's campaign was not only unique among third-party efforts, it achieved a level of grass-roots participation never before reached by the major parties in this country. Of the $6,713,524 in income covered in the February-October 1968, report,[f] the amounts and percentages by category of contributions were:

---

[f] The final report, covering February–December 1968, showed $6,697,000 in income, but it did not include under-$100 contributions for the last two months of the report period.

$500-and-over contributions	$ 458,753	6.8%
$100–$499 contributions	508,625	7.6
Under-$100 contributions	5,090,861	75.8
Sales of campaign items, refunds, reimbursements	655,285	9.8

In comparison, Henry Wallace's 1948 campaign received 38 percent of its income in contributions of under $100, and Strom Thurmond's 1948 campaign received only 11 percent of its income in small contributions.[16] LaFollette's 1924 campaign received 21 percent of its income in under-$100 contributions, and if collections are added to that amount, then 52 percent of the total income was in small contributions.[17] Roosevelt's 1912 campaign was financially the most top-heavy of the significant third-party efforts in this century: 17 percent of its income came in contributions of under $1,000.*

George Wallace's campaign report listed 551 contributions given in sums of $500 or more, which reduced to 498 individuals or husband-wife combinations. More than a third of the large contributions came in during the month of September, which was the peak of the campaign. Although there were constant rumors of large contributions from well-known right-wing personalities, few of them are confirmed by either the filed reports or other sources of information. Filed reports did show a $5,000 contribution from Leander Perez, the late political boss of Plaquemines Parish, La., and $1,000 from Edwin A. Walker, the retired army general. There were press stories that John Wayne, the movie actor (who spoke at the Republican National Convention), gave $30,000, but filed reports indicated only that he gave $2,000 to a Nixon committee, and there were other cases where persons reported to be Wallace supporters did not appear as such on Wallace reports but did so on Nixon reports. There were also numerous unverified reports about financial support from certain other right-wing individuals and organizations.

The state providing the most money from large contributors was, of course, Alabama, with $166,440 from 252 contributions. Next were Texas ($57,000 from 61 gifts) and Florida (47 gifts totalling $41,427). Apart from Southern states, only Indiana ($14,557), California ($10,950), and Pennsylvania ($10,000) supplied significant amounts in this category. The large contributors became members of the Patriots Club: Charter Members were those contributing $1,000; Distinguished Members, $2,500; and Lifetime Members, $4,500. In most states, most of the contributions were for $500, and there were only a handful of Lifetime Members. In the $100–$499 category, there were 4,032 contributions listed in the Wallace report. The report was carefully drawn, indicating the books were meticulously kept.

---

* No data are available on under-$100 contributions.[18]

Since contributors of less than $100 are not required to be individually listed on federal reports, the exact number of small contributors to the campaign is not known. But Wallace undoubtedly garnered the largest number of contributors of any candidate during 1968, pre- or post-nomination. There were claims of 900,000 contributors, but a more conservative estimate made by a top echelon worker was 750,000. The best returns came to the campaign's P.O. Box 1968 from direct-mail and television appeals, but there were also collections at rallies, a series of $25-per-plate luncheons, a few bigger dinners, and substantial sales of jewelry and campaign materials.

Fund raising was an integral part of Wallace's whole campaign, unlike most campaigns in which fund-raising events are considered and planned separately from other events, often by different aides. Wallace's typical campaign stop included an airport press conference, a closed meeting with his most important political and/or financial supporters in the area, a $25-per-plate dinner, and a rally which combined fund raising with speech-making. In some places, a $5-per-plate dinner or picnic lunch substituted for the more expensive dinner. While major-party Presidential candidates cannot afford the time to bother with such inexpensive dinners, Wallace raised significant amounts of money from them. For example, a $5-per-plate picnic dinner and 25-cents-per-glass iced tea affair in Wilson, North Carolina, reportedly netted $20,000. One series of six $25-per-plate dinners in seven days was tied in with other campaign activity. The schedule covered Memphis on June 11, Chattanooga on June 12, Atlanta on June 13, Nashville on June 14, Charlotte on June 15, and Richmond on June 17. One day in Shreveport, La., in late August, which included the usual meeting with large contributors, a $25-per-plate dinner and a rally raised $50,000.[19]

On September 16, in connection with the AIP's token convention, Wallace spent a day in Dallas, Texas, campaigning and fund raising. The day included one of the campaign's few $1,000-per-plate dinners and a 7,000-person rally.[20] Rallies were a good source of support and collections were regularly made at them, but the amounts raised were not as significant as money received through the mails. Nevertheless, Wallace and McCarthy were the two candidates in 1968 who could hold rallies and fill halls while also assisting the fund-raising operation.

Beyond the dinners and rally collections, the Wallace campaign had a computerized operation for direct mailings and for a monthly pledge system. It was estimated that there were at least 24,000 members of the pledge system; more than 2,000 new people were added in one six-week period in April-May 1968. The IBM computer sent out monthly reminders to members, including those who had pledged as little as one dollar per month. In addition, the names of persons who wrote in and those from commercial lists were also fed to the computer for fund appeals. At peak periods, the campaign sent out 50,000 pieces of mail a week in these efforts.[21] In September, at the height of the campaign, the Wallace headquarters opened its mail room to reporters, to demonstrate its claim that most of their money was coming from thousands of small contributors, and the newsmen estimated that up to $40,000 per day was being received.[22] Wallace's television appeals paid for themselves, and most of them made money.

The final source of income for the Wallace effort came from the sale of campaign materials of all kinds. While both major parties were having trouble giving away buttons, bumper stickers, and other items, the Wallace campaign was selling everything at a profit. Between January and August, an aide said that the campaign had sold three million bumper stickers at 35 cents each; four million buttons, at 10–50 cents each; and 150,000 straw hats, at up to $2.00 each.[23] In addition, there were a record of Wallace's speeches for $1.50, ties for $1.00, and commemorative coins. While the campaign financial report (to October 1968) showed a little more than $650,000 in income from the "sale of campaign materials, refunds, and reimbursements," the real figure was undoubtedly much higher. One source alleges that the system of selling campaign materials to local headquarters was "shamelessly corrupt." Since many local supporters did not have $250 for the nationally supplied kit of materials, which was priced to retail for $350, leaving $100 to the local office for campaign costs, some regional coordinators became middlemen, selling smaller quantities to local offices while "taking a handsome rake-off." The buttons which were sold individually for 10 cents, for example, had cost the local office 8 cents, but had cost the middleman only 4 cents. The straw hats which sold for $1–$2 had cost the middleman only 16½ cents each, six for a dollar.[24] With such profits, it is indeed possible that some people made money on the sale of Wallace campaign materials. But this is not the only campaign in which private profiteers abounded.

This was only one of several stories that raised questions about unethical practices in the Wallace campaign. The most famous was probably the asphalt case. In April, a civil suit was brought in Federal District Court in Montgomery alleging that State Finance Director, Seymore Trammell, who served as campaign manager for Wallace, was a party to a conspiracy to limit competition, set prices, and demand campaign contributions from companies seeking to sell asphalt to the State of Alabama. The Finance Director would be in a position to do this since he controls purchasing and disbursement of money by all state agencies. Independently of the court case, the press carried allegations of kickbacks to political friends and campaign contributions demanded of those who sold liquor to Alabama though its Alcoholic Control Board. The asphalt suit was settled out of court after Wallace's wife had died, had been succeeded by Lieutenant Governor Albert Brewer, and the state government permitted new bidding

162

by the company that brought the suit. But documentation of that and other allegations was published in the press, and questions persisted as to the sources of certain of the campaign funds.[25]

Another suit was brought by an Alabama State Representative accusing Wallace and other former state officials of using state funds in the Presidential campaign.[h] There were frequent charges both in 1964 and 1968 regarding Wallace's use of state officials in his campaign while they were on the state payroll. One story said that, excluding state troopers, the annual pay of state officials working for the Wallace campaign exceeded $175,000.[27] Eventually, some of the officials went on leave of absence or took vacation time, and the problem receded when Governor Wallace's wife died and several officials left the state payroll. While she was governor, the use of state troopers was completely legitimate since they were protecting a member of the governor's family. After her death, Governor Brewer continued the practice, with somewhat less obvious justification. There were other charges which related to the use of state airplanes, autos, credit cards, and such, but nothing substantial ever resulted from these allegations.

Large Contributions

About 13,000 individual contributions of $500 or more totalling $17.5 million were counted for the 222 national-level committees which filed reports with the Clerk of the House of Representatives. Of these, the Republicans accounted for 72 percent of the number of contributions and 73 percent of the dollars; the Democrats received 19 percent of the number of contributions and 21 percent of the dollars.[i] The Democratic contributions in sums of $500 or more at the national level decreased from 1964 to 1968. In the earlier year, the Democrats received more than 3,400 contributions totalling $5.2 million, whereas in 1968, they received 2,440 contributions totalling $3.8 million. The Republicans, by contrast, improved their showing tremendously. In 1964, the records revealed only 3,000 Republican contributions in these sums at the national level, totalling $3.7 million. In 1968, both the number and the dollar value of the total Republican contributions increased more than threefold, with the Republicans receiving 9,330 individual contributions totalling $12.7 million.

The relative importance of large gifts to selected national-level Republican and Democratic committees is shown in Table 5-6. The proportions

[h] The suit was dismissed in federal district court, but was pursued at the state level. The outcome is undetermined.[26]
[i] Contributions in sums of $500 or more to the Wallace campaign accounted for 4 percent of the contributions and 3 percent of the dollars of the 222 committees; contributions in sums of $500 or more to the Miscellaneous committees accounted for 4 percent of the contributions and 4 percent of the dollar total.

of Republican and Democratic income to national-level committees derived from individual contributions in sums of $500 or more in the last six Presidential election years are shown in the following:

National Level Committees

	1948	1952	1956	1960	1964	1968
Democratic	69%	63%	44%	59%	69%	61%
Republican	74	68	74	58	28	47

The percentages for the two major parties were much closer in 1968 than they had been in 1964.[28] However, 1964 was unusual with regard to the extent of Republican income in sums of less than $500. In 1968, as noted earlier, the Republicans did almost as well as in 1964 in gross amounts received from smaller contributions, but did much better in bringing in a larger overall total of large contributions. This brought them from a low 28 percent of individual contributions that were received in sums of $500 or more in 1964—the lowest percentage since counting began in 1948—to 47 percent in 1968. The Republican figures remain impressive, however, in the percentage of individual contributions and dollar amounts received in sums under $100.

The Democratic figures for 1968 are more difficult to determine for two reasons: one is that relatively so much more money came in from other sources than from individual contributions. For example, total Democratic receipts for the year break down as follows:

Loans	$3,125,000
"Constructive Receipts"	2,800,000
Advertising Reimbursements	280,000
Transfers from Nonreporting Committees	1,729,000
Subtotal	7,934,000
Individual Contributions	6,471,628
Total	$14,405,628

Because lenders are not included as individual contributors—even though their loans may eventually become contributions—and because so little is known about the "constructive receipts," the assessment of Democratic contributions in sums of $500 or more may well be distorted.

The second reason is that so many Humphrey-Muskie committees were set up solely for the purpose of receiving loans or large contributions. This caused the number of committees to be out of proportion to that of the Republicans in 1968 and also to the Democrats in other years. Accordingly, the test of which committees to select to give proper measure and to compare with other years must be arbitrary.

Table 5-6 covers the 80 major Humphrey-Muskie committees which were significant recipients of large contributions used in the central national

Table 5-6

The Relative Importance of Large Gifts to Major Republican and Democratic Committees, 1968

Republican Committees[a]	Total Individual Contributions	$500-&-Over Contributions	$500-&-Over —Percent	$100-$499 —Percent	Under-$100 —Percent
National Committee	2,769,857	107,099	4	5	91
National Senatorial	126,138	81,825	65	24	1
National Congressional	2,567,548	177,062	7	5	87
Congressional Boosters	796,352	768,627	97	3	—
5 Miscellaneous National	4,374,842	2,006,646	46	13	41
Subtotal	10,634,737	3,141,259	30	8	62
		(3,141,259)	(796,802)	(6,595,675)
Nixon-Agnew Campaign	2,282,429	671,744	29	6	65
Nixon-Agnew Finance	2,244,002	1,434,768	64	11	25
Nixon-Agnew TV	2,141,256	675,197	32	14	54
Victory '68	1,952,732	1,932,137	99	1	—
3 Miscellaneous	3,629,786	2,807,344	77	8	15
Subtotal	12,250,205	7,521,190	61	8	31
		(7,521,190)	(1,009,510)	(3,719,505)
Total	22,884,942	10,662,449	47	8	45
		(10,662,449)	(1,806,312)	(10,315,180)

Table 5-6 (*Continued*)

Democratic Committees[b]	Total Individual Contributions	$500-&-Over Contributions	$500 & Over —Percent	$100-$499 —Percent	Under-$100 —Percent
National Committee	890,665	172,755	19	19	62
National Senatorial	44,525	27,250	61	24	15
Congressional Campaign	29,025	14,750	51	29	20
National Congressional	4,554	2,500	55	22	23
Democrats for Sound Gov't	151,238	24,600	16	17	67
Subtotal	1,120,007	241,855	22	19	59
		(241,855)	(212,270)	(665,882)	
Humphrey for President	1,015,021	827,836	81	13	6
Humphrey-Muskie Media					
Humphrey-Muskie National Finance	402,322	378,706	94	5	1
Humphrey-Muskie Weekly TV	1,047,479	75,628	7	18	75
The 77 Other National-Level Committees	2,686,799	2,306,953	86	10	4
Subtotal	5,151,621	3,589,123	70	11	19
		(3,589,123)	(590,976)	(971,522)	
Total	6,271,628	3,830,978	61	13	26
		(3,830,978)	(803,246)	(1,637,404)	

[a] Includes the major committees listed in Table 4-13. The "5 Miscellaneous National" committees are listed in footnote c of Table 4-13, and the "3 Miscellaneous" committees are: Nixon-Agnew Committee, Nixon-Agnew Victory Committee, and Republican Victory Committee.

[b] Includes the major committees listed in Table 4-14. The "77 Other National-Level Committees" consists of the 76 committees listed in footnote c of Table 4-14, plus the Humphrey-Muskie Media Committee.

campaign. When these committees are combined with the regular party committees, as done in this analysis in previous years, the proportion of dollars received in sums of $500 or more is 61 percent.

For purposes of further analysis, information about large contributions from various other sources was added to the data from national-level committees. These contributions, totalling $11.3 million, were given in some 7,000 individual gifts to the following: Presidential prenomination committees at the national and state levels, and general election committees at the state and local levels, Congressional campaigns reported in Washington and in selected states, and other state and local prenomination and general election campaigns where information could be readily obtained.[29] The amounts added were $5.5 million in Republic contributions, $5.7 million in Democratic contributions, and $97,400 in miscellaneous gifts. Of the additional amounts, the largest dollar categories were for the McCarthy ($3.5 million), and the Rockefeller (mainly Mrs. John D. Rockefeller, Jr.'s $1.5 million) and the Romney campaigns, which will be presented in detail in the following section.

These additional amounts bring the CRF data base to a level of $28.8 million, comprised of about 15,000 persons making a total of about 21,000 different contributions in sums of $500 or more. This is a larger collection of information about large contributors than that contained in the official compilation of the Gore Committee in 1956 or in the Heard compilations for 1952 or 1956. The combined listings are distributed as follows: Republican, $18.2 million; Democratic, $9.6 million; American Independent Party, $477,200; and miscellaneous committees, $630,700.

Of these contributions, approximately $11 million, or 38 percent of the total, was derived from residents of the state of New York, while $3 million, or 10 percent, came from California.[j] The preponderance of large contributors from New York to the McCarthy campaign skews the results towards the Democratic side in New York, although this is balanced somewhat by the information obtained about the Rockefeller prenomination campaign which adds to the Republican total in New York. Without these data included, however, New York still outdistances California by more than two-to-one in information on large contributors in the CRF files. Counting contributions only at the national level as reported in Washington filings and for the Presidential general election campaigns, New York dollars lead California dollars by two-to-one, and when combined with state information, Republican contributions in those two states are more than three times greater than Democratic contributions.

---

[j] These figures are presented as contained in CRF files and are not to be interpreted as meaning that if all large contributions were known, that New York would outdistance California by so much. The last sentence in the paragraph, showing a two-to-one advantage for New York, is probably a better comparison. Campaign fund laws in California did not require listings of large contributors by name as New York law does.

In the analyses that follow, it is important to bear in mind the exclusions: data do not include contributions for less than $500, even if several gifts in the aggregate might exceed $500; contributions to state and local campaigns for other than President were only occasionally included, which means that Congressional campaigns more fully reported at the state than at the federal level, as many are, are only partially included; except in the McCarthy, Rockefeller, Romney, and Kennedy campaigns, data do not include contributions to prenomination campaigns not covered under federal or certain state laws. These exclusions also mean that many other individuals who made contributions in these amounts in primaries or at state and local levels are not included, and that some of those who are listed might well have contributed more than the compilation shows. In some cases, if warranted, verified information received in interviews was added to officially filed listings of contributions. Where precise amounts could not be verified in interviews, minimal known amounts are given with a plus sign (+) to signify that contributions may well have been larger than indicated.

Contributors of $10,000 or More

Of the approximately 15,000 persons in the Citizens' Research Foundation files of contributors for 1968, 424 made reported gifts aggregating $10,000 or more (see Appendix E). These gifts amounted to a total of $12,187,863+,[k] or 42 percent of the total of $500-and-over contributions recorded. This represents an 82 percent dollar increase from 1964, as shown in the following:

Year[30]	No. of Individuals Contributing $500 and Over	No. of Individuals Contributing $10,000 and Over	Amounts Contributed by Individuals Contributing $10,000 and Over
1952	9,500	110	$1,936,870
1956	8,100	111	2,300,000
1960	5,300	95	1,552,009
1964	10,000	130	2,161,905
1968	15,000	424	12,187,863+

---

[k] This total figure, and the total figures for the Republicans and Democrats, includes 37 cases (8 Republican, 29 Democratic) in which a dollar amount is followed by a plus (+) sign. This means that the Citizens' Research Foundation has information from at least two validated sources indicating that the individual has contributed at least as much and probably more than is shown, although precisely how much more remains unverified. Thus, the plus sign signifies that the individual gave *at least* the amount indicated, but in many cases gave more. When information was received in interviews and from private contribution lists, the minimal verified amount was used.

The 1968 largest contributors are distributed as follows:

	Number of Contributors	Amount
$10,000–19,999	250	$3,284,535+
20,000–29,999	85	2,020,131+
30,000 & Over	89	6,883,197+
Total:	424	$12,187,863+

The distribution of these gifts follows:

	Republican	Democratic	Miscellaneous[1]
$10,000–19,999	$1,823,762	$1,475,403	$ 31,000
20,000–29,999	1,201,789	558,650	26,500
30,000 & Over	4,507,234	2,172,008	114,613
Other (Under $10,000)	125,375	84,500	67,029
Total	$7,658,160	$4,290,561	$239,142

Among these contributors, there were 232 Republicans, 135 Democrats, four who gave to miscellaneous committees only, and 53 who gave to candidates or committees of both major parties or to a major party and the American Independent Party. The latter group are designated "split" contributors, and as will be seen in a later section, in many cases, these split contributions are not made to opposing candidates, but rather to candidates or committees on different levels, for example, to a Democratic Presidential candidate or committee and to a Republican Senatorial candidate. Some of the Republicans and Democrats also gave to miscellaneous committees, but they were counted as partisans if some of their money went to only one of the two major parties. Because of the split contributors, and the additional contributions to some miscellaneous committees, some contributors gave less than $10,000 to one cause or another, but in each case, the aggregate contributions totalled $10,000 or more.

The disparity in amounts received between the Republicans and the Democrats is notable and would be much greater in favor of the Republicans were it not for the information obtained about the McCarthy cam-

---

[1] The Miscellaneous committees include: Council for a Livable World; National Committee for an Effective Congress; Communications Political Action Committee; United Congressional Appeal; Americans for Constitutional Action; United Republicans of America; American Conservative Union; Exchange Firms Campaign Committee; Support Better Education Committee of Oregon; Citizens Foreign Aid Committee; the New (Fourth) Party; the campaign committees associated with the Conservative candidacies of A. L. Burnet (running in the 26th District of New York), James Buckley (running for the Senate in New York), and Frank Gaydosh (running for the Senate in Pennsylvania); and campaign committees connected with Walter Blake (running for Superintendent of Public Instruction in Oregon).

paign. Of the 424 contributors of $10,000 or more, 100 were either exclusively or partially McCarthy supporters. Of special interest, there were no Wallace supporters among the $10,000-and-over contributors. There were news reports of several Wallace contributors for that much or more, but none was verified in the records examined.

Of the 424 contributors of $10,000 or more, a hard core of 12 persons had also given an aggregate of $10,000 or more in 1952, 1956, 1960, and 1964. The members of this group gave $389,398 to the Republicans, $104,400 to the Democrats, and $8,501 to various miscellaneous committees in 1968.

Of these 12 individuals, ten have been primarily Republican with some donations of less than $10,000 to the Democratic party and to various miscellaneous committees. These ten individuals are Paul Mellon; Richard K. Mellon; John M. Schiff; John Hay Whitney; Mrs. Ailsa Mellon Bruce; Mrs. Mabel Pew Myrin; J. Howard Pew; Miss Mary Ethel Pew; E.R. Harriman, who gave $3,000 to the Democrats in 1964 and $500 to Miscellaneous in 1968; and David Rockefeller, who gave consistently to the Republicans until 1968 when his wife split their contributions by giving $5,000 to the Democrats.

The other two individuals in the hard-core group contributed as follows: Roger L. Stevens gave consistently to the Democrats and Mrs. Albert D. Lasker gave primarily to the Democrats but included a donation of $1,000 to a Republican in 1956.

Besides the hard core of twelve, it was found that 16 contributors gave in some combination of three Presidential election years in addition to 1968. Of these, eleven gave to Republicans consistently throughout the four election years, and two gave consistently to Democrats in the four years. Thomas J. Watson, Jr. gave to the Republicans in 1956, the Democrats in 1960 and 1964, and split his contributions in 1968; Harold S. Vanderbilt split his contribution in 1952 and then gave consistently to the Republicans in 1956, 1960, and 1968; and Jacob Blaustein gave to the Democrats only in 1952, 1956, and 1964, but split his contributions in 1968.

At least 13 individuals gave in some combination of two other election years in addition to 1968. Of these contributors, it was found that four gave consistently to the Republicans in the three election years and four gave consistently to the Democrats. Also, DeWitt Wallace split his contributions in 1964, but gave to the Republicans in 1960 and 1968; Harold Hochschild split his contribution in 1964, but gave to the Democrats in 1956 and 1968; Henry Ford II and John L. Loeb gave to the Republicans only in 1956, splitting their contributions in 1964 and 1968; and Frank Altshul made split contributions in all of the three election years 1952, 1964, and 1968.

Of the contributors of $10,000 or more recorded in data available to the CRF, 340 gave that much for the first time in 1968. These gifts represent \$4,474,471+ of the Republican total, \$3,324,773+ of the Democratic total, and \$219,606 of the Miscellaneous total for 1968. This extremely large number of "first-time givers" again results from the two factors stressed throughout the study: first, there were substantially more recorded contributors of large sums in 1968 than in previous years; and second, the larger CRF collection of data in 1968, especially after the inclusion of the McCarthy data, provided a much broader Democratic base from which to compile the 1968 givers of \$10,000 and over.

The difficulty in ascribing exact amounts to a given contributor should be noted. This is illustrated by the cases of large contributions from a series of people named King whose addresses are Englewood, Colorado, a suburb of Denver, or 3100 Security Life Building, Denver. Records show Nixon committees receiving \$90,000 in the general election period and \$11,000 in the prenomination period. According to the records, Mr. and Mrs. John M. King gave \$53,000, Mr. and Mrs. J. M. King gave \$27,500, Mr. and Mrs. James M. King gave \$17,500, and Mr. and Mrs. John W. King gave \$2,500. Some of these contributions were made by John M. King, the politically active chairman of King Resources Co., or by his wife.[m] The King-Resources King has a home in Englewood and offices at 3100 Security Life Building and he acknowledges that he is the John M. King who is listed for \$53,500. But he declines to accept responsibility for the gifts listed in the names of J. M., James M., or John W. John M. King says he does not know who these other Kings might be —nor do we—and declines to estimate his total political contributions in 1968 because it is a "personal" matter. There were various published stories to the effect that he contributed as much as \$250,000 to the Nixon campaigns during 1968. It proved impossible to identify with certainty the donor(s) of all the \$101,000, and accordingly, three Kings instead of one are listed separately in the \$10,000-and-over group. Thus, even when laws apply and are seemingly observed, ambiguity can result. Typographical errors or clerical carelessness aside, it is often impossible to pinpoint the sources accurately when every treasurer of every committee is allowed to report in his own way.

The contributors of \$100,000 or more in 1968 were:

	Total		*Breakdown*	
Rockefeller, Mrs. John D., Jr.	\$1,493,125	(R)		
Mott, Stewart	366,700		\$100,200	(R)
			255,500	(D)
			11,000	(Misc)
Dreyfus, Mr. & Mrs. Jack, Jr.	245,000+		76,000	(R)
			169,000+	(D)

---

[m] Another oilman, John J. King lives in Englewood also but he denies any of these contributions.

	Total	*Breakdown*
Stone, Mr. & Mrs. W. Clement	201,000+	200,000+(R)
		1,000 (Misc)
Rockefeller, Mr. & Mrs. Nelson A.	127,500+(R)	
Fisher, Mr. & Mrs. Maxwell M.	122,500+(R)	
Bernstein, Mr. & Mrs. Daniel J.	117,062	110,236 (D)
		6,826 (Misc)
Peretz, Martin	114,400+(D)	
Miller, Allan	108,000 (D)	
Carrington, Ellsworth	106,000+(D)	
Marriott, J. Willard	103,500+(R)	
Dowling, Robert W.	102,754+(D)	
Factor, Mr. & Mrs. John	102,500 (D)	
Wyly, Sam	100,000 (R)	

Of the 14 listed, only three—Stone, Dreyfus, and Factor—would be listed as contributors of $100,000 or more on the basis of their contributions in the general election period. In this group, Mr. and Mrs. W. Clement Stone gave the most to the Republican cause, contributing at least $153,916 to Nixon general election committees. Mr. and Mrs. Jack Dreyfus, who had been large McCarthy supporters, split their large general election contributions between Nixon ($72,000) and Humphrey ($63,000). Mrs. Rella Factor was the largest Democratic contributor in the general election period, giving $100,000 to Humphrey. Her husband, John Factor (who also gave $2,500 to Morse of Oregon) was one of the two largest lenders to the Humphrey campaign.

Eleven of the 14 contributors of $100,000 or more made their largest contributions during the prenomination period. These individuals, who were discussed in detail earlier, are listed below.[n]

Nelson Rockefeller Campaign

Mrs. John D. Rockefeller, Jr.	$1,482,625
Nelson Rockefeller	356,000+
Stewart Mott	100,000

George Romney Campaign

Nelson Rockefeller	100,000+ probably 300,000
J. Willard Marriott	100,000+
George Romney	100,000+ probably 200,000

Richard Nixon Campaign

W. Clement Stone	probably $500,000

---

[n] The amounts given in the prenomination list here include six cases in which a (+) designation is used to suggest that the individuals very probably contributed more than is stated, but precisely how much more is not known. In these cases, probable amounts are also given.

Eugene McCarthy Campaign

Jack Dreyfus, Jr.	100,000+
Martin Peretz	100,000+
Stewart Mott	210,000
Ellsworth Carrington	100,000+
Alan Miller	108,000

Ranging down from the $100,000-or-more contributors, there are several other very large contributors to both the Republican and the Democratic parties in the general election period.

Analysis of the contributions officially filed for 1968 resulted in the following list of the ten largest Republican contributors in the general election period. The specific contributions to Nixon in this period are noted.

	Total	Nixon	Other[o]	
Stone, Mr. and Mrs. W. Clement	$155,916	$153,916	$2,000 Rep.	1,000 Misc.
Fisher, Mr. and Mrs. Maxwell	112,500	103,000	9,500 Rep.	
Salvatori, Mr. and Mrs. Henry	90,000	83,000	7,000 Rep.	5,000 Misc.
Dreyfus, Mr. and Mrs. Jack	75,000	72,000	3,000 Rep.	69,000 Dem.
Mellon, Mr. and Mrs. Richard K.	65,000	50,000	15,000 Rep.	
Bobst, Elmer H.	56,250	55,500	750 Rep.	
Pew, Mr. and Mrs. J. Howard	63,066	50,000	13,066 Rep.	1,667 Misc.
Whitney, John Hay	57,500	31,000	26,500 Rep.	
Scaife, Mr. and Mrs. Richard M.	55,462	41,462	14,000 Rep.	
Butcher, Mr. and Mrs. Howard III	54,900	40,000	14,900 Rep.	

Among the very largest contributors to Nixon in the general election period, there were several who had given heavily to other candidates in the prenomination period. Max Fisher supported Romney in the prenomination period and then gave $103,000 to Nixon after nomination; Henry Salvatori supported Reagan in the prenomination period and then gave $83,000 to Nixon after nomination; John Hay Whitney supported Rockefeller in the prenomination period and then gave $31,000 to Nixon after

---

[o] Dreyfus was the only large Republican contributor who gave also to the Democratic party. In the amount given here for both his Republican and Democratic contributions, the prenomination contributions were not included.

nomination. J. W. Marriott and George Romney each gave the Nixon campaign $1,000, in each case presumably for purchase of tickets to dinners. Two prominent McCarthy supporters, Lester Avnet and Jack Dreyfus, split their contributions between Nixon and Humphrey in the general election period. As mentioned earlier, Dreyfus gave $72,000 to Nixon and $63,000 to Humphrey. The late Lester Avnet of Avnet Industries supported McCarthy, but then gave $4,814 to Nixon and $23,672 to Humphrey.

Similarly, there are several large Democratic contributions ranging down from the $100,000-or-more group. From officially filed reports for the general election period only, the ten largest Democratic contributors for 1968 are as follows, with contributions to Humphrey noted:

	Total	Humphrey	Others[p]	
Factor, Mr. and Mrs. John	$102,500	$100,000	$2,500 Dem.	
Lasker, Mrs. Albert D.	69,400	60,000	9,400 Dem.	
Dreyfus, Mr. and Mrs. Jack	69,000	63,000	6,000 Dem.	75,000 Rep.
Cousins, Norman	57,000	55,000	2,000 Dem.	1,000 Rep.
Allen, Mr. and Mrs. Herbert A.	56,000	56,000	1,500 Rep.	
Wasserman, Mr. and Mrs. Lew	54,096	54,096	—	
Lanier, Mrs. Doris	50,000	50,000	—	
Brandt, Mr. and Mrs. Harry	45,000	45,000	1,000 Rep.	
Guest, Raymond R.	36,000	36,000	—	
Mann, Frederick R.	35,500	30,000	5,500 Dem.	

The largest Democratic contributor in the general election period was Mrs. Rella Factor. Should her husband's loan to the Humphrey campaign be written off, the Factors would have contributed at least $340,000 to the Humphrey campaign, and that would probably add up to the largest single gift in the 1968 general election period. Mr. and Mrs. Lew Wasserman gave $54,096 to the Humphrey campaign, and he lent $240,000 to the same cause. If this loan should be written off, his total contributions to the Humphrey campaign would rise to at least $294,096.

---

[p] Whereas Mr. and Mrs. Dreyfus were the only individuals in the list of the ten largest Republican contributors who split their contributions with the Democratic party, there are four splits (counting that of the Dreyfus') in the list of ten largest Democratic contributors for 1968. Except for the Dreyfus', all the splits were for Senator Javits.

174

Split-Ticket Givers

From the list of contributors of $500 or more, an analysis was made to determine those individuals who made contributions to candidates or committees of both major parties, or to a major party and the American Independent Party (AIP) supporting George Wallace.

In 1968, according to CRF files, there were 255 split contributors. Of these, 53 were in the group of contributors who gave an aggregate of $10,000 or more, and 202 were contributors of less than $10,000. These two groups are listed in Appendix F.

Of the 255 split contributors, there were 106 cases in which an individual (or husband-wife combination) gave either to candidates running for the same office on opposing tickets, or to the same level national, state, or local political committees, such as both the RNC and the DNC.[a]

Of the 255 split contributions, 55 were husband-wife combinations. The three types of spouse combinations were: both spouses gave to both parties; one spouse gave to one party and both gave to the other; or the husband gave to one party and the wife gave to the other.

The number of individuals giving both to Republican and Democratic causes over the past few years follows:

Year	Split-Ticket Givers	Husband-Wife Combinations
1952	86	3
1956	64	3
1960	35	2
1964	80	3
1968	255	55

In the years 1956, 1960, and 1964, all but a few of the split contributions went to candidates for different offices, not to directly opposing candidates or committees. The split contributions were rarely more than a few thousand dollars. In 1964, a noticeable pattern was discerned in which individuals were giving to the Democratic Presidential candidate and to moderate Republican Senatorial candidates. In contrast, in 1968, 95, or 37 percent, of the split contributors gave to both the Nixon and Humphrey campaigns. The reasons for the large increase in the numbers of split contributors and in the number of same-level contributors in 1968 are unknown, apart from the better compilation of large contributions made by the CRF. Of course, Nixon and Humphrey were closer to the political center and to each other than were Johnson and Goldwater four years before. Humphrey may have benefited from his late campaign rise, causing some contributors to hedge their bets that he might win.

---

[a] These split contributions made on the same level are referred to as A-level splits. For further explanation of various levels of split contributors, see the introduction to Appendix F.

Of 13 split contributors involving the American Independent Party, 11 gave to Wallace and Nixon, and two gave to Wallace and Humphrey.

No impropriety on the part of an individual giving to more than one party is implied. In some cases, as in past years, contributions were clearly made for tickets to Republican and Democratic dinners, a not uncommon practice for businessmen and lobbyists. An uncommonly large number of essentially Democratic contributors, at least 23 cases, became split contributors by virtue of their contributions to Senator Javits of New York. The practice of contributing to candidates at different levels in different parties is part of the tradition of independence in voting in this country. The following record of split contributing in previous years points this out.

Among the 53 split contributors of $10,000 or more in 1968, Mr. and Mrs. Frank Altschul also split their contributions in 1952 and 1964. Mr. and Mrs. Lester Avnet, Henry Ford II, Gustave Levy, Mr. and Mrs. Henry Loeb, Mr. and Mrs. John L. Loeb, Clifford W. Michel, Richard T. Shields, and Frederick Warburg also split their contributions in 1964.

Among the 202 split contributors of less than $10,000 in 1968, R.J. Schaefer also split his contributions in 1952, 1956, and 1964; and Henry Crown split his contributions in 1956, 1960, and 1964. Thomas S. Nichols and John L. Carroll also split gifts in 1956; and Douglas Campbell, Walker L. Cisler, Edward J. Gerrity, Jr., Maxwell A. Kriendler, John L. Loeb, Jr., John D. J. Moore, and Sidney Weinberg also split their contributions in 1964.

The comprehensive data available on the McCarthy contributors made possible analyses of their response in the general election period. Of 988 contributors, 44 persons, or 4.5 percent, later contributed money to Humphrey; 14 persons, or 1.4 percent, gave to Nixon; and five persons, or 0.5 percent, gave to both the Humphrey and Nixon campaigns. In one of these 63 cases, the Nixon contribution was for a primary (Oregon), but in the other cases, the contributions marked a shift to the other candidate(s) in the general election period.

The following pattern was shown for the five McCarthy contributors who also gave to both Humphrey and Nixon:

Name	McCarthy	Humphrey	Nixon	Other
Avnet, M/M Lester Avnet Inc.	$ 26,000	$23,672	$ 4,814	$10,250R
Dreyfus, M/M Jack J., Jr. Dreyfus & Co.	100,000+	63,000	72,000	6,000D 4,000R
Loeb, John L. Carl M. Loeb, Rhoades & Co.	2,500	7,000	500	6,250R
Meckler, H.L. Bermec Corp.	1,000	10,000	15,000	500D
Murphy, Thomas S. Capital Cities Broadcasting Corp.	1,000	5,000	1,500	3,500R

Some of the McCarthy contributors who gave later to Humphrey were publicly known as Humphrey supporters in the prenomination period. In one interesting case, the brokerage partnership of Salomon Bros. and Hutzler gave $5,000 to the McCarthy campaign and $500 to the Humphrey general election campaign.

Occupational Classification of Contributors
of $10,000 or More and of Split
Contributors

Appendices G and H present the economic associations of the contributors noted in the last two sections. The $10,000-and-over contributors in Appendix G represent 42 percent of the total dollars recorded in this study, but they comprise only 424 of the 15,000 large contributors. The totals for the split contributors represent relatively fewer dollars because most were in the under-$10,000 category.

Economic identification was possible of 94.3 percent of the $10,000-and-over contributors, and of 95.3 percent of the split contributors. Primary occupation was often difficult to establish for many contributors because wealthy persons, especially those with inherited wealth, tend to have multiple interests. Some whose major occupations are readily identifiable are associated with conglomerates or other corporations that must be classified rather arbitrarily. The philanthropic category was a broad one that included, among others, numerous wealthy widows who may or may not actually be philanthropic but do have family or inherited wealth.

The dollar percentages are significant but can readily be skewed by very large contributions by one or a few persons. Because of smaller Democratic dollar totals, any Democratic contributor of, for example, $100,000 would account for a larger percentage in any occupational category than a Republican giving the same amount. For this reason, some attention should be paid to the percentages of individuals giving as well as to the dollar percentages.

Despite the differences in the composition of the two groups shown in Appendices G and H with respect to size of contributions, there were striking similarities in the percentages of dollar amounts and of individuals identified as in the investment, legal, oil, electronic and computer, and philanthropic classifications. Of course, to the extent there is overlap—53 persons in the $10,000-and-over group are also split contributors—there is duplication in the two tables.

The similarities in the two tables even extend to proportions of Republican to Democratic givers in some categories. Both Republicans and Democrats draw well from investment, legal, and the electronic and computer categories. The Republicans draw much better in insurance, oil, and manufacturing if taken in all its subcategories. The Democrats draw better in real estate, entertainment, and professional if taken in all its subcategories, including attorneys and physicians where Republicans also do well.

In finance, bankers are less well represented than brokers. If the manufacturing subcategories were combined, the proportion would be large. Except for oil, natural resources are not well represented. Nor are transportation and utility categories well represented despite their being regulated industries.

Occupational Classification of Contributors
to the Wallace Campaign

An independent effort to classify by occupation the contributors of $500 or more to the Wallace campaign was made by researchers associated with Rice University.[r] With repeat contributors and husband-wife contributors combined, the 551 contributions reduced to 498 units, of which only 40 percent were identified. Wallace contributors were much more difficult to identify than the $10,000-and-over givers or the split contributors because so many were small-town merchants or professionals not listed in standard reference works such as *Who's Who in America*. The occupational classifications of the 40 percent identified are shown in Appendix I.

The largest single group of identified contributors consisted of professionals, mainly attorneys and physicians. These contrast interestingly with two others identified as a seaman and a factory worker. As a group, the Wallace contributors seem to differ markedly in economic classification from contributors of $10,000 or more and the split contributors.

Contractors were identified as a significant group of large contributors, and the manufacturers of building materials and of cement products might tie in with the contractors. The oil operators and producers were significant contributors, as were people in the wholesale and retail sales and public official classifications. During the Wallace campaign, there were numerous stories about pressure put on state contractors and government officials to give money. Liquor is sold in Alabama in state-controlled stores, but only one wholesale distributor was identified.

Among those identified, there was no category of contributors with inherited wealth or in philanthropy.

Lenders

A description of Democratic funding requires analysis of the 43 known lenders to the Humphrey campaign. Their names, identifications, amounts

---

[r] Data were generously made available by Professor Chandler Davidson of the Department of Anthropology and Sociology.

of loans and amounts of contributions are shown in Appendix J. These are the lenders who were listed in reports filed with the Clerk of the House, and the reports indicate their loans totalled $3,087,500. This figure differs from the $3,125,000 given in the DNC report noted above, but can be explained in part by the fact that the official committee reports examined showed lesser amounts for some individual lenders than the DNC stated publicly during the campaign.

The 43 individuals identified in Appendix J can be classified according to primary occupation or economic interest as follows: seven each in manufacturing, real estate, or investment banking (including stock brokerage); five attorneys; three each in entertainment, freight-trucking, and food products; two in the oil industry; and one each in beverages, protective security, construction, clothing, and publishing. The 43rd is Mrs. Edgar Kaiser, wife of the President of Kaiser Industries, who made a loan in addition to that of her husband.

The classifications are somewhat arbitrary because several individuals could be considered under several classifications, for example, Irvin Kovens is in the clothing business but also owns a major interest in Charlestown Race Track.

The occupational distribution tells relatively little about sources of Democratic financing. Except for Kaiser aluminum, no primary industry is represented. No major defense contractor is represented. Real estate and entertainment may be considered disproportionately represented, but these are not unusual as sources of Democratic funds.

Geographic distribution is more revealing. The East Coast is well represented and 21 lenders give New York addresses. Only four are from California, but two of these—Factor and Wasserman—are the largest of the group. Minnesota, Humphrey's home state, provided five; except for Minnesota, the Midwest is represented by only one. Except for one Florida address, the South is not represented at all, and there were no Texas lenders.

There would seem to be a large number of Jews among the lenders, but this source is common in Democratic financing.

Eleven of the lenders were in the $10,000 and $5,000 categories, not startling amounts, and as contributors, these individuals would hardly be noticed.

The quick repayments to some lenders are also worth noting, particularly since those remaining unpaid would seem unlikely to get their money back any time soon. Of the 43 lenders, only 23 appeared as substantial contributors as well; the outstanding cases are Factor, lending $240,000, with Mrs. Factor giving $100,000 to Humphrey, and Wasserman, lending $240,000, and giving $54,096 to Humphrey.

Some lenders may have realized their loans would not be repaid because five gave to other Democrats but not to Humphrey committees, the loans presumably being the extent of their financial support of Humphrey. In fact, 20 lenders did not show up as contributors in sums of $500 or more at all. Surprisingly, eleven were also Republican contributors. Of these, three gave to Humphrey only as well as to Republicans, five gave to Humphrey and to other Democrats as well as to Republicans, while two gave only to the Republicans apart from the Humphrey loan.

Three lenders are especially interesting. Lester Avnet, lending $100,000 and giving $23,672 to Humphrey committees, also gave $4,814 to Nixon committees as well as giving to Senator Javits' campaign. John Loeb, lending $100,000 and giving $7,000 to Humphrey committees, also gave at least $500 to Nixon and $6,250 to Senator Javits' campaign. Arthur Houghton, lending $100,000 and giving $2,500 to a Humphrey committee, also gave $12,000 to Republican causes, including a contribution of $1,000 to Nixon and one of $1,000 to Senator Javits' campaign.

A word should be said about the lending operation. As noted, the individual listing of lenders was unusual, as was the distribution of loaned funds into $5,000 amounts per committee. Lending is perfectly legal under federal law, and the manner in which the names were officially reported was commendable.

Contributions by Family Groups.

Contributions made by members of 12 selected family groups studied by the Gore Committee in 1956[31] and the CRF in 1960 and 1964 were again checked in 1968. This group of 122 contributors includes only those persons carefully checked to be family members, including members by marriage. Husbands and wives were counted separately in this analysis, and divorced spouses of family members were not included. Table 5-7 presents the totals.[s]

---

[s] Table 32 reveals that significant political contributions are made by some prominent families. However, not all such family groups have been included in the analysis, and it is not to be concluded that all prominent families are significant political supporters. In the family groups that were analyzed, it was found that 52 individuals were contributors of $10,000 or more. These persons are: Robert R.M. Carpenter, Jr., Mr. and Mrs. Lammot DuPont Copeland, Mr. and Mrs. Reynolds DuPont, Mrs. Marshall Field, Mrs. Fiona Field Rust, Mr. and Mrs. Benson Ford, Henry Ford II, Mr. and Mrs. William Clay Ford, Mr. and Mrs. E. Roland Harriman, Mrs. Richard Bernhard, William Bernhard, Mrs. Ailsa Mellon Bruce, Mr. and Mrs. Thomas Mellon Evans, Mrs. Cordelia Scaife May, Paul Mellon, Mr. and Mrs. Richard King Mellon, Mr. and Mrs. Richard Mellon Scaife, John M. Olin, Mr. and Mrs. Spencer T. Olin, Sr., Mr. and Mrs. John C. Pritzlaff, Jr., Mrs. Mabel Pew Myrin, George T. Pew, Mr. and Mrs. John Howard Pew, John N. Pew, Jr., Miss Mary Ethel Pew, Walter C. Pew, Mr. and Mrs. David Rockefeller, Mrs. John D. Rockefeller, Jr., Mr. and Mrs. John D. Rockefeller III, Mr. and Mrs. Laurance S. Rockefeller, Mr. and Mrs. Nelson A. Rockefeller, Harold S. Vanderbilt, Vincent DeRoulet, Mr. and Mrs. Charles S. Payson, and Mr. and Mrs. John Hay Whitney. The contributions of this group amounts to $2,596,386 or 21% of the total 1968 contributions of $10,000 or more.

In the family groups, the split contributors of $10,000 or more (Appendix F) are:

Table 5-7

Contributions of 12 Prominent Families, 1968

Name	Number of Members Contributing[a]	Total Contributions	Contribution Breakdown		
			Republican	Democratic	Miscellaneous
DuPont	32	107,000	99,800	1,700	5,500
Field	4	39,000	2,000	17,000	20,000
Ford	8	109,750	57,750	52,000	—
Harriman	2	17,000	16,500	—	500
Lehman	7	51,000	2,500	48,500	—
Mellon	22	298,962	278,962	17,000+	3,000
Olin	7	70,000	70,000	—	—
Pew	11[b]	213,549	207,898	—	5,651
Reynolds	No Contributions				
Rockefeller	21	1,714,375+[c]	1,700,875	13,500	—
Vanderbilt	2	12,000	11,000	—	1,000
Whitney	6	133,500	133,500	—	—
Totals	122	2,766,136	2,580,785	149,700	35,651

[a] In this analysis, husbands and wives were counted separately. Therefore, Mr. and Mrs. ..... would constitute two (2) contributing family members.

[b] The Estate of J. N. Pew Deceased was counted as one contributing member.

[c] This Rockefeller total does not include the $356,000 contribution made by Nelson Rockefeller for his own campaign.

The following comparative analysis reveals that greater contributions by the members of the selected families were made in every party category in 1968 than in any previous year studied. Much of this dramatic leap in the Republican and the grand totals is due to the $1,482,625 Republican contribution made by Mrs. John D. Rockefeller, Jr. for Nelson Rockefeller's Presidential campaign; her contribution to Rockefeller alone accounts for 57 percent of the Republican total and 54 percent of the grand total of family contributions for 1968. However, Republican and overall totals almost doubled over 1964 without counting her gifts.[f]

	1956	1960	1964	1968
Republican	$1,040,526	$548,510	$445,280	$2,580,785
Democratic	107,109	78,850	133,500	149,700
Miscellaneous	6,100	22,000	24,146	35,651
Total	$1,153,735	$649,360	$602,926	$2,766,136

Henry Ford II, Mr. and Mrs. William Clay Ford, Mr. and Mrs. Thomas Mellon Evans, and Mr. and Mrs. David Rockefeller. The split contributors of less than $10,000 (Appendix F) are: Robert A. Bernhard and Mr. and Mrs. James H. Case III.

[f] Although the 1968 totals include Mrs. Rockefeller's contribution, they do not include the $356,000 contributed by Nelson Rockefeller for his own campaign.

Since 1956, there has been a rising trend toward Democratic contributions in the formerly all-Republican family groups. For example, in 1956, the Dupont, Ford, Mellon, Olin, Pew, Rockefeller, and Whitney families were exclusively Republican contributors. By 1968, however, only the Olin and Pew families continued to show up only as Republican supporters.

Of the family groups that became split contributors, the DuPonts and Whitneys gave considerably smaller amounts to the Democrats than to the Republicans. The Fords, on the other hand, gave $41,000 to the Democrats and only $4,100 to the Republicans in 1964 and a comparable $52,000 to the Democrats and $57,750 to the Republicans in 1968. The Mellons gave consistently more to the Republicans than to the Democrats in 1960, 1964, and 1968, but their contributions of $12,400, $17,500, and $17,000 to the Democrats still accounted for a sizeable amount of Democratic giving in the respective years. The Rockefellers gave only $1,000 Democratic versus $114,875 Republican in 1960 and $13,400 Democratic versus $1,700,875 Republican in 1968. As noted, Mrs. John D. Rockefeller, Jr.'s large contribution greatly affected the 1968 Rockefeller totals.

No family group gave exclusively to the Democrats in all of the four years examined. The Reynolds family gave to the Republicans only once, a $2,000 Republican contribution along with $11,000 to the Democrats in 1960, and the family members did not appear at all as contributors in 1968.

The Field and Lehman families gave to both parties in 1956 through 1968, contributing predominantly to the Democrats except in 1960 when the Fields gave $8,000 to the Republicans and $2,750 to the Democrats.

The Harrimans and Vanderbilts gave to both parties in 1956 through 1964, contributing predominantly to the Republicans, except in 1960 when the Vanderbilts gave $2,000 to the Democrats and $750 to the Republicans. In 1968, however, the available record showed these two families as exclusively Republican contributors.

Throughout 1956, 1960, 1964, and 1968, there have been miscellaneous (nonparty) contributions appearing for every family except the Fords, Olins, Reynolds, Rockefellers, and Whitneys. For the most part these miscellaneous contributions have averaged between $500 and $5,651, with the exceptions of a $7,000 contribution from the DuPonts in 1960, $20,000 from the Field family in 1968, $11,000 in 1960 and $11,146 in 1964 from the Mellon family, and $9,000 in 1964 from the Pews.

Thirteen Selected Groups

In 1956, the Gore Committee compared its lists of contributors against lists of officers and directors of 13 various trade associations and special-interest groups. Some groups were found to have many officials contributing large sums of money, while other groups were found to have few or none. For 1968, the CRF file of contributors was carefully checked against current lists of officers and directors of the same 13 selected groups. Appendix K presents the groups and the results.

The political interests of many of these groups are apparent. Individuals identified with these groups are assumed to contribute as individuals, not formally on behalf of the group.

A comparison of 1968, 1964, 1960, and 1956 in total giving in sums of $500 or more among members of these groups follows:

Year	Republicans	Democrats	Miscellaneous	Total[a]
1968	$1,132,982+	$136,106	$11,967	$1,281,055+
1964	200,310	225,790	4,618	468,218
1960	425,710	62,255	2,500	493,465
1956	741,189	8,000	2,725	751,914

This shows decreases from 1956 to 1964 and a reversal of trends in 1968, when giving increased substantially. In all of these years, no more than 18 percent of the officers and directors of these combined groups were found to have contributed—only twice the percentage for the population as a whole. Admittedly, the percentages among the selected 13 groups are reduced considerably by the large number of noncontributors among the top leadership of such groups as the National Association of Real Estate Boards and the American Bar Association. The ABA figures are especially revealing for members of a profession that consistently provides so many candidates for major public office. In 1968, among 297 members of the ABA House of Delegates, only 17 were found to have contributed. Their total was $13,500. Despite the attention of the medical profession to the issue of Medicare, the leadership of the American Medical Association did not appear as large contributors in either 1960 or 1964 when the issue was prominent. This may be explained in part by the practice of the American Medical Political Action Committee to seek contributions in small amounts that would not be included in this analysis, and by the tendency of physicians to support AMPAC through state affiliates for which contributor information was not available. It is clear, however, that except for John W. Galbreath of the NAREB, the individuals who appeared in the legal, medical, and real estate organizations listed here are not the same individuals who were listed in the occupational classifications for the $10,000-or-more list or for the split contributors.

The highest percentages of recorded contributors are among the mem-

---

[a] Republican and Democratic columns do not equal the total amounts because some contributors belonged to more than one of the 13 groups, and duplicated amounts have been subtracted in the overall totals.

bership of the Business Council, which has been called the elite of business and finance, the essence of the so-called establishment. Of the Council's membership, about 58 percent were listed among large contributors in 1968, 53 percent in 1964, almost 60 percent in 1960, and 40 percent in 1956. Figures for these years are shown in Table 5-8. The total contributions from the 69 contributing members in 1968 increased to a record total of $367,213. Of the 69, 67 gave a total of $280,913 to Republican candidates and committees, and five gave a total of $83,000 to Democrats. (There were three split contributors.)

Table 5-8

Business Council Contributors and Partisan Contributions among Active and Graduate Members: 1968, 1964, 1960, 1956

Year	Number of Members	Number of Contributors	Number of Contributors and Amount of Contributions		Miscellaneous
			Rep.	Dem.	
1968	119	69[a]	67	5	2
			$280,913	$ 83,000	$3,300
1964	118	63[b]	36	33	
			87,100	135,450	
1960	124	80	73	7	
			241,060	35,140	
1956	161	73	68	4	
			268,499	4,000	

Source: 1956 data from Gore Committee *Report*, Exhibit 22, pp. 86–88.

[a] Total members include 3 splits and 2 R & M.

[b] Total members include six split contributors each counted twice, once in Republican column and once in Democratic column.

Compared to 1964, when 36 gave a total of $87,100 to Republicans and 33 gave $135,450 to Democrats, the reversal is remarkable. Aggregate amounts of contributions had been decreasing between 1956 and 1964 at the same time that contributions to Democrats had been increasing. The Goldwater campaign of 1964 turned off many members who were attracted to President Johnson. The 1968 pattern reverts to Republican dominance but with Democratic amounts at still higher rates than in 1956 or 1960.

Another interesting case is recorded for the American Petroleum Institute, shown in Table 5-9. From 1956 through 1964, board members and officers of that group seemed to be giving fewer dollars; but in 1968, this pattern was reversed and 59 individuals (out of 175 members and officers) gave $461,639, of which only $30,606 went to Democrats.

Contributing patterns of officers and directors of groups such as the National Association of Manufacturers (NAM), the Chamber of Commerce of the United States, and the Iron and Steel Institute show few

184

Table 5-9

American Petroleum Institute Contributors and Partisan Contributions among Officers, Directors, and Honorary Directors: 1968, 1964, 1960, 1956

Year	Number of Members	Number of Contributors	Number of Contributors and Amount of Contributions Rep.	Dem.	Miscellaneous
1968	175	59[a]	52 $429,366	13 $30,606	1 $1,667
1964	137	24[b]	17 48,310	9 24,000	
1960	164	37	34 113,700	3 6,000	
1956	157	37	37 171,750	—	—

Source: 1956 data from Gore Committee *Report,* Exhibit 22, pp. 86–88.
[a] Total members include 6 splits and 1 R & M.
[b] Total members includes two splits, each counted twice, once in Republican column and once in Democratic column.

contributors and little money. For 1968, $154,211+ was derived from 45 individuals (out of 168) associated with the NAM, and only $20,500 went to Democrats. For the Chamber of Commerce in 1968, nine of 61 individuals were found to have contributed a total of $40,000, all to Republicans. The Iron and Steel Institute analysis revealed 12 of 36 individuals contributing $25,500, also exclusively to Republicans.

The totals for the 13 groups are particularly revealing in showing the disparity between giving to the Republicans and giving to the Democrats. Only in 1964 did the Democrats receive more funds from these groups than the Republicans, and the ratio in 1968 was eight to one in favor of the Republicans.

Other Petroleum Groups

Because of the alleged influence of the oil and gas interests on national policy, four petroleum organizations in addition to the American Petroleum Institute were examined. These are shown in Appendix L.

Although officers and directors of three of the four organizations showed a Republican preference, the overall number of persons contributing was very small. The Independent Petroleum Association of America showed contributions of $90,000 to Republican candidates and committees and $2,500 to the Democrats. However, this total was given by only four of 45 officers and directors, and one of these, Harold McClure, gave $90,000 total. The American Gas Association and the Independent Natural Gas Association of America recorded contributions only to the Republican cause; however, again the number of individuals contributing was not great and the contribution totals were fairly small. AGA showed four of 38 officers and directors contributing $3,000 to the Republicans, and INGAA showed three of 34 officers and directors giving only $2,500. The National Petroleum Refiners Association was the only organization with a Democratic advantage. In this group, five of 112 officers and directors contributed. Of these, three gave $3,500 to the Republicans, and two gave $15,500 to the Democrats.

Analysis of Largest Defense and Industrial Companies

Analysis was made of the 1968 contribution patterns of officers and directors of the 25 largest contractors in each of the following groups: the Department of Defense (Pentagon); the Atomic Energy Commission (A.E.C.); the National Aeronautic and Space Agency (NASA); and the 25 largest industrial corporations on the *Fortune* magazine list.[32] Table 5-10 presents the groups and the results.

Table 5-10

Contributions from Officers and Directors of the 25 Largest Defense and Industrial Companies in Each of Four Groups, 1968[a]

	Pentagon	A.E.C.	NASA	Fortune Industrial
Total Number of Officers and Directors	856	700	856	1,013
Number of Individual Contributors	176	105	163	228
Total Contributions	$779,753	$306,201	$626,103	$837,239
Republican				
Number of Contributors[b]	161	93	142	212
Amount of Contributions	664,252	270,200	496,602	698,839
Democratic				
Number of Contributors[b]	22	13	27	26
Amount of Contributions	110,000	30,050	129,000	132,150
Miscellaneous				
Number of Contributors[b]	2	6	1	6
Amount of Contributions	5,501	5,951	501	6,250

[a] For each of the four groups, certain individuals were officials of more than one company within that group. They and their contributions have been counted only once.

[b] Due to the presence of individuals who gave to more than one party or cause, the number of Republican, Democratic, and Miscellaneous contributors is larger than the total number of individual contributors given at the top of each column. The first total gives the actual number of individuals.

When the four lists of 25 companies are combined for a list of the 100 largest defense and industrial corporations, it becomes evident that double-counting of contributions will result because several companies appear on more than one list. There is especial congruence between corporations in the Pentagon and NASA lists. In addition, some individuals are officials of more than one company. When all such overlappings are eliminated from the analysis, and both corporations and individuals are counted only once, 70 separate companies and 378 contributing individuals are represented on the four lists. The contributors in these 70 companies gave an aggregate of $1,478,935, divided as follows: Republican, $1,250,284; Democrats, $216,200; and Miscellaneous $12,451. These represent contributions from 378 officers and directors or approximately one-fifth of the total individuals analyzed. Of these, only 53 individuals made gifts to Democrats while 339 gave to Republican causes and nine gave to miscellaneous committees. There were 17 split contributors and six contributors to Republican and miscellaneous committees. The Wallace campaign received not a single contribution.

The few companies on the *Fortune* largest industrial list which are not also among the 25 largest on the other three lists are mainly oil companies which also benefit from military- and defense-related activities. For example, Standard Oil Company of California, Mobil, Texaco, Gulf, Shell, and Standard Oil Company (Indiana) make a significant difference on the *Fortune* list, with a combined total of $186,300 in contributions. Of this total, however, $65,000 was contributed by Richard K. Mellon of Gulf Oil, who was also on the board of General Motors (Pentagon and NASA).

This is basic evidence of the extent of contributions in sums of $500 or more representing managements of the elite of the military-industrial complex. The political interests of many of these companies would seem to be apparent; however, it should be emphasized that persons identified with these companies are assumed to contribute as individuals, not formally on behalf of the corporation. The most telling commentary on Table 5-10 is the consistent disparity between contributions to Republican and to Democratic candidates and committees, ranging from 5 to 1 in the NASA list to 8 to 1 in the *Fortune* list, even in 1968 when the Democrats still controlled the White House and both houses of the Congress. It is therefore clear that most politically active managers of large corporations—even those with large government contracts—seem to share congenial views on public policy and to feel more comfortable with the Republican Party.

Of the companies studied, Litton Industries was the corporation with officers and directors making the largest aggregate contributions—$156,000, including $151,000 to Republicans, $5,000 to miscellaneous committees, and none to Democrats. It is remarkable that this company, fourteenth on the Pentagon list, had no officers or directors who made contributions to Democratic candidates or committees. The Democrats, after all, were in power and Litton had grown to prominence during years of Democratic

dominance in the 1960s. However, the two largest individual Litton contributors were directors, not company officers; these were Henry Salvatori,
who with his wife contributed a total of $95,000, and Vernon Stouffer, who
with his wife contributed a total of $27,000. Directors may have interests
quite divergent from those of the company they serve, so the analyses may
tend to exaggerate the financial participation in politics of a company's
high officials. For example, a director of an industrial firm may be a
banker, and it is difficult to assess the extent to which his banking as
opposed to his industrial interests might play a significant, or indeed any,
role in determining his contributions.

Of the total dollars given by officers and directors of the 70 corporations,
slightly more than half of the money came from directors" For this analysis,
$158,250 contributed by 13 individuals who were officers or directors of
more than one company was not included, for it was impossible to justify
eliminating their overlapping contributions from one group or another.
However, of the 364 contributors who were analyzed, it was determined that
172 directors gave $722,094, or 55 percent of the total money analyzed
($1,320,685). This finding held true in three of the four groups tested
with officers giving more than directors only in the A.E.C. group.

Another analysis included the five largest Pentagon contractors—General
Dynamics, Lockheed, General Electric, United Aircraft, and McDonnell-
Douglas—whose officers and directors contributed a total of $122,677,
splitting it $119,677 to Republicans and only $3,000 to Democrats. McDon-
nell-Douglas and United Aircraft had no Democratic contributors, and
the others had only one each. This is hardly a compelling demonstration of
the financial involvement of the so-called military-industrial complex in
politics! The disparities in giving between Republicans and Democrats
indicate that if such a complex exists, it is mainly Republican, and that
the Democrats were on the whole unsuccessful in drawing out funds from
key members. Certainly, in the face of these data, no simplistic explanation
will suffice, not even the rationalization that the contributions simply
do not surface in the records, or that this compilation is incomplete. It
is not complete, but is not incomplete to an extent that would explain the
main findings: that at the national level at least, not much money is
contributed by these individuals, and that of the money on the record in
sums of $500 or more, not much goes to Democrats.

Centimillionaires

One further analysis was done for 1968. In 1957, *Fortune* interviewed 50
of America's 250 or so persons who possessed a capital accumulation of

---

" In this analysis, officers who were also directors were counted as officers in order to
isolate outside directors.

at least $50,000,000. About two-thirds admitted to being campaign givers. *Fortune* also listed 76 persons with an estimated wealth of $75,000,000 and over, and two-thirds of them are known to have been contributors as well.[33]

In 1968, *Fortune* ran a list of 66 centimillionaires, each with wealth of at least $150,000,000.[34] The rate of contributing is very high, and 46 persons, or 70 percent, are known to have given in 1968. These individuals account for $1,138,502+[40]—more money than any other group of individuals analyzed (divided at $1,021,313+ for Republicans, $106,488 for Democrats, and $10,701 for miscellaneous committees). Of course, the wealthy are most visible, their political behavior merits attention, they are most likely to be asked to contribute, and they are most able to give. Considering the four corporate groups in Table 5-10 in relation to the *Fortune* list of centimillionaires, it is notable that total contributions of officers and directors of the group contributing the most money—the Pentagon group—are still less than the amounts given by the 46 centimillionaires. In fact, the entire group of 392 contributors in the 70 companies gave only $501,183 or 31 percent, more than the centimillionaires.

Candidates Giving $10,000 or More to
Their Own Campaigns

In the prenomination section, emphasis was placed upon the impact of wealthy candidates, both in advancing their own campaigns and in raising the ante for nonwealthy candidates. In the case of Robert Kennedy, no specific amounts could be learned. At least minimal figures were given for Nelson Rockefeller, George Romney, and Harold Stassen. Appendix M gives a partial listing of candidates who are known to have given generously to their own campaigns. The list is partial and illustrative because such information is not often published in the press, and often campaign-fund laws do not cover candidates' personal contributions to their own campaigns. There is, in fact, some distinction to be made between contributions and direct expenditures by the candidate himself. As noted in the Rockefeller section, above, federal gift tax laws are interpreted by at least some tax attorneys to mean that when a candidate gives his own funds to his own campaign, the contribution is considered an out-of-pocket expenditure and not a gift as defined in the law.

Fund-Raising Dinners and Events

A wide but by no means complete collection of newspaper clippings indicates that a minimum of $43.1 million can be accounted for as receipts

---

[40] This total and the Republican total for the centimillionaires does not include $356,000 contributed by Nelson Rockefeller for his own campaign.

at political fund-raising events in 1968 for candidates and committees at all levels. Republicans raised $21.5 million; Democrats, $17.9 million; and the American Independent Party, $3.6 million. The money was raised in different combinations at events ranging in price from $5,000 for cocktail parties to $1 tickets to galas, rallies, and clambakes.[a]

Nixon and Agnew combined in the postnomination period raised at least $7.2 million, but $6 million receipts were from a single closed-circuit event linking 22 cities. Humphrey and Muskie together were counted at $3.1 million postnomination, though Humphrey, if taken for the whole year in events for the President's Club and in his pre- and postnomination campaigns, attracted about $5.4 million. George Wallace was present at all the events when AIP money was raised, so his total is a minimum of $3.6 million. Governor Ronald Reagan was the speaker at events raising at least $2.8 million. Senator Eugene McCarthy appeared at events raising at least $2.1 million. And Robert F. Kennedy spoke at events raising at least $1.4 million in less than half a year. President Johnson appeared at events raising $1.7 million.

The wide newspaper clipping collection for 1969 indicated a minimum of $20.4 million in receipts at fund-raising events for candidates and committees at all levels. Republican receipts were $12.4 million, Democratic were $7.8 million, and miscellaneous were $161,825. President Nixon spoke at one Victory Dinner in Washington which grossed $2.6 million, and during 1969 Vice-President Agnew began to fill more fund-raising engagements, leading to his tremendous role as prime Republican fund raiser in the 1970 elections.

One factor to note about fund-raising events is that the gross receipts are not profit. Costs in promoting and staging the event may run an average of 10 percent to 20 percent. Of course, some receptions, cocktail parties, and coffee klatches are paid for by volunteer hosts, and in some cases, liquor or food is donated. For the $300 million spent for politics at all levels in 1968, at least $30 million must be considered as costs for raising the rest. Mail drives for funds are particularly expensive, but almost any other kind of fund raising, including person-to-person solicitation, entails costs as well.

Broadening the Base

Apart from the national Republican mail drive, the Neighbor-to-Neighbor campaign was again in operation in some areas of the country. Designed as a door-to-door drive for small contributions, this program has been very successful in Minnesota, primarily in Hennepin County. The

---

[a] In newspaper accounts, some figures are gross and some are net. Many events could not be included in the compilation because only amount per ticket—and not number attending—was stated, and vice versa.

Minnesota G.O.P. derived $407,000 from the source in 1968, collected from 70,068 donors. This compares with $364,000 raised in 1964 from this source, and $216,000 in 1960.

The Republican Neighbor-to-Neighbor campaign in Montgomery County, Maryland (basically a suburb of Washington, D.C.), brought in $50,637 from 7,088 contributions. This compared with $41,195 raised in 1964.

Results of Dollars-for-Democrats drives in 1968 are unknown except for Montgomery County, Maryland, where about $27,000 was raised.

6

Labor and Business in Politics

The growing concern of organized labor and corporate business with registration, get-out-the-vote, and contributions drives continued in 1968. In contributions of money and services to direct campaign activities, labor gave more powerful support to the Democrats than ever before. At the same time, significant elements of the business and financial communities were more active financially in politics than ever before.

Labor in Politics

The role of labor in 1968 is particularly difficult to assess. Numerous observers claimed the labor portion of the Democratic coalition was falling apart along with the coalition itself. For the first time in its history, the labor movement took very active sides in a Democratic Presidential prenomination fight, which certainly dissipated some of the money and effort that might have been spent in the general election. For example, almost one-third of labor's unusual allocations to the Humphrey campaign[1] were made in the prenomination period. Labor's early inflexible loyalty to Johnson and Humphrey and to Johnson's Vietnam policy meant less money was available to Humphrey for the crucial general election campaign.

Yet labor mounted a massive drive against George Wallace at a time when he was running strong among rank-and-file union members. And the belated upturn in Humphrey's fortunes just before November 5 must be credited in significant part to labor's efforts. In some respects, 1968 was a chastening experience for labor. Labor leaders spent a good deal of money and effort in directions opposed by many members who favored Robert Kennedy or George Wallace. Yet it may have been the single-minded determination of the leadership to fight Wallace that brought Humphrey as close to victory as he came. Certainly, 1968 exposed the moral issue of the leadership using voluntarily contributed political money for purposes or candidates not to the liking of substantial numbers of the givers; yet the role of leaders is to educate and lead in political as well as in economic affairs, and labor did that.

One dramatic example of the split in the Democratic coalition came early in 1968. In February, the Americans for Democratic Action, an organization which earlier had reflected the liberal-labor alliance, endorsed Eugene McCarthy for President, after a year-long struggle of trying to reconcile opposition to the Vietnam War with support for President John-

191

son. Three union presidents promptly and publicly resigned from ADA, and some union financial support for the organization was discontinued.ª

Also in February, AFL-CIO head George Meany announced that the labor organization would raise $2 million for President Johnson. In fact, labor's planning for Johnson's reelection campaign had begun months earlier, and the unions had already made a film featuring Meany in conversation with the President at the White House. The film cost $3,500 to make, and the AFL-CIO also spent more than $20,000 for prints. Before the President withdrew, AFL-CIO's Committee on Political Education (COPE) sent $5,000 to Wisconsin for the primary campaign.

After Johnson's withdrawal, many labor leaders declared their preference for Humphrey. Labor was, in general, strongly anti-Kennedy, and strove to keep local party leaders off the Kennedy bandwagon right after the President's withdrawal, giving Humphrey a chance to build his support. In April, George Meany was one of the founding members of United Democrats for Humphrey, and on May 17 he headed a group of 162 labor leaders who endorsed Humphrey.

Labor's support of Humphrey and opposition to his rivals for the Democratic nomination sometimes put labor in a most curious position. In the Indiana primary, for example, labor generally supported the favorite-son candidacy of Governor Branigan, rather than either Senator Kennedy or Senator McCarthy, although Branigan's labor record was not impressive. It was estimated that labor spent at least $15,000 in the Indiana primary. In addition, an AFL-CIO COPE official worked full time in Indiana from April 17 until the election, May 7. National representatives of the Steelworkers, Restaurant Employees, and Carpenter unions also worked for Branigan. COPE distributed 269,000 leaflets favoring Humphrey with the slogan, "Stand up for what's good in America and be counted," and some people felt that the slogan was a subtle attempt to exploit the pro-Wallace sentiment in Indiana, since Wallace's slogan was "Stand up for America".[3] However, the leadership of the UAW, one of the biggest unions in the state, worked substantially for Kennedy. As a postelection *New York Times* editorial commented: "Since both Senators [Kennedy and McCarthy] have liberal, prolabor voting records, it is hard to see what legitimate interest of the working man was served by investing funds to defeat either of them."[4]

In California, the only other primary which included a third alternative to Kennedy and McCarthy, labor supported mainly the pro-Humphrey Lynch slate. But Kennedy and even McCarthy had some significant sup-

---

ª The blow was not as strong as believed, however, because labor support for ADA had been diminishing for several years. Union contributions totalled $66,000 in 1957, but only $25,000 ten years later, which was only about 10 percent of ADA's 1967 budget. But nine other union officials stayed in ADA, most conspicuously Walter Reuther.[2]

port among middle-echelon labor leaders in the state and among the rank-and-file.

Labor's floor set-up at the Democratic Convention included walkie-talkies and mobile telephones under the direction of COPE's chief, Alexander Barkan. In addition, 221 union officials or members were delegates in 44 of the state delegations.

During the summer, the labor leadership became aware of the significant pro-Wallace sentiment among the union rank-and-file, although their response to the Wallace threat did not really take shape until after the convention. The press, too, became aware of Wallace's growing appeal, and there were many articles throughout the summer and fall about the unions' fear of Wallace and of a general swing to the right.[5] In September, as the general board of the AFL-CIO gathered to formally endorse Humphrey—which was unanimously done on September 18 (although some silent abstentions were noted)—a Gallup Poll revealed that for the first time in more than 32 years less than 50 percent of union voters were supporting the Democratic nominee. Humphrey had 42 percent of union voters to 35 percent for Nixon and 15 percent for Wallace, with 8 percent undecided.[6]

During the general election period, some Democratic Congressional candidates complained that COPE was not putting enough funds into their races and claimed that they as popular Congressmen could help the Humphrey effort. The scope of the union effort was summarized in the Humphrey section above. Few doubt that it was one of the primary reasons for the Humphrey surge in late October. In speaking to the COPE administrative committee several months after the election, George Meany claimed that organized labor had cut the Wallace vote among rank-and-file from an estimated 30 percent in September to 6–8 percent in the election.[7] Even if Meany exaggerated, the labor effort in 1968 was impressive indeed.

SCOPE, an organization not directly related to the labor movement, played a significant part in the unions' anti-Wallace campaign. Late in 1967, a group of prominent Southern moderates and Liberals formed the Southern Committee on Political Ethics (SCOPE) designed to emphasize the importance of ethics and morality in politics through public education. The chairman of SCOPE was Brooks Hays, a former Congressman from Arkansas. Many of the committee members had close ties to the Johnson Administration, and it was suggested at the time of SCOPE's formation that its real purpose was to bolster Johnson in the South for his reelection campaign.[8] When SCOPE surfaced during the 1968 general election campaign, it was as the publisher of several carefully researched and documented anti-Wallace materials, particularly "The Wallace Labor Record." The 16-page "Record" compared wages, unemployment compensation, state educational expenditures per pupil, crime rates, and taxes in Alabama and other states and cities. It was a detailed document, and SCOPE sold 475,000 copies. The purchasers, presumably, were labor unions. SCOPE's address in Washington was that of a public relations firm with close ties to the DNC and the AFL-CIO. In any case, the SCOPE materials were helpful to labor in its anti-Wallace effort.

Labor Money

To channel direct financial assistance to Federal candidates, the unions organize auxiliaries, usually managed by officials of the parent union and financed by voluntary contributions from union members. However, the amounts of money raised are relatively small: at the national level, an average of 5–6 cents per union member is collected. It takes many gifts to aggregate the big sums sometimes contributed to candidates. A single large contributor may give as much to one candidate—say $1,000 or $5,000—as a single international union representing the contributions of thousands of individuals. In fact, the actual money labor puts into politics tends to be overrated; probably more important is the manpower provided by unions, particularly for registration and election-day activities. The labor movement generally grasped early the need for strenuous precinct work, with all the drudgery of registration and vote drives, and at times has carried on the work in uncongenial atmospheres, such as in the South.

Labor Committee Expenditures

In 1968, 37 national-level labor-related political committees reported expenditures of $7.1 million.[9] This represented almost twice the amount spent four years earlier, reflecting labor's extraordinary efforts.

Table 6-1

Labor National-Level Committees Gross Disbursements, 1956, 1960, 1964, 1968

	Reporting Committees	Gross Disbursements
1956	17	$2.2 million
1960	21	2.3 million
1964	31	3.7 million
1968	37	7.1 million

All these funds come from voluntary contributions, sometimes deducted from members' paychecks under agreements with employers. They represent funds filtered up to the national or so-called international headquarters from state and local affiliates.

In 1968, there were four unions whose committees reported spending more than $500,000 each; only COPE was in that class in 1964 and 1960. There were 16 labor committees which spent more than $10,000 each (including the two separate UAW committees), an increase from ten in 1964 and four in 1960. The following table compares the ten largest labor committees in 1968—those whose gross expenditures were more than $200,000—with their total expenditures in the previous two Presidential election years.

Table 6-2

Gross Disbursements of the Ten Largest Labor National-Level Committees, 1960, 1964, 1968

	1968	1964	1960
Committee for Good Government [a]	$ 251,000	$122,000	$ 77,000
COPE (AFL-CIO)	1,207,000	989,000	794,000
DRIVE (Teamsters)	211,000	270,000	50,000
ILGWU	1,077,000	426,000	316,000
Machinists	572,000	260,000	193,000
Marine Engineers	262,000	—	—
Seafarers	947,000	121,000	—
Trainmen	215,000	43,000	10,000
UAW [a]	309,000	269,000	61,000
Steelworkers	240,000	251,000	239,000

[a] Adding the two UAW committees together, $560,000 was spent in 1968, $391,000 in 1964, and $138,000 in 1960.

In all three years, the disbursements of these committees, which are about one-third of all the labor committees reporting in each year, accounted for 75 percent of the total spent by all the committees.

COPE. Each year, COPE transfers approximately one-half of its funds to its state affiliates. While the usual reason given for these transfers is that the states can then decide to which candidates the money will be given, it is also true that the recipients of those funds will then not appear in the Federal reports which COPE files in Washington. In 1968, COPE reported transfers of $710,000 to state COPEs for redistribution to candidates.[10] Other AFL-CIO unions distributed 55 million pieces of literature (local and state unions distributed an additional 60 million pieces), and COPE made and distributed 250,000 bumper stickers and 250,000 buttons.

Seafarers. The contributions of the two political committees of the Seafarers International Union (SIU) were notable for several reasons. First, of course, their size: from 1964 to 1968, there was an eightfold increase in the SIU's political contributions. Measured another way, SIU's expenditures were three percent of the total of all national labor committees in 1964, and in 1968, when the total itself had almost doubled, SIU's share rose to 13 percent. SIU rose from eighth largest in size of expenditures in 1964 to third largest in 1968.

Second, SIU's contributions to the Presidential race were unusually large. As noted, these contributions constituted almost one-third of the total of all such labor committee contributions, and in the prenomination period, SIU's gifts were almost 40 percent of the total labor contributions to the Johnson and then to the Humphrey campaigns. Third, questions were raised about the possible link between SIU's early gifts to Johnson and Humphrey campaign committees and favorable government action on an extradition request by Canada for an SIU official who had jumped bail to this country after conviction.[b] Finally, SIU allegedly made some of their political contributions in 1968 from the union treasury rather than from separate, voluntarily contributed funds. In 1970, the SIU was indicted for violating the Federal law which prohibits the use of union dues money for political contributions.

The Gilligan Case

Labor's commitment to Humphrey and to the Administration Vietnam policy led to the strange and widely reported story of John Gilligan's Senatorial campaign in Ohio.[12] The plot was thick and there were contradictory reports, but the charge was made that labor was withholding funds from Gilligan because he was neutral in the Presidential contest during the prenomination period, and he did not vote for Humphrey at the Convention.

In the fall of 1967, the labor movement agreed to help finance a major effort in 1968 to unseat Ohio's conservative, antilabor Democratic Senator, Frank Lausche. As one part of the preparation for that effort, Ohio's unions raised the per capita quota from 5 to 10 cents per month. The challenger was John Gilligan, a liberal former Congressman. For the first time in Ohio's history, both the state AFL-CIO and the Democratic State Committee made preprimary endorsements—for Gilligan over Lausche. In that primary, the labor movement used computers to pinpoint mailings to 800,000 homes, and to prepare lists for canvassing union members, techniques which had first been employed in 1964 in Pennsylvania and two other areas.

Records of national-level labor committees show at least $109,050 in contributions to Gilligan's campaign before the May 7 primary.[c] However,

---

[b] In spite of denials by all parties in the case, and the absence of any proof, newspapers found the timing of the two events—Secretary Rusk's decision and the SIU's contributions—remarkable.[11]

[c] An additional $20,439 was contributed between March and June, but it is not known how much of this was preprimary and how much postnomination.

Gilligan actually received much more from labor, through contributions of the Ohio COPE and other state groups. An Ohio reporter put the figure at $270,000 (most, but not all, for the primary), with the Ohio COPE, the Ohio Labor Political Action Committee, and a United Organized Labor group serving as conduits for labor funds.[13] One source claimed that labor contributions accounted for 85 percent of Gilligan's primary receipts.

After Gilligan defeated Senator Lausche, labor reportedly pressured him to endorse Humphrey. Gilligan, a moderate on Vietnam whose winning primary campaign had been supported by local McCarthy and Kennedy supporters, wanted to stay neutral in the Presidential race. Over the summer, an unofficial Presidential preference primary was organized by McCarthy supporters to take place in mid-August. In an apparent attempt to deflect attention from this straw vote, Humphrey supporters called for a caucus of the state's Convention delegation, which others had wanted to postpone until the delegation was in Chicago. Humphrey received 60 of the 115 votes at that caucus, while many people—including John Gilligan—left before the voting took place. There were then charges that labor gave $250,000 for voter registration to the county chairmen whose delegates had voted for Humphrey, rather than to Gilligan as promised.

Both Humphrey and Gilligan denied that promised labor money was not forthcoming. But in the fall, labor's oft-reported promise of $250,000 was changed to a promise of $100,000. And it was only after the Ohio COPE's very late formal endorsement of Gilligan, on September 27, that $10,000 from national COPE—given to the state COPE several months earlier but reportedly "stopped" on orders of labor leaders—was released. Records show that Gilligan received $49,455 from national labor committees in the postprimary period, a little more than one-third the amount reported from these committees in the primary period.

While it is possible that Gilligan was "punished" by labor—with less money than promised and needed and with its coming late—it is also possible that labor committees simply had less to give than they had planned. While Senator Lausche could be characterized as antilabor, the Republican candidate, William Saxbe, had a moderate if not prolabor record. Hence, it is also possible that the unions feared Saxbe less than Lausche, and so were not as open-handed in their aid to Gilligan. Including both the primary and the general election, Gilligan received more from reporting national labor committees than any other Senatorial or Congressional candidate in 1968.

A very different labor-Gilligan story in 1968 concerned a "mystery committee." The Committee for the Advancement of Urban Interests (CAUI), located at the same address as national COPE headquarters but without a telephone number and disclaimed by COPE, received contributions of at least $56,900 from reporting labor committees. At least $15,950 came from COPE[14] The CAUI was believed to be a paper organization set up solely to channel labor contributions, and some observers believed all of its donations were to Gilligan.

Other Labor Cases

Morse. If some thought that labor pressured Gilligan because of his Vietnam views or his refusal to endorse Humphrey before the Convention, the case of Oregon's Senator Wayne Morse presented a strong counterargument. Morse was one of the most vocal critics of President Johnson's Vietnam policy, and he, too, stayed neutral in the Presidential race until after the National Convention. In fact, Morse did not even attend the Convention. Nevertheless, he received $137,496 from reporting national labor committees, second only to Gilligan. Had Morse won, he would have become chairman of the Senate Labor and Public Welfare Committee, and this alone could have elicited labor's strong support.

Clark vs. Dirksen. William Clark was the Democratic candidate running against Senator Everett Dirksen in Illinois. Clark's liberal, prolabor record stood in contrast to Dirksen's support of right-to-work and other antilabor measures, and yet Dirksen received almost the same amount of money from labor sources as did Clark.

Clark received $7,500 from national labor committees, and Dirksen received $6,700 from these groups, including a $5,000 contribution from the Seafarers. In addition, a local source reported that Clark received a $5,000 contribution from a Teamsters vice-president in Chicago, and that Dirksen received $5,000 from the Teamsters local in Chicago. That local had endorsed Clark, yet contributed to Dirksen, and the head of the local explained: "We live in the state, business contributes to both [sides] and we contribute to both."[15]

Registration

Expenditures for voter registration can legally be paid for from union treasuries, and those expenditures are not included in the reports of the labor political committees. In 1968, national COPE spent approximately $1 million for registration, which was about the same as was spent in 1964. Since it was reported that for every $2 spent by national COPE the states received and spent $1 (with no state receiving less than in 1966 or 1964), at least $1.5 million should have been spent by labor on registration, relating mostly to Congressional elections. Labor's registration drives concentrated on marginal Congressional districts, and were carried out selectively in labor-oriented and heavily Democratic precincts where rank-and-file strength is to be found. Unlike 1964, the Democratic National Committee did not have a separate registration drive in 1968, presumably for lack of funds. Labor's registration efforts are credited with adding 4.6 million voters to the rolls in 1968.

On election day, close to 100,000 people mobilized by labor worked, baby-sitting, driving people to the polls, distributing materials, telephone canvassing, and poll-watching. The value of this manpower is immense, and most of it is volunteered. Some of it is paid for by the political action funds of unions, such as for workers who take the day off (unpaid) from their regular employment; and, ironically, some of it is paid for by employers who sign labor contracts providing election day as a paid holiday.

As an example of how much local election-day activities can cost, a Philadelphia newspaper reported that the local Democrats had $218,000 to spend, augmented by $100,000 from labor.[16] Although these figures may be inflated, it is not unheard of to spend that much in a major city on election day.

Postelection. After 1968, labor decided to carry out annual rather than biennial voter registration drives, and $500,000 was earmarked for this in 1969. Although the union's political, voluntary funds were reported running behind 1968 (which would be expected for a nonelection year), labor's effort on behalf of Democratic candidates in several special Congressional races was significant. In Wisconsin, unions reportedly gave $20,000 as well as nine full-time and nine part-time volunteers to David Obey's campaign for Melvin Laird's seat, which Obey won. In Montana, $10,400 from labor constituted 14 percent of the cost of John Melcher's successful campaign for another Republican seat vacated by a Nixon appointment. And in California, the Machinists reportedly had 60 workers full time for the last four days of John K. Van de Kamp's unsuccessful campaign against Barry Goldwater, Jr.[17]

Labor Prosecutions

As mentioned above, a 1970 grand jury returned an indictment charging the Seafarers International Union and several of its officers and members with making and conspiring to make political contributions in violation of federal law. The indictment specifically alleges that the Seafarers, through its Political Activity Donation Account (SPAD) in 1968, contributed a total of $20,000 each to Republican and Democratic campaign committees. A continuing conspiracy since 1962 to have the union make unlawful political contributions was also alleged.

In 1968, three officers of the St. Louis Pipefitters Local Union No. 562 were convicted of conspiring to violate federal law by contributing $150,000 to political candidates during the 1964 and 1966 election campaigns.[18]

The conviction was affirmed by a Court of Appeals, but further appeals are in process. The union was fined $5,000 and each of the three officers was sentenced to one year imprisonment and fined $1,000.

A year later, in connection with the mayoral election in Baltimore, two Iron Workers Union officials were indicted for falsifying records to cover up a political contribution of $13,000.[19]

Business In Politics

Businessmen in 1968 returned to the Republican fold in large numbers, restoring the party's traditional support in the business community. The desertions from Goldwater generally returned to Nixon. As shown in the previous chapter, the contributions of officers and directors of selected corporations and business groups were heavily Republican.

During both the prenomination and general election campaigns, several newspapers conducted surveys of businessmen to determine their Presidential preferences. The earliest of these was an April *Washington Post* survey of 298 "leading executives," including members of the Business Council.[20] There were 160 responses: 91 were for Nixon; 38 for Rockefeller; 24 for Humphrey; 3 for Kennedy; 2 for Reagan; and one each for McCarthy and Wallace. Almost one-half (74) of the 160 who responded had either voted for Johnson or neither candidate in 1964, and in this group 26 were for Rockefeller; 25 for Nixon, 19 for Humphrey, 3 for Kennedy and one for McCarthy.

In early October, a *Wall Street Journal* survey of 50 business executives who had supported Johnson in 1964 found less than one-half of them were supporting Nixon, with the remainder split between Humphrey supporters and those who were undecided.[21] The article noted that Humphrey as Vice-President had cultivated support in the business community. A larger *New York Times* survey in mid-October showed significantly more support for Nixon among the 1964 Johnson supporters, and very strong Nixon sentiment among businessmen in general.[22] This poll of 1,269 of "American industry's top executives" returned 635 responses, of whom 85 percent planned to vote for Nixon. Of the 1964 Johnson supporters, the survey reported 65 percent were supporting Nixon.

Business and Professional Committees

In 1968, there were 33 national-level committees of businessmen or professionals which filed reports with the Clerk of the House. This was a threefold increase in the number of such committees from four years earlier. Of the $4.3 million reported spent by all national-level miscellaneous committees,[23] a little more than $2 million was spent by committees identified with business or professional interests. More than $1.6 million of this total was disbursed to candidates, mostly Senatorial and Congressional candidates. Only $22,000 was contributed by such committees to Nixon or Humphrey committees. The two largest business and professional committees were the Business-Industry Political Action Committee (BIPAC) and the American Medical Political Action Committee (AMPAC), which together accounted for 61 percent of the total expenditures by all such committees.

BIPAC. Spurred in part by labor's growing sophistication and ability to amass individual contributions, BIPAC was created in 1963 "to provide financial support to Congressional candidates who support the principles of constitutional government." BIPAC's political activities are supported by voluntary contributions from about 10,000 businessmen.[24] Members contribute at least $10 per year but gifts of $99 are encouraged—that is the cost of a sustaining membership and giving that amount means that the giver need not be listed by name and address in financial reports required by law. In 1968, there were only 152 contributions of $100 or more, of which seven were $500 or more.

In addition to the political funds, BIPAC receives tax-deductible contributions from individuals and corporations for year-round educational activities. In order to avoid violating the law, all of BIPAC's activities for the three months prior to a federal election are paid for from political rather than educational funds. This includes payments for staff salaries, rent, and other expenses in the period when most activities are geared to partisan campaigning. Most other business-oriented political committees and their union counterparts have not interpreted the law as requiring this procedure, although they too spend much of their time and resources on partisan electioneering in primaries as well as in general elections.

BIPAC disbursed $519,700 to candidates in 1968, an average of more than $3,000 per campaign for each of the 169 races supported. BIPAC aided candidates in 49 states (all except Vermont) and claimed a winning average of 61 percent for the endorsed. As might be expected, the recipients of BIPAC support were almost all Republicans. In the general election, only eight of the 126 House candidates supported were Democrats; all of those were from the South, seven were incumbents, and all eight won. None of the 20 Senatorial candidates supported in the general election was a Democrat, but all three candidates supported in the Senatorial primaries were Democrats, two from the South. The third case was particularly interesting: BIPAC supported the Ohio incumbent Democratic Senator, conservative Frank Lausche, in his primary battle against liberal John Gilligan, whom labor supported heavily; then, in the general election, BIPAC supported the Republican candidate, William Saxbe, who won.

AMPAC. AMPAC was created by the American Medical Association in 1961, to further the goal of "minimizing government control over the medical profession," and AMA's governing officials appoint the board of directors of AMPAC. Like most political action organizations, AMPAC engages in both political education activities, which can be funded from corporate or organizational contributions, and in partisan political activities, which are funded from dues and contributions of members and other supporters. The AMA and AMPAC have the same field staffs, and they, like BIPAC staffers, are paid from political funds when engaged in partisan political activity, and from nonpolitical funds when engaged in political education activities. The AMA gave more than $1 million to AMPAC for educational activities in 1968. Medical personnel pay dues of between $10 and $5,000 for AMPAC membership; nonmedical "friends of medicine," may also join. "Friends of Medicine," such as pharmaceutical firms, are reported to comprise 15 percent of AMPAC's membership, although the organization will not reveal its total membership.[25]

From 1962 to 1968, AMPAC spent more than $2 million on political activities, almost all of which was contributed to candidates. However, the recipients of most of AMPAC's political contributions are masked because the contributions are made to state affiliates of AMPAC, which in turn made the actual gifts to candidates. AMPAC officials privately acknowledge that the chief reason for channeling contributions from the national committee through state affiliates instead of giving directly to candidates is to relieve the local candidates of possible embarrassment. In addition, this decentralized process means that there is no way to determine from the official reports filed in Washington which candidates actually benefit from AMPAC's contributions. Of AMPAC's total expenditures of $682,000 in 1968, almost $584,000 was transferred to state affiliates.

In addition to the funds spent by AMPAC, the state and local affiliates raise and spend considerable additional amounts of money. AMPAC officials estimate that the state and local organizations spend five times as much as does the national organization, which would mean that medically related political action groups spent $3.5–$4 million in 1968. In 1968, only three incumbent Congressmen who had supported Medicare received contributions from AMPAC. In all, AMPAC supported candidates in 162 House and 23 Senate races in 1968, and local groups contributed to another 150 races.

Although few states have comprehensive disclosure laws, there is detailed information on national, state, and local medical PAC contributions for a few states. In Indiana, Congressional candidates received $4,500 from AMPAC, $33,500 from the state group, and $4,500 from local groups. In Pennsylvania, the state group contributed $32,800 to candidates, while $7,500 came from AMPAC and $5,000 from local groups. In Virginia, however, the national and state contributions almost matched: there were $15,000 from the state group and $14,500 from AMPAC.[26]

Other Business Committees. Of the other business committees, most are made up of people from one industry (often leaders of a trade association), or in some cases, from one firm, and the names of the committees are often deceptive. In many cases, the contributions of such committees are to members of the House or Senate committees which deal with legislation relating to the industry involved, or to members of the tax-writing committees in Congress. Late in the 1968 campaign, an investigative reporter presented some statistics on this practice: such so-called "special-interest groups" had contributed $500,000 to Congressional campaigns in the last three years (1965–1968), 15 of 535 Congressmen had accepted contributions of $500 to $14,000—after they had helped shaped or kill bills that affected the contributing group—and more than 150 members of "key Congressional committees" had accepted contributions from groups set up by lobbies having specific business before their committees.[27] The writer noted that there is nothing illegal in such practices as long as they do not involve any specific promises on voting.

The federal prohibition against corporate contributions does not apply to partnerships, and a new committee appeared in 1968 which represented brokerage firms, most of which are partnerships. The Exchange Firms Campaign Committee received a total of $187,000 from individuals and brokerage houses. Contributions of $5,000 each were received from such well-known partnership firms as Reynolds and Co.; White Weld and Co.; and Loeb, Rhodes and Co.; among others. The committee disbursed $146,000 to Congressional candidates in both parties, in amounts as high as $5,000. Stockbrokers at the time publicly admitted that the group's political activity was triggered by a new toughness among Federal regulators regarding brokerage commissions, use of inside information, and mutual fund management. Spokesmen said: "This is simply an attempt to support candidates who have shown . . . a willingness to listen to the industry's problems."[28]

The business or industry represented by some of the committees is apparent in their name, as the one noted above. These committees, as well as their deceptively named counterparts, often support Congressional candidates who favor or oppose one particular measure. The Life Underwriters Education Fund and Political Action Committee spent $70,000 in 1968, mainly "in support of candidates who oppose expansion of Social Security coverage."[29] The Construction Equipment Political Action Committee (CEPAC) is concerned about possible Pentagon dumping of huge quantities of surplus equipment on the market when the Vietnam War ends. Like BIPAC, CEPAC asks for $99 contributions, but its total disbursements were less than $4,000 in 1968. There is also a Scrap Iron Political Action

Committee, which spent only $1,400; a Truck Operators Non-Partisan Committee, which disbursed almost $75,000 to Congressmen concerned with interstate highways; the American Nursing Home Education and Political Action Committee, which spent $90,000 in 1968, of which about $33,000 went to candidates, including $5,600 to Nixon committees and $1,000 to a Humphrey dinner committee; and the Savings Association Political Education Committee, which disbursed more than $36,000 of its total expenditures, including $2,000 to Humphrey committees. As listed in Table 4–17, bankers, canners, automotive retailers, dentists, food processors, forest products, freezers, home furnishings, motel development, and shoe manufacturers were among other industries and professions contributing to 1968 campaigns.

Other industries have committees with innocuous-sounding names but the same general purposes in making political contributions.[30] The Committee for American Principles represents clothing and textile manufacturers, whose main interest is import quotas on foreign textiles, and disbursed $5,000 to campaigns in 1968, including $1,000 to Senator Dirksen for a speaking engagement. Dirksen also received $2,500 from the Government Improvement Group (GIG), which is identified with candy manufacturers. The GIG received no contributions of more than $99, so the contributors are not listed on filed reports, while it disbursed almost $17,000 to campaigns. The Committee for Action is composed of certain construction contractors; it spent more than $100,000 in 1968, of which $71,000 went to candidates. The Committee for Economic Growth is identified with the restaurant business; its $41,000 in disbursements (of $50,000 total expenditures) went primarily to Congressmen on tax-writing and labor committees. An only partly disguised committee is the Committee on American Leadership, whose name is an acronym for the coal industry it represents. One of the few committees to contribute to the Presidential candidates, COAL gave $1,400 to Nixon and $1,000 to Humphrey from among total disbursements of $20,000.

Among the committees whose contributors come from only one firm, the most noted in 1968 was the Effective Government Association (EGA), which was found to be composed of more than 150 employees of Merrill Lynch, Pierce, Fenner and Smith. The EGA received between $100 and $500 from each employee-contributor (only $50 was received in less than $100 contributions), and disbursement of the $46,000 raised was reportedly controlled by company executives. In mid-October, a *Washington Post* article[31] noted that as of September 1, all but one of EGA's contributions had gone to Congressmen on "relevant committees," and that the contributions were being made at a time when Merrill Lynch was charged by the SEC with illegal action concerning information on the earnings of Douglas Aircraft Company. Two weeks later, a *New York Times*[32] article noted that since the earlier *Washington Post* article, the EGA had given nothing to Congressional candidates, but instead had given identical amounts to various national Republican and Democratic organizations, including $5,000 each to the Republican and Democratic National Committees. However, the filed reports on the Presidential campaigns show $6,000 from EGA to Nixon committees and nothing to Humphrey committees.

The Fund for Good Government was made up of officials of the Chemical Bank New York Trust Company, the North Street Good Government Group was named after the main office address of General Foods Corporation, and the Citizens' Committee for Improved Government represented U.S. Plywood-Champion Papers, Inc. officials. Each of these three committees spent less than $10,000 in 1968.

Apart from the official filings of national-level committees, it is extremely difficult to obtain any information on the contributions of individual businessmen or the financial activities of business-related committees, although there is undoubtedly significant activity at the local level. There are always rumors and stories of political-financial activities on the part of corporate executives, but they can rarely be substantiated. For example, a Drew Pearson and Jack Anderson article[33] alleged that Chrysler Corporation "suggested emphatically" to 3,500 of its executives that they contribute to the party of their choice, at the rate of $5 per $1,000 in yearly income, with two top company officials disbursing those employee checks to the party chairmen in states where Chrysler has interests. Further, the article charged that it was suggested that executives in the $25,000-and-over income range contribute in cash, and that this cash was disbursed by a company vice-president to candidates. In spite of the tone of these charges, it is not illegal to organize company fund-raising activities as long as the employees are not coerced into making contributions, and as long as such activities are not carried out on company time or use no company resources. On a local level, a Good Government Fund in California was reportedly made up of contributions from Pacific Telephone Company employees, with its disbursements determined by "executives and volunteers."[34]

BEM. Not all business groups are industry-oriented or conservative. The Business Executives Move for Peace in Vietnam (BEM) is a nonpartisan organization whose purpose is to educate and involve businessmen in appropriate antiwar activities. BEM spokesmen testified before the Republican and Democratic national convention platform hearings, and BEM had hospitality suites at both the Miami and Chicago conventions.[a] BEM did not support any candidates in 1968, although its leadership was largely pro-McCarthy, and the group's only electorally related activity was to suggest where contributions could be sent to assist three Senate antiwar candidates.

---

[a] BEM's total expenditures in 1968 are estimated to have been less than $100,000.

Corporate Bipartisan Efforts

Once again, numerous corporations undertook bipartisan campaigns to encourage their employees to register, to vote, and to contribute to the party or candidate of their choice.

Aerojet. Aerojet-General's program, the oldest in the country, continued its record of success. In ten years, almost one-half million dollars has been raised from this one program.

Year	Total Raised
1958	$ 24,000
1960	60,000
1962	97,000
1964	136,000
1966	82,200
1968	90,815

The fall-off in 1966 and 1968 occurred at least in part because there were fewer employees than in earlier years. In 1968, the average contribution was $8.27 and 61 percent of employees participated; in 1964, the average had been $6.85 with 72.5 percent of employees contributing. The recipients designated by the 11,000 contributors in 1968 included 107 candidates and committees.

Hughes. Hughes Aircraft Company established its Active Citizenship Campaign in 1964 and had an outstanding first year, collecting $86,000 from more than 6,000 employees (about one-quarter of the total employment). In 1968, the Campaign again received contributions from more than 6,000 employees, and the total raised was $101,000. The average contribution was up from $13.76 in 1964 to $16.47 in 1968. Contributions in 1968 were earmarked for 150 candidates and four parties in 28 states. In addition to fund raising, Hughes operated active registration and rally programs. In 1968, more than 5,000 employees were registered to vote on company premises, up from 3,500 in 1964. There were 34 noon-hour rallies at various company sites in the state, at which 22,000 employees heard 68 candidates—one Presidential, 23 Congressional, 44 state—speak on issues. In four years, 12,000 Hughes employees were registered to vote, 255 candidates spoke at noon-hour political rallies, and more than one-quarter million dollars had been contributed to 410 campaigns and five political parties.

TRW. Thompson Ramo Wooldridge, Inc., conducts a Good Government Program. In addition to the usual program of contributions from employees who designate the recipients, employees may contribute to TRW's Good

Government Fund through a payroll-deduction system. A Disbursement Committee apportions the funds to each of four categories of recipients. The total disbursed in 1968, from both the Fund and employee-designated contributions, was $117,372; an increase from $87,000 in 1964.

	1964	1968
Raised	$85,700	$111,816
Carryover from other years	12,270	36,870
Total	97,970	148,686
Disbursed:		
To political parties—local, state and national	44,000	47,525
To candidates, partisan and nonpartisan	27,200	55,247
To special Dem. and Rep. fund-raising activities	13,300	8,000
To Dem. and Rep. Congressional Campaign Committees	2,500	6,600
Total	$87,000	$117,372

California Good Citizenship Committee. In 1968, a statewide, bipartisan committee operated in California to encourage management-sponsored, employee-directed, bipartisan in-plant political programs including registration, contributing, and voting. In 1968, more than 50 companies employing a combined total of 600,000 workers raised at least as much as the $276,000 raised in 1966 (the first year the program operated) from companies employing 500,000 workers. Some companies conducted programs in which employees sent money directly to candidates or committees, so that the company does not know who gave how much; if such amounts were known, the California program total would be significantly higher.

Michigan. In Michigan, there are Employee Citizenship Participation Programs, and the state's Democratic State Central Committee has summarized its receipts from the program for every year since 1964.

Year	No. of Firms	No. of Partici- pating Employees	Total Contributions to Democratic Party
1964	16	1,359	$24,015
1965	14	1,199	24,529
1966	22	1,251	32,801
1967	14	1,092	24,858
1968	10	Not Known	34,316

Other Forms of Corporate Contributions

Passage of the Williams Amendment, noted above, eliminated the avenue of advertising in party program books as a form of corporate political contributing, except for the major parties' convention program books every four years.

One interesting example of short-term corporate extension of credit, which is technically illegal, came to light in a prenomination campaign in 1968, and the occurrence is worth noting because it turns out not to be uncommon. An advertising agency carrying a national account worked out an arrangement with the campaign for weekly payments. It found, however, that on Wednesday or Friday it might have to pay out of its own treasury for a broadcast commitment, and it would be reimbursed by the campaign only every Tuesday. At one point when placements were heavy, the agency was out $500,000 of its own money for a period of almost a week. Unless an agency demands an advance, or refuses to place advertising without prepayment by the campaign, it can get into this bind. In the case cited, for professional reasons of wanting to do a good job and because ad firm executives were sympathetic, the agency was willing to extend itself this way.

Corporate Prosecutions

Although relating to campaigns in earlier years, a series of federal prosecutions of corporate political practices came to light during 1968 and 1969. Beginning in the Johnson Administration and continuing in the Nixon Administration, the Internal Revenue Service undertook a broad inquiry leading to 15 indictments and 14 convictions of businesses for deducting as legitimate business expenses payments that were in effect political contributions. These concealed payments violated the federal law prohibiting corporations from giving anything of value on behalf of federal candidates.

The businesses involved included three saving and loan associations, one bank, one brewery, one liquor wholesaler, two manufacturing companies, one real estate firm, one packing company, two advertising agencies, and two shipping companies. Most of these were located in southern California. Four of the companies were units of the late Howard F. Ahmanson's financial empire, and they pleaded guilty to illegally contributing a total of $50,026 to an unnamed Presidential candidate in 1964. In all, the guilty firms were fined a total of almost $200,000, but no corporate officials were penalized.

7 The Aftermath

The aftermath of an election exposes the strength and resiliency of each party. Considerable attention focused on the financial state of the two major parties in 1969.

The Republicans

After the Republicans' ideological split and shattering defeat in 1964, some observers questioned whether the party could survive, and many speculated on how long it might be before the party prospered again. While the Republicans could point to a cash balance in early 1965, in terms of political power the party was very much in trouble. The RNC was turned over to Ray Bliss, an effective, nonideological, nuts-and-bolts party man, and a turn-about was begun.

Four years later, Bliss resigned, having helped lead the Republican Party to a renaissance few thought possible. By early 1969, the Republicans not only had won the Presidency, they had increased the number of Republican Governors from 17 to 31, the highest total for the party since 1920; of Republican Senators from 32 to 43, and House members from 140 to 192, both the highest since 1956; of state legislatures from seven to 20, the highest since 1954; and elected 1,420 more county officials and nearly 100 mayors. The RNC had 190 full-time employees and a budget of $3.2 million. In short, the Republicans in early 1969 looked even better than the Democrats four years earlier, sporting a relatively unified party, an Administration in power, a strong national committee, and money.

As the Democratic experience of 1964-8 shows, the projection of future success based on present advantage is by no means a sure thing. The political results in 1969 were neither clear-cut nor one-sided. There were seven special Congressional elections, involving five seats which had been Republican and two which had been Democratic: the Democrats won five of the seats, a net loss of three for the Republicans. The November elections went the other way, with the Republicans winning the year's two gubernatorial races, in New Jersey and Virginia. John Lindsay's reelection as Mayor of New York—as the Liberal Party's candidate after having lost the Republican Party primary, and with major support from liberal Democrats—was hardly a Republican victory.

In the first flush of electoral success and political power, the Republicans talked of the possibility of winning control of both the House and

Senate in 1970. Later, the unrealistic goal of control of the House was quietly dropped, and primary attention focused on the Senate, where with seven more seats, plus Vice-President Agnew's tie-breaking vote, the Republicans would be in control. In addition, the Republicans were also planning on major efforts to win control of state legislatures, which would be drawing the lines for new Congressional districts based on the 1970 census.

During the Democratic Administrations in the 1960s, commentators and Republicans often loudly protested the secrecy and credibility gap concerning DNC finances. But once they were the ruling party, the Republicans' financial practices, while much more open, contained elements of ambiguity. One example concerned the six Illinois committees that weren't there. In March 1969, filings with the Clerk of the House revealed that eleven national-level Republican committees had received $268,610 in contributions from six different committees in Illinois.[a] The names and total amounts contributed by the Chicago committees were:

Illinois Citizens for Constitutional Government	$47,400
Illinois Citizens for Constitutional Progress	38,900
Illinois Citizens for Good Government	50,400
Illinois Committee for Good Government	50,900
Illinois Constitutional Government Committee	43,860
Illinois Free Enterprise Committee	37,150

In conformity with Federal law, each national committee received no more than $5,000 from each of the donor Illinois committees.

In trying to find out the sources of this sudden inheritance, one quickly learned that there were no telephone listings for any of the committees, and that no Republican leader in Chicago would admit ever hearing of them. An official at the RNC said that the sources of the funds could not be revealed because they would dry up. He said that the committees had been campaign groups operating solely within Illinois, and the money in question was just-discovered surplus funds from the campaign. Since Illinois had no disclosure law for political contributions, no reports were required of the committees. The treasurer of the Illinois State Republican Central Committee and an aide to the treasurer of the Illinois Citizens' Committee for Nixon-Agnew said that theirs had been the only two committees officially receiving funds for the Presidential campaign in Illinois, and that they had never heard of the six committees in question. Many suspected that, in fact, the committees were dummy fronts, as commonly used in politics: that the money was not surplus campaign funds but new

[a] Two of the receiving committees were long-standing Republican groups; the Republican Campaign Committee, which received $30,000; and the Republican National Finance Operations Committee, which also received $30,000. The other nine receiving committees were 1968 campaign groups still operative in 1969.

contributions, and that all or most of it came from just one person, one of Nixon's major financial supporters in Chicago. If these suppositions are not true, the RNC harmed its credibility by not revealing the facts in the situations, and if they are true, the attempted secrecy partly failed and the Republicans credibility was still damaged.[1]

A few months later, the Republicans used the dinner dodge to hide the names of more than 2,600 contributors to their victory celebration. The Victory Dinner, twice postponed because of President Nixon's schedule and former President Eisenhower's death, was held on May 7 and grossed about $2.6 million. Of the net profit of about $2.5 million, $500,000 went to pay for transition costs beyond the federal subsidy, about $1 million went to the RNC, and the remaining $1 million was divided 60-40 percent, respectively, for the House and Senate campaign committees. Officially, the dinner was sponsored by the Republican Victory Dinner Committee, which was exempt from federal disclosure laws because it operated in only a single jurisdiction, the District of Columbia, and the District does not require disclosure. Since the Republicans would not release a seating list, there is no way of knowing who bought tickets to the $1,000-a-plate affair. But President Nixon was informed fully when he was presented with a leather-bound one-of-its-kind book listing all the ticket-buyers. Reporters or citizens who might want to know, for example, "which erstwhile Democratic donors have been seized by desire to dine with the Party newly in power" did not have a chance, it was noted in an aptly-headlined article, "GOP Has a Turn at Hocus-Pocus."[2] Officials of Braniff Airlines, whose top executives were almost all Texans, Democrats, and friends of former President Johnson, were reported to have bought 30 tickets at a time when a case of new airline routes was being restudied.[3]

The Republican Associates program for $1,000-per-year contributors was renamed RN Associates (for Richard Nixon Associates)—while the name of the Democrats' comparable President's Club was being changed to the National Democratic Sponsors Club. At the same time, the RNC did not downgrade the small givers program, the $10-per-year Republican National Committee Sustaining Fund. Begun in 1962, the Fund has grown from an initial 70,000 contributors, and remains an important source of income. The record of the Fund since its inception, excluding Presidential general election receipts because the data are not comparable, is impressive:

1962—$	700,000	1966—$3,300,000	
1963—	1,100,000	1967—	3,500,000
1964—	2,369,000	1968—	2,400,000
1965—	1,700,000	1969—	2,125,000

While raising money from this source has been expensive—in 1968, it was close to 40 percent of the gross returns—in 1969, it was less than 20 percent of the gross income. This smaller investment may account for the somewhat lower total return than might have been expected for 1969, based on earlier years.

By 1966, income from the Sustaining Fund was sufficient to cover the day-to-day operations of the RNC, leaving the large contributors to pay for special programs. However, reduced Sustaining Fund income for 1969 and the expanded operations of the RNC, budgeted at $3.2 million, increased the reliance of the party on large contributors.

According to a document of the Republican National Finance Committee, party income for 1969 was derived as follows:

RN Associates	$1,112,363
Congressional Boosters Club	482,416
Sustaining Fund	2,125,286
Congressional Committees	1,284,107
Gala Dinners	2,024,000
Speaker Commissions	6,254
State Payments	67,037
Special Projects & Miscellaneous	102,711
	$7,204,174

The same document showed a 1970 budget for $13,162,582, but this was reduced to $11.2 million when the stock market plunge hurt fund-raising prospects.

During 1969, two incidents gave insight into the role of certain large contributors. Early in the year, when the White House seemed interested in replacing Bliss as Chairman of the RNC, certain large contributors publicly defended Bliss' record and urged that he be kept on. The party also had to select a chairman of the Republican National Finance Committee to replace Maurice Stans, Nixon's chief fund raiser, who had become Secretary of Commerce. Several prospects who were Republican moderates were reportedly blackballed by conservatives who had contributed heavily to Nixon's campaign. The job went to Jeremiah Milbank, a long-time Nixon supporter who had been a major power in the Goldwater campaigns in 1964.

Late in 1969, the investigation of late filings of various Republican campaign committees' was quietly dropped. After a year of being "still under investigation," and as everyone had expected, the case was simply closed.

The Republicans' second year in office began with another grand social fund-raising affair shrouded in secrecy and with reports of a 1968 campaign deficit arising from bills which continued to pour in throughout 1969. The affair was a January 25 belated birthday party ball for the President, hosted by RNC Chairman Morton and RNFC Chairman Milbank. The guests were supposedly those who had helped finance the 1968 campaign, but reports suggested that the "price" for attendance was a minimum of

$10,000. There were about 200 guests, but again the guest list was kept secret.

Whereas in early 1969, the Republicans claimed a cash surplus, by early 1970, the 1968 campaign deficit was said to have been $1.3 million. Of this, $400,000 was paid from 1969 income, $200,000 was paid from proceeds of the January ball, and $700,000 remained. The still-remaining debt was mentioned by some Republican officials as the reason for the belt-tightening at the RNC, which included staff cutbacks. But other sources claimed the cutbacks were an effort to make the operation more efficient and eliminate some unneeded staff. There was also no doubt that the 1969–70 stock market slump was affecting Republican as well as Democratic fund raising.

In mid-January, a RNC publication carried an article entitled "Caution: Imposters at Work" and signed by Chairman Morton.[5] In it, Morton noted that January and February are major mail-solicitation months, and that there are organizations which "pose as Republican-connected," and particularly one "using 'Republican' in its name, [which] contributed less than 10 percent of the nearly $500,000 it raised to candidates." He went on to list the four fund-raising programs run by the RNFC and the Republican Congressional Campaign Committee. Morton was referring to the United Republicans of America (URA). In 1968, URA raised $475,453 but gave only $47,100 to candidates. More than one-half of the income went to raising funds, and much of that was paid to Richard A. Viguerie Co. of Washington, a mail-order business engaged for the purpose. In addition to giving little to candidates, Evans and Novak, the columnists, charged that URA wasted much of what was given by supporting some candidates in hopeless races or those who could not win nomination.[6] The connection between URA and Viguerie was especially interesting because Viguerie had gotten some White House business in 1969. His company handled a 10,000–11,000 piece mailing on Chief Justice Burger, and some recipients said the mailing labels were identical to those for *Human Events,* a right-wing magazine.[7]

By mid-1970, the Republican Party was due to have what virtually every Washington-based organization has but no political party has had: a permanent home of its own. Although the two major political parties must be considered important and permanent institutions in American life, they have lived in rented or temporary space, while every kind of group from the Chamber of Commerce and the AFL-CIO to the National Rifle Association has an impressive building of its own.

A fund-raising drive was begun early in 1968 for a three-building Republican center on Capitol Hill in Washington. Ground-breaking ceremonies were held in Spring of 1969 and it was named the Dwight D. Eisenhower National Republican Center. The building eventually would house the RNC, the Congressional campaign committees, and the Capitol Hill Club, a Republican social organization. The new physical arrangements locating the RNC with the Congressional campaign committees could improve cooperation and coordination between these committees with favorable consequences for the party system.

Republican control of the White House necessarily meant that the RNC would shift its nonideological orientation to one reflecting Presidential policy. At the same time, the RNC and the national Republican Party generally have professionalism and money not as readily available to the Democrats. The latter permits the former, and as the 1970 election campaigns developed, it was clear that the Republicans could supply funds, skilled manpower, and know-how in Congressional campaigns that the national Democratic Party could not begin to match. Only time will tell the consequences of this for the two-party system.

The Transition

Until 1964, the costs of the transition period between Election Day and the Inauguration were borne by the political parties. In 1962, the President's Commission on Campaign Costs recommended a federal subsidy to cover certain of these costs,[8] and the resulting Presidential Transition Act of 1964 became law. For the 1964–5 transition, there was no change of party or President, and less than $75,000 was used from appropriated funds to pay the salaries of Vice-President-elect Humphrey's staff during the transition period. This enabled Humphrey to resign his Senate seat early so that his successor could be appointed in time to get seniority over the incoming freshmen Senators.

In 1968, for the first time, federal funds were available for a change involving both President and party. A total of $900,000 was appropriated for the transition period: $375,000 each for the incoming and outgoing Presidents, and $75,000 each for the incoming and outgoing Vice-Presidents. The Republicans spent $1,000,000 in addition to their half of the subsidy, bringing the total cost of the transition to about $1,500,000. This compares with known costs of more than $200,000 for the 1952–3 transition, and of at least $360,000 for the 1960–1 transition.

For their half of the subsidy, the Republicans essentially combined the costs for President-elect Nixon and Vice-President-elect Agnew. The official accounting of these funds has been made available and is shown in Table 7-1.

The additional $1,000,000 paid out by the Republicans was raised in part by the Republican Victory Dinner held in May 1969. Because of this extra cost, there was some undercurrent of criticism from Republicans that as much as one-half of the transition subsidy went to President Johnson and Vice-President Humphrey, but no known public discussion of the matter ensued. Generally, the subsidy relieves financial pressures on the parties during the postcampaign period when there may already be debts.

Table 7-1

Statement of Account—Transition Fund President-Elect and Vice-President-Elect as of May 12, 1969

Description	Pres.-Elect	Vice-Pres.-Elect	Totals
Full-Time Temporary Employees	$383,952.40	$17,697,26	$401,649.66
Civil Service Retirement	3,771.21	330.04	4,101.25
Health Benefits	283.20	42.00	325.00
Group Insurance	1,239.05	63.49	1,302.54
F.I.C.A.	14,701.64	558.59	15,260.23
Travel	1,939.78		1,939.78
Space Rental Commercial	16,986.48		16,986.48
Equipment Rental	894.75		894.75
Printing	5,760.56	261.50	6,022.06
Office Supplies	17.50		17.50
Operating Supplies	59.76		59.76
Telephone	4.20		4.20
Postage	600.00	400.00	1,000.00
Equipment	436.59		436.59
Total	$430,647.12	$19,352.88	$450,000.00

Source: General Services Administration, U.S. Government.

In 1968, the Republicans spent lavishly on transition activities, particularly in offices at the Pierre Hotel in New York City. But the subsidy did assist the incoming President in paying costs involved in selecting and assembling his administration, and in preparing to assume responsibility for taking control of the government. It is perhaps an interesting commentary that Republicans, generally opposed to government subsidies for political purposes, fully supported the legislation authorizing the funds for the transition subsidy, and wished they had received a bigger portion.

Nixon's Appointments

Traditionally, large contributors and fund raisers receive a share of the spoils. In recent administrations, numerous financial supporters received what have been called "political non-jobs," which are defined as bestowing ". . . the status symbols of high office without the job itself."[9] These are honorary positions ranging from membership on White House commissions to that of special representative of the President at foreign ceremonial functions to being honored members of inspection tours at missile ranges.

But appointments requiring Senate confirmation are another matter. Many appointments of President Nixon during 1968–69 were given to professors, technical experts, and public servants, most of whom probably could not afford large contributions. Many diplomatic appointments were given to career officers, who are restricted by law from making political contributions. The contributions of other Presidential appointees who were not career diplomats are analyzed under the heading "Chiefs of Foreign Missions and Special Missions" in Appendix K, Contributions of Officials of 13 Selected Groups, 1968.

The proportion of large contributors among Nixon appointees is not great. Of 345 major appointees,[10] only 34, or 10 percent, were found to have contributed at least one sum of $500 or more in the 1968 campaigns. Contributors among appointees are listed in Appendix N. They contributed a total of $325,975 to the Republicans, $500 to the Democrats, and $500 to miscellaneous committees. The Democratic contributor was actually a split contributor, John D.J. Moore, who gave $1,000 to a Nixon committee and $500 to a Humphrey committee, and was appointed by President Nixon as Ambassador to Ireland. Nine of the 34 contributors gave $10,000 or more.

The change in party power in 1969 can be compared with the Kennedy takeover in 1961. Of 253 major appointments made by President Kennedy through mid-1961, 35, or 14 percent, were found to have contributed and a few had actually given to the Republicans. Under President Johnson, with no change in party power, 24 of 187, or 13 percent, had given. In 1964–65, of course, many who may have been contributors stayed in the same job that Kennedy appointed them to, and did not appear on appointment lists. The amounts the Nixon appointees contributed were more than four times as much as for the Johnson appointees, and almost three times as much as for the Kennedy appointees.

The Democrats

It was possible to analyze the condition of the Democratic Party in early 1969 as neither very sick nor very healthy. On the negative side, both Harris and Gallup polls showed that, for the first time, less than 50 percent of Americans identified themselves as Democrats. The Democrats had been outspent more than two-to-one in the Presidential election, and the party had a debt of almost $6.2 million. The disruptive Chicago Convention was still a bitter and divisive memory for many. While there were at least as many potential party leaders as there were defeated or potential Presidential candidates, there in fact was no recognized and accepted leader.

On the other side, DNC Chairman Larry O'Brien's assessment of the election was that "the results . . . reveal a Democratic Party, strong and robust, and ready for victory in the 70's."[11] While this assessment was more optimistic than most, many analysts noted the closeness of the Presidential election and the fact that the Democrats had continued control of both houses of Congress. It was the first time in more than 100 years that a new President had not begun his term with his party in control of Congress.

In an interesting analysis a few months later, Jules Witcover suggested that because of these good signs the Democrats were misleading themselves about the depth of their problems and the possibility of putting the old coalition back together again. "Unlike the Republicans in 1964, who could read nothing but disaster in Goldwater's vote and hence were persuaded to put their internal war on ice for the sake of Party reconstruction, the Democrats are not hurting sufficiently to abandon all differences for the sake of unity." Since the "new politics made inroads in the 1968 election," and Humphrey's "old politics" nearly won the election, neither side was about to give up its attempt to control the party. In addition, Witcover notes: "For the first time in forty years . . . the Democratic Party finds itself denied the White House by an avowed Republican partisan . . . [who] intends to use his Presidency to consolidate and extend the Republican apparatus and increase its efficiency."[12]

The Democrats began their first year out of power with ambitious financial goals. Late in January, DNC treasurer Robert Short said that the party planned to erase its debt in 1969, raise $5 million for the 1970 elections, and raise $10 million for the 1972 elections. Since Short had already proposed that the DNC take over the Kennedy and Humphrey prenomination debts of about $1 million each (and the McGovern and McCarthy debts if they requested it), the 1969 goal of wiping out the deficit meant raising at least $8.2 million more than operating costs.

But the financial performance in the first two months was as disastrous as Short's goals had been overambitious. For January and February, the income of the DNC was a mere $22,882: in the same period, the RNC took in almost $800,000. Other Democratic committees did as poorly, receiving $45,374 in January and February, while Republican committees took in $1.6 million. The DNC had been able to meet its $7,000–$8,000 weekly payroll and pay off a few bills because several hundred thousand dollars in refunds had been received for various campaign services and advertising time paid for in advance and then not used. The only positive aspect of the party's financial condition was revealed in the comment of one DNC member, after hearing Short's January 14 report on finances: "When the Treasurer comes out and starts giving facts and figures, that's something I haven't known under LBJ. People appreciate that."[13] In party finance, at least, bad news is better than no news.

Internal political difficulties surfaced as quickly as did the financial problems. The selection of Senator Fred Harris as DNC chairman came amidst grumblings that the chairmanship should be a full-time job and not go to a sitting legislator. At the DNC meeting which confirmed Harris' selection, there was a rather bitter fight over Georgia's national committee representatives, a small replay of the Maddox-Bond delegation conflict at the Chicago Convention. Unlike the Convention compromise, however, the Georgia regulars won both DNC seats, and more wounds were opened. The meeting also approved a Humphrey-supported idea for a Democratic Policy Council, modelled after the Democratic Advisory Committee of the late 1950s, which would be a kind of shadow cabinet. There was some unhappiness with the idea, as there had been with its predecessor, particularly from Democratic Congressional leaders who expected to be the party's spokesmen or policy-makers, and it was not implemented until the Fall.

One of Senator Harris' first actions was to name the two commissions on party reform which had been mandated by the 1968 National Convention, one on Party Structure and Delegate Selection and one on Rules. Harris selected Senator George McGovern to be chairman of the first group, after Hubert Humphrey had reportedly vetoed Senator Harold Hughes, who had spearheaded the unofficial but critical committee on Party reform in the summer of 1968 which had led to the Convention resolutions. The selection of Representative James O'Hara as chairman of the Commission on Rules was one of the few Party actions which caused no dissension.

Senator Harris moved quickly on the financial front, too, trying to organize a balanced program of large and small contributors. The $1,000-per-year President's Club became the National Democratic Sponsor's Club, and Harris also organized a Young Leadership Council with the same price tag. But Harris seemed equally concerned about building a base of smaller contributors, whose importance to the party had dropped sharply during the 1960s. Although the Democrats had never raised more than $600,000 from smaller givers, Harris hoped to be able to raise enough for the basic operating budget of the DNC, covering a staff of 75, at a cost of about $1.3 million per year. For $15 to $500 per year, a Democrat could become a participating member, and receive the new biweekly publication, *Demo Memo*. While $500 per year is hardly a small contribution, $15 per year certainly is, and Harris recognized the need to try to build a base of smaller contributors.

In mid-March, DNC Treasurer Short resigned. Although Short had been expected to stay, having talked of clearing up the 1968 campaign debt, stories of unhappiness between him and Harris surfaced. Short did not leave before he paid a $51,138 bill to the Leamington Hotel in Minneapolis, which he owned. Patrick O'Connor, who had been Short's deputy, became Acting Treasurer and then Treasurer.

The first major fund-raising affair was scheduled for May 12, for the benefit of the Congressional campaign committees. Partly because the big Republican Victory Dinner scheduled for early April had been postponed to May 7, however, the Democratic affair was suffering from slow ticket sales, and so it was in turn postponed for six weeks, to June 26. Tickets were $500 each, a doubling of the price from the previous year, while the Republicans had upped their price to $1,000. Unlike the Republican affair, the Democratic dinner was strictly a Congressional effort. Congressional Democrats felt they had received no benefit from the more than $6 million the party had gone in debt, and could expect to receive little financial help from the DNC in the 1970 elections, so they were on their own. In fact, the DNC chairman quietly and effectively did help provide financial and other support for the five special House elections during the year, four of which the Democrats won.

The June Dinner netted about $800,000 of which $440,000 went to the House Campaign Committee and $360,000 to the Senate Campaign Committee. The chairman of the Senate committee, Daniel Inouye of Hawaii, decided to give $10,000 to each of the 24 Senators planning to run again, noting that in most campaigns it is important to get some money early in order to plan a good campaign. Since some of the Senators faced primary or party opposition at home, there were some loud outcries, particularly from Connecticut, Ohio, and Texas. In Connecticut, the Democratic organization was trying to dump Senator Thomas Dodd, believing that a Senator who had been censured could not win reelection. Dodd later decided not to try for the Democratic nomination but ran instead as an Independent. In Ohio, there was opposition to octogenarian Senator Stephen Young, and he later decided to retire. In Texas, conservative Democrats were planning to support a primary challenge to Ralph Yarborough, an effort that succeeded. However, one could argue that in spite of the questionable practice of taking financial sides in an intraparty dispute, Inouye's decision was understandable. As Inouye noted, the Democratic Congressional operation, consisting of an executive director, a secretary, and a receptionist, stood in stark contrast to the Republicans' numerous professional employees plus secretaries, and consequently the Democrats had to try to use their resources as effectively as possible.[14] The House Campaign Committee decided on a similar move, giving $1,000 to each Democratic incumbent.[15]

The financial position of the DNC worsened during 1969. Loan repayments of $538,000 made in January and February reduced the general election debt to $5.6 million. On August 1, the Party formally took over the debts of the Humphrey, Kennedy, and McGovern prenomination campaigns (McCarthy declined the offer). When Short had originally proposed this action in January, one reason was that then Humphrey and Edward Kennedy would not have to raise funds separately in competition with the DNC, but would be available for fund raising on behalf of the combined debts. By the summer, however, the Chappaquidick incident had severely diminished Kennedy's appeal as a fund raiser, and Humphrey scarcely proved to be an irresistible attraction for potential contributors. So the party gained $2 million in debts without increased prospects for paying off any of the deficit. In addition, a $700,000 bill for air-conditioning the Chicago Amphitheater was still unpaid, so that the Democratic debt by the fall of 1969 totalled $8.3 million.

The Democrats hired an expert to run the direct-mail fund-raising campaign for small givers. Receipts from the program increased, but without seed money to enlarge the mailings, and without the ability to reinvest all receipts from the program in further mailings, there are limits to the revenue from this source. During the summer, at least one professional fund-raising firm had submitted a proposal to the DNC for a national broad-based fund-raising drive, with a pilot test in one state. Seed money was not available for experiments of this kind either.

During 1969, the McGovern Commission was chronically short of funds, since the $75,000 promised and provided by the DNC barely covered the basic staff costs. Some members of the Commission personally covered travel costs when open hearings were held around the country. A professional fund raiser was enlisted to help solicit, but in 1969, only $36,627 was raised independently, while Senator McGovern, Mrs. McGovern, and Senator Harold Hughes each loaned $5,000 to keep the operation afloat.[b] At the same time, the national labor union leadership refused to participate in the Commission, and some state party officials were openly hostile. In spite of these difficulties, the Commission was able to continue, and in November, its report and recommendations were submitted to the states. While the proposals have the sanction of the party until they are officially accepted or rejected by the 1972 Convention, it is not clear to what extent the DNC will encourage compliance, or what will happen to those states that choose to wait and take their chances with the next Convention.

In September of 1969 the Democratic Policy Council was finally formalized, and the uproar that greeted the announcement of its 20-member executive committee revealed continuing deep divisions. As soon as the executive committee was announced, many conservative party leaders attacked it, saying it was composed of liberals except for one member, Governor McNair of South Carolina. At the same time, liberals who had supported Senators McCarthy and Kennedy in 1968 attacked the committee as being conservative and unrepresentative, because most of its members were Humphrey supporters. The full Policy Council, announced shortly thereafter, added both conservatives and non-Humphrey liberals, but it is doubtful if either wing of the party will ever accept the Council as the Democrats' policy-making body.

Some leaders suggested a midterm convention to help formulate party policy and widen participation to a broader group. Some argued that it would take money and attention away from the 1970 election, while others feared another public display of the deep schisms. In September, there

---

[b] In a 1969 filing, the Commission reported receipts of $51,627, including $15,000 in loans, and spent $47,170, of which more than half went for hearings expenses. This was a separate filing from the DNC report and the latter subsumed certain payroll and other expenses of the Commission. Also in 1969, a filing was made in the names of the Reform DNC Committee (Receipts—$11,697, and Expenditures—$8,295) and the National Democratic Policy Council (Receipts—$10,000, and Expenditures—$17,390).

221

was another fight at the DNC meeting, this time over seating the national
Committeeman from Alabama, and the regulars again won.

For their first major fund-raising affair of 1970, the Democrats seemingly tried to find a warmer setting and happier memories. The February
dinner was held in Miami Beach in honor of Harry S. Truman; the honorary chairman was former President Johnson, who did not attend. The
Democrats had planned to have a 16-city hookup via closed circuit television, and talked of netting $2 million from the affair. But leaders in
many cities wanted to save the available money for the 1970 elections,
and refused to cooperate. The Florida State Committee kept much of the
money, so that the DNC netted only about $300,000 from the 1,500
guests who had paid between $100 and $5,000 to attend.[16]

In March, DNC Chairman Harris resigned, having brought the party
only slightly closer together. The Party engaged in a public agonizing
over finding the best person, or anyone who would take the job, and
finally, Humphrey dramatically convinced Larry O'Brien only he could
do it.

O'Brien brought in Robert Strauss of Texas as treasurer and said
that reducing the debt was the first task. Unlike most recent Democratic
treasurers, except Short, Strauss talked freely about party finances, and
soon he revealed that the Democratic debt totalled $9.3 million.[c] This
included a $100,000-per-month operating deficit for each of the first
three months of 1970.

Within weeks of taking over, O'Brien and Strauss abandoned any hope
of reducing the deficit in 1970, deciding that to try to do so would only
interfere with fund-raising efforts for the Congressional elections. While
acknowledging that the DNC did not even have enough seed money to
start a major fund-raising program, Strauss insisted that all debts would
eventually be paid, on a dollar-for-dollar basis, to both individual lenders
and to vendors, mainly airlines, hotels, and telephone companies.[17] In
the first months of the O'Brien-Strauss reign, the situation was improved
in that the DNC was running on a pay-as-you-go basis, with no operating
deficit. The Democrats got about 800 persons to pledge various amounts,
some as much as $100 per month, to pay current operating costs.

In May, five Senators—Democrats McGovern, Church, and Hughes,
and Republicans Hatfield and Goodell—raised and spent $70,000 in
order to buy 30 minutes of prime-time television to present their views
on the Vietnam war and Cambodian incursion in opposition to President
Nixon's policy. At the end of the show, there was an appeal for funds to
cover costs. The response unexpectedly brought in almost $500,000,

---

[c] The total included: $2.9 million owed to individual noteholders (presumably from
the 1968 campaign); $3 million owed to vendors (presumably both from 1968 and the
1969 and early 1970 operating deficits); $2 million owed from the Humphrey and
Kennedy prenomination campaigns; and the $700,000 from the Chicago convention.

virtually all in small contributions. (The money was used to carry out bipartisan efforts in opposition to the Vietnam war.) Clearly, money was still available from small contributors on the issue of Indochina.

Wallace Aftermath

Late in October 1968, a *Washington Post* article stated: "Win, lose, or stalemate in the 1968 presidential election, George C. Wallace intends to be back campaigning again in 1972, running on the base of the third-party movement he built in the past two years."[18] The article said that some Wallace advisers expected the American Independent Party (AIP) to continue, to be well organized at the state and local level, to run AIP candidates in 1969 and 1970 elections, and to gain some converts from major-party politicians. The article also noted that the massive 1967–68 effort to get on the ballot in all 50 states would not have to be repeated in 1972 if Wallace "picks up many votes next month."

A few months later, the picture looked quite different. After winning 13.5 percent of the vote, Wallace retired from public view, and his office and staff were largely dismantled. But more significant for Wallace's possible long-range plans than his temporary quiescence, was the dissension among his former supporters.

In February, there were two national conventions of former Wallace supporters, neither of which was completely behind their 1968 leader. The first was held in Dallas early in the month, and was appropriately called a convention of The Association of Wallace Voters. The convention was organized by a former Wallace campaign operative from Los Angeles, Robert Walters, and the main speaker was Dan Smoot, the right-wing commentator. The convention pointedly refused to pass a resolution praising the "principles and ideals" of Wallace, voting instead to "commend" him.[19] Although the 250 delegates from 44 states did not agree to set up a national party, as Walters had wanted, they did agree to set up a national party group, with a national committeeman and committeewoman from every state. Wallace did not attend the convention, but it reportedly had the "unofficial blessing of his Montgomery, Alabama, headquarters,"[20] and top Wallace campaign aides were there.

Later in February, another former Wallace leader from Los Angeles, William K. Shearer, spearheaded a competing national convention in Louisville. This group was more conservative than the Dallas group, and did not have Wallace's official or unofficial support. The 226 attendees formally set up a new party, to be called "The National Committee of Autonomous State parties known as the American Independent party, the American party, the Independent party, the Conservative party, the Constitution party, the Courage party and such other political parties as desire to affiliate with this national committee." The party adopted a constitution and bylaws, and created a national committee including the state chairman and a committeeman and committeewoman from each state. Shearer was clearly intent on putting a new conservative party first and Wallace second: "A candidate properly springs from the party and not the party from the candidate."[21]

It is doubtful if either of these groups, or any other, would have any strength or even survive very long without Wallace or another charismatic candidate-leader. However, this factionalism among Wallace's followers might indicate that he would not have an unimpeded road to reconstructing his campaign for another try in 1972. Even Wallace's unprecedented ballot achievement looked somewhat less impressive: the original petitions and/or Wallace's showing in 1968 had kept his party qualified in only 19 states, and 13 of those would be lost unless party candidates ran in 1970.[22]

Wallace soon came to public attention again. In mid-March, a six-page newsletter proclaiming itself "the only official publication authorized by Governor Wallace," was issued, but it did not mention the American Independent Party. More than 1.1 million copies of the newsletter were mailed to lists of 1968 supporters and contributors, using surplus funds from the Presidential campaign.[23] People were asked to contribute to the Wallace Campaign—whose mailing address had been changed to P.O. Box 1972—and for a minimum of $12 a year they would continue to receive the monthly newsletter. Each issue contained a 500-word message from Wallace, his picture, and articles by the staff.

By June, the newsletter reportedly had 40,000–50,000 subscribers, providing a yearly income of about $500,000. The Wallace Campaign moved to a new, two-story building in Montgomery. In October, the Wallace Campaign had about 30 employees, and the newsletter was reportedly being mailed to 125,000 subscribers.[24] If the subscribers were paying the minimum $12 per year, Wallace would be receiving at least $1.5 million per year from the newsletter.

Wallace's first postelection political appearance was in March in Tennessee, on behalf of an AIP candidate in a special Congressional election. Although the District was one which Wallace carried strongly in 1968, getting almost as many votes as Nixon and Humphrey combined, he did not make an all-out effort on behalf of the AIP candidate, William Davis. He made only one live appearance in the state, and filmed some television ads. Some people suggested his limited participation would enable him to take some credit if Davis won but not be blamed if Davis lost. (Wallace had not encouraged the Davis candidacy, and had waited a month after he announced before deciding to support him personally.) The result was considered a setback, as Davis received only about one-half as many votes as the Democratic victor and barely beat the Republican candidate for second place.[25]

In May, a third national convention of Wallace's supporters was held, this time in Cincinnati, with 38 states represented. This group was a more direct descendent of Wallace's 1968 American Independent Party, and it organized a new American Party. The headquarters were located in Richmond, Virginia, and T. Coleman Andrews, Jr., who had been AIP chairman in 1968, was elected chairman. This organization did have Wallace's backing; he referred to it as the "political action" arm of the Wallace Campaign.[26]

Throughout 1969, Wallace continued to maintain he was not a candidate for anything, and that any decision on 1972 would depend on the actions of the Nixon Administration. But in July, it was reported that his aides were again compiling information on the requirements for ballot qualification,[27] and in November, Wallace took a three-week trip to South Vietnam and eight other Asian nations.

Wallace's decision to run for Governor of Alabama in 1970 confirmed what many political analysts had been saying: that in order seriously to consider another Presidential effort, Wallace would have to have an elective office as a base. While Wallace's close win in that primary may have looked like less than an overwhelming mandate, it was expected that once elected he would be able to use the Governor's office to again wield a strong, effective, political organization. And it seemed that at least in the early stages of a 1972 campaign, Wallace would not have many financial difficulties. Whether or not he would be able to rekindle the fervor of 1968 was a major question, and would seem to depend in part on the actions of the major parties as well as on conditions at home and abroad.

8

The Financial Future

1968 was an unusual year politically and financially. Campaign expenses were the greatest in history. The Democratic Party witnessed a series of challenges during the primaries, the withdrawal of an incumbent from seeking renomination, the assassination of one of its front-runners, and the nomination of its candidate in a tumultuous and politically disastrous national convention.

Without the anti-Vietnam sentiment and activity, there would probably not have been an internal party challenge to President Johnson, and 1968 might have been a normal year with a prenomination contest only in the "out," Republican, party. George Wallace might have run independently, but without the violence at Memphis, Los Angeles, and Chicago, his challenge could well have taken a different form. The challenge to Vietnam policy caused protest movements that shook the political system to the core. The candidacies of McCarthy, Kennedy, and McGovern were based essentially on that issue, and even Romney's and Rockefeller's challenge to Nixon would have been less likely without the Vietnam issue.

Whatever eulogy one may speak over the demise of the McCarthy movement, it achieved a great deal though lacking strong and steadily focussed leadership. It started a new liberal politics of participation, brought Robert Kennedy into the fray, dislodged an incumbent President, crystallized the issue of Vietnam and helped legitimize opposition to the nation's policy there, and channelled some alienated and some young into partisan politics within a traditional framework of action that promised new hope and new directions in the context of the two-party system, without violence and street demonstrations.

The kind of campaign a candidate chooses is determined by his position vis-à-vis his opponents, by his own perception of how to win, by his financial resources, and by his own personality and style. The kinds of campaigns in 1968 included President Johnson's ostensible noncandidacy; McCarthy's one issue, one state at a time primary road; Kennedy's blitz campaign; Humphrey's dubious inheritance and his avoidance of the primaries; Nixon's rich, smooth, balanced campaign; Romney's abortive campaign; Rockefeller's media-mainly attempt; and Reagan's diversion at Miami Beach. The lack of money dictated McCarthy's one-at-a-time approach. The availability of money made possible both Kennedy's and Rockefeller's short and intensive efforts. One can only speculate how the paucity or abundance of money affected any outcomes.

The Democratic Presidential campaign began in disorder and debt, and ended in considerable disarray and unprecedented debt. Despite Democratic control of the Presidency, the campaign had great difficulty in raising money, and ended with a big deficit that was compounded by the assumption by the Democratic National Committee of portions of the Humphrey and Kennedy prenomination debts. Essentially, the Democrats failed during their supremacy in the 1960s either to develop stable and ample sources of funds or to enact legislation that would ease their financial plight. Undue dependence on the President's Club led to inevitable trouble when prospects of winning the Presidency dimmed. Failure to develop a broader base of financial support hurt when the crunch came in 1968. The Presidential Election Campaign Fund Act, enacted in 1966, would have provided federal subsidies for Presidential general elections starting in 1968.[1] The law was disenacted after seven month's life, and the fact that nothing took its place attests to the lack of attention paid to the subject of legislation on political finance in high places. The Democrats faced 1969 and 1970 without any realistic chance to reduce the debt and barely kept their current operations funded. In the 1970 election, without labor funds and contributions to candidates from peace-oriented groups, the Democratic effort would have suffered seriously. The financial plight of the Democratic Party is serious indeed.

The Republican Party was better organized in its solicitation of funds in 1968, and more strategic in their deployment—a luxury permitted by the availability of money. The Republican Presidential campaign outspent the Democrats by better than two to one. The disparity in Republican to Democratic sources among corporate managers and other groups detailed in this study has been shown in most cases to be even greater than two to one and in fact, greater than one might anticipate given Democratic ascendancy since 1932. The Republican financial advantage was heightened in 1969 and 1970 by control of the White House. Republicans depend on large contributions, but their financial underpinnings are strengthened by the success of their small contributions drives. The financial future of the Republican Party is bright indeed.

1968 also witnessed the campaign of the most financially successful third party in modern American history. The party raised, primarily through small contributions, enough money to finance its operations, including the lengthy and tedious fight in each of the states to place their candidate's name on the ballot, and to finish the campaign out of debt.

1968 was a year of turmoil and transition. The parties and their candidates reflected this in their fund raising, and in their expenditures.

Notes

Chapter 1
Introduction

1. Alexander Heard, *The Costs of Democracy* (Chapel Hill: The University of North Carolina Press, 1960), pp. 7–8. This volume contains most data comparisons prior to 1960 used in this book.

2. Herbert E. Alexander, *Financing the 1964 Election* (Princeton: Citizens' Research Foundation, 1966), p. 13, hereinafter cited Alexander, *1964*. This volume contains most data comparisons for 1964 and 1960, and certain earlier years, used in this book; but also see Alexander, *Financing the 1960 Election* (Princeton: Citizens' Research Foundation, 1962), hereinafter cited as Alexander, *1960*.

3. In these calculations, the total vote for each Presidential election is taken from: for 1912 and 1916, Louise Overacker, *Money in Elections* (New York: The Macmillan Company, 1932), p. 80; for 1920–1964, Richard M. Scammon, ed., *America at the Polls* (Pittsburgh: Governmental Affairs Institute, 1965), pp. 1–23; for 1968, Theodore H. White, *The Making of the President 1968* (New York: Atheneum Publishers, 1969), Appendix A. Labor and miscellaneous expenditures are not included in these calculations.

4. *Survey of Political Broadcasting, Primary and General Election Campaigns of 1968* (Washington: Federal Communications Commission, August, 1969), Table 3. Publication hereinafter cited as FCC, *Survey 1968;* the FCC publications for the 1964 and 1960 elections are cited as FCC, *Survey 1964* and FCC, *Survey 1960*.

5. FCC, *Survey 1968*, pp. 1–2.

Chapter 2
Prenomination Campaigns

1. Alexander, *1960,* pp. 16–19.

2. Heard, *Costs*, pp. 334–5.

3. Alexander, *1964*, pp. 17–18, 23–24.

4. For an interesting brief discussion of the comparative wealth of the Kennedy and Rockefeller families, see Lewis Chester, Godfrey Hodgson, and Bruce Page, *An American Melodrama: The Presidential Campaigns of 1968* (New York: The Viking Press, 1969), pp. 214–5.

5. See White, *Making*, pp. 35, 38–40, 50–52.

6. White, *Making*, p. 57.

7. Rowland Evans and Robert Novak, "Inside Report: Romney's Diminishing War Chest," *The Washington Post*, August 2, 1967.

8. *The New York Times*, September 18, 1967.

9. White, *Making*, pp. 58–60.

10. For details, see T. George Harris, "What Makes Romney Run," *Look*, December 12, 1967.

11. Jules Witcover, *The Resurrection of Richard Nixon* (New York: G.P. Putnam's Sons, 1970), p. 124–154.

12. White, *Making*, pp. 50–2.

13. *Summary Report of Campaign Contributions and Expenditures: 1968 Primary Election* (Compiled and published by Clay Myers, Secretary of State of Oregon, undated), p. 12. Hereinafter referred to as *Oregon 1968 Primary Summary*.

14. Witcover, *Resurrection*, p. 299.

15. For a discussion of the President's Club, see Alexander, *1964*, pp. 77–81.

16. *The New York Times*, June 28, 1968.

17. See White, *Making*, pp. 224–33.

18. For a discussion of this strategy and its effects, see Chester, Hodgson, and Page, *Melodrama*, pp. 382–93.

19. According to Chester, Hodgson, and Page, *Melodrama*, p. 387.

20. Witcover, *Resurrection*, p. 307.

21. Chester, Hodgson, and Page, *Melodrama*, p. 391.

22. White, *Making*, pp. 35–6.

23. Chester, Hodgson, and Page, *Melodrama*, pp. 197–208.

24. Chester, Hodgson, and Page, *Melodrama*, p. 199.

25. Written by Lee and Ann Edwards (San Diego: Viewpoint Books, 1967).

26. "Deadline Near In Fund Case," Boston *Herald-Traveler*, March 6, 1969.

27. "Johnson Makes Early Bid for N.H. Vote," *The New York Times*, September 15, 1967.

28. "Gov. King, McIntyre to Run for Johnson in New Hampshire," *The New York Times*, October 31, 1967.

29. White, *Making*, p. 113.

30. *Ibid.*, p. 159.

31. *Ibid.*, pp. 159–60.

32. Rowland Evans and Robert Novak, "LBJ Drops Out," *The Washington Post*, March 10, 1968.

33. See Chapter 6, section, The Seafarers.

34. See Chester, Hodgson, and Page, *Melodrama*, pp. 68–77, and White, *Making*, pp. 76–80.

35. Richard Harwood, "McCarthy Men See No Money Problem," *The Washington Post*, December 1, 1967.

36. Chester, Hodgson, and Page, *Melodrama*, p. 85.

37. White, *Making*, p. 83.

38. Leonard Sloane, "Advertising: McCarthy Men Do Own Spots," *The New York Times*, August 12, 1968.

39. Tom Wicker, "In the Nation: Free Ride for McCarthy," *The New York Times*, March 7, 1968.

40. "Ill Wind Blows Good," *The New York Times*, March 20, 1968.

41. Dial Torgenson, "Oregon Victory Opens Purses for McCarthy," *The Los Angeles Times*, May 30, 1968.

42. Robert Walters, "Third of McCarthy Staff Cut in Economy Drive," *Washington Star*, July 18, 1968.

43. For a complete list of Mott's political contributions, see Appendix B.

44. Chester, Hodgson, and Page, *Melodrama*, p. 81.

45. See White, *Making*, pp. 157–66 and Chester, Hodgson, and Page, *Melodrama*, pp. 64–5 and 105–126 for somewhat varying accounts of Kennedy's long indecision and final decision to enter the race.

46. Peter Goldman, "Politics: RFK Against Himself," *Newsweek*, February 17, 1969.

47. Chester, Hodgson, and Page, *Melodrama*, pp. 128–9.

48. Robert Walters, "Kennedy Stepping Up Indiana Radio-TV Bid," *Washington Star*, May 2, 1968.

49. Chester, Hodgson, and Page, *Melodrama*, pp. 129–30.

50. *Ibid.*, pp. 317–19.

51. *Oregon 1968 Primary Summary, op. cit.*

52. Allen L. Otten, "Vice-President Slows Kennedy's Drive, Edges Into Race Himself," *The Wall Street Journal*, April 12, 1968. See also Chester, Hodgson, and Page, *Melodrama*, p. 144.

53. Eve Edstrom, "Party Workers Shift to HHH," *The Washington Post*, May 2, 1968.

54. Chester, Hodgson, and Page, *Melodrama*, pp. 143–4.

55. Roy Reed, "Humphrey's Donations Have Dropped Since Kennedy's Death; Staff Cut By 25%," *The New York Times*, June 20, 1968.

56. Rowland Evans and Robert Novak, "The Humphrey Strategy," *The Washington Post*, April 14, 1968.

57. See section on labor allocations to Presidential candidates, pp. 191–194, below.

58. Chester, Hodgson, and Page, *Melodrama*, p. 164.

59. See Alexander, *1964*, pp. 25–6.

60. Chester, Hodgson, and Page, *Melodrama*, pp. 149, 556.

Chapter 3
Financing the Conventions

1. For a comparison with the funding of the 1960 and 1964 Republican and Democratic Conventions, see John F. Bibby and Herbert E. Alexander,

The Politics of National Convention Finances and Arrangements (Princeton: Citizens' Research Foundation, 1968), Table 7, p. 49.

2. See *Ibid.*, pp. 16–17, 58–62; and Alexander, *1964*, pp. 40–42.

3. 80 (Part I) Stat. 38.

4. 82 Stat. 251.

5. Harold Hughes, Chairman, *The Democratic Choice, A Report of the Commission on the Democratic Selection of Presidential Nominees* (1968).

6. See Alexander, *1964*, pp. 41–2.

Chapter 4
The General Election Campaigns

1. See tables 19, 20, and 21, below.

2. *Time*, November 15, 1968.

3. White, *Making*, p. 363.

4. Chester, Hodgson, and Page, *Melodrama*, p. 629.

5. For details and discussion of Nixon's media campaign, see Political Broadcasting and Newspaper Advertising, below.

6. Chester, Hodgson, and Page, *Melodrama*, p. 617.

7. Described in detail in Private Public Opinion Polls, below.

8. Chester, Hodgson, and Page, *Melodrama,* p. 619.

9. White, *Making*, p. 327.

10. Chester, Hodgson, and Page, *Melodrama*, p. 645–6.

11. Chester, Hodgson, and Page, *Melodrama*, p. 160; *Congressional Quarterly*, October 18, 1968; *Time*, October 11, 1968, October 25, 1968; White, *Making*, p. 356.

12. See section on Political Broadcasting, below.

13. Don Oberdorfer, "Humphrey has Bilingual Day in South Texas," *The Washington Post*, October 23, 1968.

14. Chester, Hodgson, and Page, *Melodrama*, pp. 637, 709.

15. White, *Making*, p. 339.

16. Quoted in *Ibid.*, p. 357n.

17. See White, *Making*, pp. 367–8.

18. "Wallace's Army: The Coalition of Frustration," *Time*, October 18, 1968.

19. "Wallace's Workers: Right-Wing Extremists Provide Vital Manpower for Third-Party Drive," *The Wall Street Journal*, October 24, 1968.

20. Overacker, *Money*, p. 79.

21. Heard, *Costs*, p. 54, Table 4.

22. See section on Political Broadcasting, below.

23. Chester, Hodgson, and Page, *Melodrama*, p. 289.

24. *Ibid.*, p. 287.

25. J. M. McFadden, "Wallace Ponders Future: Race Cost $9 Million," *The Washington Post*, December 26, 1968.

26. Alexander, *1964*, Table 6, p. 48.

27. FCC, *Survey 1968*, p. 1.

28. *Ibid.*, Table 1, and FCC, *Survey 1964*, Table 1.

29. See Robert Kent Durkee, *Pervasive Persuasion, Presidential Campaigning in an Electronic Era* (Senior Thesis, Princeton University, 1969), p. 172.

30. FCC, *Survey 1968*, Table 1.

31. *Ibid.*, Table 3.

32. *Ibid.*, p. 1.

33. *Ibid.*, Tables 1, 9, 20.

34. *Ibid.*

35. *Ibid.*, and FCC, *Survey 1964*, Tables 1, 9A, 22A.

36. *Ibid.*

37. For a detailed view of these shows, see Joe McGinniss, *The Selling of the President 1968* (New York: Trident Press, 1969).

38. Durkee, *Persuasion*, p. 291–2.

39. *Ibid.*, p. 178.

40. *Ibid.*, pp. 294–5.

41. See McGinniss, *Selling*, pp. 149–50, 156, and Durkee, *Persuasion*, p. 295.

42. Durkee, *Persuasion*, p. 178.

43. *Ibid.*, p. 295.

44. Jack Gould, "TV: Viewing Candidates," *The New York Times*, June 3, 1968.

45. "TV Caught in Political Middle," *Broadcasting*, August 26, 1968, p. 28.

46. Jack Gould, "TV: California Gets 3 Candidates on Air Together," *The New York Times*, August 28, 1968.

47. Durkee, *Persuasion*, p. 312.

48. *Ibid.*, p. 265.

49. "L.B.J. Should Debate on TV," *Saturday Evening Post* (Speaking Out), June 27–July 4, 1964, p. 12.

50. Durkee, *Persuasion*, p. 266.

51. FCC, *Survey 1968*, p. 1.

52. Durkee, *Persuasion*, p. 315.

53. For a recent series of proposals regarding broadcasting in Presidential elections, see *Voters' Time, Report of the Twentieth Century Fund Commission on Campaign Costs in the Electronic Era* (New York: The Twentieth Century Fund, 1969).

54. FCC, *Survey 1968*, Table 4.

55. *Ibid.*, Table 6.

56. *Ibid.*, Tables 5 and 6.

57. *Ibid.*, Table 5.

58. *Ibid.*

59. *Ibid.*, p. 3.

60. *Ibid.*, Table 5.

61. *Ibid.*, Table 8.

62. *Ibid.*, Table 17.

63. FCC, *Survey 1962, 1964, 1966, 1968.*

64. FCC, *Survey 1968*, Table 2.

65. *Ibid.*

66. *Ibid.*, Table 11 and 22.

67. *Ibid.*, Tables 12 and 23.

68. For 1956, see *1956 General Election Campaigns,* Report to the Senate Committee on Rules and Administration, Subcommittee on Privileges and Elections, 85th Congress, 1 Session (1957), Exhibit No. 8, pp. 54–63. (hereafter cited as Gore Committee, *Report.*)

69. The most detailed reports of the ORC operation can be found in Don Oberdorfer, "Unsung Poll Helped GOP Chart Path to Victory," *The Washington Post*, December 29, 1968, and "Political Polling 1968," *The Analyst*, March, 1969.

70. Michael Stern, "Poll Indicates that Nixon Trails in State, with McCarthy Ahead," *The New York Times*, August 22, 1968.

71. Roy R. Silver, "Nassau Poll Gives Nixon 66% as Humphrey Drops 19 Points," *The New York Times*, October 4, 1968.

72. "Do Polls Help Democracy," *Time*, May 31, 1968.

73. See Chapter 2, Rockefeller, above.

74. See *The Analyst*, and "GOP Planning Series of Polls," *Washington Star*, May 2, 1968.

75. See Table 1–1 above.

76. For a discussion of labor's role, see Chapter 6, below.

77. For a discussion of business in politics, see Chapter 6, below.

78. For an interesting postelection story on URA, see Chapter 7, The Republicans, below.

79. For a complete list of committee allocations, see Herbert E. Alexander and Caroline D. Jones, eds., *Contributions of National-Level Political Committees to Incumbents and Candidates for Public Offices, 1968* (Princeton: Citizens' Research Foundation, 1971); hereafter cited as *1968 Committee Contributions.*

80. For comparable data and detailed analyses of such committee allocations in the 1964 elections, see Kevin L. McKeough, *Financing Campaigns for Congress: Contribution Patterns of National-Level Party and Non-Party Committees, 1964* (Princeton: Citizens' Research Foundation, 1970).

81. *Electing Congress, The Financial Dilemma,* Report of the Twentieth

Century Fund Task Force on Financing Congressional Campaigns (New York: The Twentieth Century Fund, 1970), p. 16.

82. Alexander, *1960*, pp. 44–49.

83. For a discussion of labor support to Morse and Gilligan, both acknowledged doves, see Chapter 6, below.

Chapter 5
Sources of Funds

1. Roper Public Opinion Research Center, Williams College.

2. White, *Making*, p. 329.

3. *Ibid.*

4. David R. Jones, "Humphrey Seeks $1,000 Supporters," *The New York Times*, October 25, 1968.

5. Alexander, *1964*, pp. 77–81.

6. See below, Chapter 5, Lenders.

7. See Walter Pincus, "Party Hid Donors, Aide Says," *The Washington Post*, January 9, 1969.

8. See Appendix J.

9. Chester, Hodgson, and Page, *Melodrama*, p. 716.

10. White, *Making*, pp. 365–6.

11. See Appendix D.

12. White, *Making*, pp. 339–40.

13. For a fuller explanation, see Alexander, *1964*, pp. 99–104.

14. Periscope Section, *Newsweek*, September 30, 1968.

15. *The Washington Post*, October 4, 1968.

16. Heard, *Costs*, p. 54.

17. Overacker, *Money*, p. 145.

18. *Ibid.*, p. 144.

19. "The Wallace Phenomena," *U.S. News and World Report*, August 26, 1968.

20. "Wallace Sets Fire to the '68 Campaign," *U.S. News and World Report*, September 30, 1968.

21. Jim Hampton, "Behind the Curtains, the Wallace Campaign is Laboring Hard," *National Observer*, May 20, 1968.

22. *Congressional Quarterly*, September 27, 1968.

23. Chester, Hodgson, and Page, *Melodrama*, p. 666.

24. *Ibid.*, p. 664–5.

25. Walter Pincus, "Suit Alleges Kickbacks for Wallace Campaign," *The Washington Post*, April 15, 1968; J. M. McFadden, "Firm That Sued Alabama Gets State Asphalt Pact," *The Washington Post*, May 30, 1968; "Agencies

Weigh Price-Rigging, Kickback Charges in Alabama," *The Washington Post*, April 29, 1968; Jerry Landauer and Kenneth Slocum, "Loss of Statehouse Control Cuts Donations to Alabamian's Drive: Pinch on Wallace," *The Wall Street Journal*, June 10, 1968; Morton Mintz, "Liquor Sales to State Benefit Wallace Friends: Liquor and Favoritism Fund-Raiser, Payoff Linked," *The Washington Post*, November 25, 1968; Jack Anderson, "Insiders Whisper Alabama Liquor Payoff," *The Washington Post*, November 26, 1968; Drew Pearson, "Liquor Kickback Probe Backed," *The Washington Post*, December 6, 1968.

26. See *Congressional Quarterly*, October 25, 1968, p. 2954.

27. Neil Maxwell, "Wallace Commandeers Officials in Alabama for His Campaign Bid," *The Wall Street Journal*, December 7, 1967.

28. For commentary on the earlier years, see Alexander, *1964*, p. 86.

29. A summary of the official sources of data used follows. In the case of the information filed at the Federal level with the Clerk of the House and the Secretary of the Senate, the data obtained are complete. For the states, the data are only partial.

Depository	*Data Obtained*
Federal (filed with the Clerk of the House of Representatives and the Secretary of the Senate)	General Election and quarterly committee filings
Connecticut	General Election
Florida	General Election
Kansas	Primary and General Election
Kentucky	Primary and General Election
Maryland	General Election
Michigan	General Election
Nebraska	General Election
New Hampshire	General Election
New Jersey	General Election
New Mexico	General Election
New York (city) Board of Elections	General Election
New York (state)	Primary and General Election
Oregon	Primary and General Election
Pennsylvania	Primary and General Election
South Dakota	Primary
Wisconsin	Primary

For an extensive commentary on methods and scope, see Alexander and Jones, *Political Contributors of $500 or More in 1968* (Princeton: Citizens' Research Foundation, 1971). Regarding use of special lists and interview data added to the Alexander and Jones compilation exclusively for this study, see explanation above, Chapter 2.

30. The universe of filings and lists from which were derived data about individual contributors of $500 or more was not the same for each of these five years. Data for 1952 and 1956 derived from Heard, *Costs,* p. 53, note 37.

31. Gore Committee, *Report,* Exhibit 11, pp. 65–67.

32. The four lists of 25 corporations each were printed in Richard F. Kaufman, "As Eisenhower Was Saying . . . 'We must Guard Against Unwarranted Influence by the Military-Industrial Complex,' " *The New York Times Magazine,* June 22, 1969, p. 70. These lists were derived from the following sources: For the Pentagon, 100 Companies and Their Subsidiary Corporations Listed According to Net Value of Military Prime Contract Awards (Fiscal Year 1968), Department of Defense; For A.E.C., Annual Report for 1968, Atomic Energy Commission; For NASA, Annual Procurement Report, NASA (Fiscal Year 1968); For the industrial list, 500 Largest U.S. Industrial Corporations, Fortune Directory (1968). The four groups are as follows:

Largest Defense Contractors			Largest Industrial Corporations
Pentagon	A.E.C.	NASA	
1 General Dynamics	1 Union Carbide	1 North American Rockwell	1 General Motors
2 Lockheed	2 Sandia Corp.	2 Grumman	2 Standard Oil (N.J.)
3 General Electric	3 General Electric	3 Boeing	3 Ford
4 United Aircraft	4 DuPont	4 McDonnell-Douglas	4 General Electric
5 McDonnell-Douglas	5 Reynolds Electrical	5 General Electric	5 Chrysler
6 A.T.&T.	6 Westinghouse	6 I.B.M.	6 Mobil
7 Boeing	7 Bendix	7 Bendix	7 I.B.M.
8 Ling Temco Vought	8 Holmes & Narver	8 Aerojet-General	8 Texaco
9 North American Rockwell	9 Douglas United Nuclear	9 RCA	9 Gulf Oil
10 General Motors	10 Dow Chemical	10 Chrysler	10 U.S. Steel
11 Grumman	11 Goodyear Atomic	11 General Dynamics	11 A.T.&T.
12 AVCO	12 Idaho Nuclear	12 TRW	12 Standard Oil (Calif.)
13 Textron	13 Aerojet-General	13 General Motors	13 DuPont
14 Litton	14 Atlantic Richfield	14 Ling Temco Vought	14 Shell Oil
15 Raytheon	15 E.G.&G.	15 Lockheed	15 RCA
16 Sperry-Rand	16 Gulf General Atomic	16 Philco-Ford	16 McDonnell-Douglas
17 Martin Marietta	17 Monsanto	17 Sperry Rand	17 Standard Oil (Ind.)
18 Kaiser Industries	18 Kerr-McGee	18 Martin Marietta	18 Westinghouse
19 Ford	19 National Lead	19 T.W.A.	19 Boeing
20 Honeywell	20 Mason & Hanger	20 Federal Electric	20 Swift
21 Olin Mathieson	21 North American Rockwell	21 Catalytic-Dow (joint venture)	21 I.T.&T.
22 Northrop	22 Homestake-Sapin	22 United Aircraft	22 Goodyear Tire & Rubber
23 Ryan Aeronautical	23 United Nuclear	23 Brown Engineering	23 General Telephone & Electronics
24 Hughes	24 Pan American	24 Honeywell	24 Bethlehem Steel
25 Standard Oil (N.J.)	25 Phillips Petroleum	25 Control Data	25 Union Carbide

33. Richard Austin Smith, "The Fifty-Million-Dollar Man," *Fortune,* November, 1957, pp. 176–177, 236.

34. Arthur M. Louis, "America's Centimillionaires," *Fortune,* May, 1968, pp. 152–157, 192–96.

Chapter 6
Labor and Business in Politics

1. See above, Chapter 2, Humphrey.

2. Felix Kessler, "The Liberal ADA Shows Signs of Disintegrating Over Vietnam Issue," *The Wall Street Journal,* February 8, 1968.

236

3. Wallace Turner, "Labor Group Backs Branigan in Effort to Press Humphrey Drive," *The New York Times*, May 6, 1968.

4. May 8, 1968.

5. See, for example, Richard Critchfield, "Crossroads of Labor: Unions Fear Swing to Right," *Washington Star*, July 9, 1968; Joseph A. Loftus, "Labor Leaders for Humphrey Concerned by Wallace Support," *The New York Times*, September 14, 1968; A. H. Raskin, ". . . And the Pro-Humphrey Labor Chiefs are Worried," *The New York Times*, September 15, 1968; and Helen Delich Bentley, "What Makes Labor Run," *The Baltimore Sun*, October 20, 1968.

6. As reported in "How Wallace Campaign is Splitting the Labor Vote," *U.S. News and World Report*, September 23, 1968.

7. Frank C. Porter, "AFL-CIO Takes Credit for Cutting Wallace Vote," *The Washington Post*, February 20, 1969.

8. Walter Rugaber, "Southerners Ask Political Ethics," *The New York Times*, November 10, 1967.

9. Listed in Table 4-16.

10. For a complete listing of COPE transfers to states, see Alexander and Jones, eds., *1968 Committee Contributions*.

11. See, for example, Jerry Landauer, "Union's Political Gifts Follow Administration Aid to Fugitive Official," *The Wall Street Journal*, July 19, 1968; "A Lesson from One Union on How to Finance the Campaign," *U.S. News and World Report*, August 5, 1968; "Rusk Denies Political Links in Banks Extradition Case," *The Baltimore Sun*, July 20, 1968; "Fannin Sees Party Deal Over Unionist," *The Washington Post*, September 21, 1968; Richard Wilson, "Labor Leaders See Trouble if Nixon Wins," *Washington Star*, September 27, 1968.

12. Ken Clawson, "Labor Strength Rises in Ohio," *The Washington Post*, May 16, 1968; Joseph A. Loftus, "Labor in Ohio Making Major Drive to Oust Lausche," *The New York Times*, May 6, 1968; Abe S. Zaidan, "HHH Drive Splits Ohio Democrats," *The Washington Post*, August 14, 1968; Steven V. Roberts, "Humphrey Uses Pressure in Ohio," *The New York Times*, August 15, 1968; "Humphrey Denies Asking Labor to Cut Off Funds in Ohio Case," *The New York Times*, August 16, 1968; James M. Naughton, "HHH Men Buy Ohio for $250,000, Insiders Report," *Cleveland Plain Dealer*, August 16, 1968; Robert Walters, "Conservative Mood in Ohio a Bad Omen for Democrats," *Washington Star*, October 2, 1968.

13. Gordon C. Raeburn, "Out-of-State Unions Contributed $271,011 to Gilligan Campaign," Cincinnati *Post and Times-Star*, June 25, 1968.

14. Richard Halloran, "Mystery Organization Funnels Unionists' Funds to Candidates," *The Washington Post*, September 23, 1968.

15. Robert Gruenberg and William J. Eaton, "Dirksen's $5,000 Club," *Chicago News*, June 16, 1969.

16. Joseph H. Miller, "Democrats Get Labor Funds for Poll Aid in Negro Areas," *The Philadelphia Inquirer*, November 5, 1968.

17. Richard Levine, "Unions vs. The GOP: Labor Maps Big Drive to Assist Democrats in Races for Congress," *The Wall Street Journal*, October 3, 1969.

18. Walter Pincus, "Three Union Aides Indicted in Political Funds Case," *The Washington Post,* May 10, 1968.

19. "Lie About Political Gift Charged to Union Aides," *The Washington Post,* June 20, 1969.

20. Hubert Rowan, "Businessmen Pick Nixon, Reject RFK," May 2, 1968.

21. "Nixon & Business: Nominees Fail to Win Some of the Executives Who Bolted GOP in '64," October 16, 1968.

22. Terry Robards, "Poll of Executives Puts Nixon Ahead," October 27, 1968.

23. Listed in Table 4-17.

24. See Jonathan Cottin, "Washington Pressures/BIPAC Seeks to Elect Pro-Business Members to Congress," *National Journal,* July 18, 1970, pp. 1525–1531.

25. See Judith Robinson, "Washington Pressures/AMA's Political Action Arm Trades Campaign Aid for Dialogue With Lawmakers," *National Journal,* August 1, 1970, pp. 1659–1665.

26. *Ibid.*

27. Joseph Albright, "Special Interests Pay Off," *Newsday,* October 28, 1968.

28. Jerry Landauer, "Business-Backed Groups Seeking to Elect Friendly Candidates, Offset Labor," *The Wall Street Journal,* October 17, 1968.

29. *Ibid.*

30. See Albright, "Special Interests," "Business-Backed Groups," and Eileen Shanahan, "Corporation Executives Contribute to Political Candidates Through Groups With Unrevealing Names," *The New York Times,* October 25, 1968.

31. Walter Pincus, "Merrill Lynch Raises Campaign War Chest," October 18, 1968.

32. "Merrill Lynch Officers Give Money to a House Candidate Who Has No Rival," November 3, 1968.

33. "Mills Leaves in Arkansas Tax Loophole," *The Washington Post,* June 1, 1968.

34. "An Unusual Political Pot," San Francisco *Chronicle,* May 23, 1968.

Chapter 7
The Aftermath

1. Robert Walters, "Six GOP Mystery Donors," *Washington Star,* March 14, 1969; "Donors Mystery Grows," *Washington Star,* March 15, 1969; David S. Broder, "Six GOP Fund Groups in Illinois Veil Contribution of $268,250," *The Washington Post,* March 15, 1969.

2. Jerry Landauer, *The Wall Street Journal,* May 7, 1969.

3. Rowland Evans and Robert Novak, "GOP Taps the Airlines," *The Washington Post,* February 23, 1969.

238

4. See Chapter 5, The Republicans, above.

5. *Monday,* January 19, 1970.

6. "1970 Fund-Raising Drive of URA Way Out Front in Sheer Audacity," *The Washington Post,* April 10, 1969.

7. William Grieder, "Direct-Mail Fund Raiser Gets White House Client," *The Washington Post,* May 28, 1969.

8. See *Financing Presidential Campaigns,* Report of the President's Commission on Campaign Costs (Washington: Government Printing Office), pp. 23–24.

9. Don Oberdorfer, "The New Political Non-Job," *Harper's Magazine,* October 1965, p. 108.

10. Listed by *Congressional Quarterly* in various issues, January 31, February 28, May 9, May 16, May 30, and December 12, 1969, and in the *Congressional Quarterly Almanac* (1969), and from the State Department's list of appointed ambassadors as of January 2, 1970.

11. "Election Showed Party is Robust Says Democratic Chief O'Brien," *The Washington Post,* December 27, 1968.

12. "Transfusions for the Democrats," *The Progressive,* April, 1969.

13. As quoted in "Singing in the Rain," *The New Republic,* January 25, 1969.

14. Joseph Daughen, "Democrats Are Broke and Debt is $7.5 Million," Philadelphia *Evening Bulletin,* September 19, 1969.

15. William Chapman, "Democrats Advance Fund Aid," *The Washington Post,* September 18, 1969.

16. "Democrats: Divided and Dispirited," *Time,* February 16, 1970.

17. William Chapman, "Democrats Won't Dent Huge Debt in '70," *The Washington Post,* March 23, 1970.

18. "Alabamian Set to Run in 1972" (Third of a four-part series), October 22, 1968.

19. Nicholas C. Chriss, "Wallace Backers Balk at Leader's Principles," *The Los Angeles Times,* February 2, 1969.

20. Arlen J. Large, "Wallace's Loyalists Meet to Shape Plans for Another Try in '72," *The Wall Street Journal,* February 3, 1969.

21. " '68 Wallace Backers Urge a Conservative Party," *The New York Times,* February 23, 1969.

22. Large, "Wallace's Loyalists."

23. J. M. McFadden, "Wallace Issues Newsletter Saying 'I Shall Continue,' " *The Washington Post,* March 13, 1969.

24. "Wallace Expects Vietnam War to Be Key Issue in '72 Election," *The New York Times,* October 28, 1969.

25. Martin Waldron, "Wallace Man is Defeated in Tennessee Congressional Election," *The New York Times,* March 26, 1969.

26. Homer Bigart, "Wallace Has No Political Plans but His Staff in Ala-

bama is Larger than that of National Democrats," *The New York Times,* June 22, 1969.

    27. Stewart Alsop, "Br'er Rabbit Wallace," *Newsweek,* July 14, 1969.

Chapter 8
The Financial Future

    1. For a full account of the Long Amendment and its aftermath, see Herbert E. Alexander, "The Presidential Election Campaign Fund Act: The American Subsidy That Wasn't," paper presented at the Political Finance Panel of the 7th World Congress of the International Political Science Association, held in Brussels, Belgium, September 23, 1967.

Appendixes

Appendix A

Receipts and Expenditures
McCarthy Campaign, Massachusetts, 1968

RECEIPTS (THROUGH 11/30/68)

		Committee		
		Mass. McCarthy	*Volunteers*	*Eleven Votes*
General Contributions				
Actually received	$152,707			
Transferred to Volunteers	13,705	$139,002		
Actually received	220,222			
Transferred to Mass.				
McCarthy	1,020	_____	$219,202	_____
Total General Contributions	$358,204			
Special Receipts[a]				
$100 Cocktail Parties		29,147		
Symphony Hall Benefit Concert		8,865		
Art Auction		16,510		
Women for McCarthy Luncheon		4,917		
Kenney ad		8,156		
Eugene's II (cabaret)		5,712		
Fenway Park Rally		153,790		
Boston Garden Rally		_____	_____	$ 61,411
Total Special Receipts	$288,508			

[a]These figures are gross receipts. For the expenses involved in these functions, see Expenses section of this Appendix.

Transfer of Funds from
   Other Committees

	Mass. McCarthy Volunteers	Eleven Votes
Coalition for McCarthy: Boston, Mass.	$ 234	
Volunteers for McCarthy: Boston, Mass.	1,500	
Florida McCarthy for President: Miami (?), Fla.		$ 1,000
No. California Youth for McCarthy: San Francisco, Calif.		3,000
So. California Health Professionals for McCarthy: Los Angeles, Calif.		3,000
No. California Citizens for McCarthy: San Francisco, Calif.		3,000
Faculty for McCarthy: New York, N.Y.		3,000
Economists for McCarthy: New York, N.Y.		3,000
Lawyers for McCarthy: New York, N.Y.		3,000
Businessmen & Professionals for McCarthy: New York, N.Y.		3,000
Campaign Associates: New York, N.Y.		3,000
Business Community for McCarthy: New York, N.Y.		3,000
Friends of McCarthy: New York, N.Y.		3,000
Businessmen for McCarthy: New York, N.Y.		3,000
Investors' Committee for McCarthy: New York, N.Y.		3,000
Financial Community for McCarthy: New York, N.Y.		3,000
Committee of 100 for McCarthy: New York, N.Y.		3,000
Business Leaders for McCarthy: New York, N.Y.		3,000
Business & Professional Men for McCarthy: New York, N.Y.		3,000

	Mass. McCarthy	Volunteers	Eleven Votes

Transfer of Funds from
Other Committees, cont.

William Street Committee for McCarthy: New York, N.Y.		$ 1,000	
Mass. McCarthy for President: Boston, Mass.		10,000	
Eleven Votes for Peace: Boston, Mass.		29,300	
Missouri State McCarthy for President Committee: St. Louis, Mo.		316	

Total Transfers of Funds: $ 91,350

Contributions from Other Committees

Dissenting Democrats Boston, Mass.	$ 400		
Massachusetts Political Action for Peace (MassPAX)	1,685		
Bus Fares & contributions for Poor Peoples' March	3,732		

Total Contributions from
Other Committees: $ 5,817

Total Receipts: $743,879

DISBURSEMENTS (THROUGH 11/30/68)

		Mass. McCarthy	Volunteers	Eleven Votes
Actual Expense:				
State Headquarters		$ 65,512	$ 0	$ 0
Districts (31 district operations; 18 headquarters)		51,455	0	0
Publicity		82,872	15,886	11,220
Fees (includes all payments to staff)		25,915	7,202	200
Travel and Transportation		7,549	12,633	0
Chicago Convention		4,079	(15,000)*	0
Miscellaneous		5,549	0	0
Fenway Park Rally Operation (see Schedule 1, attached)		29,215	2,500	0
Boston Garden Rally Operation (see Schedule 2, attached)		0	0	15,403
		$272,146	$ 38,221	$ 26,823
Total Actual Expense:	$337,190			
Transfers Out: (see Schedule 3, attached)		$163,413	$123,520	$ 29,300**
Total Transfers Out:	$316,233			
Other Candidates: (see Schedule 4, attached)		0	$116,000	$ (29,300)
Total Other Candidates:	$116,000			
Other Committees: (see Schedule 5, attached)		1,062	3,500	0
Total Other Committees:	$ 4,562			
		$436,621	$281,241	$ 56,123
Total Disbursements:	$773,985			

*Not an expense; transferred to McCarthy Special Projects (see Schedule 3, attached).
**All transfers made to Volunteers for McCarthy and designated for other candidates (see Schedule 3, attached).

Schedule 1 - Fenway Park Rally Operation

	Mass. McCarthy	Volunteers	Eleven Votes
Fenway Park:			
Rental; services; lights:	$ 11,104	$ 2,500	
Other: Additional seating in field; sound system; special lighting; signs and decor; stage and scaffolding:	4,292	0	
Sound System & Closed-Circuit T.V.:			
For overflow crowd outside Fenway Park	2,539	0	
Telephone and Telegraph:	1,644	0	
Concession:			
McCarthy campaign souvenirs:	2,676	0	
Publicity:	(8,791)	(14,478)	
Fees	(878)	(122)	
Cocktail Party:	3,000	0	
Accomodations & Travel:			
Senator McCarthy and staff, entertainers and platform guests:	1,279	0	
Miscellaneous:			
Printing; office supplies; postage:	2,681	0	
Total Mass. McCarthy Fenway Operation	$ 29,215		
Total Volunteers Fenway Operation		$ 2,500	
Total Fenway Park Rally Operation $31,715			

*Allocated elsewhere

Schedule 2 - Boston Garden Rally Operation

	Mass. McCarthy Volunteers	Eleven Votes
Boston Garden:		
Rental & services:		$ 9,000
Special security:		426
Other:		41
Entertainment:		1,500
Printing & Postage:		3,719
Accomodations & Travel:		
Senator McCarthy and other candidates:		418
Miscellaneous:		299
*Publicity		(11,220)
*Fees		(200)
Total Eleven Votes Boston Garden Rally Operation		$ 15,403
Total Boston Garden Rally Operation	$ 15,403	

*Allocated elsewhere

Schedule 3 - Transfers Out

		Mass. McCarthy	*Volunteers*	*Eleven Votes*
3/22/68	Volunteers for McCarthy: Boston, Mass.	$ 705		
3/22/68	McCarthy for President: Milwaukee, Wisc.	100		
3/26/68	Scientists & Engineers for McCarthy: Wisconsin	500		
4/5/68	High School Students for McCarthy: Brunswick, Maine	100		
4/11/68	Volunteers for McCarthy: Boston, Mass.	3,000		
4/12/68	McCarthy for President: Washington, D.C.		$ 10,000	
4/17/68	Citizens for McCarthy: Wisconsin ?		8,000	
4/24/68	Citizens for McCarthy: Wisconsin ?	5,000		
4/26/68	McCarthy for President: Washington, D.C.	3,500		
4/30/68	McCarthy for President: Washington, D.C.	4,100		
5/1/68	McCarthy for President: Washington, D.C.	1,000		
5/3/68	McCarthy for President: California	5,000		
5/9/68	McCarthy for President: Washington, D.C.	10,000		
5/10/68	McCarthy for President: Washington, D.C.	1,483		
5/16/68	McCarthy for President: Washington, D.C.	5,000		
5/20/68	McCarthy for President: Washington, D.C.	3,000	3,000	
5/23/68	McCarthy for President: Portland, Oregon	425		
5/25/68	Mass. McCarthy for President: Boston, Mass.		1,020	
5/28/68	McCarthy for President: California	8,500		
5/29/68	McCarthy for President California		3,000	

Schedule 3 - Transfers Out, cont.

		Mass. McCarthy	Volunteers	Eleven Votes
6/3/68	McCarthy for President: New York, N.Y.	$ 500		
7/10/68	McCarthy for President (C.D.A.): New York, N.Y.		$ 20,000	
7/10/68	McCarthy for President: New York, N.Y.		500	
7/17/68	McCarthy for President: New York, N.Y.		25,000	
7/17/68	McCarthy for President: Louisville, Ky.		10,000	
7/29/68	McCarthy for President: Washington, D.C.		5,000	
8/1/68	McCarthy for President: New York, N.Y.	100,000		
8/2/68	McCarthy for President: Chicago, Ill.	1,500		
8/16/68	Volunteers for McCarthy: Boston, Mass.	10,000		
8/21/68	McCarthy Special Projects: Chicago, Illinois		15,000	
9/4/68	McCarthy for President: New York, N.Y.		3,000	
10/28/68	Volunteers for McCarthy: Boston, Mass.			$ 15,000
10/30/68	Volunteers for McCarthy: Boston, Mass.			14,300
10/68	Madison Square Garden Rally Committee: New York, N.Y.	———	20,000 ———	———

Total Mass. McCarthy Transfers Out $163,413

Total Volunteers Transfers Out $123,520

Total Eleven Votes Transfers Out $ 29,300

Total Transfers Out $316,233

Schedule 4 - Other Candidates

			Volunteers	
		Campaign Advance	Loan	Contribution
5/21/68	Paul O'Dwyer: New York	$ 1,000		
8/30/68	Elder for Congress: Massachusetts			$ 2,000
9/68	Stevens for Congress: Massachusetts			2,500
9/68	Gilligan for Senate: Ohio		$ 10,000	
10/68	O'Dwyer for Senate: New York	25,000		
10/68	Rosenblith for Congress: Massachusetts			1,000
10/68	O'Dwyer for Senate: New York	25,000		
10/22/68	Missourians for Eagleton: Missouri	5,000		
10/23/68	Morse for Senate: Oregon			2,000
10/28/68	Gilligan for Senate: Ohio	10,000		
10/28/68	Stevens for Congress Massachusetts			1,000
10/28/68	Eagleton for Senate: Missouri			2,500
10/30/68	D.C. Committee for Better Gov't. (Hughes for Senate): Washington, D.C.	10,000		
10/30/68	Gilligan for Senate: Ohio			10,000
10/30/68	D.C. Committee for Better Gov't. (Hughes for Senate): Washington, D.C.	2,000		
10/31/68	Morse for Senate: Oregon			2,000
10/31/68	Chavez for Governor: New Mexico			1,000

252

Schedule 4 - Other Candidates, cont.

	Campaign Advance	Volunteers Loan	Contribution
10/31/68 Clark for Senate: Illinois	$	$	$ 3,000
11/1/68 Gruening for Senate: Alaska			1,000
Total Campaign Advances	$ 78,000		
Total Loans		$ 10,000	
Total Contributions			$ 28,000
Total Other Candidates	$116,000		

Schedule 5 - Other Committees

	Mass. McCarthy	
	Campaign Advance	*Contribution*
6/28/68 Southern Christian Leadership Conference: Atlanta, Ga.		$ 562
8/7/68 National Democratic Party of Alabama: Montgomery, Ala.		500
For McCarthy delegates		

Total Mass. McCarthy *Other Committees*	$ 1,062

	Volunteers
10/68 Madison Square Garden Rally Committee: New York, N.Y.	$ 3,500

Total Volunteers *Other Committees*	$ 3,500

Total Other Committees	$ 4,562

Appendix B

Memorandum by Stewart R. Mott Stating His Political Contributions in 1968*

stewart rawlings mott

8 November 68

MEMORANDUM

TO:

During 1968, I made donations to various political committees on behalf of the following candidates:

Presidential

Eugene McCarthy		$210,000 (approx - incl expenses)
Nelson A. Rockefeller		100,000 (approx - all expenses)

Senate

Alan Cranston	Calif.	500
J. W. Fulbright	Ark.	1,000
John J. Gilligan	Ohio	11,000
Ernest Gruening	Alaska	1,000
Harold Hughes	Iowa	1,500
George McGovern	S. Dak.	1,000
Wayne Morse	Oregon	1,500
Paul O'Dwyer	New York	18,000 (approx - incl expenses)

House of Representatives

John Bingham	New York	500
William Blue	Michigan	2,000
Mel Dubin	New York	1,000
Ed Koch	New York	2,000
Al Lowenstein	New York	1,000
Wm. Fitz Ryan	New York	500
Don Weeden	New York	200
Ted Weiss	New York	1,000

In addition I made donations of approx. $5,000 to a variety of national political committees and organizations, including, for example, $2,000 to the National Committee for an Effective Congress.

Also I made donations or paid in expenses approx. $6,000 for a variety of state and local political campaigns and organizations.

Altogether I estimate that I spent a total of about $365,000 for the above-mentioned political purposes during the past ten months. And just to put things in perspective, let me comment that political donations of this amount--for me--are not easy, inasmuch as the total $365,000 is more than three times my annual after-tax income, or equivalent to about 7% of my total assets. I have not yet met anyone who has contributed an equivalent proportion of his assets or income!

*Reprinted with permission of Stewart R. Mott.

Appendix C

**Kennedy for President Committee for California
Consolidated Statement, Receipts and
Expenditures, 1968**

The following reproduction of a computer accounting of expenditures for the Robert Kennedy Campaign in California (pp. 258–261) is an example of highly responsible and highly unusual political record-keeping. This is only one of many such reports on the California Kennedy campaign, and it presents expenditures matched against budget estimates on an item-by-item basis. The degree of detail in this report has been all too rare in political record-keeping.

This example may be an indication of increasing sophistication in the handling of political financial records at a time when the computer is playing several new and important roles in political campaigning.

PAGE NO. 1

175 503

KENNEDY FOR PRESIDENT

COMMITTEE FOR CALIFORNI

CONSOLIDATED

STATEMENT

RECEIPTS & EXPENDITURES

PERIOD ENDING 06/15/68

OPERATIONS

	EXPENDITURES		TOTAL	VARIANCE %	
	CURRENT	YR TO DATE	BUDGET	UNDER	OVER
SALARIES AND FEES	18,056.92	76,835.47	71,319.96	5,515.51-	7.7-
PAYROLL TAXES	944.07	1,579.37	1,970.36	390.99	19.8
TRAVEL	1,788.91	5,800.11	9,007.36	3,207.25	35.6
TELEPHONE & TELEGRAPH	1,999.13	29,695.35	62,996.93	33,301.58	52.9
OFFICE & EQUIP RENTAL	6,431.06	53,542.30	54,782.01	1,239.71	2.3
FREIGHT EXPRESS & DEL	1,937.90	4,626.68	1,133.90	3,492.78-	308.0-
STATIONERY & SUPPLIES	8,676.90	30,911.68	19,137.55	11,774.13-	61.5-
INSURANCE	100.00	1,485.00	2,440.27	955.27	39.1

	EXPENDITURES		TOTAL	VARIANCE	
	CURRENT	YR TO DATE	BUDGET	UNDER OVER	%
POSTAGE	662.94	7,606.03	4,566.13	3,039.90-	66.6-
VOLUNTEER EXPENSE	2,331.67	5,610.97	3,344.61	2,266.36-	67.8-
MISCELLANEOUS	1,886.40	3,499.80	3,170.63	329.17-	10.4-
TOTAL OPERATIONS	44,815.90	221,192.76	233,869.71	12,676.95	5.4
SALARIES AND FEES	•	•	5,000.00	5,000.00	100.0
TRAVEL	.00	239.10	10.55	228.55-	176.7-
TOTAL PUBLIC RELATIONS	.00	239.10	5,010.55	4,771.45	95.2
SALARIES AND FEES	1,799.06	12,796.75	11,154.61	1,642.14-	14.7-
PAYROLL TAXES	338.64	474.69	397.25	77.44-	19.5-
TRAVEL	696.07	5,718.95	4,860.21	858.74-	17.7-
DIRECT AREA SUPPORT	7,227.43	57,688.98	72,568.51	14,879.53	20.5
MISCELLANEOUS	6,544.90	19,214.14	26,357.83	7,143.69	27.1
TOTAL SPECIAL GROUP EXP	16,606.10	95,893.51	115,338.41	19,444.90	16.9
SALARIES AND FEES	1,291.53	23,268.30	25,308.86	2,040.56	8.1
PAYROLL TAXES	245.81	416.98	87.47	329.51-	377.0-
TRAVEL	680.46	1,908.22	2,025.07	116.85	5.8

259

260

| | EXPENDITURES | | TOTAL | VARIANCE | |
	CURRENT	YR TO DATE	BUDGET	UNDER OVER	%
CUTS CLIPS MATS SUBS	2,146.73	2,426.04	1,507.92	918.12-	60.9-
MISCELLANEOUS	404.14	3,897.64	1,982.57	1,915.07-	96.6-
TOTAL NEWS BUREAU	4,768.67	31,917.18	30,911.89	1,005.29-	3.3-
REGISTRATION	.00	27,698.06	25,759.55	1,938.51-	7.5-
TOTAL REGISTRATION	.00	27,698.06	25,759.55	1,938.51-	7.5-
TRAVEL CANDIDATE	.00	3,039.65	.	3,039.65-	-
TRAVEL CANDIDATE STAFF	284.58	3,628.74	56,664.44	53,035.70	93.6
MISCELLANEOUS	4,241.67	28,103.81	71,325.17	43,221.36	60.6
TOTAL CANDIDATES EXP	4,526.25	34,772.20	127,989.61	93,217.41	72.8
GET OUT THE VOTE	77,134.48	175,822.64	250,000.00	74,177.36	29.7
TOTAL GET OUT THE VOTE	77,134.48	175,822.64	250,000.00	74,177.36	29.7
CAMPAIGN MAILING	655.87	6,920.37	15,213.65	8,293.28	54.5
TOTAL DIRECT MAILING	655.87	6,920.37	15,213.65	8,293.28	54.5
POLLS & SPECIAL SURVEYS	1,040.47	10,289.52	17,544.34	7,254.82	41.4
TOTAL POLLS & SPECIAL	1,040.47	10,289.52	17,544.34	7,254.82	41.4
BUMPER STRIPS	.00	12,695.67	16,194.42	3,498.75	21.6

| | EXPENDITURES | | TOTAL | VARIANCE | |
	CURRENT	YR TO DATE	BUDGET	UNDER OVER	%
BUTTONS	38.11-	10,307.67	20,131.32	9,823.65	48.8
BROCHURES	.00	35,325.57	10,712.68	24,612.89-	229.8-
OTHER	1,718.02	16,847.82	16,130.93	716.89-	4.4-
TOTAL ORGANIZATIONAL	1,679.91	75,176.73	63,169.35	12,007.38-	19.0-
NEWSPAPER ADV GENERAL	.00	1,000.00	1,000.00	.00	.0
NEWSPAPER ADV MINORITY	•	•	4,000.00	4,000.00	100.0
RADIO ADV PRODUCTION	.00	.00	•	.00	•
RADIO ADV TIME	1,000.00	1,000.00	4,000.00	3,000.00	75.0
TV ADV PRODUCTION	.00	250.00	250.00	.00	.0
OTHER ADVERTISING	.00	1,827.85	3,500.00	1,672.15	47.8
MISCELLANEOUS	.00	238.40	•	238.40-	• -
TOTAL MASS MEDIA	1,000.00	4,316.25	12,750.00	8,433.75	66.1
GRAND TOTAL	152,227.65	684,238.32	897,557.06	213,318.74	23.8 *

Appendix D

Letter from Stewart R. Mott to
Hubert H. Humphrey*

STEWART RAWLINGS MOTT

13 Oct. 1968

Hubert H. Humphrey
Vice-President of the U.S.A.
The White House
Washington, D.C.

Dear Mr. Vice-President:

On Wednesday, October 16th, at 8pm in your suite at the Waldorf Towers (42H) here in New York, you will be meeting with the people whose names are listed on the following page. Let me tell you just how this meeting came about:

First, about myself.... As a native of Flint, Michigan, last Fall at the age of 30, I was considering running for Congress in the 7th District against the Republican incumbent, Donald Riegle. I decided not to run (as a Democrat) because I did not feel I could support the Johnson Administration's conduct of the war in Vietnam. Then later, in March of this year, I came out as a strong supporter of Rockefeller for President, because he seemed to be the only reasonably liberal Republican who could possibly defeat Mr. Johnson and also bring an early end to the Vietnam war. Not only did I pay for 21 full pages of advertising for Rockefeller, I also set up the Coalition for a Republican Alternative, which was the only national citizens coordinating office for a period of six weeks during the early part of the Rockefeller campaign, and spent over $90,000 of my own money in supporting his candidacy.

When McCarthy suceeded so well in New Hampshire and Wisconsin, my interest in the Democratic Presidential campaign revived, and soon I found myself spending an increasing amount of time and money in the McCarthy campaign. By June 6th I had become the National Coordinator for Special Gifts and eventually I found I had given more than $200,000 towards the McCarthy candidacy. I spent full time during the summer months soliciting donations for the McCarthy campaign and helped to raise well over one million dollars. Altogether, including the $25,000 or so that I've given to Senatorial, Congressional, and local races, I've spent over $325,000 this year in politics, an amount that far exceeds my "ability" to give, since it equals three times my after-tax income or about 6% of my total assets! I mention all this to assure you that I am indeed very much concerned about national politics and that I'm willing to put my money where my mouth is. And I've spent some seven months in full-time work as well.

I cannot give you a full and adequate description of the others with whom you'll be meeting. I do know that ever since June we've been working together very closely in the McCarthy National Finance Committee and our work has been very effective. Most of the others, like myself, are political newcomers--we are not part of any regular Democratic Party organization. Collectively, the group whom you'll be meeting is responsible for having raised some $3-4,000,000 for the McCarthy campaign, and we individually have given an aggregate of over $1.5 million to the campaign. Each person, except for a couple, has given

*Reprinted with permission of Stewart R. Mott.

263

$50,000 or more to the McCarthy candidacy. Each one was a key person in contributing to the amazing success of the McCarthy phenomenon.

In the aftermath of our experience in Chicago--a most disagreeable experience especially for those of us quartered with the McCarthy staff on the 15th floor of the Hilton--we have stayed together as a group, meeting often here in N.Y.C. Our focus has been primarily on the Senatorial and Congressional campaigns where candidates of the McCarthy-Kennedy tradition have mounted campaigns with some strong hope of success. We have been working together now for some six weeks since Chicago in this new role and I expect that we will continue to stay together as a group in some informal fashion even after the November election.

In these past six weeks since Chicago, we have had virtually no contact with your office or your National Finance Committee, although various ones of us have been invited to miscellaneous $100-a-plate dinners and that sort of superficial activity. Only one or two of us has ever met you in person and we have not had a chance to meet with you following your Chicago victory.

One would think that your National Finance Committee--in as much need of funds as it apparently is--would seek out the key McCarthy supporters and attempt to recruit us on behalf of your campaign. This has not happened. We have not been invited to meet with you on a private, personal basis and we have not been asked to serve on your National Finance Committee.

To my knowledge, none of us has declared his support for you and your candidacy. Again, as far as I know, none of us has contributed towards your campaign. Although we each have the capability to contribute something more towards political campaigns in 1968, most of us are reserving our donations to give towards the campaigns of the "peace" candidates, such as Church-Clark-Cranston-Eagleton-Fulbright-Gilligan-Gruening-Hughes-McGovern-Morse-O'Dwyer and others.

My only contact with you has been through the press: TV, radio, newspapers. I have been a student of your domestic and foreign policy positions, but you have not yet convinced me to come forth and support you. Like yourself, I am not convinced that a conservative martini (four parts Nixon, one part Wallace) would be the best concoction for the future of our country. It seems to me that you are the only electable alternative to this prospect. Yet I am still not convinced that I should give money and time to your campaign, especially when the "peace" candidates so urgently need help.

In talking with Ted Lamb and Bill Connell, I came to the conclusion that the least we on the McCarthy Finance Committee could do for you would be to give you a hearing--a personal private interview of an hour's length--in order to question you about our own view of the nation's future and what it ought to be. We will be meeting you next Wednesday evening with an open mind and a sense of fair-play. We would "like" to be able to support you, but we certainly do need to be convinced.

I cannot promise you that any of us will be willing to give a thin dime towards your campaign. And we certainly will not be functioning as a group--each will make his own decision individually. We realize that you would like to have us become contributors towards your campaign, but you should not expect an immediate decision from any of us, checkbook-in-hand. If we become "turned on" and enthusiastic towards your candidacy, we have the capacity to give $1,000,000 or more to your campaign--and raise twice or three times that amount. But we will each make our own individual judgements on the basis of how you answer our several questions and how you conduct your campaign in the coming weeks.

So much for the introductions. We look forward to meeting with you this
Wednesday evening and I personally am very pleased that we are taking the
initiative to meet with you--even though your own Finance Committee has
virtually ignored the opportunity to arrange such a meeting. I am glad to
be the one who has set it up and arranged it--the results we shall see in the
next few weeks.

Sincerely yours,

Stewart R. Mott

cc: each person named on the following page
    William Connell, Aide to HHH
    James Thornton, Scheduler for HHH
    Dwayne Andreas, HHH Finance Committee
    Robert Short, HHH Finance Committee

P.S. We understand that you may invite either Mr. Andreas or Mr. Short to
join you for this meeting next Wednesday.

Appendix E

Contributors of $10,000 or More, 1968

This Appendix lists those individuals who in 1968 contributed in the aggregate $10,000 or more. It also shows those individuals in the 1968 compilation who contributed $10,000 or more in 1952, 1956, 1960, and 1964. (1952 list from Gore Committee, *Hearings*, part 2, pp. 527-29; 1956 list from Gore Committee, *Report*, Exhibit 12, pp. 67-71, and Exhibit 26, pp. 2-192; 1960 list from Herbert E. Alexander, *Financing the 1960 Election*, Appendix A, pp. 95-103; 1964 list from Herbert E. Alexander, *Financing the 1964 Election*, Appendix A, pp. 128-131. Husbands and wives are counted as one.

Contributions in 1964, 1960, 1956, and 1952 were made to the same party as in 1968 unless otherwise noted (R-Republican; D-Democratic; M-Miscellaneous). Husband and wife combinations refer to 1968 records only; in some cases, spouse combinations have varied through the years.

An asterisk (*) indicates that some or all of the information on the given amount was received from interviews or special lists, rather than from official campaign fund reports.

267

Contributors of $10,000 or More, 1968

Name and Address	Total	1968 Breakdown Republican	Democratic	Misc.	1964 Total	1960 Total	1956 Total	1952 Total
Abplanalp, Robert H. Bronxville, New York	$ 31,000	$28,000		$ 3,000				
Abramson, Dr. Harold A. New York, New York	10,000		$ 10,000					
*Alanson, Mrs. Lionel Mason San Francisco, California	10,000		10,000					
Aldrich, Mr. and Mrs. Winthrop W. New York, New York	16,000	16,000						
Alessio, Mr. and Mrs. John S. San Diego, California La Mesa, California	10,000	10,000						
Allen, Mr. and Mrs. Herbert A. New York, New York	57,500	1,500	56,000					
Altschul, Mr. and Mrs. Frank New York, New York	14,500	1,000	13,500		$ 1,000R 26,000D			$ 2,500R 14,059D
*Amory, Mr. and Mrs. Copley Lincoln, Massachusetts	21,250	1,000	19,750	500				
Anderson, Robert O. Roswell, New Mexico	44,000	44,000						
Andreas, Mr. and Mrs. Dwayne O. Excelsior, Minnesota New York, New York	11,000		11,000		10,000			
*Arkus-Duntov, Yura New York, New York	20,500+[a]		20,500+					

Name					
Armour, Mr. and Mrs. Laurance H. Chicago, Illinois Lake Forest, Illinois	11,000	11,000			
Arroyo, Nicholas R. Washington, D.C.	12,000	12,000			
Astor, Mrs. Vincent New York, New York	14,000	9,000	5,000		$15,000R
Autrey, Mr. and Mrs. Gene North Hollywood, California	15,000	15,000		20,000D	
*Avnet, Mr. and Mrs. Lester New York, New York	64,736	15,064	49,672		
Baker, George F. Jr. New York, New York	41,000	41,000			
Baker, Michael Jr. Rochester, Pennsylvania	14,000	10,000	4,000		
Barnett, Mr. and Mrs. Bernard H. Louisville, Kentucky	25,000	25,000			
Barrett, George F. Chicago, Illinois	20,000	20,000			
Bassine, Mr. and Mrs. Charles C. New York, New York	17,500		17,500		
*Beck, Louis New York, New York	20,000+		20,000+		
Beffa, Harvey Sr. Normandy, Missouri	12,000	12,000			
*Benjamin, Mr. and Mrs. Robert S. New York, New York Kings Point, New York	33,000	1,000	32,000		12,500D 1,000M

Name and Address	Total	1968 Breakdown			1964	1960	1956	1952
		Republican	Democratic	Misc.	Total	Total	Total	Total
Benner, Claude J. Dallas, Texas	$ 13,500		$ 13,500					
Benton, William Fairfield, Connecticut New York, New York Southport, Connecticut	12,538		12,538		$ 13,000		$ 23,675D 250M	$ 15,033
Berlinger, Mr. and Mrs. George F. New York, New York	14,000	$ 14,000						
Berman, Mr. and Mrs. Philip I. Allentown, Pennsylvania	16,000		16,000					
*Bernhard, Mrs. Richard J. New York, New York	16,500		16,500					
*Bernhard, William L. New York, New York	19,000		19,000					
*Bernstein, Mr. and Mrs. Daniel J. Scarsdale, New York	117,062		110,236	$ 6,826				
Berry, Mr. and Mrs. Loren H. Dayton, Ohio Lima, Ohio Miami Beach, Florida	47,500	46,500		1,000				
Bewley, Mr. and Mrs. George W. Lockport, New York	10,500	10,500						
Biggs, Mr. and Mrs. William R. Washington, D.C.	11,000		11,000					
Blaustein, Mr. and Mrs. Jacob Pikesville, Maryland Baltimore, Maryland	18,000	1,000	17,000		17,000D		14,150D	13,000D

Name and Location							
*Bloch, Allan R. Chicago, Illinois	10,000	10,000					
Bloomingdale, Mr. and Mrs. Alfred S. Los Angeles, California New York, New York	10,000	10,000					
Bobst, Elmer H. Morris Plains, New Jersey	63,250	63,250			$ 13,000		
*Bostrom, Mr. and Mrs. Harold W. Milwaukee, Wisconsin	25,000	25,000					
Boyar, Louis Beverly Hills, California	15,000	15,000					11,250
Boyar, Mr. and Mrs. Mark Beverly Hills, California	18,500	18,500					
Brandt, Mr. and Mrs. Harry New York, New York	46,000	45,000	1,000				
Bratti, Peter I. New York, New York	12,500	2,500	10,000				
*Brimberg, Mr. and Mrs. Robert H. Scarsdale, New York	10,000	10,000					
Brock, Mrs. George C. Los Angeles, California New Orleans, Louisiana	22,000	8,500	1,500				
*Bronfman, Mr. and Mrs. Edgar M. New York, New York	21,250	17,250	4,000				
Brown, Mr. and Mrs. Edward W. Jr. Orange, Texas	30,000	30,000				35,000R 1,500D	
Bruce, Mrs. Ailsa Mellon New York, New York	33,000	30,000	3,000	15,000R	16,500R	23,200R	14,500R

Name and Address	Total	1968 Breakdown			1964	1960	1956	1952
		Republican	Democratic	Misc.	Total	Total	Total	Total
Bubb, Henry A. Topeka, Kansas	$ 10,000	$ 10,000						
Buchanan, Wiley T. Jr. Washington, D.C. Dallas, Texas Newport, Rhode Island	13,000	13,000						
Buck, Mr. and Mrs. Richard J. New York, New York	25,000	25,000						
Bugas, Mr. and Mrs. John S. Dearborn, Michigan Bloomfield Hills, Michigan	20,000	20,000						
Burden, Hon. William A.M. New York, New York	14,500	14,500					$ 10,750	
Burns, Mr. and Mrs. Fritz B. Los Angeles, California	13,000	13,000						
Burton, Mr. and Mrs. Courtney Cleveland, Ohio	14,000	14,000						
Butcher, Mr. and Mrs. Howard III Villanova, Pennsylvania Philadelphia, Pennsylvania	55,400	54,900		$ 500				
Cabell, Henry F. Portland, Oregon	11,500	11,500						
Cantella, Vincent M. Boston, Massachusetts	10,000	10,000						
*Carlson, Chester F. Pittsford, New York Stanford, California	32,200	1,000	$ 30,700	500				
Carpenter, R.M. Jr. Wilmington, Delaware	10,000	10,000						

Name				
*Carrington, Ellsworth T. New York, New York	106,000+		$106,000+	$
*Carter, William	12,500		12,500	
Casey, James J. New York, New York	10,500	10,500		
Casey, Mr. and Mrs. William J. New York, New York	17,750	17,750		
Christopher, Mr. and Mrs. George San Francisco, California	12,600	12,600		
*Clark, Blair New York, New York	75,000+		75,000+	
*Clynes, Dr. Manfred Palisades, New York	30,000		30,000	
Cohen, Mr. and Mrs. Arthur New York, New York	15,500	500	15,000	
Coleman, Mr. and Mrs. James Daniel Stetson The Plains, Virginia Chicago, Illinois	25,086	25,086		
*Compton, Randolph Scarsdale, New York	10,000		10,000	
Copeland, Mr. and Mrs. Lammot duPont Greenville, Delaware Wilmington, Delaware	14,000	14,000		$ 13,000
*Cornfeld, Bernard Geneva, Switzerland	30,000		30,000	
*Coslow, Sam Palisades Park, New Jersey	10,900		10,900	
Cousins, Norman New York, New York	58,000	1,000	57,000	$ 10,800

Name and Address	Total	1968 Breakdown Republican	Democratic	Misc.	1964 Total	1960 Total	1956 Total	1952 Total
*Cox, Mr. and Mrs. Gardner Cambridge, Massachusetts	$ 10,700		$ 10,700					
Craigmiles, Mr. and Mrs. Adrian Rich Hill, Missouri	10,000		10,000					
*Cromwell, Mr. and Mrs. P. McEvoy Baltimore, Maryland	11,800		11,800					
*Cunningham, Miss Priscilla New York, New York	18,900		18,900					
*Dakin, Henry S. San Francisco, California	26,167+		25,500+	$ 667				
Danskin, Merlyn E. Oregon	16,000		16,000					
*Davidson, Mrs. Crow Girard New York, New York	20,050		20,050					
Davis, Walter Royal Midland, Texas	25,000	$ 25,000						
DeBartolo, Edward J. Youngstown, Ohio	10,000		10,000					
*Degnan, Mrs. June California	60,000		60,000					
Dehlendorf, Robert O. II Los Altos Hills, California Menlo Park, California	11,000	11,000						
Denckla, D. Bethesda, Maryland	10,000			10,000				
*DeNeufville, Hugo Mendham, New Jersey	10,000		10,000					

Name					
DeRoulet, Vincent New York, New York	44,500	44,500			
*Dilbeck, Walter J. Evansville, Indiana	50,000+	50,000+			
Disney, Mr. and Mrs. Roy E. Burbank, California	10,561	10,561			
Donnelley, Mr. and Mrs. Gaylord Chicago, Illinois Libertyville, Illinois	13,000	13,000			
Dorrance, John T. Jr. Camden, New Jersey Gladwyne, Pennsylvania	20,100+	20,100+		$ 13,000	
*Dowling, Robert W. New York, New York	102,754+	102,754+		17,000	$ 12,500
*Dreyfus, Mr. and Mrs. Jack J. Jr. New York, New York	245,000+	76,000	169,000+	33,000R	
Dudley, Mr. and Mrs. Guilford Jr. Nashville, Tennessee	51,000	51,000			
Dunn, Mrs. J.R. Coconut Grove, Florida	12,500	12,500			
DuPont, Hon. and Mrs. Reynolds Wilmington, Delaware	13,500	11,500	2,000	$ 11,000R 500M	
*Dutcher, Mr. and Mrs. Cornelius G. Phoenix, Arizona	12,000	12,000	12,000		
Dyson, Mr. and Mrs. Charles H. New York, New York Scarsdale, New York	16,500	1,500	15,000		
*Edgar, George P. New York, New York	17,000	17,000	17,000		

Name and Address	Total	1968 Breakdown Republican	1968 Breakdown Democratic	1968 Breakdown Misc.	1964 Total	1960 Total	1956 Total	1952 Total
*Edison, Mr. and Mrs. Theodore M. West Orange, New Jersey	$ 10,000		$ 10,000					
Ehrman, Frederick L. New York, New York	41,136	$ 41,136						
*Eldridge, Mr. and Mrs. Donald F. Witherton, California	10,000 (loan)		10,000 (loan)					
Elkus, Mr. and Mrs. Richard J. Redwood City, California Woodside, California	41,500	41,500						
Erpf, Armand G. New York, New York	13,500	3,500	10,000					
*Evans, Mr. and Mrs. Thomas Mellon New York, New York Pittsburgh, Pennsylvania Greenwich, Connecticut	23,500+	6,500	17,000+			$ 10,000R		
Factor, Mr. and Mrs. John Hollywood, California	102,500		102,500			20,000		
Farkas, Mr. and Mrs. George Lewis New York, New York	10,000	10,000						
Farley, Edward New York, New York	25,000	25,000						
*Faulkner, Dr. and Mrs. James Brookline, Massachusetts	25,500		25,000	$ 500				
Field, Mr. and Mrs. Charles D. San Francisco, California	10,000	10,000						
*Field, Mrs. Marshall							$ 20,000D	$ 28,000

Name					
*Fife, Martin New York, New York	72,000	72,000			
Finch, Mr. and Mrs. Edward R. Jr. New York, New York	25,000	25,000			
*Finkelstein, Mr. and Mrs. Jerry New York, New York	24,150+	24,150+			
Firestone, Mr. and Mrs. Roger S. Pottstown, Pennsylvania Bryn Mawr, Pennsylvania	39,000	39,000	$ 12,000	11,500	11,150
*Fisher, Mr. and Mrs. Maxwell M. Detroit, Michigan Franklin, Michigan	122,500+	122,500+		15,000	
Fixman, Ben Creve Coeur, Missouri	10,000	10,000			
Flanigan, Mr. and Mrs. Horace C. New York, New York	13,000	13,000			
*Folger, Hon. J. Clifford Washington, D.C.	19,000+	19,000+	12,000	13,600	11,500
Ford, Mr. and Mrs. Benson Grosse Pointe Shores, Michigan	41,000	41,000			
Ford, Henry II Grosse Pointe, Michigan Detroit, Michigan New York, New York Washington, D.C.	37,250	30,000 7,250	4,100R 40,000D		18,899R
*Ford, Mr. and Mrs. William Clay Dearborn, Michigan	21,000	20,000 (Mr.) 1,000 (Mrs.)			
*Forgash, Morris New York, New York	12,500	12,500			
Frankel, George Greenwich, Connecticut New York, New York	16,500	15,500 1,000			

Name and Address	Total	1968 Breakdown Republican	Democratic	Misc.	1964 Total	1960 Total	1956 Total	1952 Total
Freeman, Mr. and Mrs. Stanley M. Beverly Hills, California Los Angeles, California	$ 17,000	$ 17,000						
Frick, Miss Helen Clay Pittsburgh, Pennsylvania	19,500	19,500			$ 18,570R 1,000M		$ 26,300	$ 20,000
Galbreath, Mr. and Mrs. John W. Columbus, Ohio	24,000	24,000						
Galvin, Mr. and Mrs. Robert W. Franklin Park, Illinois Barrington, Illinois	13,000	13,000			25,000			
Garland, Mr. and Mrs. John Jewett Los Angeles, California San Marino, California	15,000	15,000						
Gary, Mr. and Mrs. Theodore S. Miami Beach, Florida Chicago, Illinois	13,500	13,500						
Gauer, Mr. and Mrs. Edward H. San Francisco, California	41,000	41,000						
Gaydosh, Frank W. Union Dale, Pennsylvania	26,500			$ 26,500				
Gelatt, Mr. and Mrs. J.S. La Crosse, Wisconsin	28,500	28,500						
Gholson, Elmo McLeansboro, Illinois	10,000		$ 10,000					
Gilbert, Mr. and Mrs. Benjamin D. Stamford, Connecticut New York, New York	13,000	3,000		10,000				
*Gimbel, Robert New York, New York	50,250+	50,250+						

Name						
Gimma, Mr. and Mrs. Joseph A. New York, New York	10,000	10,000				
*Glekel, Newton New York, New York	25,500+		24,500+	1,000		
Gordon, Mr. and Mrs. Albert H. New York, New York	38,750	38,750				
Gordon, Milton A. New York, New York	15,000		15,000			
Goulandris, Alexandre N. New York, New York	10,000	10,000				
Gould, Mr. and Mrs. Kingdon Jr. Laurel, Maryland Washington, D.C.	22,000	22,000				
Grant, Mr. and Mrs. Arnold M. New York, New York	25,500		25,500		31,000	$ 13,500
*Green, Mr. and Mrs. Louis New York, New York	27,000	27,000				
*Green, S. William New York, New York	11,000	11,000				
Greenwall, Mr. and Mrs. Frank K. New York, New York	27,020	27,020			10,000D	
*Grimson, Mrs. Samuel B. New York, New York	18,500	1,000	17,500			
Gruber, Edward L. Pennsylvania	12,000	12,000				
Guest, Raymond R. Dublin, Ireland King George, Virginia	36,000		36,000		11,000	
Harnischfeger, Walter Milwaukee, Wisconsin	11,000	10,000		1,000		

Name and Address	Total	1968 Breakdown			1964	1960	1956	1952
		Republican	Democratic	Misc.	Total	Total	Total	Total
Harriman, Mr. and Mrs. Edward Roland, New York, New York	$ 17,000	$16,500		$ 500	$ 25,000R 3,000D	$22,750R	$ 34,350R	$ 22,000R
Haskell, Henry G. Jr. Wilmington, Delaware	11,017	11,017						
*Hefner, Hugh Chicago, Illinois	10,000+		$ 10,000+					
Heinz, Henry J. II Pittsburgh, Pennsylvania	11,000+	11,000+					12,500	
Helis, William G. Jr. New Orleans, Louisiana	20,000		20,000		15,000			
*Hiatt, Mr. and Mrs. Arnold Newton, Massachusetts	10,000+		10,000+					
Hirsch, Mr. and Mrs. Clement L. Los Angeles, California Newport Beach, California	29,000	29,000						
*Hochschild, Mr. and Mrs. Harold K. New York, New York	27,000+		27,000+		3,000R 26,000D			
Hoffman, Mr. and Mrs. H. Leslie El Monte, California	15,411	15,411					26,000	
Holmes, John A. St. Louis, Missouri	18,000	18,000						
Homan, Rudolf Cincinnati, Ohio	15,850	9,000		6,850				
Hooker, John J. Jr. Nashville, Tennessee	35,000		35,000					
Hope, Mr. and Mrs. Bob North Hollywood, California	16,000	16,000						

Name						
Houghton, Mr. and Mrs. Amory Corning, New York	19,500	19,500		12,000		
Houghton, Arthur A. Jr. New York, New York	14,500	12,000	2,500	16,000R		
Houtchens, Mr. and Mrs. Delton L. Clinton, Missouri	10,000		10,000			
Humes, Mr. and Mrs. John P. New York, New York	43,000	43,000		35,900		
Ingalls, Mr. and Mrs. David S. Cleveland, Ohio	12,000	12,000				
Irwin, Mr. and Mrs. John N. II New York, New York	15,000	15,000				
Ittleson, Henry Jr. New York, New York	28,500	28,500			10,200	
*Jakobson, Mr. and Mrs. John New York, New York	14,700		14,700			16,000
*Janeway, Eliot New York, New York	10,000+		10,000+			
Johnson, Dorothy Oregon	20,723	20,723				
Johnson, Mark Oregon	30,723	30,723				
*Jones, Alfred Winslow New York, New York	11,500		11,500			
*Jordan, Sherman	10,000		10,000			
Jorgensen, Mr. and Mrs. Earle M. Los Angeles, California	22,500	22,500				
Judelson, David N. New York, New York	16,000	16,000				
Judy, Mr. and Mrs. Paul R. Chicago, Illinois	10,000	10,000				

282

Name and Address	Total	1968 Breakdown Republican	Democratic	Misc.	1964 Total	1960 Total	1956 Total	1952 Total
Kaiser, Mr. and Mrs. Edgar Oakland, California Lafayette, California	$ 25,000		$ 25,000					
Kaiser, Mr. and Mrs. Leland M. San Francisco, California	31,000	$ 31,000						
*Kaplan, Mr. and Mrs. Jack M. New York, New York	16,500	1,000	15,500					$ 19,000D
Kearney, Mr. and Mrs. William J. Birmingham, Alabama	12,000	12,000						
Kearns, Henry New York, New York	14,000	14,000						
Keith, Mr. and Mrs. Willard W. Beverly Hills, California	19,880	19,880						
Kellogg, Francis L. New York, New York	25,000	25,000						
Kerwitz, J.C. Oregon	10,000	10,000						
*Kimball, Dan Washington, D.C.	15,000		15,000					
King, Mr. and Mrs. J.M. Denver, Colorado	27,500	27,500						
King, Mr. and Mrs. James M. Denver, Colorado Englewood, Colorado	17,500	17,500						
King, Mr. and Mrs. John M. Denver, Colorado Englewood, Colorado	53,500	53,500						

Name							
Knight, Mr. and Mrs. Bruce Lister Miami Beach, Florida Spring Lake, New Jersey	30,000	30,000					
Kononoff, Mr. and Mrs. Alexis B. Coral Gables, Florida	12,000	2,000 (Mrs.)	10,000 (Mr.)				
Kreeger, David L. Washington, D.C.	25,000		25,000		$ 10,000		
Krim, Mr. and Mrs. Arthur B. New York, New York	11,000		11,000			$ 10,000D 500M		
Krulewitch, Mr. and Mrs. Melvin L. New York, New York	11,000	11,000					
*Kuhn, Mr. and Mrs. Samuel L. New York, New York	10,300		10,300				
*Lamb, Edward Toledo, Ohio Maumee, Ohio	18,500		18,500				
*Lamont, Mr. and Mrs. Corliss New York, New York	10,000		10,000				
Lancaster, Mr. and Mrs. Burt Malibu, California	10,000		10,000				
Lane, Mr. and Mrs. Edward H. Altavista, Virginia	21,650	19,650	1,500	$ 500			
Lanier, Mrs. Doris Bal Harbour, Florida	50,000		50,000				
Lasdon, William S. New York, New York	27,000	27,000					
Lasker, Mrs. Albert D. New York, New York	69,400		69,400		22,500	19,300	$ 1,000R	64,400D
*Lawrence, Larry	30,000		30,000				
Lawson, D.J. Fort Worth, Texas	15,000		15,000				21,000

284

Name and Address	Total	1968 Breakdown Republican	Democratic	Misc.	1964 Total	1960 Total	1956 Total	1952 Total
*Lederer, Mr. and Mrs. Saul Detroit, Michigan	$ 10,100		$ 10,100					
*Lee, Robert P. Rumson, New Jersey	10,000		10,000					
Lefrak, Samuel J. New York, New York Forest Hills, New York	14,250	$ 13,250	1,000					
Leithead, Barry T. New York, New York	17,200	17,200						
Leslie, Mr. and Mrs. John W. Chicago, Illinois Evanston, Illinois	11,000	10,000		$ 1,000				
Levin, Mr. and Mrs. Howard S. New York, New York	30,000		30,000					
Levin, Mr. and Mrs. Philip J. Warren, New Jersey North Plainfield, New Jersey	22,000	3,000	19,000					
Levine, Joseph E. New York, New York	22,250	22,250						
*Levine, Lawrence New York, New York	16,815		16,815					
Levitt, Mr. and Mrs. William J. Lake Success, New York	37,500	37,500						
*Levy, Gustave New York, New York	10,000	7,000	3,000		$ 5,000R 7,000D			
Lewis, Mr. and Mrs. Lawrence Jr. Richmond, Virginia Palm Beach, Florida	19,000	19,000						

Name / Location							
*Lidow, Eric Los Angeles, California	19,000		16,000	3,000			
Liedtke, J. Hugh Midland, Texas	18,000	18,000					
Liedtke, W.C. Jr. Houston, Texas	14,000	14,000					
Linen, Mr. and Mrs. James A. III Greenwich, Connecticut New York, New York	12,500	12,500					
Litchfield, Edward H. Coudersport, Pennsylvania	10,000		10,000				
Loeb, Mr. and Mrs. Henry A. New York, New York	17,500	2,500	15,000		6,000R 13,500D		
*Loeb, Mr. and Mrs. John L. New York, New York	16,250	6,750	9,500				$ 10,000R
Long, Mr. and Mrs. Jack Hyattsville, Maryland	10,200		10,200				
Love, John A. Jr. Sheridan, Wyoming	10,000	10,000					
Luckman, Mr. and Mrs. Charles Los Angeles, California	15,000	15,000			16,250D		
Mandel, Mr. and Mrs. Milton H. New York, New York	12,000	12,000					
Mann, Hon. Frederick R. New York, New York Philadelphia, Pennsylvania	35,500		35,500		27,500	$ 10,000	
*Marks, Mrs. Caroline C. New York, New York	10,000		9,000	1,000			
Marks, Louis New York, New York	15,000		15,000				
*Marriott, J. Willard Washington, D.C.	103,500+	103,500+					

Name and Address	Total	1968 Breakdown Republican	Democratic	Misc.	1964 Total	1960 Total	1956 Total	1952 Total
Marshall, Mr. and Mrs. Anthony D. New York, New York	$ 25,000	$ 25,000						
*Marshall, Mr. and Mrs. James New York, New York	19,000		$ 19,000					
*Martindell, Mrs. Jackson Princeton, New Jersey	12,250		12,250					
Massey, Jack C. Nashville, Tennessee	16,500	16,500						
May, Mrs. Cordelia Scaife Ligonier, Pennsylvania Pittsburgh, Pennsylvania	52,000	52,000						
Maytag, Lewis B. Jr. Miami, Florida	27,000	27,000			$ 19,000			
*McAllister, Mrs. Frances B. Flagstaff, Arizona	10,000+		10,000+					
McCabe, Thomas B. Swarthmore, Pennsylvania Philadelphia, Pennsylvania	18,300	18,300				$ 16,000		
*McClure, Harold M. Jr. Alma, Michigan	90,000	87,500	2,500				$ 19,500	$ 13,000
McCormick, Fowler Chicago, Illinois	16,000	16,000					13,100	
McCulloch, Robert P. Los Angeles, California	27,297	27,297						
McDaniel, Mr. and Mrs. Glen Los Angeles, California	11,500	11,500						
McGovern, Mr. and Mrs. Eugene Long Island, New York New York, New York	19,000	19,000						

Name								
McGowen, Jackson R. / Long Beach, California / Santa Monica, California	18,700	18,700						
McKnight, William L. / St. Paul, Minnesota	44,000	44,000						
McMullen, John J. / New York, New York	12,000	12,000						
McVitty, Mr. and Mrs. Edward W. / New York, New York	10,000		9,500	$ 500				
*Meckler, Mr. and Mrs. Herman L. / New York, New York / Kings Point, New York	26,500	15,000	11,500					
Mellon, Paul / Pittsburgh, Pennsylvania / Washington, D.C.	47,000	47,000			11,000	18,500	29,500	22,000
Mellon, Mr. and Mrs. Richard K. / Pittsburgh, Pennsylvania	65,000	65,000			23,500	20,000	33,000	25,500
Metaxo, Spiro / New York, New York	10,000	10,000						
Michel, Clifford W. / New York, New York	10,500	500	10,000					
Middendorf, John William II / New York, New York / Greenwich, Connecticut	15,500	15,500						
Millard, Mark J. / New York, New York	12,500	2,500	10,000					
*Miller, Allan / Boca Raton, Florida	108,000		108,000					
*Miller, Edward J. / New York, New York	10,000		10,000					
Miller, Mr. and Mrs. Lloyd I. / Cincinnati, Ohio	11,000	11,000						

Name and Address	Total	1968 Breakdown			1964 Total	1960 Total	1956 Total	1952 Total
		Republican	Democratic	Misc.				
Monell, Edmund C. New York, New York	$ 22,000	$ 22,000						
Morrison, Dr. and Mrs. Thomas J. New York, New York	52,000	52,000			$ 29,000	$ 15,000		
*Morse, Joseph New York, New York	15,100		$ 15,100					
Moscoso, Teodoro Santurce, Puerto Rico	18,000		18,000					
*Mosler, John New York, New York	12,250	11,750	500		10,000D			
*Mott, Stewart New York, New York	366,700	100,200	255,500	$ 11,000				
*Murphy, Thomas S. New York, New York	11,000	5,000	6,000					
Myrin, Mrs. Mabel Pew Philadelphia, Pennsylvania Kimberton, Pennsylvania	35,833	34,166		1,667	24,000R 3,000M	15,750R	$ 47,125R	$ 35,500R
Neipp, Morton Toledo, Ohio	10,000		10,000					
Newington, Dr. and Mrs. John C. Greenwich, Connecticut	21,500	21,000		500	48,000R			
Newman, Frank Boca Raton, Florida	10,500	10,500						
Newman, Howard A. New York, New York	30,000	30,000			12,500D			
Nielsen, Mr. and Mrs. Arthur C. Chicago, Illinois	38,000	32,000		6,000				

	1	2	3	4	5	6
North, John Ringling New York, New York Sarasota, Florida	10,000					
Noyes, Mr. and Mrs. Nicholas H. Indianapolis, Indiana	18,000				10,250	
Nye, Charles B. Durham, North Carolina	10,000					
Olin, John M. East Alton, Illinois St. Louis, Missouri	31,500			31,000	12,500	14,950
Olin, Mr. and Mrs. Spencer T. St. Louis, Missouri	12,500			11,900	24,500	34,600
*Ostrow, Samuel Los Angeles, California	10,000	10,000				
Packard, Mr. and Mrs. David Los Altos Hills, California Palo Alto, California	11,000					
Paley, William S. New York, New York	10,000					12,600
Patterson, Hon. and Mrs. Jefferson Washington, D.C.	10,000					21,000
Pawley, Mr. and Mrs. William Douglas Miami, Florida	22,000					
Payson, Mr. and Mrs. Charles S. Manhasset, New York	28,000			20,500	20,000	71,850
*Peretz, Martin Cambridge, Massachusetts	114,400+	114,400+				
Pew, George T. Haverford, Pennsylvania	10,650		650			

Name and Address	Total	1968 Breakdown Republican	1968 Breakdown Democratic	1968 Breakdown Misc.	1964 Total	1960 Total	1956 Total	1952 Total
Pew, Mr. and Mrs. John Howard Philadelphia, Pennsylvania Ardmore, Pennsylvania	$ 64,733	$ 63,066		$ 1,667	$ 29,000R 3,000M	$ 16,750R	$ 51,125R	$ 38,250R
*Pew, John Newton Jr. Chester, Pennsylvania Bryn Mawr, Pennsylvania Hodis, Pennsylvania	41,000	41,000						
Pew, Miss Mary Ethel Philadelphia, Pennsylvania Bryn Mawr, Pennsylvania	32,833	31,166		1,667	24,000R 3,000M	16,750R	47,125R	36,250R
Pew, Walter Crooker Philadelphia, Pennsylvania	14,000	14,000						
Phipps, Mr. and Mrs. Ogden P. Palm Beach, Florida New York, New York	18,000	18,000						
Pickett, R. Atlanta, Georgia	12,000	12,000						
Pike, Mr. and Mrs. Thomas P. Los Angeles, California	10,805	10,805						
*Pirie, Robert Hamilton, Massachusetts	10,000+		$ 10,000+					
Pistell, Mr. and Mrs. Richard C. New York, New York	50,000	50,000						
Polk, Louis Jr. Dayton, Ohio	10,000	10,000						
*Pomerance, Mr. and Mrs. Ralph New York, New York Cos Cob, Connecticut	19,350+	750	18,600+		7,300D 15,500M	17,500D 10,000M	30,700D	
*Pratt, Mr. and Mrs. George D. Jr. Bridgewater, Connecticut	17,500+		15,000+	2,500				

291

Name							
Price, Mr. and Mrs. James R. Lafayette, Indiana	34,000	30,000	4,000				
Pritzker, Mr. and Mrs. Jay A. Chicago, Illinois Winnetka, Illinois	10,000	10,000					
Pritzlaff, Mr. and Mrs. John C. Jr. New York, New York Phoenix, Arizona	23,000	23,000					
Ray, Mr. and Mrs. James C. Bozeman, Montana	11,653	11,653					
Regan, Mr. and Mrs. D. New York, New York	10,000	10,000					
Resnick, Joseph Y. Washington, D.C. New York, New York	18,500		18,500				
Revson, Charles New York, New York	26,000	15,500	10,500				
Reynolds, Mr. and Mrs. Robert O. Hollywood, California	33,000	33,000					
Riklis, Mr. and Mrs. Meshulam New York, New York	25,000	25,000	25,000				
Rockefeller, Mr. and Mrs. David New York, New York	25,500	20,500	5,000	12,500R	13,975R	22,000R	20,000R
Rockefeller, Mrs. John D. Jr. New York, New York	1,493,125	1,493,125			15,000	19,000	34,500
Rockefeller, Mr. and Mrs. John D. III New York, New York	17,500	17,500			13,500	14,250	14,000
Rockefeller, Mr. and Mrs. Laurance New York, New York	23,500	23,500			15,975	25,550	35,000

Name and Address	Total	1968 Breakdown			1964	1960	1956	1952
		Republican	Democratic	Misc.	Total	Total	Total	Total
*Rockefeller, Mr. and Mrs. Nelson A. Albany, New York New York, New York	$127,500+ b	$127,500+				$ 16,000	$ 35,600	$ 32,000
Rollins, John W. Wilmington, Delaware	15,000	15,000						
Roman, Mr. and Mrs. Stephen B. Toronto, Canada	10,000	10,000						
Rosen, Carl New York, New York Dedham, Massachusetts	10,000		$ 10,000					
Rosenthal, Lawrence M. New York, New York	10,000	10,000						
Rosenstiel, Lewis S. Miami Beach, Florida New York, New York	10,000	10,000						
*Roth, Harry Los Angeles, California	11,000		11,000					
Rothberg, Mr. and Mrs. Samuel Peoria, Illinois	25,000		25,000					
*Rubin, Mr. and Mrs. Reed New York, New York	18,500+		18,500+					
*Rubin, Mr. and Mrs. Samuel New York, New York	76,000		76,000					
*Rubin, Mrs. Vera D. New York, New York	14,450		14,450					
Ruckelshaus, Mr. and Mrs. Conrad Indiana	10,000	10,000						

Name					
Ruffin, Mr. and Mrs. Peter B. Scarsdale, New York New York, New York	30,890	30,890			
Runnells, Mrs. Clive Lake Forest, Illinois Chicago, Illinois	17,000	17,000			
Russell, Fred J. South Gate, California Los Angeles, California	21,000	21,000			
Russell, Mrs. Margery F. Oregon	94,613		$ 94,613		
*Rust, Mrs. Fiona Washington, D.C.	20,000		20,000		
*Ruttenberg, Derald H. New York, New York	11,000+	10,000		$ 1,000+	
Salvatori, Mr. and Mrs. Henry Los Angeles, California	95,000	90,000	5,000		
Sawyer, Grant Las Vegas, Nevada	25,000	25,000			
Scaife, Mr. and Mrs. Richard Mellon Pittsburgh, Pennsylvania	55,462	55,462			
*Scheiner, Mr. and Mrs. Martin L. Pleasantville, New York	13,250	11,750	1,500		
Schiff, Mr. and Mrs. John M. New York, New York	24,500	24,500			$ 10,000
Schmidt, Benno C. New York, New York	13,000	13,000			11,500
Schrader, Abe New York, New York	14,000	14,000			18,550
Schulman, Mr. and Mrs. Samuel Los Angeles, California	23,000	23,000			15,000

Name and Address	Total	1968 Breakdown			1964 Total	1960 Total	1956 Total	1952 Total
		Republican	Democratic	Misc.				
Schweiker, Mr. and Mrs. Malcolm A. Worcester, Pennsylvania	$ 38,000	$ 38,000						
Sears, Mrs. Lester M. Shaker Heights, Ohio	47,000	47,000						
Sesnon, Mr. and Mrs. W.T. Jr. Los Angeles, California Beverly Hills, California	24,000	24,000						
*Settel, Mrs. Elmer New York, New York	25,100		$ 25,100					
Shaheen, John M. New York, New York	16,500	16,500						
Sharp, Mrs. Evelyn New York, New York	22,000	22,000						
Sharples, Mr. and Mrs. Philip T. Haverford, Pennsylvania Philadelphia, Pennsylvania	21,000	21,000						
Sheldon, Mr. and Mrs. Alan III Grosse Pointe, Michigan	12,100	12,100						
*Shields, Richard T. New York, New York	20,000	2,000	18,000					
Simon, Joel New York, New York	17,000		17,000					
Singer, Mr. and Mrs. Edwin Corpus Christi, Texas	10,000	10,000						
Singer, Mr. and Mrs. Herbert M. New York, New York	15,000		15,000					

Name and Location							
Singleton, Mr. and Mrs. Henry, Los Angeles, California	23,735	23,735					
Skouras, Spyros P., New York, New York	17,450	17,450					
Smith, Mr. and Mrs. Kent H., Gates Mill, Ohio / Cleveland, Ohio	10,000	10,000					
*Spanel, Mr. and Mrs. A.N., Princeton, New Jersey	11,000+		11,000+				
Spencer, Jack K., Columbia, Georgia	47,500	47,500					
*Sperling, Miklos, Indianapolis, Indiana	11,500+		11,500+				
Sproul, Elmer C., Orange, New Jersey	11,000		11,000				
*Stein, Howard, New York, New York	10,500+		10,500+				
Stein, Mr. and Mrs. Jules, Beverly Hills, California / New York, New York	11,250	9,250	2,000				
Steinman, Miss Frances, Lancaster, Pennsylvania	19,000	19,000					
Steinman, Mrs. James Hale, Lancaster, Pennsylvania	16,000	16,000					
Stevens, Mr. and Mrs. Roger L., Washington, D.C.	30,000		30,000	$ 18,000	$ 20,000	$ 15,000	$ 11,000
Stone, Mr. and Mrs. E.M., Denver, Colorado	10,000		10,000				
*Stone, Martin, Los Angeles, California	40,000		40,000				

Name and Address	Total	1968 Breakdown Republican	Democratic	Misc.	1964 Total	1960 Total	1956 Total	1952 Total
*Stone, Mr. and Mrs. W. Clement Chicago, Illinois New York, New York	$201,000+	$200,000+		$ 1,000				
Stouffer, Mr. and Mrs. Vernon Cleveland, Ohio	27,000	27,000						
Swift, John H. Columbus, Georgia	25,000	25,000						
Swigert, Ernest G. Portland, Oregon	16,000	11,000		5,000				
Taylor, P.G. Pennsylvania	10,000		$ 10,000					
Taylor, Col William B. III Washington, D.C. Arlington, Virginia	10,000	10,000						
*Thomas, Michael New York, New York	10,000		10,000					
Thornton, Charles B. Beverly Hills, California Los Angeles, California	19,500	19,500						
Timken, W.R. Cleveland, Ohio Canton, Ohio	13,500	13,500						
*Towbin, A. Robert New York, New York	20,000		20,000					
Towsley, Dr. and Mrs. Harry A. Ann Arbor, Michigan	18,000	18,000			$ 12,000			
*Tuchman, Dr. and Mrs. Lester New York, New York	20,500+		20,500+					

Name	1	2	3	4	5	6	7	8
Tuttle, Mr. and Mrs. Holmes, Los Angeles, California	10,500	10,500						
Valle, Mr. and Mrs. Anthony E., Los Angeles, California	10,000	10,000						
Vanderbilt, Harold S., New York, New York, Lantana, Florida	11,000	11,000				$ 12,000	$ 51,000	$ 41,000R / 3,000D
Van Alstyne, David Jr., New York, New York	25,000	25,000						
Vesco, Mr. and Mrs. Robert L., Boonton, New Jersey	20,000	20,000						
Virtue, Mr. and Mrs. Julian A., Rolling Hills, California	10,000	10,000						
Wallace, Mr. and Mrs. DeWitt, Mount Kisco, New York, Pleasantville, New York	40,101	35,900		4,201	8,250R / 1,750D	12,500R / 8,000M		
*Wallach, Mr. and Mrs. Ira, Scarsdale, New York	18,000	1,000	17,000					
*Warburg, Frederick, New York, New York	13,000	2,000	11,000					
*Warburg, James, New York, New York	24,850		24,850					
Warner, Jack L., Burbank, California	25,000	25,000					11,000	
Wasserman, Mr. and Mrs. Lew R., New York, New York, Beverly Hills, California	54,096		54,096		28,000			
*Wasserman, William Stix, New York, New York	11,000		11,000					
Watson, Mr. and Mrs. Arthur K., Armonk, New York, New York, New York	54,875	54,875			13,000D			

Name and Address	1968 Breakdown				1964	1960	1956	1952
	Total	Republican	Democratic	Misc.	Total	Total	Total	Total
Watson, Thomas J. Jr. Armonk, New York	$ 28,875	$ 7,875	$ 21,000		$ 37,000D	$ 10,500D	$ 10,000R	
Watson, Welcome H. Henry Fort Lauderdale, Florida	10,000		10,000					
Watt, Mr. and Mrs. R.A. Beverly Hills, California Washington, D.C.	27,500	25,000	2,500					
Watzek, Aubrey R. Portland, Oregon	12,500	12,500						
*Weaver, Mr. and Mrs. John J. San Francisco, California Hillsborough, California	17,500+		17,500+					
*Weber, F. Palmer Brooklyn Heights, New York	11,000+		11,000+					
Weiner, Ted Fort Worth, Texas	22,282	22,282						
*Weiselberg, Marvin Lido Beach, New York	20,000		20,000					
*Wellington, Thomas D. New York, New York	15,000		15,000					
Weyerhaeuser, Frederick K. St. Paul, Minnesota	21,796	21,796						
Wheeler, Mr. and Mrs. Coleman H. Portland, Oregon	10,400	10,400						
Wheeler, Edwin P. New York, New York	12,000	12,000						
White, William M. Jr. New York, New York	19,000	19,000						

Name							
Whitney, John Hay New York, New York	57,500	57,500		22,500	17,550	47,100	$ 31,000
Widener, George D. Philadelphia, Pennsylvania	11,000	11,000			13,500R 1,000M	24,200	
Widener, P.A.B. Versailles, Kentucky	21,000	21,000					
Wien, Lawrence A. New York, New York	15,000		15,000				
*Willens, Mr. and Mrs. Harold Los Angeles, California	25,000+		25,000+				
Wilson, Mr. and Mrs. David K. Nashville, Tennessee	48,000	48,000					
Winston, Mr. and Mrs. Harry New York, New York	10,000	5,000	5,000	10,000D			
Winston, Norman K. New York, New York	11,000		11,000	11,000	11,000		
Winthrop, Mr. and Mrs. Robert Old Westbury, New York	10,500	10,500					
Wishnick, Mr. and Mrs. Robert I. New York, New York	32,625	32,625					
Wishnick, William New York, New York Scarsdale, New York	17,625	17,625					
Woldenberg, Malcolm New Orleans, Louisiana	10,000		10,000				
Wood, Gen. Robert E. Chicago, Illinois	12,930	11,096	$ 1,834		10,500R 1,545M		
*Work, Horace H. Locust Valley, New York	16,300		16,300				

		1968 Breakdown			1964	1960	1956	1952
Name and Address	Total	Republican	Democratic	Misc.	Total	Total	Total	Total
Wrather, Mr. and Mrs. John D. Jr. Beverly Hills, California Newport Beach, California	$ 15,000	$ 15,000	$	$	$	$	$	$
*Wyly, Sam Dallas, Texas	100,000	100,000						
Wyman, Mr. and Mrs. Thomas G. New York, New York	13,000	13,000			$ 17,000D			
Yarmuth, Stanley Louisville, Kentucky	10,000	10,000						
*Zaffaroni, Dr. Alejandro Atherton, California	12,500		$ 12,500					
Zurn, Everett Fairview, Pennsylvania	20,000	5,000	15,000					
Zurn, Melvin A. Erie, Pennsylvania	20,000	5,000	15,000					
1968 Totals:	$12,187,863+	$7,658,160+	$4,290,561+	$239,142				

[a]In the $10,000-or-more list there are 37 cases (8 Rep., 29 Dem.) in which a plus (+) was added to the recorded amount. In these cases, the amount has been increased from the original figure as a result of additional information from at least two valid sources.
[b]The amount given in this list for Nelson A. Rockefeller does not include $350,000 which he contributed to his own campaign. See Appendix M.

Appendix F

**Individuals Who Contributed $500
and Over to Candidates and Committees
of Both Parties, 1968**

This Appendix lists those 255 individuals (or husband-wife combinations) who contributed $500 or more to candidates and committees of both major parties, or to one or both major parties and the American Independent Party.

In cases in which a contributor gave to the Republicans, the Democrats, and a miscellaneous committee other than A.I.P., the miscellaneous contribution is noted and counted within the totals. However, the split itself is made up only of the Republican and Democratic contributions. Only miscellaneous contributions to A.I.P. can stand alone as part of a split with a Republican or Democratic contribution. A.I.P. donations are indicated in the lists of split contributors by an asterisk (*). They occur only in the list of split contributors of less than $10,000.

A-level splits are those split contributions in which an individual (or husband-wife combination) gave to candidates running for the same national, state, or local office on opposing tickets. A-level split contributions may be made to individual candidates or to political committees such as the RNC and DNC. Specifically, the following types of a-level splits occurred in the 1968 records. (The abbreviations in parentheses for these types of a-level splits are used in the lists of split contributors below.)

1. Presidential level (a Pres). Splits in which contributions were given to the individual candidate committees of Nixon, Humphrey, or Wallace during the general election period.

2. Presidential Mixed (a Pres Mixed). Splits in which one party contribution was given to a specific presidential candidate committee (e.g., Humphrey for President Club, Nixon-Agnew Committee), and the opposing party contribution was given to a general party committee (e.g., Democratic National Committee, Republican National Finance Committee). Always the general party committees were checked with regard to the date of the contribution. Only contributions dated after the conventions in Chicago and Miami were considered definite party committee contributions to the nominated presidential candidates. If a party committee was strictly designed for a specific candidate (e.g., Victory 68 Committee – Nixon, A.I.P. – Wallace), it was considered to be in the a Pres category.

3. Presidential Prenomination (a Pres Prenom). Splits in which contributions were given to the presidential candidates who ran in the prenomination period before the conventions.

4. National Party Committee (a Nat'l Party Comm. — Gen or Prenom). Splits given to opposing national party committees. Gen refers to contributions in the period after the conventions; prenom refers to the prenomination period.

5. Congressional (a Cong). Splits in which contributions were given to specific Congressional candidates on the same level.

6. Congressional Party Committee (a Cong Party Comm). Splits in which contributions were given to Congressional party committees on the same level (e.g., Democratic Senatorial Campaign Committee, National Republican Congressional Campaign).

When both spouses gave to both parties, they are listed as Mr. and Mrs. When both spouses gave to one party, but only one gave to the other, they are listed as Mr. and Mrs., and either (Mr.) or (Mrs.) is added in parentheses after the particular contribution which belongs only to the one. When the husband gave to one party and the wife to the other, the husband is listed first with his contribution, and the wife is listed separately under his name with her gift. In these cases, the total for the couple is found in the Total column following the husband's name.

Split Contributors of $10,000 or More, 1968

Name	Republican	Democratic	Miscellaneous (*A.I.P.)	Total Contributions
Allen, Mr. and Mrs. Herbert A. New York, New York	$ 1,500 (Mr.)	$ 56,000		$ 57,500
Altschul, Mr. and Mrs. Frank New York, New York	1,000 (Mr.)	13,500		14,500
Amory, Mr. and Mrs. Copley Lincoln, Massachusetts	1,000 (Mrs.)	19,750	$ 500 (Mrs.)	21,250
Astor, Mrs. Vincent New York, New York	9,000	5,000		14,000 a Pres
Avnet, Mr. and Mrs. Lester New York, New York	15,064	49,672 (Mr.)		64,736 a Pres
Baker, Michael Jr. Rochester, Pennsylvania	10,000	4,000		14,000 a Cong
Benjamin, Mr. and Mrs. Robert S. New York, New York Kings Point, New York	1,000 (Mr.)	32,000		33,000
Blaustein, Mr. and Mrs. Jacob Pikesville, Maryland Baltimore, Maryland	1,000 (Mr.)	17,000		18,000
Brandt, Mr. and Mrs. Harry New York, New York	1,000 (Mr.)	45,000		46,000
Bratti, Peter I. New York, New York	10,000	2,500		12,500 a Pres
Brimberg, Mr. and Mrs. Robert Scarsdale, New York New York, New York	1,500 (Mr.)	8,500		10,000
Bronfman, Mr. and Mrs. Edgar New York, New York	4,000 (Mr.)	17,250		21,250

Name	Republican	Democratic	Miscellaneous (*A.I.P.)	Total Contributions
Carlson, Chester F. Pittsford, New York Stanford, California	$ 1,000	$ 30,700	$ 500	$ 32,200
Cohen, Mr. and Mrs. Arthur New York, New York	500 (Mr.)	15,000		15,500
Cousins, Norman New York, New York	1,000	57,000		58,000
Dreyfus, Mr. and Mrs. Jack A. Jr. New York, New York	76,000	169,000+ (Mr.)		245,000+ a Pres (Also a Pres Prenom)
Dyson, Mr. and Mrs. Charles H. New York, New York Scarsdale, New York	1,500 (Mr.)	15,000		16,500
Erpf, Armand G. New York, New York	3,500	10,000		13,500
Evans, Mr. and Mrs. Thomas M. New York, New York Pittsburgh, Pennsylvania Greenwich, Connecticut	6,500 (Mr.)	17,000+		23,500+
Ford, Henry II Grosse Pointe, Michigan Detroit, Michigan New York, New York Washington, D.C.	7,250	30,000		37,250 a Pres
Ford, William Clay Dearborn, Michigan		20,000		21,000
Ford, Mrs. William Clay Dearborn, Michigan	1,000			—

Name				
Frankel, George New York, New York Greenwich, Connecticut	1,000	15,500		16,500
Grimson, Mrs. Samuel B. New York, New York	1,000	17,500		18,500
Houghton, Arthur A. Jr. New York, New York	12,000	2,500		14,500
Kaplan, Mr. and Mrs. Jack M. New York, New York	1,000 (Mr.)	15,500		16,500 a Cong
Kononoff, Alexis Coral Gables, Florida		10,000		12,000 a Pres
Kononoff, Mrs. Alexis Coral Gables, Florida	2,000			—
Lane, Mr. and Mrs. Edward H. Altavista, Virginia	19,650	1,500 (Mr.)	500 (Mr.)	21,650
Lefrak, Samuel J. New York, New York Forest Hills, New York	13,250	1,000		14,250 a Pres
Levin, Mr. and Mrs. Philip J. Warren, New Jersey North Plainfield, New Jersey	3,000	19,000		22,000
Levy, Gustave New York, New York	7,000	3,000		10,000
Loeb, Mr. and Mrs. Henry A. New York, New York	2,500 (Mr.)	15,000		17,500
Loeb, Mr. and Mrs. John L. New York, New York	6,750	9,500 (Mr.)		16,250 a Pres
McClure, Harold M. Jr. Alma, Michigan	87,500	2,500		90,000
Meckler, Mr. and Mrs. Herman L. New York, New York Kings Point, New York	15,000 (Mr.)	11,500		26,500 a Pres

Name	Republican	Democratic	Miscellaneous (*A.I.P.)	Total Contributions
Michel, Clifford W. New York, New York	$ 500	$ 10,000		$ 10,500
Millard, Mark J. New York, New York	2,500	10,000		12,500
Mosler, John New York, New York	11,750	500		12,250
Mott, Stewart New York, New York	100,200	255,500	$ 11,000	366,700 a Pres Prenom
Murphy, Thomas S. New York, New York	5,000	6,000		11,000 a Pres (Also a Pres Prenom)
Pomerance, Mr. and Mrs. Ralph New York, New York Cos Cob, Connecticut	750 (Mr.)	18,600+		19,350+
Price, Mr. and Mrs. James R. Lafayette, Indiana	30,000	4,000 (Mr.)		34,000 a Pres
Revson, Charles New York, New York	15,500	10,500		26,000 a Pres
Rockefeller, Mr. and Mrs. David New York, New York	20,500	5,000 (Mrs.)		25,500 a Pres
Ruttenberg, Derald H. New York, New York	10,000	1,000+		11,000+ a Pres Prenom
Shields, Richard T. New York, New York	2,000	18,000		20,000
Stein, Mr. and Mrs. Jules Beverly Hills, California	9,250	2,000 (Mr.)		11,250 a Cong Party Comm.
Wallach, Mr. and Mrs. Ira Scarsdale, New York	1,000 (Mr.)	17,000		18,000

Warburg, Frederick New York, New York	2,000	11,000	13,000
Watson, Thomas J. Jr. Armonk, New York	7,875	21,000	28,875
Watt, Mr. and Mrs. R. A. Beverly Hills, California Washington, D.C.	25,000	2,500 (Mr.)	27,500 a Pres
Winston, Mr. and Mrs. Harry New York, New York	5,000	5,000 (Mr.)	10,000 a Pres
Zurn, Everett Fairview, Pennsylvania	5,000	15,000	20,000 a Pres
Zurn, Melvin A. Erie, Pennsylvania	5,000	15,000	20,000 a Pres
Totals	$ 584,789	$1,185,472+	$ 12,500	$1,782,761+

Split Contributors of Less Than $10,000

Name	Republican	Democratic	Miscellaneous (*A.I.P.)	Total Contributions
Ackerman, Martin S. New York, New York East Hills, New York	$ 1,000	$ 2,000		$ 3,000
Alcorn, Charles W. Houston, Texas	1,000	1,105		2,105
Allen, Charles Jr. New York, New York	1,500	3,000		4,500
Altmayer, Jay P. Mobile, Alabama		1,000	$ 500*	1,500 a Pres
Altschul, Harold New York, New York	1,000	5,000		6,000
Anderson, Phillip D. Palm Beach, Florida	1,000	1,000		2,000
Barkes, Curtis Hillsdale, Illinois				
Elk Grove Township, Illinois	1,000	500		1,500
Barta, Mr. and Mrs. Wesley J. St. Louis, Missouri	1,000	1,000 (Mr.)		2,000 a Pres Mixed
Beggs, E. Dixie Pensacola, Florida	500	501		1,001
Beinecke, Edwin J. New York, New York	1,500	1,100		2,600 a Pres
Bemis, Judson Minneapolis, Minnesota	500	500		1,000 a Pres Mixed
Benestad, Torleaf New York, New York	500	500		1,000
Bennett, R.E. Fort Lee, New Jersey	650	650		1,300 a Pres Mixed

309

Name			
Bernard, Robert A. New York, New York	2,500	1,000	3,500
Blaine, Walter F. New York, New York	1,000	5,000	6,000 a Pres
Bluhdorn, Charles G. New York, New York	500	2,000	2,500
Blumberg, Herschel Hyattsville, Maryland	501	2,000	2,501
Boulton, Schroeder New York, New York	1,000	1,700	2,700
Bowden, Alfred E. New York, New York	3,000	4,000	7,000 a Cong Party Comm.
Boykin, Mr. and Mrs. Sam M. Birmingham, Alabama	6,000	500 (Mr.)	6,500
Brandenthaler, Anthony Oregon	500	500	1,000
Briggs, R.W. San Antonio, Texas	5,000	1,000	6,000
Bullard, Mrs. John M. Nonquitt, Massachusetts	2,000	1,000	3,000
Bullock, Hugh New York, New York	5,000	500	5,500 a Nat'l Party Comm. (Prenom)
Burns, Robert H. Downey, California	1,500	1,500	3,000 a Pres
Butler, Monroe Los Angeles, California	500	500	1,000
Calder, Stephen A. Fort Lauderdale, Florida	500	500	1,000
Campbell, Douglass New York, New York	500	1,000	1,500

Name	Republican	Democratic	Miscellaneous (*A.I.P.)	Total Contributions
Cancelliere, Marion A. Pittsburgh, Pennsylvania	$ 2,000	$ 1,000		$ 3,000 a Pres Mixed
Carey, Walter F. Bloomfield, Hills, Michigan	500	500		1,000 a Pres Mixed
Carlton, Winslow New York, New York	1,000	2,000		3,000
Carroll, John L. McLean, Virginia Brighton, Massachusetts	1,000	1,000		2,000 a Pres Mixed
Cates, Dudley F. New York, New York		500		1,500
Cates, Mrs. Dudley F. New York, New York	1,000			—
Chapin, Roy D. Jr. Detroit, Michigan	1,000	2,000		3,000 a Pres
Charno, Harold New York, New York	1,000	500		1,500
Cisler, Walker L. Grosse Pointe, Michigan Detroit, Michigan	2,000	1,500		3,500 a Pres
Clifford, Mr. and Mrs. Patrick J. New York, New York	500 (Mr.)	500		1,000
Cole, Mrs. C. Grenes Houma, Louisiana	1,000		$ 500*	1,500 a Pres
Cone, Edward T. Princeton, New Jersey	500	1,000+		1,500+
Connor, John T. New York, New York	500	1,000		1,500

Name				
Cowles, Gardner New York, New York	3,750	1,000		4,750
Crawford, O.R. Jasper, Texas	2,000	1,000		3,000 a Pres
Crown, Henry Chicago, Illinois	1,000	2,500		3,500
Cudlip, David Rockwell Greenwich, Connecticut	1,200	750		1,950
Cullman, Mr. and Mrs. Edgar Meyer New York, New York	7,266	1,000 (Mr.)		8,266 a Pres
Culverhouse, Mr. and Mrs. Hugh F. Jacksonville, Florida	2,000		500* (Mr.)	2,500 a Pres
Daniell, A.E. Pittsburgh, Pennsylvania	1,000		500*	1,500 a Pres
Davis, Champion McDowell Wilmington, Delaware	500	1,500		2,000
Decker, Harold Houston, Texas	2,000	1,000		3,000
Degenstein, Mr. and Mrs. Lester E. New York, New York	2,000	2,000 (Mr.)		4,000 a Pres
DeMeglio, Julian Hyattsville, Maryland	1,000	1,000		2,000
Dewey, Mr. and Mrs. Gordon C. New York, New York	6,000	500 (Mr.)		6,500
Dial, Morse G. Jr. Washington, D.C.	1,500	1,000		2,500 a Pres
Dick, Edison Lake Forest, Illinois Chicago, Illinois	1,000	1,000		2,000
Doherty, W.T. Houston, Texas	1,000	1,000		2,000

Name	Republican	Democratic	Miscellaneous (*A.I.P.)	Total Contributions
Dresser, Robert B. Providence, Rhode Island	$ 500		$ 2,000 * (Mr.) 5,000 (Mr., Mrs.)	$ 7,500 a Pres
Dresser, Mrs. Robert B. Providence, Rhode Island				—
Driscoll, Joseph P. Dallas, Texas	1,000	$ 1,000		2,000 a Pres
Dunleavy, F.J. Philadelphia, Pennsylvania	500	500		1,000 a Pres Mixed
Dwyer, James F. New York, New York	2,500	2,500		5,000 a Pres
Eaton, Frederick M. New York, New York	1,500	2,500		4,000
Elliott, Vince Vinita, Oklahoma	500	500		1,000
Ely, Nathaniel J. Bethesda, Maryland		500		1,000 a Pres
Ely, Mrs. Nathaniel J. Bethesda, Maryland	500			—
Englehard, Charles W. Jr. Newark, New Jersey	250	5,750		6,000
Evans, Robert B. Detroit, Michigan	1,000	1,000		2,000 a Pres
Fain, Irving Jay Providence, Rhode Island Pawtucket, Rhode Island	1,000	5,000		6,000
Fisher, Donald W. Detroit, Michigan	2,100	1,000		3,100

Name				
Fisher, J. Robert New York, New York	3,500	1,000		4,500 a Pres
Forman, Dr. and Mrs. Charles Fort Lauderdale, Florida		500 (Mr.)	1,000*	1,500
Foster, David H. Dallas, Texas	1,000	1,000		2,000 a Pres
Foster, Glen S. II New York, New York	1,000	500		1,500 a Pres
Foster, Robert McKnight Palm Beach, Florida	1,000	250		1,250
Fox, Robert Pennsylvania	500	500		1,000 a Cong
Frankel, William V. New York, New York	500	500		1,000
Fribourg, Mr. and Mrs. Michel New York, New York	3,501 (Mr.)	4,000		7,501
Funderburk, M.L. Houma, Louisiana	1,000	500		1,500 a Nat'l Party Comm. (Gen)
Furr, Roy Lubbock, Texas	1,000	2,000		3,000
Garcia, Salustiano Miami, Florida	1,000	500		1,500
Garfinkle, Henry New York, New York	2,500	500		3,000
Gerrity, Edward J. Jr. New York, New York	2,500	2,000		4,500 a Pres
Goldston, W.J. Houston, Texas	1,000	1,000		2,000
Greene, David J. New York, New York	500	1,000		1,500

Name	Republican	Democratic	Miscellaneous (*A.I.P.)	Total Contributions
Gruss, Joseph S. New York, New York	$ 1,000	$ 3,000		$ 4,000 a Pres
Gruss, Mrs. Joseph S. New York, New York	$ 1,000			—
Gruzen, Barnett Sumner New York, New York	2,000	1,000		3,000
Harrington, Robert D. Worcester, Massachusetts	500	1,000		1,500 a Pres
Hart, Thomas H. Miami, Florida	1,300		$ 1,000*	2,300 a Pres
Harvey, M.J. Tyler, Texas	2,000		1,000*	3,000 a Pres
Harvey, M.J. Jr. Dallas, Texas	1,500		1,000*	2,500 a Pres
Helliwell, Paul L.E. Miami, Florida	1,000	1,000		2,000
Henry, Leonard New York, New York	2,000	500		2,500 a Pres
Herzog, George Cleveland, Ohio	1,000	1,000		2,000 a Pres
Higgins, George T. Washington, D.C.	750	500		1,250
Hirshhorn, Joseph J. New York, New York	2,000	5,000		7,000
Hoart, Francis X. New York, New York	1,000	500		1,500 a Pres

Name			
Holmes, Walter S. Jr. / Glen Ridge, New Jersey / New York, New York	1,750	500	2,250
Hult, Nils B. / Eugene, Oregon	3,500	500	4,000
Hurok, Mr. and Mrs. Sol / New York, New York	500 (Mr.)	5,000	5,500
Hussa, L.R. / Oregon	1,500	1,000	2,500
Isbrandtsen, Mr. and Mrs. Jacob / New York, New York	2,500 (Mr.)	5,000	7,500 a Pres
Jacobson, Mr. and Mrs. Robert J. / New York, New York	2,000	1,500 (Mr.)	3,500 a Pres
Jaglom, Simon / New York, New York	500	500	1,000
Johnson, Edward C. II / Boston, Massachusetts / Washington, D.C.	1,900	950	2,850
Johnson, Samuel / Racine, Wisconsin	3,000	1,200	4,200
Joyce, James / Andover, New York	4,000	1,000	5,000 a Pres Mixed
Juda, Felix / Los Angeles, California	1,000	1,000	2,000
Katz, Joseph M. / Pittsburgh, Pennsylvania	1,000	1,500	2,500
Katz, Solomon / Fairless Hills, Pennsylvania	500	1,000	1,500
Kelly, Carl D. / Winnetka, Illinois	2,500	500	3,000

Name	Republican	Democratic	Miscellaneous (*A.I.P.)	Total Contributions
King, Kerryn New York, New York	$ 1,000	$ 1,000		$ 2,000
Klein, Sam W. Cleveland, Ohio Shaker Heights, Ohio	1,000	2,500		3,500
Klutznick, Philip Chicago, Illinois	500	500		1,000
Kogod, Robert P. Washington, D.C.	2,000	3,000		5,000 a Pres
Korth, Howard J. Oakland, California	1,000	2,750		3,750 a Pres
Koshland, Stephen A. New York, New York	1,000	500		1,500
Kriendler, Maxwell A. New York, New York	4,000	2,000		6,000
Lachman, Charles R. New York, New York	1,000	1,000		2,000 a Pres
Lasker, Bernard J. New York, New York	8,500	1,000		9,500
Lennon, F.A. Cleveland, Ohio Chagrin Falls, Ohio	4,000	1,000		5,000
Lewis, Salim L. New York, New York Lewis, Mrs. Salim L. New York, New York	4,000	2,600		6,600
Lilienthal, Mr. and Mrs. David New York, New York				–
Princeton, New Jersey	200 (Mr.)	2,500		2,700

Name				
Loeb, John L. Jr. New York, New York	1,500		1,000	2,500
Lovelace, Jon B. Los Angeles, California	500		800	1,300
Lundell, L.W. New York, New York	1,750		500	2,250
MacBain, Gavin K. Mt. Kisco, New York New York, New York	1,000		838	1,838 a Pres
Manning, Richard de Y New York, New York	500		500	1,000
Marr, M.H. Dallas, Texas	2,000	$ 1,000*		3,000 a Pres
Marx, Louis New York, New York	1,000		1,000	2,000
Matthews, Richard J. Grosse Pointe, Michigan	500		750	1,250
Maull, Baldwin Buffalo, New York	500		500	1,000
McConnell, Joseph H. Richmond, Virginia	1,000		1,000	2,000 a Pres
McErlean, Charles F. LaGrange, Illinois	1,000		2,000	3,000
McHugh, Joseph M. New York, New York	1,000		1,000	2,000 a Pres
Meyer, Andre New York, New York	1,000		5,500	6,500
Meyer, Dr. Eugene III Baltimore, Maryland	500	500	3,000	4,000
Meyer, Mrs. Eugene III Baltimore, Maryland				—

Name	Republican	Democratic	Miscellaneous (*A.I.P.)	Total Contributions
Milner, R.E. Dumas Jackson, Mississippi	$ 1,000		$ 1,000*	$ 2,000 a Pres
Money, William C. Phoenix, Arizona	500	$ 1,000		1,500 a Pres
Moore, John D.J. New York, New York	1,000	500		1,500 a Pres
Mulcahy, J.A. Palm Beach, Florida New York, New York	1,000	1,000		2,000
Nash, Jack New York, New York	1,500	2,000		3,500
Neuberger, Mr. and Mrs. Roy New York, New York	5,000	1,000+ (Mr.)		6,000+ a Pres Prenom
Nevius, John A. Washington, D.C.	800	500		1,300
Newton, James St. Petersburg, Florida	1,000	850		1,850
Nichols, Thomas S. New York, New York	4,000	3,000		7,000 a Pres
Nicholson, Ralph Tallahassee, Florida	500	990	500*	1,990 a Pres
Nielsen, Arthur C. Jr. Chicago, Illinois	1,000			1,500
Nielsen, Mrs. Arthur C. Jr. Chicago, Illinois		500		–
Nunn, Ira H. Washington, D.C.	1,000	1,000		2,000 a Pres

Name			
Opstad, Donald O. Washington, D.C. Great Falls, Virginia	2,000 a Pres	1,000	1,000
Orell, Bernard L. Tacoma, Washington	1,000	500	500
Orloff, Monford A. Portland, Oregon	3,000 a Pres Prenom	2,500	500
Ottenstein, Joseph Washington, D.C.	7,000	5,500	1,500
Ottenstein, Victor H. Washington, D.C.	1,500	1,000	500
Paris, Julius Cleveland, Ohio	2,000 a Pres	1,000	1,000
Peterson, Charles Baltimore, Maryland Timonium, Maryland	1,500	500	1,000
Peterson, Robert O. San Diego, California	3,000 a Pres	1,000	2,000
Petrie, Milton J. New York, New York	2,000 a Pres Mixed	1,000	1,000
Post, Mrs. Marjorie Merriweather Washington, D.C.	3,100 a Pres	2,500	600
Rabb, Maxwell M. New York, New York	1,500	500	1,000
Richardson, Arthur L.B. New York, New York	2,500	1,500	1,000
Root, Morris J. Philadelphia, Pennsylvania	1,500	500	1,000
Ross, Arthur New York, New York Mamaroneck, New York	5,500 a Pres	1,000	4,500

Name	Republican	Democratic	Miscellaneous (*A.I.P.)	Total Contributions
Roth, Chester New York, New York	$ 1,000	$ 1,000		$ 2,000
Rothenberg, Albert New York, New York	1,000	500		1,500 a Pres
Rouse, James W. Baltimore, Maryland	1,000	600		1,600
Rubloff, Arthur Chicago, Illinois	1,000	1,000		2,000
Russell, W.L. Houston, Texas	1,500	500		2,000
Saltzman, Maurice Cleveland, Ohio	1,000	2,500		3,500 a Pres
Salzman, Mr. and Mrs. Herbert Washington, D.C.	5,000 (Mrs.)	2,000		7,000
Schaefer, R.J. Brooklyn, New York	2,250	1,000		3,250
Schuster, Mrs. Anne Storrs New York, New York	4,750	500		5,250
Schwartz, Marvin New York, New York	1,000	500		1,500 a Pres
Scott, George A. San Diego, California	2,000	1,500		3,500 a Pres
Shannon, Thomas F. Washington, D.C.	1,000	500		1,500
Shay, Edward Los Angeles, California	2,000	500		2,500
Simon, William G. San Marino, California	1,000	500		1,500 a Pres

Name			
Sinatra, Frank Burbank, California	1,000	1,000	2,000
Slick, Earl F. Winston-Salem, North Carolina	4,000	500	4,500
Smith, Charles E. Washington, D.C.	3,000	2,500	5,500 a Pres Mixed
Smith, Robert H. Washington, D.C.	1,000	4,500	5,500 a Pres
Spiegel, M.L. Minneapolis, Minnesota	500	500	1,000 a Pres
Spiegel, Sam New York, New York	1,250	1,000	2,250
Stepelton, Norman A. Wilmette, Illinois	2,000	2,000	4,000 a Pres Mixed
Stern, E.H. New York, New York	7,000	2,000	9,000
Stewart, L.L. Oregon	3,000	1,500	4,500 a Cong
Stoddard, Howard J. Lansing, Michigan	1,000	1,000	2,000 a Pres
Stoddard, Stanford C. Detroit, Michigan	1,000	1,000	2,000
Stone, Mr. and Mrs. Edward Durell New York, New York	4,500	1,000 (Mr.)	5,500 a Pres
Stone, Edward Durell Jr. Fort Lauderdale, Florida	500	500	1,000 a Pres
Strelsin, Alfred A. New York, New York	1,500	3,000	4,500
Tankoos, S. Joseph Jr. New York, New York	2,000	500	2,500 a Pres

Name	Republican	Democratic	Miscellaneous (*A.I.P.)	Total Contributions
Terres, Ed A. Washington, D.C.	$ 2,000	$ 3,000	$	$ 5,000 a Pres
Tonks, Mr. and Mrs. Raymond M. Miami, Florida	7,000 (Mr.)	2,000		9,000 a Pres
Underwood, Milton R. Houston, Texas	1,000			1,500 a Pres
Underwood, Mrs. Milton R. Houston, Texas			$ 500*	–
Uris, Harold New York, New York	2,500			3,500+
Uris, Mrs. Harold New York, New York		1,000+		–
Usen, Irving Boston, Massachusetts	1,000	1,000		2,000 a Pres
Usina, Leonard Florida	500	3,000		3,500
Vollmer, Arnold H. New York, New York	2,500	500		3,000
Volpe, Joseph Jr. Washington, D.C.	1,000	1,000		2,000 a Pres
Walker, George Gholson New York, New York	500	1,000+		1,500+
Walton, John Riverdale, Maryland	1,501	1,000		2,501
Weinberg, John L. New York, New York	500	1,000		1,500

Weinberg, Sidney New York, New York	1,250	3,000		4,250
Weld, David New York, New York	4,000			5,000
Weld, Mrs. David New York, New York		1,000		–
Wilson, Joseph C. Rochester, New York	500	8,195		8,695
Totals	$322,269	$271,329	$ 16,500	$610,098

Appendix G

**Occupational Classification of Contributors
of $10,000 or More, 1968**

The following analysis presents the occupational classifications of the contributors of $10,000 or more in the Citizens' Research Foundation compilation.

Of the 424 individuals or husband-wife combinations, 400 or 94.3 percent were classified into 18 major categories and their subdivisions. One of these categories, Miscellaneous, consists of those individuals who do not fall into any of the other major occupations or professions. The areas involved in Miscellaneous are listed in footnote b.

In some cases, the multiple interests of certain contributors necessitated arbitrary decisions as to their primary classifications. There is no double classifying, and each contributor has been designated to only one occupation or profession.

Twenty contributors, representing $446,609 or 3.7 percent of the total contributions, remain unidentified.

Occupational Classification of Contributors of $10,000 or More, 1968

Occupational Classification	Contributions Republican	Democratic	Miscellaneous	Total[a] (Indiv.)	Amount
Finance					
Banking & Trust Companies	$ 207,500 2.7%	$ 45,000 1.0%	$ 500 0.2%	(11) (2.6%)	$ 253,000 2.1%
Investment Banking & Brokerage	588,786 7.7%	862,686 20.1%	17,826 7.5%	(56) (13.2%)	1,469,298 12.1%
Insurance	340,000 4.4%	38,500 0.9%	1,000 0.4%	(7) (1.7%)	379,500 3.1%
Professional					
Artists & Architects	27,750 0.4%	29,300 0.7%	—	(4) (0.9%)	57,050 0.5%
Attorneys	298,750 3.9%	239,265 5.6%	—	(31) (7.3%)	538,015 4.4%
Authors	—	120,350 2.8%	—	(3) (0.7%)	120,350 1.0%
Clergy	—	17,500 0.4%	—	(1) (0.2%)	17,500 0.1%
Consultants & Researchers	133,153 1.7%	25,000 0.6%	6,000 2.5%	(6) (1.4%)	164,153 1.3%
Educators	—	124,400 2.9%	—	(2) (0.5%)	124,400 1.0%
Engineers	12,000 0.2%	14,000 0.3%	—	(2) (0.5%)	26,000 0.2%
Physicians & Psychologists	92,000 1.2%	82,500 1.9%	1,000 0.4%	(7) (1.7%)	175,500 1.4%
Communications					
Broadcasting	15,000 0.2%	6,000 0.1%	—	(2) (0.5%)	21,000 0.2%
Printing	13,000	—	—	(1)	13,000

Publishing & Editing	84,400 1.1%	126,838 3.0%	4,201 1.8%	(10) (2.4%)	215,439 1.8%
Real Estate: Land & Housing Development	204,140 2.7%	313,254 7.3%	1,000 0.4%	(18) (4.2%)	518,394 4.3%
Natural Resources					
Mining	68,000 0.9%	37,000 0.9%	—	(5) (1.2%)	105,000 0.9%
Oil	739,485 9.7%	45,000 1.0%	10,651 4.5%	(23) (5.4%)	795,136 6.5%
Timber	21,796 0.3%	—	—	(1) (0.2%)	21,796 0.2%
Utilities	81,500 1.1%	16,000 0.4%	1,000 0.4%	(5) (1.2%)	98,500 0.8%
Transportation	141,700 1.9%	28,500 0.7%	5,000 2.1%	(10) (2.4%)	175,200 1.4%
Leasing	112,500 1.5%	11,500 0.3%	—	(4) (0.9%)	124,000 1.0%
Food & Beverage					
Food Processing & Distribution	75,200 1.0%	35,000 0.8%	—	(7) (1.7%)	110,200 0.9%
Distillery	36,000 0.5%	42,250 1.0%	—	(5) (1.2%)	78,250 0.6%
Restaurant & Hotel-Motel	149,500 2.0%	—	—	(3) (0.7%)	149,500 1.2%
Wholesale & Retail Sales: Food, Department, Jewelry Stores; Automobile Agency, etc.	61,596 0.8%	118,750 2.8%	28,334 11.8%	(11) (2.6%)	208,680 1.7%

Occupational Classification	Contributions			Total[a]	
	Republican	Democratic	Miscellaneous	(Indiv.)	Amount
Manufacturing					
Automobile	$ 96,250 1.3%	$ 50,000 1.2%	—	(4) (0.9%)	$ 146,250 1.2%
Chemicals & Pharmaceuticals	256,817 3.4%	34,000 0.8%	—	(12) (2.8%)	290,817 2.4%
Clothing & Accessories	23,000 0.3%	106,000 2.5%	—	(5) (1.2%)	129,000 1.1%
Consumer & Household Products	172,200 2.2%	80,700 1.9%	$ 3,500 1.5%	(13) (3.1%)	256,400 2.1%
Electronics & Computers	260,460 3.4%	178,422 4.2%	4,500 1.9%	(13) (3.1%)	443,382 3.6%
Factory & Industrial Components & Equipment	72,500 0.9%	110,000 2.6%	1,000 0.4%	(9) (2.1%)	183,500 1.5%
Glass	31,500 0.4%	2,500 0.1%	—	(2) (0.5%)	34,000 0.3%
Iron, Steel, Aluminum	72,000 0.9%	35,000 0.8%	—	(6) (1.4%)	107,000 0.9%
Rubber	39,000 0.5%	—	—	(1) (0.2%)	39,000 0.3%
Textiles	42,200 0.6%	—	—	(2) (0.5%)	42,200 0.3%
Other	85,900 1.1%	55,700 1.3%	500 0.2%	(7) (1.7%)	142,100 1.2%
Entertainment	127,511 1.7%	154,096 3.6%	—	(13) (3.1%)	281,607 2.3%
Public Officials during 1968	150,500 2.0%	84,500 2.0%	—	(6) (1.4%)	235,000 1.9%

Philanthropy; Family & Inherited Wealth	2,135,804	27.9%	619,750	14.4%	39,000	16.3%	(36)	(8.5%)	2,794,554	22.9%
Retired	130,000	1.7%	138,500	3.2%	—		(13)	(3.1%)	268,500	2.2%
Miscellaneous[b]	272,316	3.6%	115,100	2.7%	1,667	0.7%	(23)	(5.4%)	389,083	3.2%
Unidentified	186,446	2.4%	147,700	3.4%	112,463	47.0%	(24)	(5.7%)	446,609	3.7%
Total	$7,658,160		$4,290,561		$ 239,142		(424)		$12,187,863	

[a] In the Total column, the figures and percentages in parentheses refer to the number of contributors (individuals).

[b] Within the Miscellaneous category are included those occupational classifications which do not fall into the other categories. These include businessmen involved in numerous business areas or conglomerates, owners or presidents of baseball teams, a student, and individuals involved in such areas as toy import-export, the funeral business, and interior decoration.

Appendix H

Occupational Classification of Split
Contributors, 1968

The following presents the occupational classification of the 1968 split contributors. This group consists of the 53 individuals or husband-wife combinations
in the $10,000-and-over group and the 202 individuals in the under-$10,000
category who split their contributions in various amounts among the Republican,
Democratic, and American Independent Party causes.

In the analysis, the split contributors fell into 20 major occupational or professional categories and their subdivisions. Efforts were made to follow the
categories developed in the occupational classification of the contributors of
$10,000 or more (Appendix G), but complete uniformity was not possible.

For the 255 split contributors, the largest percentage of both individuals
and gifts was found in the Investment Banking & Brokerage subdivision of
Finance. In this category, 47 (18.4%) of the contributors gave $582,800
(24.4%) of the gifts. The second largest percentage of total individuals was found
in the Attorney group in which 25 (9.8%) of the contributors were found.
However, the second largest percentage of total contributions was found in the
Philanthropy; Family & Inherited Wealth category in which only six (2.4%) of
the split contributors gave $415,550 (17.4%) of the total gifts.

Occupational Classification of Split Contributors, 1968

Occupational Classification	Republican	Democratic	Miscellaneous[a]	Total[b] (Indiv.)	Total[b] Amounts
Finance					
Banking & Trust Companies	$ 32,500 3.6%	$ 31,000 2.1%	—	(12) (4.7%)	$ 63,500 2.7%
Investment Banking & Brokerage	177,400 19.6%	403,400 27.7%	$ 1,500* 13.6% / 500 2.8%	(47) (18.4%)	582,800 24.4%
Insurance	2,500 0.3%	2,000 0.1%	—	(3) (1.2%)	4,500 0.2%
Professional					
Architects	7,250 0.8%	20,600 1.4%	—	(3) (1.2%)	27,850 1.2%
Attorneys	28,050 3.1%	55,251 3.8%	2,500* 22.7% / 5,000 27.8%	(25) (9.8%)	90,801 3.8%
Certified Public Accountants	1,000 0.1%	500 0.03%	—	(1) (0.4%)	1,500 0.1%
Composers	500 0.1%	1,000 0.1%	—	(1) (0.4%)	1,500 0.1%
Consultants	6,700 0.7%	4,500 0.3%	—	(4) (1.6%)	11,200 0.5%
Educators	1,501 0.2%	1,000 0.1%	—	(1) (0.4%)	2,501 0.5%
Engineers	14,500 1.6%	14,500 1.0%	—	(3) (1.2%)	29,000 1.2%
Physicians	2,500 0.3%	21,000 1.4%	1,500* 13.6% / 500 2.8%	(4) (1.6%)	25,500 1.1%

Communications					
Broadcasting	$ 5,000 0.6%	$ 6,000 0.4%	—	(1) (0.4%)	$ 11,000 0.5%
Publishing & Editing	5,250 0.6%	58,990 4.0%	$ 500* 4.5%	(3) (1.2%)	64,740 2.7%
Magazine, Newspaper, Book Distribution	4,500 0.5%	7,000 0.5%	—	(3) (1.2%)	11,500 0.5%
Real Estate: Land & Housing Development	51,551 5.7%	31,500 2.2%	1,000* 9.1%	(12) (4.7%)	84,051 3.5%
Construction	9,000 1.0%	2,000 0.1%	—	(2) (0.8%)	11,000 0.5%
Natural Resources					
Mining	2,250 0.2%	10,750 0.7%	—	(2) (0.8%)	13,000 0.5%
Oil	98,500 10.9%	39,605 2.7%	2,000* 18.2%	(10) (3.9%)	140,105 5.9%
Timber	4,000 0.4%	1,000 0.1%	—	(2) (0.8%)	5,000 0.2%
Utilities	15,650 1.7%	5,650 0.4%	—	(5) (2.0%)	21,300 0.9%
Transportation	19,000 2.1%	14,750 1.0%	—	(11) (4.3%)	33,750 1.4%
Leasing	16,000 1.8%	11,500 0.8%	1,000* 9.1%	(2) (0.8%)	28,500 1.2%

Occupational Classification	Contribution			Total[b]	
	Republican	Democratic	Miscellaneous[a]	(Indiv.)	Amounts
Food & Beverage					
Food Processing & Distribution	$ 1,000 0.1%	$ 1,000 0.1%	—	(1) (0.4%)	$ 2,000 0.1%
Distillery	10,250 1.1%	20,250 1.4%	—	(3) (1.2%)	30,500 1.3%
Tobacco Industry	10,266 1.1%	5,000 0.3%	—	(2) (0.8%)	15,266 0.6%
Wholesale & Retail Sales: Food, Department, Jewelry Stores	10,000 1.1%	10,500 0.7%	—	(4) (1.6%)	20,500 0.9%
Manufacturing					
Automobile	9,250 1.0%	52,000 3.6%	—	(3) (1.2%)	61,250 2.6%
Chemicals & Pharmaceuticals	7,000 0.8%	10,000 0.7%	—	(4) (1.6%)	17,000 0.7%
Clothing	3,000 0.3%	4,500 0.3%	—	(3) (1.2%)	7,500 0.3%
Consumer & Household Products	67,400 7.4%	23,038 1.6%	$ 500 2.8%	(12) (4.7%)	90,938 3.8%
Electronics & Computers	29,939 3.3%	72,172 5.0%	—	(4) (1.6%)	102,111 4.3%
Factory & Industrial Components & Equipment	16,500 1.8%	33,000 2.3%	—	(5) (2.0%)	49,500 2.1%
Glass	12,000 1.3%	2,500 0.2%	—	(1) (0.4%)	14,500 0.6%
Steel	1,000 0.1%	—	500* 4.5%	(1) (0.4%)	1,500 0.1%

Wood Products	500 0.1%	2,500 0.2%	—	(1) (0.4%)	3,000 0.1%
Other	33,500 3.7%	46,395 3.2%	500 2.8%	(5) (2.0%)	80,395 3.4%
Entertainment	16,000 1.8%	89,500 6.1%	—	(8) (3.1%)	105,500 4.4%
Public Officials during 1968	6,000 0.7%	3,000 0.2%	—	(2) (0.8%)	9,000 0.4%
Philanthropy; Family & Inherited Wealth	123,050 13.6%	281,500 19.3%	11,000 61.1%	(6) (2.4%)	415,550 17.4%
Retired	12,000 1.3%	18,500 1.3%	—	(7) (2.7%)	30,500 1.3%
Miscellaneous[c]	18,701 2.1%	26,350 1.8%	500* 4.5%	(14) (5.5%)	45,551 1.9%
Unidentified	14,600 1.6%	11,600 0.8%	—	(12) (4.7%)	26,200 1.1%
Total	$ 907,058	$1,456,801	$ 11,000* 18,000	(255)	$ 2,392,859

[a] In the column labeled Miscellaneous, those contributions which were to George Wallace of the American Independent Party are indicated by an asterisk.

[b] In the Total column, the figures and percentages in parentheses refer to the number of contributors.

[c] Within the Miscellaneous category are included those occupational classifications which do not fall into the other classifications. In this group, Miscellaneous includes businessmen involved in numerous business areas or conglomerates and individuals involved in such areas as trading stamps, travel agencies, building maintenance, grain brokerage, credit corporations, and professional organizations.

Appendix I

Occupational Classification of Wallace Contributors of $500 or More, 1968

Occupational Classification	Contribution[a]	
Finance		
Banking, Trust, & Loan Companies	(5)	$ 5,500
	(1.0%)	1.2%
Stocks & Investments	(5)	4,500
	(1.0%)	1.0%
Insurance	(4)	2,500
	(0.8%)	0.5%
Professional		
Architects	(3)	2,000
	(0.6%)	0.4%
Attorneys	(19)	19,119
	(3.8%)	4.2%
Consultants	(1)	1,000
	(0.2%)	0.2%
Educators	(1)	500
	(0.2%)	0.1%
Engineers	(4)	4,500
	(0.8%)	1.0%
Geologists	(1)	500
	(0.2%)	0.1%
Physicians	(17)	13,500
	(3.4%)	2.9%
Communications		
Advertising	(1)	500
	(0.2%)	0.1%
Broadcasting	(2)	1,000
	(0.4%)	0.2%
Publishing	(2)	1,500
	(0.4%)	0.3%
Oil Operators & Producers	(10)	15,000
	(2.0%)	3.3%
Lumber & Lumber Products	(5)	4,000
	(1.0%)	0.9%
Cattle & Ranching	(2)	2,000
	(0.4%)	0.4%
Real Estate	(7)	7,500
	(1.4%)	1.6%

Occupational Classification	Contribution[a]	
Contracting		
Heavy Construction: Road Building & Paving	(19)	23,500
	(3.8%)	5.1%
Electrical Contracting & Engineering	(4)	5,000
	(0.8%)	1.1%
Water Well Drilling	(2)	$ 2,000
	(0.4%)	0.4%
Manufacturing		
Building Materials	(1)	1,000
	(0.2%)	0.2%
Cement Products	(3)	2,000
	(0.6%)	0.4%
Chemicals & Pharmaceuticals	(3)	2,500
	(0.6%)	0.5%
Clothing	(1)	500
	(0.2%)	0.1%
Electric Products	(1)	1,000
	(0.2%)	0.2%
Factory & Industrial Components & Equipment	(5)	3,500
	(1.0%)	0.8%
Farm Implements & Equipment	(3)	3,000
	(0.6%)	0.7%
Steel	(1)	1,000
	(0.2%)	0.2%
Other	(4)	5,000
	(0.8%)	1.1%
Wholesale & Retail Sales	(11)	10,000
	(2.2%)	2.2%
Wholesale Liquor Distribution	(1)	500
	(0.2%)	0.1%
Retail Services (Dry Cleaning, Plumbing, Exterminating)	(3)	1,700
	(0.6%)	0.4%
Utilities	(2)	1,500
	(0.4%)	0.3%
Transportation & Storage	(5)	3,300
	(1.0%)	0.7%
Food Processing & Distribution	(4)	2,500
	(0.8%)	0.5%
Motel	(1)	500
	(0.2%)	0.1%
Marine Related Services (Tugs, Equipment Chartering, Inspection)	(3)	2,000
	(0.6%)	0.4%

Occupational Classification	Contribution[a]	
Seaman	(1) (0.2%)	500 0.1%
Factory Worker	(1) (0.2%)	$ 1,000 0.2%
Public Officials during 1968	(13) (2.6%)	9,000 2.0%
Retired	(7) (1.4%)	8,000 1.7%
Miscellaneous	(12) (2.4%)	8,000 1.7%
Unidentified	(298) (60.0%)	275,104 60.0%
Total	(498)	$458,723

[a]The figures in parentheses refer to the number of contributors in each category; the percentages in parentheses refer to the number of these contributors as a percentage of all large contributors to Wallace.

Appendix J

**Lenders to Democratic National Campaign with
Amounts of Loans and Contributions, 1968**

| | *Loans* | *Contributions* | |
		To Humphrey Committees	*To Other Democrats*
John Factor Real Estate Los Angeles, California	$240,000	$100,000 (Mrs.)	$ 2,500
Lew Wasserman Music Corporation of America Universal City, California	240,000	54,096	–
† *Herbert A. Allen Allen & Co. (Investment Banking) New York, New York	100,000	56,000	–
†Lester Avnet Avnet Inc. (Electronics) New York, New York	100,000	23,672	26,000
†Robert Benjamin United Artists Corporation New York, New York	100,000	31,000	500
†Jacob Blaustein Pan-Am. Petroleum & Transport Co. Pikesville, Maryland	100,000	14,500	2,500
†Arthur G. Cohen Arlen Properties, Inc. (Real Estate) New York, New York	100,000	15,000	–
Robert Dowling City Investing Co. (Real Estate) New York, New York	100,000	100,000	2,754
Milton Gilbert Gilbert Systems Inc. (Trucking) New York, New York	100,000	–	500
*Milton Gordon M.A. Gordon Co., Inc. (Investment Banking) New York, New York	100,000	15,000	–
H.E. Gould Universal American Corporation (Diversified Industrial Manufacturing) New York, New York	100,000	–	–
Leon Hess Hess Oil & Chemical Co. New York, New York	100,000	–	5,500

341

	Loans	Contributions	
		To Humphrey Committees	To Other Democrats
† Arthur Houghton Corning Glass Works New York, New York	100,000	2,500	-
Francis S. Levien Universal American Corporation (Diversified Industrial Manufacturing) New York, New York	$100,000	–	–
†John Loeb Carl M. Loeb, Rhoades & Co. (Investments) New York, New York	100,000	$ 7,000	$ 2,500
Arthur F. Murphy House of Seagram, Inc. New York, New York	100,000	–	–
Pat O'Connor Attorney Minneapolis, Minnesota	100,000	–	–
*Jeno Paulucci R.J. Reynolds Foods Duluth, Minnesota	100,000	–	1,000
† Arnold M. Picker United Artists Corporation New York, New York	100,000	–	–
Robert E. Short Admiral-Merchants Motor Freight, Inc. Minneapolis, Minnesota	100,000	–	–
*Edwin L. Weisl Attorney New York, New York	100,000	–	–
Samuel Friedland Food Fair Stores, Inc. Miami, Florida	95,000	5,000	–
*Deil Gustafson Summit State Bank of Richfield- Bloomington Minneapolis, Minnesota	70,000	–	–
*Irvin Kovens Irvin Kovens (Clothing Store) Baltimore, Maryland	70,000	–	–
*Richard Millman Attorney Washington, D.C.	70,000	–	1,000

	Loans	Contributions	
		To Humphrey Committees	To Other Democrats
*Howard A. Weiss Attorney Chicago, Illinois	$ 70,000	–	–
*Philip I. Berman Fleet Systems, Inc. Industry, Pennsylvania	50,000	$ 10,000	$ 6,000
† *Norman Cousins[a] *Saturday Review* New York, New York	50,000	55,000	2,000
*S. Harrison Dogole Globe Security Systems Philadelphia, Pennsylvania	50,000	–	–
*J.J. Wolgin Atlas Credit Corporation (Real Estate) Philadelphia, Pennsylvania	50,000	–	1,000
Edgar F. Kaiser Kaiser Industries Corporation Oakland, California	37,500	12,500	–
Mrs. Sue M. Kaiser Lafayette, California	37,500	12,500	–
*(Mr. and Mrs.) George Backer Real Estate New York, New York	10,000	5,500	–
*Seon P. Bonan Real Estate Greenwich, Connecticut	10,000	–	–
*John E. Collins Brincefield Co. (Construction) Washington, D.C.	10,000	–	–
† *Charles H. Oestreich CHO Enterprises, Inc. (Real Estate) New York, New York	10,000	–	–
*Kenneth J. Pezrow Pezrow Sales Co. (Food Brokers) Maspeth, New York	10,000	–	–
*Arnold A. Saltzman Seagrave Corporation (Diversified Industrial Manufacturing) New York, New York	10,000	2,443	–

	Loans	Contributions	
		To Humphrey Committees	To Other Democrats
*Mitchell Siegel United Investors Corporation New York, New York	$ 10,000	–	–
*Robert S. Sinn Ultronic Systems Corporation (Electronics) Moorestown, New Jersey	10,000	$ 5,000	–
Dwayne Andreas First Interoceanic Corporation (Grain Brokerage) Minneapolis, Minnesota	5,000	11,000	–
*Richard J. Rubin Real Estate Philadelphia, Pennsylvania	5,000	–	–
*(Mr. and Mrs.) Jerome J. Shestack Attorney Philadelphia, Pennsylvania	5,000	–	–

† Also gave to Republicans.

* Loan returned. Loans returned entirely with the following exceptions: Berman – $2,500 of $5,000; Oestrich – $7,000 of $10,000; Pezrow – $7,800 of $10,000; Saltzman – $5,000 of $10,000; Siegel – $7,000 of $10,000.

aPresumably a loan, because $50,000 was reported repaid, but no record of original contribution reported.

Appendix K

**Contributions of Officials of
13 Selected Groups, 1968**

There are cases throughout the 13 groups in which individuals serve in more than one capacity in the organization. For example, an officer may also be a director or a trustee. This situation occurs in the American Medical Association, Association of American Railroads, Manufacturing Chemists Association, National Association of Electric Companies, and the National Association of Real Estate Boards. In these cases, the official number of officers, directors, trustees, etc. is given, but the individual's contribution is counted only in the first category in which he appears.

Some individuals are officials of more than one of the 13 groups. In these cases, the contributions are included in each individual group; however, the final cash total eliminates all contribution duplications.

Contributions of Officials of 13 Selected Groups, 1968

Group or Association	Total Members	Contributions [Number of contributors in parentheses]				Additional Factors
		Republican	Democratic	Miscellaneous	Total	
American Bar Assn.						
House of Delegates	297	(12) $ 10,000	(4) $ 2,500	(2) $ 1,000 Includes $500 AIP	(17) $ 13,500	1 R&M
American Medical Assn.						
Officers	7	–	–	–	–	
Trustees	12	–	–	–	–	
American Petroleum Institute						
Directors	136	(40) 335,800	(13) 30,606	–		6 Splits
Honorary Directors	39	(12) 93,566	–	(1) 1,667		1 R&M
		(52) 429,366	(13) 30,606	(1) 1,667	(59) 461,639	6 Splits 1 R&M
American Iron & Steel Institute						
Directors	36	(12) 25,500			(12) 25,500	–
Association of American Railroads						
Officers	15	–	–	–	–	–
Directors	20	(8) 14,000	–	–	(8) 14,000	–
Business Council						
Active Members	64	(39) 191,713	(3) 57,000	(2) 3,300		2 Splits 2 R&M
Graduate Members	55	(28) 89,200	(2) 26,000	–		1 Split
		(67) 280,913	(5) 83,000	(2) 3,300	(69) 367,213	3 Splits 2 R&M

Chiefs of Foreign Missions and Special Missions						
Non-career Officers	34	(15) 241,675	(1) 500	(1) 500	(15) 242,675	1 Split, 1 R&M
Manufacturing Chemists Assn.						
Officers	6	(1) 500				—
Directors	34	(8) 8,050				—
		(9) 8,550			(9) 8,550	
National Association of Electric Companies						
Officers	6	–				—
Directors	30	(2) 2,000			(2) 2,000	—
National Association of Manufacturers						
Officers	5	(3) 2,500	(1) 500			—
Divisions VP's	5	–				
Regional VP's	12	(4) 4,000	(2) 2,000			1 Split
Honorary VP's	20	(7) 87,544+	(5) 18,000	(3) 7,167		2 R&M, 2 Splits
Directors	126	(25) 32,500				
		(39) 126,544+	(8) 20,500	(3) 7,167	(45) 154,211+	3 Splits, 2 R&M
National Association of Real Estate Boards						
Officers	6	–				—
Directors	312	(4) 26,500			(4) 26,500	—
National Coal Assn.						
Directors (Active & Honorary)	48	(4) 7,000			(4) 7,000	—
United States Chamber of Commerce						
Officers	11	(1) 1,500				—
Directors	50	(8) 38,500				—
		(9) 40,000			(9) 40,000	
Totals		$1,132,982+	$136,106	$ 11,967	$1,281,055+	

Appendix L

Contributions of Officials of Four Selected Petroleum Organizations, 1968

The following four petroleum groups were analyzed in addition to the officer and director membership of the American Petroleum Institute in Appendix K, Contributions of Officials of 13 Selected Groups, 1968. The lists of officers, directors, and officers who were also directors were obtained from the 1968 lists of officials published by each organization. The names were subsequently analyzed against the CRF listings of 1968 large contributors.

Analysis revealed that whereas 34 percent of the officials of the American Petroleum Institute were contributors, only 11 percent of American Gas Association, nine percent of Independent Natural Gas Association of America, 10 percent of Independent Petroleum Association of America, and five percent of Natural Petroleum Refiners Association total officers and directors were recorded political contributors.

For the most part, the Republicans received more money than the Democrats from the petroleum groups. The officials of the first two groups in this Appendix gave to the Republicans only, and the officials of the third gave 36 times more cash to the Republicans than to the Democrats ($90,000R; 2,500D). Even the one individual who gave to the Democrats split his contributions. This is in keeping with the giving pattern of the officers and directors of the American Petroleum Institute who gave 14 times more money to the Republicans than to the Democrats ($429,366R; 30,606D). Six of the 13 Democratic contributors of API split their contributions.

The fourth group in this Appendix, Natural Petroleum Refiners Association, reversed the money trend by giving only $3,500 to the Republicans and $15,500 to the Democrats with no splits. However, even in this group, the Republican contributors numbered three, and the Democratic givers numbered two.

Contributions of Officials of Four Selected Petroleum Organizations, 1968

Group or Association	Total Members	Contributions [Number of contributors in parentheses]				Additional Factors
		Republican	Democratic	Miscellaneous	Total	
American Gas Assn.						
Officers	2					
Directors	31	(3) $ 2,500	—	—		
Officers & Directors	5	(1) 500	—	—		
		(4) 3,000			(4) $ 3,000	
Independent Natural Gas Assn. of America						
Officers	4					
Directors	25	(3) 2,500	—	—		
Officers & Directors	5					
		(3) 2,500			(3) 2,500	
Independent Petroleum Assn. of America						
Officers*	7					
Directors	32	(3) 2,500	(1) $ 2,500	—		
Officers & Directors	1	(1) 87,500	—	—		1 Split
		(4) 90,000	(1) 2,500		(4) 92,500	
Natural Petroleum Refiners Assn.						
Directors	103	(3) 3,500	(2) 15,500	—		
Officers & Directors	9	—	—			
		(3) 3,500	(2) 15,500		(5) 19,000	

Appendix M

Candidates who Gave $10,000 or More for
Their Own Campaigns, 1968

In 1968, at least 9 political candidates gave $10,000 or more for their own campaigns. The following information is verified in the Citizens' Research Foundation files.

Name	Party	Office Being Sought	Amount
Briscoe, Dolph Uvalde, Texas	Democratic	Governor of Texas (Primary)	$460,000
Kinney, David B. Arlington, Virginia	Democratic	10th Congressional District of Virginia (General Election)	77,000
Mahoney, George P. Baltimore, Maryland	Miscellaneous (Independent Candidate)	United States Senate (General Election)	15,449
Pierpont, Dr. Ross Z. Baltimore, Maryland	Democratic	United States Senate (Primary)	18,300
Rockefeller, Nelson A. Albany, New York New York, New York	Republican	President of United States (Prenomination)	356,000[a]
Romney, George Detroit, Michigan	Republican	President of United States (Prenomination)	100,000+[b]
Stassen, Harold Philadelphia, Pennsylvania	Republican	President of United States (Prenomination)	40,000
Whittenburg, Edward Houston, Texas	Democratic	Governor of Texas (Primary)	200,000
Wineland, Fred Prince Georges County, Maryland	Democratic	5th Congressional District of Maryland (Primary)	10,000

[a]As noted in Appendix E, Nelson A. Rockefeller also gave $127,500+ to other candidates and committees, including a $100,000+ contribution to George Romney's campaign.
[b]Mr. Romney also gave $2,500 to other candidates and committees.

351

Appendix N

Contributions among Selected Nixon Appointees, 1968-1969

The following list names those 34 individuals who contributed $500 or more in 1968 and who were appointed to offices in the Nixon administration in 1968-1969. Contributions which include wives' contributions are indicated by an asterisk (*). It is not suggested that a contribution was a reason for any appointment.

In all, a total of 345 appointees were analyzed for contributions. The names were taken from lists of appointments published by the *Congressional Quarterly* (January 31, February 28, May 9, May 16, May 30, and December 12, 1969), the *Congressional Quarterly Almanac* (1969), and from the State Department's list of appointed ambassadors as of January 2, 1970. In the analysis, only noncareer ambassadors were analyzed for contributions. For a specific breakdown of these totals, see the section on Chiefs of Foreign Missions and Special Missions (Noncareer), Appendix K.

Name	*Appointment*	*Contribution*
*Annenberg, Walter H. Wynnewood, Pennsylvania	Ambassador to Great Britain	$ 2,500 Rep.
Ash, Roy L. Los Angeles, California	Special Advisor on Management and Efficiency in Government, Executive Office	8,500 Rep.
DeRoulet, Vincent New York, New York	Ambassador to Jamaica	44,500 Rep.
*Dudley, Guilford Jr. Nashville, Tennessee	Ambassador to Denmark	51,000 Rep.
Ellsworth, Robert F. Washington, D.C.	U.S. Permanent Representative on the Council of the NATO	675 Rep.
Gilbert, Carl J. Dover, Massachusetts	U.S. Special Representative for Trade Negotiations, Executive Office	1,000 Rep.
*Gould, Kingdon Laurel, Maryland Washington, D.C.	Ambassador to Luxembourg	22,000 Rep.
*Humes, John P. New York, New York	Ambassador to Austria	43,000 Rep.
Kearns, Henry San Marino, California	President, Export-Import Bank	7,000 Rep.
*Marshall, Anthony D. New York, New York	Ambassador to Melagasy Republic	25,000 Rep.
Melady, Thomas Patrick New York, New York	Ambassador to Republic of Burundi	500 Rep.

Contributions among Selected Nixon Appointees, 1968-1969, cont.

Name	Appointment	Contribution
*Meyer, Charles A. Gladwyne Park, Pennsylvania	Assistant Secretary (Inter-American Affairs), State Department	4,000 Rep.
Middendorf, J. William II New York, New York	Ambassador to Kingdom of the Netherlands	$ 15,500 Rep.
Moore, John D.J. New York, New York	Ambassador to Ireland	1,000 Rep. 500 Dem.
Mosbacher, Emil Jr. White Plains, New York	Chief of Protocol, State Department	500 Rep.
Nunlist, Frank J. Jr. Harrison, New Jersey	Assistant Post Master General (Operations)	1,000 Rep.
*Packard, David Los Altos Hills, California Palo Alto, California	Deputy Secretary, Defense Department	11,000 Rep.
*Pritzlaff, John C. Jr. Phoenix, Arizona Scottsdale, Arizona	Ambassador to Malta	23,000 Rep.
*Replogle, Luther I. Oak Park, Illinois	Ambassador to Iceland	6,500 Rep.
Rinehart, D. Eldred Smithsburg, Maryland	Member, Renegotiation Board	1,750 Rep.
Rogers, William P. Bethesda, Maryland	Secretary of State	3,000 Rep.
Romney, George Bloomfield Hills, Michigan	Secretary, Department of Housing and Urban Development	2,500 Rep.
Rossides, Eugene T. New York, New York	Assistant Secretary (Customs, Engraving and Printing, Mint, Law Enforcement), Treasury Department	500 Rep.
Rush, Kenneth New York, New York	Ambassador to Federal Republic of Germany	1,000 Rep.
Russell, Fred J. South Gate, California Los Angeles, California	Deputy Director of Office of Emergency Preparedness, Executive Office	21,000 Rep.
Samuels, Nathaniel New York, New York	Deputy Under Secretary for Economic Affairs, State Department	500 Rep.
Schmidt, Adolph W. Pittsburgh, Pennsylvania	Ambassador to Canada	500 Rep.
Smith, Gerard C. Washington, D.C.	Director, U.S. Arms Control and Disarmament Agency	8,000 Rep.
Stans, Maurice H. New York, New York	Secretary, Commerce Department	4,950 Rep.
*Symington, J. Fife Lutherville, Maryland	Ambassador to Trinidad and Tobago	5,000 Rep. 500 Misc.

Contributions among Selected Nixon Appointees, 1968-1969, cont.

Name	*Appointment*	*Contribution*
Train, Russell E. Washington, D.C.	Under Secretary, Interior Department	1,000 Rep.
Van Dusen, Richard C. Detroit, Michigan	Under Secretary, Department of Housing and Urban Development	$ 1,100 Rep.
Volpe, John A. Winchester, Massachusetts Boston, Massachusetts	Secretary, Transportation Department	1,000 Rep.
*Warner, John W. Washington, D.C.	Under Secretary, Navy Department	6,000 Rep.
Subtotals	Republican Democratic Miscellaneous	$325,975 500 500
Total		$326,975

*Indicates inclusion of wife's contribution.

About the Author

Herbert E. Alexander has been the Director of the Citizens' Research Foundation since 1958. He received his B.A. from the University of North Carolina, M.A. from the University of Connecticut, and Ph.D. in Political Science from Yale University in 1958. He taught in the Department of Politics at Princeton University in 1956-58, and subsequently has been a Visiting Lecturer at Princeton and at the University of Pennsylvania. During 1961-62, he was Executive Director of the President's Commission on Campaign Costs, and from 1962-64 he was a Consultant to the President of the United States.

Dr. Alexander has written extensively on matters relating to money in politics. He is the author of *Financing the 1960 Election* (1962), *Financing the 1964 Election* (1966), "The Switch in Campaign Giving" (with Harold B. Meyers), *Fortune,* Nov., 1965, and "A Financial Landslide for the G.O.P." (with Harold B. Meyers), *Fortune,* March, 1970. He has authored several articles for books, among them: "Financing the Parties and Campaigns," in Milton C. Cummings (ed.), *The National Election of 1964* (Washington: The Brookings Institution, 1966); "Broadcasting and Politics," in M. Kent Jennings and L. Marmon Ziegler, *The Electoral Process* (Englewood Cliffs: Prentice-Hall, Inc., 1966). Dr. Alexander has edited and contributed to *Studies in Money in Politics, Volume I* (1965) and *Volume II* (1970), published by the Citizens' Research Foundation. He has also written articles for *Encyclopaedia Britannica* and for the *Encyclopedia Year Book.*